AF477803

SHAKESPEARE'S MEDIEVAL CRAFT

SHAKESPEARE'S MEDIEVAL CRAFT

Remnants of the Mysteries on the London Stage

KURT A. SCHREYER

CORNELL UNIVERSITY PRESS
Ithaca and London

First published 2014 by Cornell University Press

Printed in the United States of America

Library of Congress Cataloging-in-Publication Data

Schreyer, Kurt A., author.
   Shakespeare's medieval craft : remnants of the mysteries on the London stage / Kurt A. Schreyer.
      pages cm
   Includes bibliographical references and index.
   ISBN 978-0-8014-5290-1 (cloth : alk. paper)
  1. Mysteries and miracle-plays, English—History and criticism. 2. Shakespeare, William, 1564–1616—Sources.
3. Shakespeare, William, 1564–1616—Criticism and interpretation. I. Title.
   PR2953.M54S37   2014
   822'.0516—dc23   2014004188

For my parents, and for Kim

Contents

❧ ILLUSTRATIONS

Acknowledgments

I must first thank my colleagues in the English department at the University of Missouri—St. Louis, particularly the department chair, Richard Cook, who from the beginning was committed to supporting my research on this project in every way possible. No one could have a better colleague than I do in Frank Grady, and thanks to his generosity I am the decided beneficiary of his intellect, expertise, and humor. He gave his keen attention to most of the pages of this book, and many of its insights were prompted by his comments and suggestions. The generosity of the University of Missouri Research Board allowed me to give my full attention to this project, and the College of Arts and Sciences provided the funding necessary to travel and present my work to my peers.

I have been fortunate indeed to receive professional training at three academic institutions, the University of Notre Dame, the University of Pennsylvania, and Fordham University, where medievalists and early modernists routinely and cooperatively "think across" the divide that has traditionally separated their disciplines. I thank the faculty and graduate students at these institutions for their generous support and encouragement, especially Peter Stallybrass, Emily Steiner, Zachary Lesser, David Wallace, Cy Mulready, Jared Richman, Scott Krawczyck, Marissa Greenberg, Elizabeth Williamson, Jennifer Higginbotham, Jane Degenhardt, Jon Hsy, Erika Lin, Graham Hammill, Jesse Lander, Maura Nolan, Mary Erler, Katie Little, Suzanne Yeager, and Mary Bly. My thanks also go to Rob Barrett, Theresa Coletti, Richard Emmerson, Jonathan Gil Harris, Emma Lipton, Michael O'Connell, and Paul Whitfield White for their suggestions and encouragement.

Chapter 3 appeared as "Balaam to Bottom: Artifact and Theatrical Translation in the Sixteenth Century," *Journal of Medieval and Early Modern Studies* 42, no. 2 (Spring 2012): 421–59 (copyright 2012, Duke University Press. All rights reserved). It is gratifying to thank the journal's editors as well as Duke University Press for their support. I am also grateful for the comments and critical insights of the organizers and participants of several conferences held at the University of Toronto, including the Queen's Men and Renaissance

Medievalisms conferences held in the fall of 2006 and the Chester 2010 conference held in May 2010. Special thanks are owed to David Klausner, Helen Ostovich, Jessica Dell, Jennifer Roberts-Smith, and Alexandra Johnston, who organized the last of these wonderfully engaging academic events. Part of chapter 2 was published as "'Erazed in the Booke'? Periodization and the Material Text of the Chester Banns," in *The Chester Cycle in Context, 1555–1575,* edited by Jessica Dell, David Klausner, and Helen Ostovich (Farnham, UK: Ashgate, 2012), 133–45. I am grateful that Elizabeth Rivlin at Clemson University was the first editor to show interest in my work and publish a portion of chapter 5 in *Shakespearean Hearing,* a 2010 special issue of *The Upstart Crow.* I thank copy editor Jamie Fuller and the staff at Cornell University Press, especially Karen Hwa and Katherine Liu. I am particularly obliged to the editor in chief, Peter Potter, for his insights and suggestions as well as for his encouraging support.

I have met only a few of the editors and scholars responsible for the incredible resources of the Records of Early English Drama (REED) project housed at the University of Toronto, yet I would like to express my sincerest gratitude and respect to them. Quite simply, this book would not have been possible without their efforts.

Long before I chose literature as a career, my friend Lou Volpe, like god-sent Mentes, prompted this delightful odyssey into the beauty and wonder of Shakespeare's plays. I owe a special debt to Paul Rathburn, who first inspired me to consider the significance of early English drama to the professional London stage.

My most grateful thanks are, above all, owed to Margreta de Grazia. My admiration and esteem for her has, over the years, been outmatched only by my gratitude and affection.

My parents, Bill and Corrine Schreyer, have stood faithfully behind me since my earliest struggles and accomplishments, and in my wife, Kim, I am blessed with the dearest companion and friend that I could (and did) hope and pray for. That is why this book is dedicated to them.

❧ NOTE ON THE TEXT

With the exception of Shakespeare's plays, which have become familiar as products of the modern critical tradition, italicized characters in early English works, and the Middle English letters thorn and yogh, which have been updated to *th* and *gh,* respectively, to aid publication, I have elected not to modernize the spelling or punctuation of the Chester Banns or other early English texts. My use of archaisms is not, like so much dust on the sleeve of the studious archivist, a testimony to the author's scholarly credentials or, perhaps worse, any sort of claim to recovering past texts in their own terms. It is hoped, rather, that old spellings will reinforce for the reader, at the level of orthography, the book's keen interest in the way that past things (in this case words) can be lifted out of their previous contexts, be fitted into new cultural edifices to meet present interests and perhaps even acquire new signification, yet still appear out-of-date and even obsolete.

Unless otherwise noted, all citations from Shakespeare, the Chester mystery plays, and the York plays are taken from the following editions, respectively, and will be cited by line number in the body of the text: *The Norton Shakespeare: Based on the Oxford Edition,* ed. Stephen Greenblatt et al. (New York: Norton, 1997); *The Chester Mystery Cycle,* ed. R. M. Lumiansky and David Mills, EETS Supplementary Series 3 and 9 (Oxford: Oxford University Press, 1974; repr. 1986); *The York Plays: A Critical Edition of the York Corpus Christi Play as Recorded in British Library Additional MS 35290,* ed. Richard Beadle, EETS Supplementary Series 23 (Oxford: Oxford University Press, 2009).

EETS	Early English Text Society
JMEMS	*Journal of Medieval and Early Modern Studies*
OED	*The Oxford English Dictionary*
REED	Records of Early English Drama
REED: *Cheshire*	Records of Early English Drama, *Cheshire including Chester,* ed. Elizabeth Baldwin, Lawrence M. Clopper, and David Mills
REED: *Chester*	Records of Early English Drama, *Chester,* ed. Lawrence M. Clopper
REED: *Coventry*	Records of Early English Drama, *Coventry*, ed. R. W. Ingram
REED: *York*	Records of Early English Drama, *York*, ed. Alexandra F. Johnston and Margaret Rogerson
SQ	*Shakespeare Quarterly*

SHAKESPEARE'S MEDIEVAL CRAFT

Introduction

In nova fert animus mutatas dicere formas corpora.

—Ovid

This book explores the relationship between Shakespeare's plays and a tradition of late medieval English biblical drama known as mystery plays. Although the mysteries have often been narrowly defined as annual "Corpus Christi plays," they were in fact a broad tradition that took many shapes and sizes on a variety of occasions, not necessarily seasonal or annual, and in different localities throughout fifteenth- and sixteenth-century England.[1] Until recently, the mysteries, like other manifestations of English festival culture, were obscured by the simplistic term "medieval drama," which encouraged early modernists to ignore them.[2] They were also believed, according to an outdated yet tenacious view, to have suddenly vanished because of the Reformation or the advent of commercial London theater. However, we now know that they enjoyed both secular and ecclesiastical sponsorship and participation by Protestants and Catholics. This book demonstrates the central importance of the material culture of the mystery play tradition to Shakespearean dramaturgy.

Contemporary scholarship seems to have reached a consensus in its search for continuities rather than disjunctions between the professional London companies and the earlier drama and culture of the sixteenth century. The treasure of archival material brought to light by the Records of Early English Drama (REED) project housed at the University of Toronto has encouraged early English drama specialists to enter into cross-period engagement.[3]

Having recognized, moreover, that what is often labeled "medieval" drama survives in sixteenth-century manuscripts, many scholars of the "Middle Ages" feel quite at home in the latter decades of their traditional disciplinary field.[4] Scholarship on the Queen's Men and on the practices of touring has blurred distinctions between the drama of London and that of the provinces, and in the process helped us to rethink critical categories and distinctions.[5]

Shakespeare's Medieval Craft joins these scholarly undertakings by asking whether and how Shakespeare's plays recalled the late medieval mystery plays. It proposes that certain material features of Shakespeare's stage—including the ass's head of *A Midsummer Night's Dream,* the theatrical space of Purgatory in *Hamlet,* and the knocking at the gate in the Porter scene of *Macbeth*—constitute remnants of the earlier mysteries transformed to meet the exigencies of the commercial London playhouses. Rather than viewing the Reformation as a barrier separating religious and secular English theater, I see it as a cultural re-formation and re-membering of bonds between early modern subjects and medieval artifacts. I contend, therefore, that Shakespeare's stage paradoxically distinguishes itself from the mysteries precisely through its transformative incorporation of elements of that dramatic tradition.

In this way, my book shares Jonathan Gil Harris's keen interest in the temporality of dramatic objects yet not in their untimeliness per se; it examines, rather, a particular temporal transformation of matter, namely, the afterlife of medieval artifacts in early modern English culture.[6] For this same reason I will not provide "object biographies" that diachronically trace the perpetual recycling of objects both as commodities and more singularly valued cultural artifacts.[7] Identifying a material link between Shakespeare and the mysteries, I want to think more carefully about the way we temporally frame the properties and practices of early English drama before Shakespeare. For we early modernists have too long sequestered these objects and dramaturgies from our scholarly consideration—and in fact have created the myth of the singularity of our authors and field of study precisely through our derogation of medieval artifacts. This error arises from a kind of historiographical forgetfulness. As students of Renaissance culture, we tend to think that the objects of our study are Renaissance objects and that they belong to the temporal moment or period under consideration. But they do not, or at least not entirely.[8] The implications of this insight are far-reaching, for they challenge long-standing theories about historical origin and style. And pursuing these inquiries requires us to put pressure on comfortable notions of the identity of an object or work, of historicity, originality, and inspiration as well as the converse of these: anachronism, forgery, and plagiarism. It means above all challenging accepted ideas about that most sacred tenet of our discipline: Shakespearean authorship.

Asserting a material link between Shakespeare and the mysteries is important for two methodological reasons as well. First, literary historians tend to view Shakespeare almost exclusively as a poet and thereby elevate him above the material practices of his stagecraft.[9] This view of Shakespearean drama persists in popular editions like *The Norton Shakespeare.* While acknowledging that "costume was a vital element in the plays," it tells readers, "for all the games with magic tricks and devils spouting fireworks that were part of the Shakespearean staging tradition, spectacle was a limited resource on the scene-free Elizabethan stage. Shakespeare in this was a poet more than a player."[10] I urge instead that we strive to recover a sense of the substantial artisanal undertakings involved in most if not all forms of early English drama, especially Shakespeare's.[11] Like the contributors to *Subject and Object in Renaissance Culture,* I see Shakespeare as "a *playwright,* a craftsman who, like a shipwright or cartwright, fashions his material for practical use."[12] This book will show that one important yet overlooked aspect of Shakespeare's playwright joinery was the fusion of pieces from the "old" mystery plays to his theatrical works.

Second, attending to the significant ways in which late medieval material culture influenced the commercial London stage is helpful in that we may initially prevent Shakespeare, the peerless author of Renaissance literature, from precipitously consuming our scholarly attention. Indeed, the structure of this book reflects a considered approach to early English drama that only gradually brings the professional London playhouses and their most famous playwright into view. Today, both medievalists and early modern scholars are rightly skeptical of teleological narratives that value sixteenth-century drama only for its anticipation of Shakespeare. I am suggesting, however, that this critical awareness is not enough and that perhaps we need to be bolder in our assertions about the material significance of the mystery plays for the professional theaters that emerged in London in the late sixteenth century. I therefore argue that we should continue to interrogate the privileging of the London stage over its predecessors as well as to raise further questions about the abstraction of the authorial subject from the theatrical object. This book aims, moreover, to unsettle the casual periodization of early English drama that results from corresponding assumptions about the relative superiority of the Renaissance author over the medieval object.

I am not suggesting that we ignore historical difference by supposing that Shakespeare was working within a mystery or morality play tradition, for this approach runs the risk of being mired in E. K. Chambers's language of hybrids, precursors, and secularization.[13] Rather, I wish to contribute to a growing body of scholarship that is attempting to address the widespread disinclination to see the mystery plays as having any relationship to the professional London stage. To do so, we need to reexamine the manner in which the Reformation reconditioned the subjective responses of audiences to traditional dramatic objects by looking within the plays themselves as well as in the surrounding culture.[14] Consequently, this book asks what it would mean if in fact the material remnants of the mysteries were vital and direct agents, not rude precursors, in the production of some of the most famous plays in the Shakespeare canon.

The technological conditions of early English drama remained relatively constant in the sixteenth and early seventeenth centuries, and therefore tradesmen-players and professional actors alike relied on tried-and-true materials and methods of staging. Creativity was not lacking; in fact, the great cost of manufacturing and maintaining costumes, for example, might ensure their preservation and stage presence by encouraging professional London companies to produce plays about them. A particularly exotic and expensive costume or property like an ass's head might almost demand incorporation in a performance. On the other hand, something as cheap to make as the sound effect of loud pounding or thunder could be as readily reproduced on a pageant wagon as in a playhouse and was therefore carried over to the London stages as well.

Whereas late medieval dramatic materials and technologies remained unchanged in the early modern period, the cultural circumstances in which they were staged and perceived were ever-changing and uneven. Indeed, the symbolic systems that these dramatic objects and practices represented had never been universally fixed in the first place but varied greatly across England during the fifteenth and sixteenth centuries.[15] More important, the mystery play tradition endured long enough for audiences to observe and appreciate the symbolic transformations that these materials underwent before and after their migration to the London stage. Whether from direct experience or general familiarity, many London spectators recognized dramatic objects and practices from their provincial manifestations and enjoyed seeing them re-created by urban acting companies. Undoubtedly this claim will make many readers uncomfortable, yet as several scholars have observed, early modernists too readily overlook the mystery tradition's contemporaneity with the London stage.[16] Some dismiss it as provincial when, to the contrary, the massive immigration to England's capital city in the late sixteenth century meant that there were thousands of people whose first and perhaps defining experience of drama was the sights and sounds of the mysteries. Shakespeare wrote for theatergoers who, like himself, brought with them fond and often very particular and tangible recollections of those plays, such as the ranting of Herod and the color of beard worn by the first murderer, Cain. I argue that in fact, long after Shakespeare, writers composed plays that both relied on and catered to audience recognition of older dramatic materials and practices.

The significance of immigration from the provinces to London does not (or should not) imply that urban drama surpassed rural performances in the minds of either actors or audiences. To the contrary, it encourages us to look for points of contact, interaction, and exchange between provincial and metropolitan forms of sixteenth-century English drama yet simultaneously recognize the singular playing spaces and local politics involved in each. And those connections are, I believe, chiefly artisanal. Few players were born into the craft of professional acting; they came to it as members of other crafts and therefore must have related to one another as guildsmen whether or not they had learned their respective trades in London.[17] Moreover, they approached their new profession practically—that is, as praxis—with a craftsman's eye toward its physical assets and demands. Actors and poets alike were attentive to the many ways in which they could exploit the materiality of their medium.

Modern criticism has been slow to credit the artisanal culture of the London stage for a number of reasons. One obvious explanation has already been mentioned: manual craft is often casually associated with the provinces while commercial enterprise is seen as proper to the city. Similarly, we are comfortable linking the poet Shakespeare with nobility and royalty but not with tradesmen. In this we reassure ourselves that he was a prosperous entrepreneur who achieved the status of a gentleman, but in doing so we conveniently overlook the fact that he was also the son of a glover and may have practiced the trade himself. Being modern or postmodern, moreover, we tend to view art, including drama, ideationally. Perhaps, too, as citizens in a global economy of circulating capital, we have a tendency to view commercial enterprise as modern and sophisticated in contrast to the supposed bygone simplicity of manual craft. And since we are culturally invested in Shakespeare, we form him in our own image.[18]

To uncover the material connections between Shakespeare's stage and the mysteries, and indeed to argue for the centrality of late medieval dramatic objects to later professional stagecraft, I will introduce a somewhat obscure (from the traditional Renaissance scholar's point of view) sixteenth-century document. The Chester Late Banns, which comprise a fascinating post-Reformation proclamation that relishes the Old Faith's plays and calls for their continued performance, highlight the customary trappings of each pageant, or episode, in the Creation to Doom cycle of plays. As in their earlier (often called "Catholic") version, the later ("Protestant") Banns urge the tradesmen not to alter the plays "in many points from the old fashion." The vintners are directed to ensure that the star that guided the "wise kinges three" be prominently displayed; the butchers must present the Devil in his "accustomed" black, feathery costume; the water drawers are to see that "all poyntes" of Noah's Ark are prepared.[19] The props, costumes, and pageant displays of the Chester mystery plays captivate nearly every stanza of the Banns proclamation. These repeated and emphatic demands not only encourage us to consider whether Shakespeare underscores the materiality of the dramatic remnants he borrows but also suggest that the materiality of the mysteries continued to influence and inspire post-Reformation theatrical production. In this way, the Chester Banns challenge us to approach the history of early English drama in a radically different way: not as a canon of influential authors but as a history of theatrical objects whose stage presence demanded the skills of craftsmen-actors and play-wrights.

Crucially, the Banns not only direct attention to the material features of the mysteries but also point the way in another important respect: they historicize theatrical objects. With their historiography—their sense that English drama, though still beloved and familiar, has somehow progressed—the Banns illustrate how Shakespeare's theater might have looked upon, and borrowed from, antecedents in the mystery plays. They encourage their audience to believe that because the plays are so hopelessly old-fashioned, their present theatrical significance must be harmless and benign or else may now be interpreted in new ways, even in ways that contradict their previous signification. They are new insofar as they are old.

At first reading, this historiography sounds like a sixteenth-century version of Hegel's dialectical *Aufhebung* whereby the past is first contained, then canceled or sublated, and finally transcended, though never entirely superseded. But the Banns differ in crucial and productive ways from Hegel, not least because they trade in sixteenth-century theatrical objects, not modern conscious subjects. And they do not presume that historical progress is necessarily positive. In fact, their conservatism holds the key to understanding their resourceful manipulation of progressive rhetoric. Whereas Hegel extols progress and puts history to work for the future fulfillment of spirit, the Banns commend tradition and attempt to use historical change for the preservation of past material artifacts and practices. The Banns seem initially to celebrate the progress of history out of a benighted time of ignorance, but closer study shows that they find all of Chester history laudatory and its "ancient" theatrical history particularly exceptional.

The rhetorical formation of historical difference exempts the mysteries from current religious values in an effort to quiet religious opponents, restrain meddling authorities, and thus avert the outright suppression of the plays. To achieve these ends, the Chester Banns proclamation deftly performs what I term synchronic diachrony: it urges the guild players to perform their pageants "as custom ever was" (synchrony) yet distinguishes the present time of performance from the city's Catholic past (diachrony). Diachronic change is in this way the guarantor of synchronic contact with the past.[20]

With their synchronic diachrony, the Chester Banns help us to grasp an important phenomenon regarding the artifacts of the mystery play tradition: namely, that the proscription of Catholic objects and practices did not prevent the professional theater companies from using the remnants of mystery drama but almost guaranteed that they did so. Novelty (or at least the appearance of it) was not an ideological concern for the London theater companies so much as a commercial necessity. Visually striking props, machinery, costumes, and architecture could help to attract audiences to the public stages, and as their display brought commercial success, they became important investments. Just as playwrights adorned their play texts with newly coined English words and foreign phrases to grab the ear of audiences, so too they wrote plays that called for lavish costumes and eye-catching stage objects.[21] But extravagance was expensive, and familiar sights and sounds might lose their charm. As a result, theater companies found themselves in constant need of new and memorable stage properties. They also needed to fully exploit the machinery, architecture, and material features of the playhouses, for these structures were costly capital investments. Church and state regulations unintentionally provided a windfall. By outlawing the mysteries, Reformers freed theatrical objects from their previous religious associations (though not entirely, as we will see), making them available to a London theater market eager for new means of dramatic expression. Thus prohibition meant profit for Shakespeare and his contemporaries.

Once assigned to the past, and particularly to a blinkered, superstitious age, dramatic material can be safely recuperated and restaged. The plays considered at length in this book all take place in the distant past: *Macbeth* and *Hamlet* in pre-Norman Scotland and Denmark, respectively, and *A Midsummer Night's Dream* in ancient Athens. Beyond this antiquation, however, Shakespeare, like the Chester Banns, explicitly denigrates the stage practices of the mysteries and the Old Religion that sponsored them. In each of these plays there is a moment when the mystery play remnant that has been resurrected is then eluded, disparaged, or rejected. Nearly the entire duration of act 5, scene 1 of *Dream,* for example, sets up the rude, mechanical dramaturgy of provincial tradesmen-actors as the buffoonish foil to the supposedly magical, dream-like fantasy staged by the professional "shadows" of the Lord Chamberlain's Men. Shakespeare does this, I argue, first, to preserve the appearance of modish sophistication in a theater market that places a premium on novelty, and second (and for much the same reason), to mask his indebtedness to the mystery play tradition. As I suggest in chapter 5, the suspicion aroused by puritan antitheatricalists may have encouraged Shakespeare to conceal his borrowings from pre-Reformation religious drama. Yet practical considerations probably mattered more than ideology for a professional playwright and company shareholder. Shakespeare benefited from the fact that the Reformation freed the stage materials of the mysteries from their exclusively religious significance and thus permitted their migration to the London stages. He therefore had a commercial interest in perpetuating the synchronic diachrony between his public playhouse and the mystery pageants. As with the Chester Banns, it would be advantageous for Shakespeare to antiquate the materials he borrowed from the mystery plays so as to ensure that they remained presently available for continued dramatic performance.

Having raised the question of provincial ties to Shakespeare's theater, I am not suggesting that Shakespeare ever heard or read the Chester Banns. I have adopted that document as a critical paradigm for two reasons: first, to correct a long-standing bias on the part of Renaissance scholars toward medieval craft, and second, to show that early modern subjects did not always share this preconception. Yet if we are disposed to accept the substantial amount of scholarship that has endeavored to link Shakespeare to the northwest of England, then we have further grounds for accepting the Banns' heuristic access to English Renaissance historical thinking about pre-Reformation culture.[22]

The Chester Banns draw our attention to the handcrafted elements of the guilds' pageants and their afterlife on the Shakespearean stage, but it is difficult to encapsulate this material borrowing with a single, practical term. First, the two theaters share more than stage properties. Their performance spaces and stage architecture incorporate the same, three-tiered cosmography of Heaven, Earth, and Hell. The mysteries and professional London theaters also shared sound effects and sound-making technology. One material carryover that this work does not address but that other studies have explored is scent.[23]

The diversity of the theatrical elements being borrowed by Shakespeare complicates the need for succinct terminology, but the legacy of Chambers's teleology is a greater challenge. The use of the term "leftover," for example, is unsatisfactory.[24] Following Michael O'Connell, I argue for the continued vitality of the mystery play tradition.[25] But if the props, dramaturgy, and stage architecture of the mysteries remained in some ways available to the London theater companies, it is also true that they were not what they had once been. For secular and ecclesial authorities did ultimately put a stop to mystery drama, and when the plays that we shall examine were first staged, that older tradition was beginning to fade into memory. Indeed, the commercial success of permanent theater structures widened that historical distance by divorcing performance from the church's religious calendar. In addition, performance space became the fixed property of acting companies rather than borrowed and provisional.[26] But those same playhouse structures also preserved some of the technologies and material properties of the mysteries. Our critical terminology must account for the waning of this older dramatic tradition rather than serve as an anodyne for cultural loss by asserting only continued vitality. I will often rely on neutral terms like "objects" and "artifacts" as I explore the overlap between provincial pageant wagons and the London playhouses. Considering historical difference as well as synchronous influence, however, I will also refer to the material elements and practices Shakespeare borrowed from the mysteries as "remnants," for his use of the term could express both diminution and lingering vitality.

Remnants in Shakespeare's plays seem to occupy, or constitute, in-between times. They are polychronic: their ruined or diminished features record diachronic change, but they simultaneously preserve what once was. For Lady Anne in *Richard III,* the corpse of King Henry VI is a "bloodless remnant of that royal blood" of the house of Lancaster, but it remains an "honourable" and "holy load" all the same. She wonders "if honour may be shrouded in a hearse," and we may wonder too, and yet she believes that the "poor key-cold" body in the coffin still retains the "figure of a holy king" (1.2.1–32). Objects in this culture do not easily lose their historicity. As a detached piece of a once-complete institutional edifice, the remnant lingers on in the wake of upheaval and, significantly, recalls both the remote time and the period elapsed in between. It may even help to revive the past in some altered way. Though Richard has the old king buried hugger-mugger, the name of Henry and the blood-red rose of Lancaster are resurrected at the end of this play in the figure of Henry VII, who marries Elizabeth of York. The "true succeeders of each royal house" will "conjoin together" and "unite the white rose and the red" to begin the Tudor dynasty (5.8.30, 31, 19).[27]

Remnants have the ability to produce memory even as they are being resituated in new cultural contexts. I will explore how this mnemonic force evoked early modern audiences' recollection of mystery drama and catalyzed dialogue and action in Shakespeare's plays.[28] I suggest, for example, that an audience's response to the Ghost in *Hamlet* needs to be evaluated in the context of the *Last Judgment* plays of the mysteries, where the dead emerge from trapdoor graves in the stage floor, perhaps from two distinct traps leading separately to Purgatory and to Hell. Few today would be reminded of Balaam's talking ass upon seeing Bottom emerge from behind the brake, yet Globe audiences may well have recalled that biblical beast along with other appearances of the ass in the liturgies of the church and polemical Reformation pamphlets. In *Macbeth,* Shakespeare dramatizes the act of remembering mystery drama. The same sound of knocking that alarms Macbeth and Lady Macbeth following the murder of Duncan prompts a sleepy, inebriated gatekeeper to imagine himself the "devil-porter" of Hell's gate and to perform the well-established role of the devils in the *Harrowing of Hell.*

The post-Reformation Banns' unmitigated enthusiasm for the mystery plays as well as Chambers's relative diminution of them within an already denigrated historical period has encouraged me to look more closely at the mystery tradition itself. It is not my intention to suggest, however, that the mysteries were exclusively important to Shakespeare's professional stage. I argue, in fact, that the Banns can help us to become more cognizant of the contributions of other sixteenth-century dramatic traditions—notably Tudor moral interludes—to the London playhouses.

According to the *Middle English Dictionary,* the word "misterie" could refer to "hidden symbolism, doctrine, or spiritual significance in matters of religion; mystical truth," or a "rite, happening, or feeling with religious or mystical significance" like the Eucharist. It could also refer to "a handicraft, an art" or "a guild." But I must emphasize that I have chosen this now-unfashionable word to refer to a kind of play, although it was never used as such in the late medieval or early modern period.[29] That connotation appeared around the middle of the eighteenth century, perhaps, as the *Oxford English Dictionary* suggests, in relation to the Latin *mysterium,* or hidden truths of a religion. This coinage suggests that what was important for literary historians during the Enlightenment was the fact that the plays were religious and therefore fundamentally different from the secular commercial theater that followed.[30] After the industrial revolution, however, their association with manufacturing seems to have been more important. As a result, the word "mystery," as relating to a craft or occupation, was chosen by nineteenth-century scholars who sought to underscore their production by tradesmen.

During the centuries when the plays were being performed, terms such as "Corpus Christi Play" or "Whitson Plays" might be used, not as generic designators but simply to mark the occasion of their performance, namely, around the feast of Corpus Christi (the Thursday after Trinity Sunday) or else Whitsunday (White Sunday, or Pentecost).[31] The more generic "cycle plays" is now often used with regard to Chester and other cities with larger play sequences. As I will usually be addressing individual plays within the cycle, I have chosen the word "pageant" for its association with the wagon, or "pageant," manufactured by the craft guilds as well as for its subtle distinction between this older dramatic tradition and later professional "theater"—that is, staged productions within fixed architectural structures like the Globe.[32] When speaking of the pageants as a group, I will most often refer to them as "mysteries" in order to hold on to the historicity of that term—its affinities with both material labor and religious rites. I may occasionally speak of play "cycles" to emphasize their processional characteristics or to address a particular pageant's place within the broader serial narrative. I rarely employ the term "biblical drama" for, as we'll see, some of the most interesting plays are uncanonical.

My first chapter demonstrates the manner in which traditional criticism—not only literary (Thomas Warton, E. K. Chambers) but also historical (G. W. F. Hegel, Jacob Burckhardt) and art historical (Erwin Panofsky)—has worked to associate the Middle Ages with objects while abstracting Renaissance artists and authors from the materiality of their craft. I then identify and discuss three historiographical modalities—exemplarity, palimpsests, and anachronism—in order to highlight the various ways in which post-Reformation culture was still in close material contact with pre-Reformation forms and antecedents and, furthermore, to argue that medieval artifacts were often indispensable to Renaissance authorship. Chapter 2 then introduces the Chester Banns, which commission a performance of the mysteries despite growing puritan antagonism. I also demonstrate how the Banns participate in each of the historiographical modes of afterlife, recuperation, and re-membering discussed in chapter 1. The edited, rewritten, censored, and annotated material texts of these Chester proclamations, for example, may serve as an ink-and-parchment model of the complex historiography of the Shakespearean stage.

The next three chapters trace the medieval provenance of specific elements of Shakespeare's stage in order to show how his plays invite the audience to recall the mystery plays even as they supply these remnants with new theatrical significance and context. The epilogue, "Riding the Banns beyond Shakespeare," tests the scope of the book's central thesis by asking how the Chester Banns may further help us to appreciate the theatrical provenance and material agency of dramatic objects in the stagecraft of Shakespeare's contemporaries, including Jonson, Webster, and Middleton. Here, too, we'll see that the adoption of mystery—as well as morality—play properties and conventions continued well into the seventeenth century, long after traditional religious drama is thought to be significant.

 # Chapter 1

Toward a Renaissance Culture
of Medieval Artifacts

> It is not history, but direct and personal observation
> [*autopsía*] and living presence [*parousía*] of all the
> things that happened then.
>
> —Manuel Chrysoloras

To understand Renaissance authorship, Shake-
speare's in particular, we need to appreciate medieval artifacts. But medieval
objects have long played a definitive yet deprecatory role in the history of
early English drama. In his three-volume *History of English Poetry* (1774–81),
the first comprehensive account of English literature from the eleventh to
the seventeenth century, Thomas Warton confesses an irresistible yet somewhat embarrassed interest in them. "There is a curious passage in Lambarde's
Topographical Dictionary written about the year 1570, much to our purpose,
which I am therefore tempted to transcribe." Succumbing to the temptation, he quotes the Elizabethan lawyer and antiquary William Lambarde
(1536–1601) at considerable length and in great detail:

> In the dayes of ceremonial religion, they used at *Wytney* (in Oxford-
> shire) to set fourthe yearly in maner of a shew, or interlude, the resur-
> rection of our Lord, &c. For the which purposes, and the more lyvely
> heareby to exhibite to the eye the hole action of the resurrection, the
> priestes garnished out certain smalle puppettes, representing the per-
> sons of Christe, the watchmen, Marie, and others; amongst the which,
> one bare the parte of a wakinge watcheman, who espiinge Christe to
> arise, made a continual noyce, like to the sound that is caused by the
> metynge of two stykes, and was therof commonly called *Jack Snacker of*

Wytney. The like toye I myself, beinge then a childe, once saw in Poule's churche at London, at a feast of Whitsuntyde; wheare the comynge downe of the Holy Gost was set forthe by a white pigion, that was let to fly out of a hole that yet is to be sene in the mydst of the roofe of the greate ile, and by a longe censer which descendinge out of the same place almost to the verie grounde, was swinged up and downe at such a lengthe, that it reached with thone swepe almost to the west-gate of the churche, and with the other to the quyre staires of the same; breathinge out over the whole churche and companie a most pleasant perfume of such swete thinges as burned therein. With the like doome [dumb] shewes also, they used everie where to furnishe sondrye partes of their churche service, as by their spectacles of the nativitie, passion, and ascension, &c.[1]

Warton transcribes this passage into an account of how drama migrated from churches to other public spaces, and thus its lengthy description of physical objects, let alone such spectacular pageantry, seems extraneous to his immediate purpose. Besides the level of detail, what is important to note is the absence of any commentary, as if the objects alone could account for themselves. Warton accepts without question Lambarde's post-Reformation bias against the childish toys of the Old Faith.[2] More important, he has no problem with the association of an Oxfordshire resurrection play with a London church service at Whitsuntide. Both are typical of "the dayes of ceremonial religion," days infused with dramatic sensory experiences: lively toys and puppets that dazzle the eye, sweet-smelling censors of incense, and the "continual noises" of music and sound effects.

The presence of stage objects also shapes Warton's account of English drama's origins. Discussing a fourteenth-century *ludus* performed by the guild of Corpus Christi at Cambridge, he observes: "Our drama seems hitherto to have been almost entirely confined to religious subjects, and these plays were nothing more than an appendage to the specious and mechanical devotion of the times."[3] Early English theater, according to this description, is little more than a physical spectacle that suspiciously resembles that other medieval show, the Catholic Mass. Warton's pejorative terms, which are all the more derogatory considering he was perhaps "the most devoted and sympathetic eighteenth-century reader of medieval English literature," are worth noting for they will enjoy a long career in literary history and criticism.[4] "Confined" in its subject matter, pre-Reformation drama is described as the hollow show of an age of superficial devotion. Associated with manual craft, it is not merely thoughtless but is an appendage on the unholy body of popish practice.[5] Just as Rome subjugated spiritual faith and devotion to the practice of corporeal works, here pre-Reformation plays are themselves synecdochically reduced to the stage properties they dramatize, thus becoming "specious" and "mechanical" toys.

I begin with these passages from Warton not only to foreground the kinds of dramatic objects that will be the focus of this book but also to call attention to the way in which medieval artifacts in particular are, as it were, made to tell time. They serve as chronographic indexes differentiating between past and present. Warton, in other words, is not simply observing the importance of stage properties to early English dramatic practice; rather, he distinguishes premodern drama by tying it to the idols of the Old Faith. He manufactures the historicity—the benightedness—of early drama by underscoring its materiality.

If the primacy of objects is characteristic, even constitutive, of pre-Reformation drama for Warton, so too is the absence of individual subjectivity both on stage and off:

> It is certain that these Miracle-plays were the earliest of our dramatic exhibitions. But as these pieces frequently required the introduction of allegorical characters, such as Charity, Sin, Death, Hope, Faith, or the like, and as the common poetry of the times, especially among the French, began to deal much in allegory, at length plays were formed entirely consisting of such personifications. These were called Moralities. The miracle-plays, or Mysteries, were totally destitute of invention or plan: they tamely represented stories according to the letter of scripture, or the respective legend.

Morality plays, he continues, "indicate dawnings of the dramatic art; they contain some rudiments of a plot, and even attempt to delineate characters, and to paint manners. From hence the gradual transition to real historical personages was natural and obvious."[6] Significantly, the achievement of individuality coincides with an epochal shift: the personifications of late medieval moralities mark the dawn of what will undoubtedly become, in the noontide of eighteenth-century theater, full-fledged dramatic figures. But in Warton's narrative, "real" characters displaying inwardness must wait until enlightened modernity sheds more light on the English stage.[7] The consciousness of history itself will also have to wait. As ignorant of historical difference as they are "destitute of invention," the Middle Ages are deemed oblivious to the (modern) discipline of history per se and instead "tamely" and obediently adhere verbatim to legend and scripture.[8]

Warton's account of the Shakespearean stage, though couched in a similar idiom, tells a very different story: "Shakespeare's aim was to collect an audience, and for this purpose all of the common expedients were necessary. . . . His representations abound with the usual appendages of mechanical terror, and he adopts all the superstitions of the theatre. This problem can only be resolved into the activity or the superiority of a mind, which either would not be entangled by the formality, or which saw through the futility, of this unnatural and extrinsic ornament."[9] The appendages of the proximate dark ages still reach out and grasp—even terrorize—the Shakespearean stage. As Warton later explains, "the reformation had not yet destroyed every delusion, nor disenchanted all the strong holds of superstition. . . . Every goblin of ignorance did not vanish at the first glimmerings of the morning of science."[10] Shakespeare's mind, however, is said to hold itself masterfully above the base world of mechanical objects left over from popish forms of play and retained merely "to collect an audience." In this way Shakespeare stands apart not only from his own time but from the pre-Reformation past as well. What is more, he anticipates and is fundamentally sympathetic with Warton's own eighteenth-century present: "The Shakespeare of a more instructed and polished age, would not have given us a magician darkening the sun at noon, the sabbath of the witches, and the cauldron of incantation."[11] As in the transcription of Lambarde's account of *Jack Snacker of Wytney*, a benighted past is distinguished from a brighter, more "polished" modernity through a metonymy of physical objects (cauldrons), sensory experiences (darkness and incantation), and idolatrous rituals similar to popish hocus pocus (the witches' Sabbath). Shakespeare, however, is viewed as a liminal figure who, by virtue of his mind, stands on the threshold of the Enlightenment and heralds the dawn of Reason. In this way, Warton rescues the Renaissance author par excellence from his own age.

The derogation of medieval artifacts extends to other disciplines besides the study of English literary history. It is precisely the divorce of the subject from the object that, in Jacob Burckhardt's widely influential *The Civilization of the Renaissance in Italy* (1860), drives a temporal wedge between the Renaissance and the Middle Ages. Burckhardt maintained that, beginning in the fourteenth century, the ancient civilizations of Greece and Rome "obtained so powerful a hold on Italian life" that, with their peculiar political status as city-states, they "combined to produce the modern Italian spirit, which was destined to serve as the model and ideal for the whole western world."[12] As a result, the medieval veil "woven of faith, illusion, and childish prepossession" melted so that, on the one hand, "an *objective* treatment and consideration of the State and of all the things of this world became possible" and, on the other hand, "man became a spiritual *individual,* and recognized himself as such."[13] Objects, of course, remain present and important to the Renaissance genius, but this historical awakening endows the subject with both objective detachment from all the things in the world and a recognition of one's own autonomy.[14]

Attendant on that consciousness is a newfound interest in the objects of antiquity (and decidedly not those of the Middle Ages) on their own terms. Burckhardt relates the story of the accidental excavation near Rome of an ancient marble sarcophagus containing the well-preserved body of a young woman. "It was said that she still kept the colours of life, with eyes and mouth half open. She was taken to the palace of the 'Conservatori' on the Capitol; and then a pilgrimage to see her began." The point of the story, he says, is not its veracity "but the firm belief that an ancient body, which was now thought to be at last really before men's eyes, must of necessity be far more beautiful than anything of modern date."[15] The classical object occludes the medieval.

Or does it? Burckhardt's excavation story conforms quite closely to the hagiographic genre of *inventiones,* that is, narratives concerning the finding or discovery (*inventio*) of a saint's relics. Beginning with the fifth-century *Revelatio Sancti Stephani,* these stories were popular throughout Europe for the duration of the Middle Ages.[16] Burckhardt, then, borrows a widely practiced medieval genre to tell the story about the irrelevance of the Middle Ages. In fact, his account includes several of the major plot elements of the *inventiones,* most notably the body's miraculous preservation, its odor of sanctity, and its subsequent *translatio* to a shrine, though here a site for aesthetic rather than religious pilgrimage.[17] This passage is worth noting for the way it pulls back the curtain on Burckhardt's historiography: we see him enacting the fiction of the Renaissance author he helps to create, the author who, though clearly indebted to medieval antecedents, ignores, abjures, or silently borrows them in an effort to exult classical forms and constitute the Renaissance itself.

Inventiones are narrative supplements designed to consolidate varying accounts in an oral tradition or to fill in the gaps between sporadically documented histories.[18] Burckhardt, however, ingeniously uses this narrative to open a historical chasm. The young woman's corpse serves as a temporal index, a sign not of bodily decay but of the decline of the civilization that has intervened between her death and rediscovery. There cannot, after all, be a cultural renaissance unless it ensues upon a period of decadence and decay. Thus not only medieval artifacts but also classical objects, in their luminosity, may serve to derogate the Middle Ages and separate them from the Renaissance subject.[19]

However fascinating the classical artifact was to the Renaissance mind, it never, according to Burckhardt, entirely held sway over it. As Erwin Panofsky articulates in his powerful Burckhardtian account of the Renaissance revolution in historical consciousness, the Renaissance artist's relation to the world of objects was one of mastery; unlike his medieval predecessors, he could keep things in perspective.[20] "In the Italian Renaissance," he writes, "the classical past began to be looked at from a fixed distance, quite comparable to the 'distance between the eye and the object' in that most characteristic invention of this very Renaissance, focused perspective."[21]

According to Panofsky, the technology of perspectival visual representation reflects the Renaissance's historical perspective: "The men of the Renaissance were convinced that the period in which they lived was a 'new age' as sharply different from the medieval past as the medieval past had been from classical antiquity and marked by a concerted effort to revive the culture of the latter."[22] Like Burckhardt, Panofsky attributes to the Renaissance a mastery over past objects that the Middle Ages lacked. "Medieval art, for Panofsky, had been incapable of joining historical subject matter with its proper historical form: Eve was portrayed in the pose of a *Venus pudica,* for example, and the Trojan priest Laocoön tonsured like a monk."[23] The new "cognitive distance" he ascribes to the Renaissance is absent from the protorenaissances of the ninth and twelfth centuries.[24]

It is important to reemphasize the manner in which artifacts serve chronographic purposes. Mixing ancient and contemporary objects, medieval art is anachronistic; placing objects in their proper visual and temporal place, Renaissance art is properly historicist.[25] Panofsky readily admits "that the Renaissance was linked to the Middle Ages by a thousand ties," but in his narrative medieval artifacts themselves testify to a historical break—and therefore to their own obsolescence:

> Something rather decisive, then, must have happened between 1250 and 1550. And when we consider two structures erected during this interval in the same decade but on different sides of the Alps—Alberti's Sant'Andrea at Mantua, begun in 1472 and the choir of St. Sebaldus at Nuremberg, completed in that very year—we strongly suspect that this decisive thing had happened in the fifteenth century and on Italian soil.[26]

Locked into a progressive chronology of artifacts where the neoclassical occludes the medieval, the Gothic choir is dead on arrival. Works like the architecture of Sant'Andrea as well as examples borrowed from Vasari (the *Laocoön,* the *Torso of the Belvedere,* the *Venus,* and the *Apollo*) supersede "the imperfections still present in the style of the Quattrocento"[27] and "'caused the disappearance . . . of that dry, rude and cutting manner' which, 'by too much study,' had come to prevail" in the fourteenth century.[28]

What the medieval artifact renders inert, the Renaissance genius enlivens—and not, Panofsky says, in the visual arts alone. In literature as well he believes the Renaissance "succeeded in resurrecting the soul of antiquity instead of alternately galvanizing and exorcising its corpse."[29] A hapless necromancer, the medieval artist can neither bury nor revive the dead objects of the past, but the Renaissance master, like Christ at the tomb of Lazarus, first stands "weeping at the grave of antiquity" before miraculously resurrecting it.[30]

The most influential twentieth-century history of early English drama, E. K. Chambers's 1903 *The Mediaeval Stage,* likewise contrasts dead medieval objects with invigorating Renaissance genius.[31] Chambers was hardly thinking of the famous pageant wagons of great cycle sequences when he gave his book its title. In his account, mystery drama signifies only to the extent that it awakens a "deep-rooted" popular dramatic instinct that was manifest in many other forms of entertainment. To the question, "What then, in sum, was the heritage which the early Elizabethan writers and players of interludes received from their immediate predecessors?" Chambers responds by glorifying Shakespeare and reducing the Middle Ages to a mere conduit—worse, a sepulchre—of pagan antiquity. In the early years of Elizabeth's reign, he writes, "a heterogeneous welter of all the dramatic elements of the past and future" began to emerge so that "belated morals and miracle-plays jostle with adaptations of Seneca and Plautus." This confused and jumbled mass constitutes "precisely the dry bones which one day, beneath the breath of genius, should spring up into the wanton life of the Shakespearean drama."[32]

Chambers is noted and criticized above all for his secularization thesis, a diachronic narrative of how the professional London stage came about through the gradual, linear progression of popular dramatic forms from the church nave to the marketplace and eventually the Globe itself.[33] It is important to note, however, that as in Warton's account, medieval religious drama ultimately contributes very little to the professional English stage according to Chambers. It is the dross that is siphoned out in his dialectical narrative of the forging process of history.[34] Consequently, only village festivals, May games, mummings, and so forth, and not the mystery cycles, are what truly qualify for him as "medieval drama."[35] After a millennium in which the ancient art of drama was left to wither into mere "dry bones," early Elizabethan playwrights began to exhume its ancient remains buried in various elements of folk culture and so the stage is set for the flourishing "palmy days" of Shakespeare and his contemporaries.[36]

The disciplines of literature, history, and art history have, therefore, long dismissed the significance of medieval objects to Renaissance artists and authors, let alone "The Author" William Shakespeare.[37] The narrative of diachronic change by which we abstract the latter from the former is predicated upon a bias against the materiality and craft of the Middle Ages. Exploring material connections between early sixteenth-century drama and the later professional London stage, this book is not predisposed to accept the schism between Renaissance subject and medieval object that has reinforced the great historical divide in early English drama. I contend, rather, that if we overturn the traditional Burckhardtian view of the subject's lordship or mastery over the object, then we may expose the artificiality of the subject-object binary and, with it, the very title of "Renaissance author" that has secured Shakespeare's place in the canon. My purpose is not to obscure Shakespeare's considerable abilities but to insist that the medieval objects he molds into early modern drama be allowed to assert their agency on both the playmaker and his audiences such that Shakespeare emerges less as an author—an originator or founder—than as a play-wright, a builder or maker of plays whose stagecraft is often inspired by medieval artifacts.

Before turning to the question of Shakespeare and the mystery plays, however, I would like to counterbalance the traditional view of early modernity as a world newly set free from the trifles of medieval religion and culture and to show how thoroughly saturated with medieval artifacts and antecedents Renaissance culture really was. Though of course not all early modern works are indebted to medieval objects or concepts, this chapter does rather audaciously claim that it was nearly impossible for an early modern author not to be influenced (whether positively or negatively) by medieval objects. In what follows, therefore, I explore sixteenth- and seventeenth-century historiographies that complicate the traditional narrative of diachronic historical difference between a supposedly naive, mechanical Middle Ages and a sophisticated, intellectual Renaissance that disdained contact with the crude materials of a benighted past. I identify three overarching modes of early modern discourse that, by deploying tropes of recuperation, return, and afterlife, preserve contact with past matter: exemplarity, palimpsests, and anachronism.

There are many examples in addition to those from Shakespeare that demonstrate the degree to which medieval objects helped to define Renaissance culture. Of particular interest is the way in which objects both denote and deny temporality and historical difference—that is, the roles that artifacts play within these histories and, above all, in articulating them.[38] Exemplarity, palimpsests, and anachronism each configure history in different ways. If we were to imagine the present and the past as two texts on the desk of an early modern student, we might say (with the partial success that analogies always offer) that exemplarity situates the past as an open text adjacent to the present one in which the student writes; he draws inspiration and culls anecdotes and sententiae from the old text but also writes about his encounters with it. A palimpsestic approach imagines the student inscribing his text on the leaves of the old; what he reads influences what he writes so that sometimes gaps and entire pages of the past text remain legible, partly edited, or marginally glossed—others are ripped out. In anachronism, perhaps the oddest of the three, the two texts, covering very different subjects, are widely separated on the desk and yet appear to be one and the same.

I don't see these historiographies as autonomous, competing, or mutually exclusive, however: they resemble and reinforce each other in many ways. Palimpsestic overwriting of medieval dogma by Reformation or Counter-Reformation polemicists may, for example, require the consultation of authoritative exemplars. The aim of my discussion is to illustrate early modern culture's various and complex encounters with the medieval past and to call particular attention to the manner in which it re-formed its attachments to artifacts that we have long sequestered from our scholarly consideration.

Exemplarity

Early modern reading practices, pedagogy, and technologies like the commonplace book encouraged students to look to the past as a storehouse of models for present action in the world. On the one hand, exemplarity necessarily implies historical difference; in fact, the authority of a model may accrue as it recedes further and further from the present. This proverbial wisdom—*Et bonum quo antiquius, eo melius*—is recited in the opening chorus of Shakespeare's *Pericles* (I. Cho., 10), a play that dramatizes its reliance on the authority of the medieval text of John Gower's *Confessio Amantis*. On the other hand, exemplarity, premised as it is on the repeatability of the past, proposes that historical distance can be—must be—overcome.[39] To facilitate recuperation, a Renaissance student or reader must first break or fragment and epitomize history. The word "exemplum" comes from the Latin verb *eximere*, "to extract" or "to take away." Once detached, the historical antecedent may, with all of its applicability as well as its incongruity, be brought to bear on the present situation or crisis.

When I use the term "exemplarity" to describe a mode of historiography, I am referring to its divergent manifestations in ethics, rhetoric, and poetry (the exposition of ideal moral behavior through exempla, say, or an older text that serves as a model for poetic invention). More important, however, I employ the term to refer to the fundamental historiographical posture or attitude that these various practices cumulatively foster in late medieval and early modern culture. Whereas an agonistic model of aesthetic production demands originality and therefore a diachronic break from past authors and conventions, exemplarity imagines a transhistorical community more akin to the generous reciprocity among friends that early modern readers would have gleaned from Cicero and Seneca.[40] It encourages social, cultural, and literary contact and exchange.[41]

The exemplary model or author is often explicitly, even fondly, acknowledged, as when Shakespeare brings Gower on stage in *Pericles* or when he cites Chaucer as the "noble breeder" of the *Two Noble Kinsmen*. But exemplarity's amicable climate of disinterested sharing may also mean that, as with Shakespeare's indebtedness to Chaucer's *Troilus and Criseyde* and Chapman's *Homer,* borrowings remain anonymous because they need not be acknowledged.[42] For this reason it is helpful to include the topoi of literary genres and even borrowed stage practices as forms of exemplarity. As we will see, unacknowledged borrowing is particularly characteristic of the syntax or structure of representation of the professional London playhouses.

Exemplarity is associated almost exclusively with Renaissance humanists, but it is an ancient exercise practiced throughout the Middle Ages.[43] As Larry Scanlon has established, exemplary narrative form, once rooted in pagan Roman notions of political *auctoritas,* was co-opted, first by the medieval church but then again by late medieval vernacular poets who chafed against clerical authority. Its widespread influence in English culture by the middle of the fourteenth century may be seen in Chaucer's *Canterbury Tales,* Gower's *Confessio Amantis,* Hoccleve's *Regement of Princes,* and Lydgate's *Fall of Princes.*[44] According to Scanlon, moreover, Shakespeare's status as the principal author of English letters arises directly from the secular poetic authority founded upon these four canonical works in the Chaucerian tradition.[45]

But what interests me is Scanlon's account of the performativity of the exemplum, past authority's ability to empower rather than restrict the present, for this provides further cultural evidence for the profound reliance on theatrical antecedents by the fledgling professional theaters.[46] While exemplarity was a pedagogical system designed to prepare the student for practical worldly and especially political action, it also fostered broader habits of thinking, reading, and writing that assimilated medieval as well as ancient models. In their grammar school and in some cases university education, early modern playwrights were encouraged to look to the past for examples and, by decontextualizing them from their historical particulars, adapt them to present circumstances. Combined with the unrehearsed *disputatio* routinely performed by English schoolboys, exemplarity placed the past within relatively easy mental reach of the debater/orator who needed to offer authoritative precedents for or against a stated viewpoint or course of action.[47] Nearly every scene Shakespeare wrote reflects this system of education, particularly those moments of debate between a protagonist and her adviser-friend. Indeed, it was a highly effective rhetorical training system for the many contingencies of professional acting and playwriting. The demands of staging up to forty plays per season in large, fixed, public theaters competing for audiences with various other forms of entertainment would have fostered a culture of exemplarity among playwrights—and noneducated actors as well—who felt compelled to look for tried-and-true models. In short, the need for novelty on the professional London stage meant that England's dramatic past was held close at hand.

The early modern theater's assimilation of medieval dramatic examples manifested itself in structural, thematic, and material forms. That it did so was, for Glynne Wickham, not only a matter of "common sense" but also evidence of the fact that "the public theatres of Elizabethan London were the crowning glory of medieval experiment."[48] Far from rejecting medieval dramatic practice, Shakespeare, according to Robert Weimann, was notably accomplished at blending originality and tradition.[49] Indeed, the professional London stages were uniquely situated in time and place to conjoin (and thereby capitalize upon) the oral and body-centered spectacles of older performance traditions as well as the literary art of humanist poetry newly learned in grammar schools and universities.[50] It was only the gradual ascendancy of humanism during the course of the English Renaissance that, for Weimann, drew attention to the author's pen at the expense of the actor's voice and body and thus tipped the scales against the "performant function" inherited from popular native theatrical traditions.

But according to Helen Cooper, the ascendancy of classical literary culture hardly diminished Shakespeare's reliance on medieval dramatic examples, which, in her estimation, freed him from the "narrowing and exclusive" restrictions of humanist drama.[51] These borrowings range from abstract theories to expedient technologies that are often invisible, she argues, to drama historians trained to annotate direct quotations and other verbal echoes. Textual connections rarely exist, Cooper explains, and we must look under our scholarly noses for dramaturgical assumptions and approaches that were carried over from late medieval drama and culture yet have so long been deemed early modern and uniquely characteristic of the professional London stage that they have escaped our notice.[52]

As is often pointed out, for example, the London playhouses ignored classical rules of genre and decorum: Shakespeare and his contemporaries mixed tragic and comic action. Less often noted, however, is that the professional stage, like the mystery play tradition, "acted its action," rather than rhetorically conveying offstage events after the manner of ancient Greek and Roman drama.[53] Staging the action is just one feature of what Cooper calls "total theatre," an ambitious dramaturgical method Shakespeare shared with the mysteries that transcends literal mimesis by attempting to stage God and other immaterial beings, invisible persons and objects, vast stretches of time, and wide expanses of space. Even Shakespeare's transformation of, or complete departure from, traditional English exemplars bespeaks his indebtedness.[54]

Shakespearean narrative and characterization are fundamentally informed by thematic patterns borrowed from the still-vital mystery play tradition. For example, Michael O'Connell demonstrates how the frequently occurring theme of male sexual jealousy, and particularly the unjustifiable persecution of a virtuous woman, follows the exemplar of Joseph's distrust regarding Mary's conception of Jesus.[55] In the same way that the mystery play characters of Herod and Pilate inform tyrants like Macbeth and Richard III, the figure of Joseph serves as a model for suspicious husbands like Othello and Leontes.[56] Characters like Kent/Caius in *King Lear* may be patterned after figures from the morality play tradition such as Plain Speech and, more important, the "narrative stages" of that tragedy are modeled after "Summons of Death" morality plots.[57] For John D. Cox, stage devils were not merely inherited medieval patterns for early modern characters such as Iago and Richard III but wholesale importations—an explicit, though vestigial, borrowing or remnant of that older dramatic tradition. This extraordinarily protracted career meant that long after sacred beings like God and angels were banned from English dramatic performance, spectators regularly witnessed onstage dramatic manifestations of evil—right up to the moment that the commercial theaters were closed in 1642.[58]

The Old Drama did not merely offer models for individual characters or character types but structurally underpinned some of the most famous scenes in Shakespeare's plays.[59] Accordingly, the dramaturgy of true and false resurrections from the *Antichrist* pageants of the mystery cycles impresses its mark upon such moments as Falstaff's phony resurrection on the Shrewsbury battlefield. As we will see in chapter 5 with respect to *Macbeth,* scenes involving dramaturgy borrowed from earlier (and especially pre-Reformation) forms of English drama offered Shakespeare an apparently irresistible opportunity to rebuke Puritan antitheatrical prejudices.[60] Shakespeare may therefore be said to adopt, in an exercise of theatrical exemplarity, traditional stage practices and adapt them to suit new theatrical and political purposes.[61]

The significance of the London stage's widespread exemplarity is, to return to Scanlon, that it empowered rather than shackled present dramatic practices. For in choosing what to exemplify—to lift out of the past as worthy of imitation—the present selects or brackets a piece of the past to suit and, more importantly, to authorize and enable its own purposes. The past itself does not constitute authority; the past acquires authority when applied to present circumstances.[62] The exemplar may therefore be said to possess a double-edged efficacy: to resist innovation and to become the very means of modernization. As we'll see in the next chapter, this insight will be crucial to understanding the afterlives of dramatic remnants from the mystery plays.

The production of literary texts according to accepted forms and conventions is fundamentally a kind of exemplarity. And certain genres, such as miracle plays and hagiography, overtly advertise their metonymic use of biblical figures as exemplars. Dynamic and flexible, genres allow a wide variety of political and social concerns to be handled using familiar literary and rhetorical tools.[63] On the other hand, genres reassure readers and audiences by promising conformity to expectations, and in doing so, effectively synchronize historically and culturally diverse texts.[64]

Renaissance culture was well read in medieval genres and literary forms. Even that most medieval of literary categories, the saint's life, was not buried by Reformers but, according to Julia Lupton, raised to new life. She traces a generic genealogy of hagiographic and typological conventions and themes between apparently dissimilar Renaissance texts.[65] *The Winter's Tale,* for instance, dramatizes a hagiography that is distinctively pagan as well as Catholic, but the play cannot be said to do so without the ascendency of Protestant historiography, which bankrupted these older discourses and thereby aided and enabled their rebirth.[66] The play's famous statue scene both powerfully re-creates traditional Marian iconography and yet definitively challenges it. Consequently, Lupton argues, "*The Winter's Tale* neither melancholically glorifies the icons of the Church nor manically participates in their smashing; rather, it takes up the fragments of the idols *as* fragments, stones of Rome whose vestigial thaumaturgy and iconographic redeployments animate Shakespearean drama."[67] To do so presupposes a thorough familiarity with narratives of saint's lives on the part of Shakespeare and his audience.

The conventions of medieval romance were dramatized on the boards of the London stage as well. Unlike the social satire of classical Plautine comedy or contemporary London plays by Jonson and others, the signature feature of Shakespearean comedy, the romantic plot culminating in marriage, is a medieval borrowing. Many who visited the playhouses were familiar with this pattern of story from hugely popular vernacular narrative romances, which had become available as never before since the advent of printing.[68] *The Comedy of Errors,* acutely indebted to Plautus as it is, nevertheless imports significant elements from Gower's fourteenth-century account of *Apollonius of Tyre* in his *Confessio Amantis,* a text still popular enough among Tudor readers and Jacobean audiences to be printed in 1554 and adapted to the stage in *Pericles* (c. 1608).[69]

With their pattern of contrition, long-suffering atonement, and eventual redemption, not *Pericles* alone but all of Shakespeare's romances are particularly indebted to medieval literary conventions.[70] Central to this dramatic model is the presence of strong female protagonists who, like their male counterparts, have the fortitude and wisdom to venture on their own quests rather than serving as mere prizes for their successful completion.[71] For Cyrus Mulready, medieval narrative romance does not merely afford Shakespeare numerous exemplars but becomes a popular stage genre in its own right—offering, by virtue of its fantastical voyages and quests of knightly errantry, formal and material models that fueled English imaginings of overseas commercial and imperial expansion.[72] A study of Mercator's historic 1569 wall map demonstrates that romance narratives, far from being discredited, materially determined how early modern cartographers viewed the great globe itself.[73]

Medieval romance exerted a broad influence on early modern culture that was not confined to the professional theater. Edmund Spenser's *The Faerie Queene* is keenly aware of its place within both literary and historiographical narrative traditions, especially Middle English romance. According to Andrew King, Spenser's great epic poem represents a dialogue or witty debate between Spenser and Chaucer rather than a unidirectional line of indebtedness or influence from past to present. More important, the conventions of Middle English romance set the terms of this discussion. Torn between his active interest in native romances and his admiration for Chaucer, who disparaged them, Spenser ingeniously composes a "'Chaucerian' misreading of *Sir Thopas.*"[74] Consequently, the text of *The Faerie Queene* antiquates itself as it reproduces for its readers the experience of reading a fifteenth-century manuscript anthology in which Spenser (re)appropriates the very same romances that Chaucer's *Sir Thopas* had ridiculed.[75]

More than cultivating archaism for the sake of literary nostalgia, this generic engagement by Spenser is an exercise in exemplarity: it facilitates his participation in a contemporary religious debate. Antiquarians like Matthew Parker, John Bale, William Camden, John Dee, and John Stow desired to put historiography to the service of English Protestant nationalism. Spenser's writings open a new front that both complements and complicates this endeavor, for though he may achieve, as King suggests, a kind of literary reformation—an assimilation of a medieval English literary heritage "in order to gain 'prophetic' authority for the Reformation"—yet it is also true that he recovers a "monkish" pre-Reformation genre that Reformers like Parker and Bale had neglected.[76]

Just as religious Reformers would cite Duns Scotus, Peter Lombard, or Thomas Aquinas to refute their Roman Catholic adversaries, early modern discourses condemning romances borrowed medieval exemplars to craft their arguments. The result was that Protestant antiromance polemics were temporally hybrid composites applying old rhetoric to a new cause and context.[77] The next section of this chapter will revisit this phenomenon as we examine the palimpsestic texts of the Reformation; for now, however, it is sufficient to note that doctrinal allegiance often mattered far less to later writers seeking narrative exemplars and argumentative strategies. Medieval romances were thus kept in close proximity to the early modern present even as they were being censured.

Associating exemplarity with Renaissance humanism, we may lose sight of the numerous ways in which early modern writers constructed medieval authors and texts as "antique" models for imitation. They may even, as when Tudor poets encountered the works of Chaucer, have viewed their modern writings as uncouth imitations of revered medieval exemplars.[78]

Palimpsests

A palimpsest is a material object that testifies to several temporal moments of inscription. But it is also a complex system, or network, of material agency, whose embedded yet partially visible histories impinge on the writer even as it receives a new impression. If, like Julian Yates and Jonathan Gil Harris, we bear in mind this actor-network model of the palimpsest, we may further unsettle our casual yet absolute distinction between subjects and objects and begin to consider Renaissance authorship in terms of its connectedness to, and profound investment in, medieval artifacts.[79]

It has long been observed that the Reformation was fought in the margins of books, but if that is the case, then it materializes not as an erasure, purgation, or return that occludes the Middle Ages but as a palimpsest that bears witness to the ongoing accretion of glosses on abiding points of debate inherited from that earlier period. A wide variety of popular devotional activities, objects, and buildings furnish us with a dynamic picture of the negotiations and renegotiations with pre-Reformation ritual and belief performed by both English Protestants and Catholics.

Libraries were perhaps the most important sites for the Reformation's contact with the medieval past. To view this cultural and ideological revolution as a historic break, or merely in terms of iconoclastic destruction, is to overlook the creation and circulation of new texts and practices out of the textual legacy of the Middle Ages.[80] Early modern libraries facilitated this material production. In their contact with medieval books, Jennifer Summit argues, later readers were confronted with medieval modes of reading, including *lectio divina, allegoresis,* and *compilatio,* which, though they opposed at first, they nevertheless selectively adapted to suit their own practices and purposes.[81] In this way, memory and the textual past were inherently inscribed in Protestant literary efforts of self-definition. One such work is, again, Spenser's *Faerie Queene.* With its "poetics of wreckage," the allegory of Protestant nationhood in book 2 represents an extended reflection upon the work of cultural recovery and transformation performed in and upon English libraries.[82]

Medieval texts and textual practices directly influenced the way that early modern printers made books and early modern readers consumed them. We might expect the medieval practice of ornamenting religious books with embroidered bindings featuring devotional images to have died out when *sola scriptura* displaced holy images with the sacred word, not only in the texts of Bibles but in prayer books as well. William Sherman, however, has noted the persistence of iconography in Protestant prayer books. He studies a fascinating devotional volume that, with its curious blending of manuscript and early print conventions, is "stubbornly transitional."[83] As it bridges the gap between printed page and written manuscript, Protestant scripturalism and Catholic images, the early modern present and the medieval past, it clears a material space for other middle grounds:

> It is a manuscript copy of the entire printed Book of Common Prayer and Psalter—the two texts that together formed the established script for the ritual conversations between a minister and his congregation, on the one hand, and between individuals and God, on the other. It was made in the early 1560s and it features an elaborate decorative scheme drawing on the visual conventions of both printed books and manuscripts . . . including some seventy capitals devised in the style of woodcuts from contemporary printed books, and another seventy illuminated letters that were recycled from three or more late medieval manuscripts using scissors and paste.[84]

As private and custom-made as any manuscript, the book diligently declares its common and contemporary allegiances both by its ornamental Tudor roses and by fully and carefully copying out the entire text of the Act of Uniformity. Its recycled decorative initials, however, lend a "retro" appearance and may suggest loyalty to older institutions, a desire to tangibly preserve the past, and above all an earnest investment in, and perhaps even a fervent devotion to, the sacred efficacy of illuminated letters.[85]

Official Protestant books also found it difficult to erase the past. Elizabeth commissioned a Latin prayer book in 1560 that featured a calendar of saints reminiscent of traditional Catholic primers, and the 1561 Book of Common prayer included sacred as well as secular calendars, so that traditional saints' days were found inscribed together with the dates of legal terms, astrology, and royal accession anniversaries. Zealous reformers were undoubtedly disappointed to see the lingering residue of popery in the sanctioned prayer book of the English Church, but they would have to wait a century before the verbal and visual traces of the Old Faith were more completely excised.[86]

Palimpsests do more than tell the story of the past's refusal to go quietly. They also illustrate the powerful material forces used by the present to subdue and contain it. As Siân Echard's study of the use of Saxon font in early modern texts demonstrates, medieval artifacts may retroactively serve to confine and demote their own history. On the one hand, texts such as archbishop Matthew Parker's 1566 *Testimonie of Antiquitie,* the first printed book to contain Anglo-Saxon characters, deployed that script as part of a larger effort to provide the Church of England with an ancient pedigree. In this sense, the material reproduction of the font lends the weight and authority of the English past against Roman letters and doctrines. On the other hand, the Saxon characters of the Old English text may have had the potential both to alienate early modern readers and to foster disparaging associations with the uncivilized and benighted "Gothish" past.[87] Even if the category of the gothic was still largely neutral and descriptive, the Saxon script contrasted sharply with the attractive and familiar italic font of contemporary English books, which took Latin humanist texts as their model and authority. Typography discriminates: by visually setting Old English apart, it confirms assumptions, connections, and implications very different from those of modern English characters and confers or denies cultural cachet.[88] The material presence of the past is not a guarantee of its sustained proximity. Its very presence may both signal and contribute to its gradual detachment from the present.

To turn the question around, cultural recovery may come about both in spite of and as an unintended consequence of reform and even erasure. Seventeenth-century religious polemicist attempts to extinguish the traces of

Catholic folklore legends quite often ensured the preservation of these tales. Pamphlets, books, and sermons condemning popery, satanic artifice, and witchcraft thus serve as palimpsestic records of spells, prophylactic rhymes, and forbidden rites.[89] In fact, Alison Shell argues, the very fear and condemnation of old popish practices bears witness to the ongoing uneasiness about their possible efficacy.[90] Rejected ideologies thus often find refuge not merely alongside but within refuting texts.[91] Though written to disprove or purify the main body of an adversary's text, marginal glosses may serve instead as manicules, indexes that highlight illicit views that would otherwise have remained buried and hard to find. As we will see in chapter 2, the annotations of a previous reader or compiler might draw the reader's attention to forbidden material and even help to preserve it.

We might also say that English Catholic recusancy and the Counter-Reformation did not expunge what they considered newly inscribed heresies. Rather, new ideological glosses were accreted onto old texts and old liturgical practices acquired new contexts. According to Phebe Jensen, sixteenth- and seventeenth-century commonplace books containing late medieval Christmas carols were centerpieces in the communal festivities of recusant families. The carols in these collections revive late medieval English Christmas traditions yet also revise them to suit Counter-Reformation spiritual priorities and obligations.[92] The commonplace book of the Blundells of Little Crosby, for example, records carols authored by William Blundell during the 1620s and 1630s as well as earlier English songs. When composing his carols, Blundell borrowed from Counter-Reformation sermons and thereby created a temporally composite text that bears the imprint of post-Tridentine recusancy as well as traces of the older fifteenth-century caroling form.[93]

With their Latin tags, Marian devotion, and casual mixing of the sacred and profane, carols were often used to articulate religious recusancy and political opposition. Their very presence on the pages of manuscript commonplace books suggests that they were recorded as part of a broader, perhaps multigenerational, struggle for religious expression.[94] Edmund Bolton's 1600 *England's Helicon,* for instance, records a carol entitled "The Sheepheards Song: A Caroll or Himme for Christmas" that reinscribes Elizabethan pastoral allusions to Elizabeth, the May queen, with more conventional religious references.[95] The Blundell and Bolton carol collections are good illustrations of the palimpsestic complexity of the English Reformation. Through the writing over of a Reformed text, recusancy may be visible as the most recent impression, or it may simply be glimpsed in the preservation of an earlier inscription, a significant though often unseen agent in early modern English religious culture.[96]

Early modern palimpsests need not be textual. The Renaissance's peculiar sensitivity to "untimeliness" means that London architecture and even the bodily histrionics of the Lord Chamberlain's Men may display polychronicity akin to the palimpsest's inadequate material erasure.[97] Like Pierre Nora's *lieux de mémoire,* landscape features such as holy wells inscribe the countryside with traces of its idolatrous and superstitious past.[98] So pervasive was this inscription that vegetation bore impressions as well. Seasonal flowers gathered to festoon church altars, shrines, and statues on the many saints' days, feasts, and liturgies in the Catholic calendar acquired, over time, religious names connoting their sacred and later, after the Reformation, their idolatrous purpose.[99]

Medieval monastic ruins were particularly evocative palimpsestic texts that informed long-standing oral traditions and, eventually, the Gothic novel. Orally transmitted "sacrilege narratives"—that is, supernatural stories in which "sacred stones cry out against sacrilege, calling down divine vengeance on the perpetrator"—were, in Shell's words, "*attached to* ruined abbeys, martyrs' relics, and other highly visible signs of Reformation violence."[100] Decorative emblems or mottoes were displayed on or in buildings as a means of exorcising, so to speak, such sacrilegious histories. A commonplace example was the image of an eagle unwittingly bearing a flaming coal from a sacred altar and thus destroying its nest and offspring. Ephraim Udall's *Noli Me Tangere* (1642) chose this emblem as its frontispiece, and in the text Udall urges wealthy landowners to display it in their homes.[101]

The early modern experience of living in a house with a monastic or religious history must therefore have been rather uncanny. Later residents were obliged to assert their right to the property against its former owners, whose presence was believed to be mysteriously yet substantively attached to the building. In fact, new material objects such as engraved mottoes and other textual embellishments were crafted to speak on behalf of modern subjects and to give them the final word in response to the medieval edifice. In this way, the walls of the house displayed a mute though sometimes contentious dialogue between its current and former occupants.[102] Just as early modern readers, in touching medieval books, were touched by them in turn, so too the buildings, landmarks, and flora of Renaissance England were potential material sites of contact with the Middle Ages.[103] The fact that early modern subjects felt the necessity to refute the historical reproach of medieval artifacts should encourage us to listen to what those objects may have had to say.

London playhouses may also be seen as palimpsests, though the tension between past and present histories was more productive than combative. The great sequences of biblical drama in larger cities like York and Chester required open, public spaces to accommodate their large audiences and, often, streets to facilitate the procession of pageant wagons. These wagons and sometimes the surrounding playing area, including the street below and the windows and balconies above and behind them, were used to represent the *mise-en-scène* of the salvation story: Heaven, Earth, and Hell. Later public playhouses did not frequently need to bring devils and deities on stage, yet large sums were spent nonetheless on the structures and machinery—spangled ceilings, trapdoors, and hoisting mechanisms, for example—required to incorporate this same, three-tiered cosmography. A wide variety of new commercial plays, from tragedies and histories to city comedies and romances, are written on and for this old dramatic surface. Professional playwrights seem especially to have enjoyed writing plays that, in effect, peel back the layers of the playhouse-palimpsest and remind audiences of its earlier history. We see Heaven open for Jupiter to appear in Marlowe's *Dido, Queen of Carthage* and Shakespeare's *Cymbeline.* Heywood's *A Woman Killed with Kindness* reminds the audience that God is "the ultimate spectator and judge," while Lodge and Greene "substitute an enthroned Hosea to take his place and watch over the events on stage" in *A Looking-Glass for London.*[104] Hell gapes in a number of plays, including Marlowe's *Dr. Faustus* and Shakespeare's *Henry VI, Part 1,* while Jonson begins *The Devil Is an Ass* in Hell. My discussion of *Hamlet* in chapter 4 offers a further opportunity to explore the embedded yet partly visible histories of these palimpsestic theatrical spaces.

Perhaps the chief medieval palimpsest—its very status as a work of human hands fiercely debated—is the Eucharistic host. A polychronic object, it joins the biblical moment of the Last Supper to the present moment of devotional eating; and it is achronic, outside time as it anticipates the eschatological banquet of the Lamb. With the introduction of the Lutheran doctrine of *sola fide,* the manner of the presence of Christ's body in the Eucharist was placed under enormous scrutiny. Battle lines were drawn over the manner of Christ's presence: Was he carnally and objectively present, *ex opere operato,* through the Roman Catholic notion of transubstantiation? Was he present together with the substances of bread and wine (Lutheran consubstantiation)? Was Christ's presence "real" yet not local (Calvin)? Or was the Lord's Supper just that, a supper, which merely memorialized Christ's passion and death (Zwingli)?[105]

Few literary historians have been more fascinated by or written more eloquently about this scrutiny of the Eucharist than Stephen Greenblatt. Throughout his career, he underscores the indebtedness of Shakespeare's theater to medieval culture, and particularly religious ritual and liturgy, by first asking, "What happens when a piece of cloth is passed from the church to the playhouse?" and later making the bold assertion that "apparently secular works" like *Hamlet* "are charged with the language of eucharistic anxiety" as to the status of leftover communion bread.[106] In a similar fashion, institutions like exorcism that before had a literal now have a "literary use."[107] The vast machinery of Purgatory is no longer institutionally promulgated in England. Nevertheless, its "poetry" survives in an Elizabethan theater world crammed with ghosts, devils, and spirits.[108] According to Greenblatt, then, the cultural energy once invested in pre-Reformation sacraments and rituals is redirected, after the Reformation, to secular professional theater, as if Reformed liturgies were mere spiritual exercises hopelessly unable to assuage skepticism and nostalgia for embodied ritual.

Yet most Reformers were deeply committed to the sacraments and sought ways to reinscribe Christ's Eucharistic body, not elude it. As Sarah Beckwith reminds us, it is mistaken to anticipate Enlightenment secularism, as Greenblatt tends to do, and assume that the Reformation ushers in an absolute dualism between matter and spirit.[109] There is, in fact, much that Reformed Christianity, particularly in England, retained from the sacramental theology of the Old Religion, including a desire for ritual encounter with the body of Christ. The English Church taught that the Eucharist communicated Christ's real presence, not a bare memorial of the Last Supper.[110] Far from rejecting the flesh, Archbishop Thomas Cranmer's 1550 "Defence of the True and Catholic Doctrine of the Sacrament of the Body and Blood of Our Saviour Christ," for example, underscores the Eucharist's material sustenance.[111]

The other theologian whose writings influenced Reformed Christianity in sixteenth- and seventeenth-century England, though belatedly and often unofficially, is John Calvin. And Calvin, too, was eager to preserve the doctrine of Christ's true and not merely symbolic presence in the sacrament of the Eucharist. In his *Treatise on the Lord's Supper* he declares, "We all confess with one mouth that, in receiving the sacrament in faith, according to the ordinance of the Lord, we are truly made partakers of the real substance of the body and blood of Jesus Christ."[112] Calvin urged weekly participation in the Lord's Supper as a means of strengthening faith in God's mercy. Addressing the importance and efficacy of the sacraments and emphasizing that to receive "in faith" is not merely to use "the understanding and imagination," Calvin claims, "In fact, I see not how any man can attain a solid confidence that he has redemption . . . unless he first has a real communion with Christ himself."[113] According to Calvin, Christ's flesh itself never enters the communicant's body; rather, the person who receives the communion bread in faith is lifted up into the divine presence.[114]

Like Cranmer, therefore, Calvin sees a profound analogy, not a divorce, between body and spirit. Accordingly, one important project of the English Reformation is the recuperation of the material object of the Eucharistic host. To accomplish this, Reformers viewed the history of theology on the Eucharist as a palimpsest whereon they needed to overwrite the theory of transubstantiation, which they saw as a modern addition to the texts of the Fathers, while allowing older teachings on Christ's real presence—by the ancient church, certainly, but also by medieval commentators like Augustine and Bernard—to remain legible.[115]

But the Eucharist is, materially speaking, more than the bread and wine broken and shared on the altar or communion table. It is also a liturgical celebration of Christian community or common-union, and as such it extended beyond the church doors and acquired physical presence through other ritual practices, including biblical drama and, as many scholars have argued, later supposedly secular drama as well.[116] This Eucharistic body also resembles a palimpsest, which plays like the York mysteries interpretatively gloss. "The very gap between an amateur (known) local actor and sacred role, and the juxtaposition of word and thing on stage, help to make the Corpus Christi theater," Beckwith writes, "a commentary upon and an interaction with the Mass and the offices."[117] In a similar fashion the social and sacramental *corpus mysticum* of the medieval church deeply informs, according to Jennifer Rust, the political settlement of the early modern English commonwealth. She argues that the idea of the mystical body was not abandoned but innovatively imagined to have migrated from the Catholic Mass to the body of the Reformed martyr even as it retained its sacramental and mystical features.[118] As the Christian church in England was reformed, its sacraments and rituals were re-formed as well. Reinscribed, not erased, late medieval sacraments form the palimpsestic subtext, or in Beckwith's terms, the grammar and idiom of later early modern discourses, including Shakespearean theater.[119]

Anachronism

Anachronism, Margreta de Grazia observes, is "one of the many ways in which the Whiggish Augustan age asserts its literary superiority over its less refined predecessors."[120] We have glimpsed this acute sensitivity to chronology in the passage from Warton at the beginning of this chapter. But the real problem, as de Grazia explains, is not simply that the Renaissance did not share the Enlightenment's preoccupation with chronology but that we do.[121] Recent art historical study, however, is helping to free us from our assumed diachronic sophistication by showing that the Renaissance was, contrary to Panofsky's account, as thoroughly anachronic as the often-maligned Middle Ages.[122]

Medieval and Renaissance artifacts occupied various modes of temporality, or lived different kinds of "temporal lives."[123] According to Alexander Nagel and Christopher Wood, artists and viewers were able to perceive an artifact not only, as Panofsky argued, in an authorial way—that is, as a unique representation of a particular artist's style and therefore of a definite historical moment.[124] They were also capable of looking past the accidents of an artwork's manufacture and seeing certain artifacts as instantiations, as provisional links in a long chain of substitutable replicas extending back in time. Viewing artifacts in this substitutional mode acknowledges and accepts their polychronicity, for it assumes that the work genuinely replaced its lost and unrecoverable predecessors and, for that very reason, is connected to an unknowable point of origin in antiquity. In fact, it *is* ancient and, equally as important, it lends antiquity a concrete presence.[125] Late medieval and early modern European artists began to explore the productive tension between authorial and instantiated modes of representation. Like their patrons and spectators, they were very well aware that certain artifacts were recently crafted, and yet they might prize these objects as if they were very old.[126]

Nagel and Wood's revision of Panofsky's long-standing (yet tenacious) view of Renaissance art is helpful to this discussion for two reasons. First, it overthrows the theory of disinterested cognitive distance between subject and object that has underpinned author-centered approaches to literary as well as art historical scholarship. Second, it helps us to begin to recuperate a whole category of artifacts that have been dismissed as temporal oddities, namely anachronistic objects, many of which are of medieval origin. Henceforth I will use the term "anachronic" as opposed to the disparaging term "anachronistic," which assumes Panofsky's historicist claim that the moment of material execution sears its brand on every object as a constitutive feature and chains it to the literal circumstances of its making.[127]

The clash of historicities that constituted Renaissance art is visible in the many anachronisms in *St. Augustine in His Study* (c. 1503) by the Venetian painter Vittore Carpaccio, including modern furniture, the trinkets and codices on the shelves, the regalia of a fifteenth-century (not fifth-century) bishop, and a nude Venus unlikely to have belonged to the Bishop of Hippo. The painting very much asserts, in other words, the authorial moment of performance. Yet the substitutional model is simultaneously at work on Carpaccio's canvas. The statue of the resurrected Christ on Augustine's private altar could have been seen in the Venetian church of Santa Maria della Carità at the time the portrait was being painted. While the bronze figure would seem to blend in with the other anachronisms in the room, Nagel and Wood argue that it is not quite the same, for it is a venerated object situated on an altar. In fact, its significance as a cult image believed by contemporary Venetians to be of ancient origin is well documented. For Carpaccio, then, the church statue that served as his model was more than a modern approximation of a lost ancient original: "The bronze Christ did not just 'stand for' or refer poetically to antiquity. Rather, for him the statue *was* an antique work."[128] In a culture that so highly valued the material evidence offered by relics—ancient Christian as well as pagan—and that was adept at reading modern events and objects typologically as well as sacramentally, this paradoxical yet powerful double vision must have seemed quite natural.

Hans Holbein the Younger's famous painting *The Ambassadors* (1533) offers an English example of Renaissance anachronism (figure 1). Two young Frenchmen sent by Francis I to the English court—Jean de Dinteville, seignor

FIGURE 1.   Hans Holbein the Younger, *Jean de Dinteville and Georges de Selve (The Ambassadors)*, 1533. © National Gallery, London/Art Resource, NY.

de Polisy, and Georges de Selve, later bishop of Lavaur—are shown adorned and surrounded by a variety of material objects, including jewels and books as well as scientific and musical instruments. A number of sophisticated readings of the painting discuss the relation between the aristocratic subjects and the meticulously detailed objects.[129] Holbein's subtle suggestion of discord, most notable in the lute with the broken string, is also well established.[130] But attention to the painting's temporal discordance has not been sufficiently noted.

For Kenneth Charlton, the painting frames a particular moment in early modern European history: the age of discovery when voyagers and scientists transformed land, sea, and sky—and, with them, time itself as the Middle Ages gave way to the modern era. The scientific instruments signify the New Science's rejection of medieval scholasticism in favor of British empiricism, "a new chapter in the history of ideas and in the study of those ideas."[131] Greenblatt also claims that Holbein's panel captures and celebrates the authorial moment of the painting's material execution. "Dinteville and Selve are depicted," he writes, "in the context of the highest hopes and achievements of their age," and the intrusive anamorphic skull is "a bravura display of Holbein's virtuosity" as well as a symbol of a Renaissance subject, Thomas More.[132]

But Holbein includes several objects that are temporally out of joint with these authorial readings, which bind the painting to a single historical moment. The torquetum, for example, is hardly evidence of new scientific achievement; it is an astronomical instrument invented in the late twelfth century, around the time that legends of Prester John, whose fantastical kingdom is depicted on the supposedly modern geopolitical globe (on the left of the bottom shelf), began to be popular. Comfortable with our perception of Holbein as a Renaissance artist, we may underestimate his indebtedness to the memento mori tradition and its critique of the vanity of secular power and learning. The anamorphic technique may have arisen from meditative practices popular in the Middle Ages that, through the contemplation of a skull or other emblem of mortality, reminded an introspective person of the brevity of human life and the ephemerality of the world.[133]

The death's-head, though prominent, may not be the most important medieval remnant in this Renaissance portrait. The ceremonial mosaic pavement of colored marble disks, squares, whorls, and guilloches is typical of medieval floors in Rome's major churches, as the connoisseur Henry III (1207–72) well knew when he directed the sanctuary of Westminster Abbey to be similarly paved.[134] Holbein may have used the English floor as a model or he may have had more direct knowledge of Roman Cosmati, as they were called after the family who dominated the craft. The cosmatesque surface in *The Ambassadors* is incongruous both because of its anachronism and because in twelfth- and thirteenth-century Rome these ornamental floors were reserved for sacred spaces.[135] The Roman pavements consisted of the spolia of previous floors and ancient marble leftovers, and thus, when viewed substitutionally, grounded the church in antiquity much more literally than did its claims of apostolic succession. The fact that Holbein's anamorphic skull is situated—or rather is discovered like the medieval *inventio* of a saint's relics—in a sacred floor that has been relocated to a profane setting may suggest that Henry VIII's defiance of Rome is, like the morbid death's-head, a grotesque distortion of worldly authority. But if the mosaic tile is intended to signify Westminster Abbey, then as a substitutional symbol it lends the weight of antiquity to the English crown, and the French embassy may be seen to wrongfully profane holy ground.[136] Either way, the medieval artifact asserts its polychronicity in spite of the fact that scholars have cataloged it as a mere curiosity—or else as further evidence of the historical moment of Holbein's presence at the English court, in which case the cosmatesque floor is silently translated from a thirteenth- to a sixteenth-century object, a colonization of the medieval by the early modern.

Early modern English books are also anachronic. The Anglo-Saxon typography in archbishop Parker's 1566 *Testimonie of Antiquitie,* discussed above, is a powerful illustration. That the archbishop earnestly believed that the Anglo-Saxon characters could, by means of their substitutional temporality, confer ancient authority on his text cannot be doubted, and his need for it must have been great, for the material investment in the typeface was considerable.[137] As Richard Clement states, "the font had a subliminal ability to authenticate the antiquity and authority of a text."[138]

Not only rare Anglo-Saxon typeface but widely used black-letter print also began to signify both Englishness (the "English letter") and, given its antiquated appearance by the seventeenth century, a definite past-ness capable of inducing what Zachary Lesser calls "typographic nostalgia" in some readers.[139] Anachronically updated medieval texts were also empowering. Sixteenth-century printers fashioned Chaucer as a "learned, cosmopolitan contemporary, suitable for the king's library" as well as a proto-Protestant reformer in order to appeal both to Henry VIII's humanist interests and to his desire for church reform.[140]

Spenser's *The Shepheardes Calender* offers a secular, and more lighthearted, example of textual anachronism. King argues that Spenser adorned the book with a deliberately archaic apparatus of woodcuts and marginal annotations to make it appear, like its archaic language, as if it were an older work that he merely chanced upon in Eumnestes's library and edited for his readers' benefit.[141] In doing so, Spenser granted a native English text the status of a classical work, for only the latter was deemed worthy of such apparatuses. Yet we might also think of the *Calender*'s archaic features in substitutional terms. The woodcuts and glosses do not merely recall or refer to antiquity; they *are* ancient and their presence on the page—wryly to be sure—bestows classical status on Spenser's contemporary book. Aside from the expense involved, substitutional anachronism, in addition to authorial determination, may explain why successive printers would carefully preserve the woodcuts as well as the complicated layout and organization of *The Shepheardes Calender* during the course of five quarto editions as well as the 1611 folio.[142]

Sandro Botticelli's *Portrait of a Young Man Holding a Medallion* (c. 1485) further demonstrates the constitutive role of anachronism in Renaissance art; more important, it offers a distinct emblem of the central argument of this chapter, namely, that Renaissance authors often considered medieval artifacts indispensable to their own work (figure 2). The portrait depicts a young man holding a roundel of an unknown saint, but the icon being conspicuously presented to the viewer is not a painted reproduction—it is a genuine relic that has been embedded in a cavity carved out of the modern wood panel. Italy in the late fifteenth century was experiencing a vogue for Byzantine-style icons; this artifact, however, is neither Eastern nor ancient. It is only about a century older than the portrait. Like a jeweler setting a precious gem, Botticelli inserted a prized remnant of gold-ground painting from an altarpiece probably executed by the Sienese master Bartolommeo Bulgarini during the fourteenth century.[143]

The significance of the painting for Nagel and Wood is that it demonstrates the temporal instantiation of icons.[144] From this point of view, the modern, secular figure of the young man is clearly delineated from an object that would have been, in the substitutional mode, considered antique and sacred. Yet the icon is demonstrably not ancient, and if, as an instantiation, it differs from the representation of the youth who holds it, it is likewise removed from its role as a cult image. In fact, Botticelli's decision to encase a piece of a fourteenth-century altarpiece aims, in my opinion, to playfully disturb the substitutional reception of the icon by underscoring its detachment from the ancient past. Tilted slightly to show its bottom frame and the contact it makes with the edge of the painting and the youth's fingers, the roundel is held so as to reveal that a collector, perhaps the painting's sitter, has carved it into its present shape. The embedded object demonstrates, in other words, the historical transformation of Byzantine icons to collectible pieces

FIGURE 2. Sandro Botticelli, *Portrait of a Young Man Holding a Medallion*, c. 1485. Private collection. Reproduced with permission.

of art. The viewer appreciates the artifact both for itself and for its status as a portable object that may be held and admired. The object commands attention though it is not, ostensibly, the "subject" of the portrait. There is, in other words, no sense that Botticelli is proclaiming his mastery or superiority over the Bulgarini artifact. Quite the opposite is true. Underscoring the past-ness of the icon, its diachrony, seems to enliven and synchronize it so that we almost expect the saintly figure to turn his upward gaze toward us and speak.[145]

While the framed icon is markedly different from the painted image of the young man holding it, Botticelli's painting offers an intersecting and overlapping history of portraiture in which the medieval artifact demands recognition as an essential link to classical forms. Both Renaissance subject and medieval object exchange historicities. First of all, the trecento fragment is also a collectible piece of art that situates the painting in the context of a recent modern vogue. Next, the half-length view of the young man is modeled after the Madonnas and saints of the Byzantine icon tradition, and while it would be inaccurate to say that he, too, symbolizes substitution, his truncated torso suggests a closer proximity between the portrait's youthful subject and the object he holds. Furthermore, it was a commonplace medieval practice to include the portraits of friends, patrons, and admired contemporaries as marginal figures in a Crucifixion fresco or Nativity panel. Botticelli cleverly recalls this custom by rendering the secular subject of his portrait still "marginal" in the sense that he is outside the frame of the gold-ground holy scene. Finally, the other major historical influence on early modern portraiture was the sculptural bust, which during the Middle Ages frequently contained a saint's relic. With its encased fragment, Botticelli's painting is therefore both a manifestation of the signature artwork of the Renaissance—the secular portrait—as well as that most medieval of artifacts—the sacred reliquary.

Botticelli's *Portrait of a Young Man Holding a Medallion* illustrates the nature of Renaissance authorship in a way that is crucial to my exploration of Shakespearean drama. In order to emphasize the profound manner in which late medieval and early modern subjects believed that material objects could provide a direct, physical encounter with the past, the epigraph to this chapter cites the fifteenth-century Greek scholar Manuel Chrysoloras. He vividly related his experience of Rome's ancient ruins, including the ekphrastic scenes on monuments like the Arch of Titus, saying, "Herodotus and the other historians did great things with their works; but only in images is it possible to see everything as if in the time at which it happened, and thus this [image-based] history is absolutely and simply exact: or better, if I may say so, it is not history, but direct and personal observation [*autopsía*] and living presence [*parousía*] of all the things that happened then."[146] With an eye toward Shakespearean drama, I'd like to consider Botticelli's portrait as an ek-phrasis, that is, a speaking out of a material vestige of the past. Our entrenched critical instincts may encourage us to view this painting in terms of a Hegelian *Aufhebung:* the trecento fragment (the medieval object) is the inert remnant of a dead tradition of religious portraiture that Botticelli's handsome young man, as proxy for the artist himself (the Renaissance subject), sublates through the masterful assertion of his new, secular presence. Given Chrysoloras's insight, however, we can see that artistic agency works in the opposite way: it is the material artifact, in this case a medieval icon, which sets the conditions for and inspires the creativity of the Renaissance author. Far from thoughts of novelty or originality, the author lives in the presence [*parousía*] of the thing that has inspired, and possibly commanded, his direct and personal observation [*autopsía*]. No wonder the youth proudly displays the icon yet dares not let his fingers touch its surface. This may also explain why Botticelli did not merely paint an imitation of the icon but carved out a space in the panel to receive this aesthetically living and sacred object.

Contrary to Burckhardt and Panofsky, who imagine the Renaissance artist ignoring medieval artifacts (or distracted by them) and focusing instead on classical models, I argue that early modern artists were often preoccupied with medieval artwork. And even when faced with an object that was supposedly ancient yet clearly more modern, they viewed it in such a way that its temporalities cohabitated reciprocally rather than agonistically. The outdated yet tenacious view of the Reformation that we first glimpsed in Warton's account of *Jack Snacker of Wytney* sees a binary dividing Catholicism, superstition, scholasticism, good works, objects, and matter on the one hand from Protestantism, rationalism, humanism, faith, subjects, and spirit on the other. Rather than accept such a "massive value judgment," this book proposes to view the Reformation (in England at least) as a re-formation of the bonds between early modern subjects and medieval artifacts.[147] Despite several determined waves of reform, purgation, prosecution, and iconoclasm (which were unquestionably considerable and devastating), people in sixteenth- and seventeenth-century England continued to live in daily contact with artifacts of medieval culture—in their buildings, tombs, paintings, books, maps, statues, prayers, songs, festivals, and topographical features of the countryside.

But as students of early modern culture, we are predisposed to ignore the historicity of this sweeping array of artifacts. Undoubtedly this is due in part to our disciplinary preparation, but we also have a tendency to either modernize or ignore medieval objects, to suppose them to belong singularly to the period that interests us or to overlook them altogether. Our comfortable, widely held view of the Renaissance artist or author as an *auctor,* a founder or originator, is contingent on this theory of artifacts, as is the very notion of artistic style. Indeed, our idea of the Renaissance artist has emerged ipso facto by the sequestration of medieval objects.

And yet, I argue, medieval objects and practices sparkled with the possibility of reinvention precisely because they could be regarded as displaced, and this reengagement brought them into closer contact, for their obsolescence was not tantamount to their supersession. Having examined a wide spectrum of medieval artifacts, I will presently consider more closely the polychronicity of the dramatic objects of the mystery play tradition so that we may uncover whether and how they were available to Shakespeare. According to Nagel and Wood, "'Renaissance art' was a machine for the production of 'medieval art.'"[148] As we will see, the Shakespearean stage was one of the most productive of these machines.

🍂 CHAPTER 2

The Chester Banns

A Sixteenth-Century Perspective on the Mysteries

> The plays comonlie called the Whitson Plays at
> Mydsommer next cominge shal be sett furth and
> plaide in such orderly manner and sorte as the same
> have bene accustomed.
>
> —Chester City Certificate, 1575

On 10 May 1572, an outspoken Reformed clergyman named Christopher Goodman wrote a letter to the earl of Huntingdon urging that he, as president of the Council of the North, suppress Chester's annual mystery plays. One of a minority of university-educated Protestant divines in the region, Goodman, who had helped to translate the Geneva Bible during his exile, was an eloquent and determined reformer and increasingly successful in turning the local gentry against drama, minstrelsy, dancing, and animal sports.[1] Hinting at mayor John Hankey's collusion with recusant factions, the letter begins with a brief historical sketch of the Chester mystery plays: "certain plays were devised by a monk about 200 years past in the depth of ignorance, & by the Pope then authorized to be set forth, & by that authority placed in the city of Chester to the intent to retain that place in assured ignorance & superstition according to the Popish policy. against which plays all preachers & godly men since the time of the blessed light of the gospell have inveyed and impugned." Goodman's religious views obligate him to divide Chester history, not simply into ancient and modern or past and present periods but rather into Catholic and Protestant epochs, a "past time of monkish ignorance" and a "godly present time of the blessed light of the gospel."[2] This history is, of course, hardly neutral; it is ideologically driven and has as its goal the destruction of the Chester cycle. Not until the Enlightenment of the eighteenth century and Hegel's world history in the following century would a decisive historical break between the Middle Ages and the Renaissance, with the Reformation as the pivotal epochal moment, be assumed as a matter of course.[3] Goodman's letter, therefore, asks us to consider how late sixteenth- and early seventeenth-century Cestrians viewed their city's past, particularly their theatrical history.

Such a consideration might seem irrelevant given current trends urging early English drama scholars to search for continuities rather than disjunctions between the professional London stage and the earlier drama and culture of the sixteenth century. But our eagerness to elide the once sacrosanct medieval-Renaissance divide must not overlook the fact that centuries before E. K. Chambers's 1903 *The Mediaeval Stage* accounted for the growth and evolution of the Renaissance stage at the expense of earlier dramatic forms, pre-Reformation English drama was, if not disparaged, often ignored. Goodman was not alone in his desire "for the repressing of Papacy, & advancing of godliness" through the suppression of drama.[4] In what immediately follows, I briefly consider other early modern English theatrical histories with particular attention to the place afforded (if any) to the mystery play tradition in those narratives.

In his 1607 sermon, the Protestant preacher William Crashaw offered a genealogy of the English stage in which medieval mysteries, the popish progeny of ancient heathen theater, were seen as direct conduits of the ungodly errors put on display in London's public playhouses: "The vngodly Playes and Enterludes so rife in this nation; what are they but *a Bastard of Babylon,* a daughter of error and confusion, a hellish deuice . . . deliuered to the *Heathen,* from them to the *Papists,* and from them to vs?"[5] Reminding King James that the primitive church had condemned plays, Crashaw called for the destruction of this "tower of Babel" as part of a larger program of religious reformation.

Decades before Crashaw, Stephen Gosson, Anthony Munday, and Phillip Stubbes offered histories of English drama that were similarly continuous. Gosson's 1579 *Schoole of Abuse* reflects upon the degeneracy aroused by plays and playgoers in ancient Rome before turning to England itself. Citing Cassius Dio's *Roman History,* he claims that pre-Roman Britain was inhabited by hearty men who "fed vppon rootes and barkes of trees, they would stand vp to the chin many dayes in marishes without victualles." The behavior of contemporary theatergoers, by contrast, leads him to descant pejoratively in terms similar to Shakespeare's Richard III: "Oh what a wonderfull chaunge is this? Our wreastling at armes, is turned to wallowyng in Ladies laps, our courage, to cowardice, our running to ryot. . . . Compare London to Rome, and England to Italy, you shall finde the Theatres of the one, the abuses of the other, to be rife among us."[6]

Following Gosson's lead under the guise of the self-styled "Anglo-phile Eutheo," Anthony Munday claimed that his pamphlet represented the latest "blast" of a righteous trumpet in an uninterrupted history of God-fearing antitheatricality warning Christians to beware the perils of playgoing: "For in al ages the most excellent men for learning haue condemned them by the force of eloquence, and power of Gods worde."[7] Phillip Stubbes similarly took up where Gosson left off, arguing that plays "are quite contrarie to the Word of grace, and sucked out of the Deuills teates, to nourish vs in ydolatrie hethenrie, and sinne."[8] Adding secular authorities, including Scipio and Constantine, he claimed that "all Writers both diuyne and prophane, euer since the beginning haue disalowed them, and writ (almost) whole volumes against them."[9] Gosson, Munday, and Stubbes, thus drew no distinction between heathen and Catholic drama: from the pagan dramas introduced by Caesar's armies to the public plays and interludes of their own time, England, they claimed, had been incessantly plagued with one form of theatrical degeneracy or another.

As several studies have established, the views of Reformed antitheatricalists and iconoclasts are to some extent a carryover from medieval clerical apprehension, not necessarily with theater per se but with the various festivities that fill the ritual church calendar.[10] Plays and other secular pastimes had long been included alongside liturgical celebrations and came in time to be associated with the church calendar itself, so that many reformers later cited theatrical activities as one of many examples of the profanation of Catholicism.[11] What gradually emerged, therefore, was a theatrical genealogy whereby the idolatry of plays was ascribed both to their pagan Greek and Roman origins and to the so-called popery of the late Middle Ages.

By 1633, more extreme Reformed views had so far displaced the old consensus of tolerance that William Prynne's *Histrio-Mastix* could further connect popish ceremony and drama to the London playhouses by, on the one hand, claiming that most professional actors were "professed Papists" and, on the other hand, underscoring the theatricality of Catholic ritual.[12] Just as "Popish Priests and Iesuites in forraigne parts . . . have turned the Sacrament of Christs body and blood into a Masse-play; so they have likewise transformed their Masse it-selfe, together with the whole story of Christs birth, his life, his Passion, and all other parts of their Ecclesiasticall service into Stage-playes."[13] As with his antitheatrical predecessors, Prynne's continuous history of pre- and post-Reformation drama makes no distinctions between the fifteenth-century biblical drama and the professional London stage on the eve of the English Civil War.

We ought to view Reformation narratives with considerable suspicion whether they promote novelty and chronological difference or historical continuity.[14] Yet defenders of the public playhouses were also uneasy about pre-Reformation English religious drama. Written in response to Gosson, Thomas Lodge's *Defence of Poetry, Music, and Playes* (1579) candidly treasures classical Greek and Roman drama for its "ancient custome." While defending poetry, moreover, he approvingly notes, "Chaucer in pleasant vein can rebuke sin vncontrold." But his defense of stage plays offers no corresponding example from the religious drama of the Middle Ages.[15] His discussion of tragedy and comedy leaps from the classical past over those offensive intervening centuries to the modern English present: "Let me apply those dayes to ours, their actors to our players, their autors to ours."[16] Like Chaucer and ancient drama—but conspicuously not Catholic drama—contemporary English stage plays "can rebuke sin vncontrold."

Like Lodge, Thomas Heywood's 1612 *Apology for Actors* responded to antitheatricalists by simply ignoring pre-Reformation English drama altogether. Holding up pagans (not the early church) as the bearers of "antiquity and dignity" to English theater, he wrote, "Thus our Antiquity haue we brought from the *Grecians* in the time of *Hercules,* from the *Macedonians* in the age of *Alexander,* from the Romans long before Iulius Caesar."[17] Embracing theater's pagan origins, Heywood is careful to exclude popish forms of drama: "I omit the shewes and ceremonies euen in these times generally vsed amongst the Catholikes, in which by the Churchmen & most religious, diuerse pageants, as of the Natiuity, Passion, and Ascension, with other Historicall places of the Bible, are at diuerse times & seasons of the year vsually celebrated."[18]

While both theater antagonists and advocates ignore mystery drama and agree that London playhouses revive antiquity in some way, their conflicting accounts raise questions about the place of pre-Reformation plays in the history of early English drama. According to antitheatricalists, the public stages carry on an unbroken history of corruption and heathen degeneracy. In Lodge and Heywood's narratives, on the other hand, commercial theater has disclaimed a dark ages of Catholic drama in order to recuperate respectable pagan virtues. Neither opponents of the professional London acting companies nor their supporters, it would seem, had much use for mystery plays. And yet the very existence, to say nothing of the earnestness, of seventeenth-century narratives like Crashaw's sermon, Heywood's *Apology,* and above all Prynne's violent contempt—expressed at the late date of 1633—for biblical drama suggests that this powerful dramatic form was apparently not easily suppressed and forgotten.

Considering the theatrical genealogies outlined above, the current scholarly push for historical continuity in early English drama is less straightforward than it first appears. As theater historians, we find ourselves in the rather awkward position of concurrence with the views of Puritan antitheatrical-ists. I propose an additional historical perspective. A proclamation made in the city of Chester around 1575, perhaps in response to Goodman's force-ful objections, did in fact find use and value in the public performance of biblical drama. Known as the Late Banns, this post-Reformation document affords a place for mystery plays by appealing to civic pride and an antiquar-ian desire to preserve local customs. The 1619 *Breviary of Chester History* calls the Banns "the breeife of the whole playes," for this proclamation not only advertised the upcoming performance of the plays and encouraged audi-ence attendance but also promoted the contributions of the various guilds.[19] Surviving plays—or pageants, as they are sometimes called as if to reinforce the association between the dramatic action and the custom-made wagon upon which that action was often staged—depict the major events of bibli-cal history from Creation to Doomsday, with the scenes of Christ's Passion receiving particular dramatic elaboration. Performed at least as early as 1422, the Chester mysteries survived Henry's break from Rome, his son Edward's sweeping reforms, and much of Elizabeth's reign.[20] Divided into poetic stan-zas, the Banns announce which guilds will present each pageant, draw at-tention to significant events in each performance, and highlight noteworthy pieces of craftsmanship such as carriages, props, or costumes. The Banns also articulate what I believe to be a productive alternative to the accounts of sixteenth-century theatrical history mentioned above, a narrative that seeks to preserve synchronic contact with past theatrical objects and practices even as the Banns themselves record and perform diachronic historical change.

"The Breeife of the Whole Playes"

One factor that make the Chester mystery plays so helpful to our study of sixteenth-century histories of early English drama is the fact that the city was so rich in antiquarian activity during that period and well into the seventeenth century—which is to say, during Shakespeare's lifetime and the decades following. As the REED projects for Chester and Cheshire attest, a wide range of original documents—Cathedral records; churchwarden ac-counts; parish archives including accounts, lists of church officers, minutes of meetings, and so forth—has been preserved.[21] These records survive thanks to antiquarians such as Archdeacon Robert Rogers, whose *Breviary* included a history of the city. Though he died in 1595 before completing it, his son David not only finished the work but also produced five copies of four different versions. In addition to the two Rogerses, four successive genera-tions of the Holme family bequeathed to posterity hundreds of volumes of antiquarian records detailing the civic history of early modern Chester.[22] All together, these manuscripts tell the story of the town's vibrant ceremonial and dramatic past and of its ongoing investment and pride in that history.

Chester antiquaries, as they may have called themselves, wanted to believe that their annual biblical pageants had begun around the time of the city's founding.[23] With the records that survive for us today, however, we can be sure only that a well-established civic play was being enacted by 1422.[24] That year, the "Play of Corpus Christi" was an abridged, one-day, fixed-set production most likely held at the Church of St. John outside the city walls. That it may have been a Passion play rather than a complete biblical cycle is consistent with the fact that it would have been performed following a procession of the Eucharistic host to mark the feast of Christ's body and blood. The period between 1519 and 1531 witnessed not only the shift in performance dates to the week following Whitsunday (Pentecost)—for reasons that remain uncertain—but also considerable additions of Old Testament material.[25] Further revisions and alterations followed the ebb and flow of Reformation ideologies and English monarchs. In 1548, Edwardian reform suppressed the clergy's Corpus Christi play, and Whitsun play scenes such as the bakers' *Last Supper* were either heavily amended or deleted entirely. Not surprisingly, annual production became increasingly less assured in the late sixteenth century. That the pageants were staged one final time in 1575 is noteworthy given that the church hierarchy had forbidden their performance several years before.[26] Yet the end of the mysteries did not mean the end of dramatic activity in Chester. The Midsummer Show, an annual fair believed to have begun in 1499, included not only the giant likenesses of animals on stilts parading through Cestrian streets but also the appearance of well-known characters from the pageants, such as Balaam's talking ass, the devil, Judas, and Simeon. These too were eventually prohibited, yet their afterlife extended well into the first decade of the seventeenth century.[27]

In addition to the play texts themselves, city and guild officials in Chester preserved a large number of materials associated with their performance. Among these documents were the Banns, a proclamation or public notice announcing the upcoming cycle of pageants, which were most likely read publicly by the town crier at various points throughout the city of Chester in the days leading up to their performance.[28] To be "banned" in this sense is not to be prohibited but quite the opposite: it is to be officially sanctioned, warranted, or commissioned. Two versions of the Banns survive: the first (often called "Early" or "Catholic") was originally composed at an unknown date and survives in a 1540 copy (MS Harley 2150).[29] The second ("Late" or "Protestant") version was unquestionably written after Henry's break from Rome, probably after Corpus Christi celebrations were suppressed in 1548 and possibly as late as 1572.[30] The Late Banns are recorded in four manuscripts: Harley 2013 (1600), Bodley 175 (1604), and two 1609 copies of Rogers's *Breviary,* one in the Chester City Archives and one in the British Library (Harley 1944). The two versions of the Banns reflect the historical changes brought on by the Reformation. The Early Banns, for instance, clearly contain references to traditional beliefs later deemed idolatrous by Reformers and omitted by the Late Banns, such as "our Lady thassumpcion" not to mention Catholic rituals including a "Solempne procession [of] . . . The blessed sacrament."[31] Yet the Late Banns closely rely on the Early Banns as well. Indeed the two documents share a devotion to civic custom as well as a guildsman's eye for handiwork. It may seem strange to us that a "Protestant" document like the Late Banns would value pre-Reformation dramatic custom and craft—to say nothing of allowing God to be impersonated on stage. But that is precisely the reason they were commissioned: as an attempt both to claim, somewhat incongruously, that the plays have been sufficiently revised and updated and to emphasize their theological benignity as an age-old local custom.[32]

"As Custome Euer Was"

For the Early Banns the mysteries are "Auntient" pieces of Chester civic history that supposedly date from the city's earliest days. "[F]irst Inuented & putt into English by Randle Higden a monck of chester Abby," the plays "were begon truly" when "Sur Iohn Aneway was maire of this Citie."[33] "Randle Higden" was Ranulf Higden, a monk from about 1299 to 1364 in the city's Benedictine Abbey of St. Werburgh's (later the starting point of the Chester mysteries), and author of the "most commonly cited chronicle in late medieval England, the *Polychronicon.*"[34] The assertion that Sir John Arneway was mayor when Higden composed the plays is suggestive, though without historical basis. At the time of the Banns, Arneway was popularly believed to have been the city's first mayor, and Chester antiquarians claimed that he initiated them—which is to say that the mysteries were nearly old as the city's other Norman institutions. Never mind that the date of his supposed interaction with monk Higden (1328) doesn't coincide with the city's founding and ignores its Roman past.[35]

The Early Banns seek both to proclaim and to justify the present performance of their plays, and they do so on a number of fronts:

> ffor asmyche *as of old tyme* not only for the Augmentacion & incresse of
> the holy and catholyk ffaith of our sauyour cryst Iesu and to exhort the

> myndes of the comen people to gud deuocion and holsom doctryne
> ther of but Also for the comen welth and prosperitie of this Citie A
> play and declaracion of many and dyuers stories of the bible begyn-
> nyng with the creacion & fall of lucifer & endyng with the generall
> Iugement of the world to be declared & playde now in this whison
> weke . . . at the costys of the craftys men and occupacons of the said
> Citie *whiche hereunto haue from tyme to tyme vsyd and performed the same*
> Accordingly.[36]

The guilds are urged to perform these plays as much for the sake of
tradition—their ancestors have "from tyme to tyme vsyd and performed
the same"—as for their city's moral and economic benefit. If the Early Banns
begin by dwelling upon the "old tyme" of Chester history, their final concern is the perpetuation of dramatic traditions:

> god grunt vs merely
> And see theym many A yere
> Now haue I done that lyeth in me
> To procure this solempnitie
> That these playes contynued may be
> And well sett fourth Alway[37]

Though probably composed after the introduction of Henrician reforms, the
Early Banns appear to have little doubt that these "solemn" annual performances will continue as they have from time out of mind—or, in the words
of their post-Reformation counterpart, "as custome euer was."[38]

The Late Banns also hold on to the mystery plays as immemorial civic
practice. Rather than leave the uncomfortable elements of the old religion
without remark, the post-Reformation document immediately draws attention to them, beginning with their monastic authorship:

> Reuerend Lordes and Ladyes all
> That at this tyme here assembled be
> By this message vnderstande you shall.
> That sometymes there was Mayor of this Cittie
> Sir Iohn Arnewaye knighte whoe moste worthelye
> Contented him selfe to sett out in playe
> The deuise of one Rondoll Moncke of Chester Abbaye
> This Moncke not Monckelyke, in scriptures well seene
> In stories traueled with the beste sorte[39]

As with the Early Banns, the Late Banns perpetuate the fabricated notion
of a distinguished mayor's involvement in the history of the plays. Indeed,

the mysteries are worthy of staging, the Banns argue, in part because of the role played by this "knighte whoe moste worthelye" inaugurated their performance. But the Late Banns' treatment of Ranulf Higden is distinct from that of their predecessor: they view the author-monk as a kind of proto-Protestant figure.[40] In the passage above he is said to be "not Monckelyke, in scriptures well seene"—in other words, surprisingly knowledgeable of scripture by comparison with other monks, who in Reformist discourse were commonly said to be hopelessly superstitious and ignorant of scripture. The distinction is reiterated a few lines later:

> ffor at this daye an euer. He desearued the fame
> Which fewe Monckes deserue[d] proffessinge the same[41]

The Banns further associate him with the history of the Reformation by noting his efforts to impart the true faith ("good belefe") through the translation of scripture into the vernacular:

> These storyes of the testamente at this tyme you knowe
> In a common englishe tonge neuer reade nor harde
> yet thereof in these Pagiantes to make open showe
> This Moncke and noe moncke was nothinge affrayde
> With feare of burninge. hangeinge. or cutting of heade,
> To sett out that all may Deserne and see
> And parte of good belefe. beleue ye mee[42]

Braving persecution and death to spread the gospel in the English tongue, Higden might have been drawn from Foxe's sixteenth-century *Book of Martyrs*. Called "This Moncke and noe moncke," the reputed author of the Chester mysteries appears no ordinary cleric, and the events of the past seem not so distant. The Banns prologue recalls the turbulence of recent English history: defiant production of vernacular Bibles, "feare of burninge" for one's religious practices, and radical monks who repudiate orthodoxy were commonplaces in the history of the mid-sixteenth-century English Reformation. Perhaps that is why the next historical move by the Late Banns is so startling:

> Condemne not oure matter where groosse wordes you heare
> which Importe at this daye smale sence or vnderstandinge
> As sometymes postie, bewtye, in good manner or in feare
> with suchlike wilbe vttered in theare speaches speakeing
> At this tyme those speches caried good lykinge
> Thoe if at this tyme you take them spoken at that time
> As well matter as words, then all is well[43]

Now the city's plays and their author are hardly contemporary or even recent but undoubtedly long gone. So much time has past that audiences of
"this daye" and "this tyme" can make "smale sence or vnderstandinge" of
the "groosse," archaic words they hear on stage. The Banns encourage historiographical awareness; auditors must appreciate the historical difference
between themselves and the time the plays were written. At stake in this
historiography is far more than the appreciation of archaic words and phrases:
it's the survival of the plays (and with them Chester's unique civic identity) in
a climate of increasing Protestant suspicion and Tudor centralism. To defuse
this hostility, the Late Banns present the plays as relics of a bygone age. The
historical distance of the mystery plays is their saving virtue, preserving and
protecting them from contemporary criticism. The Early Banns reveled in
the past (the "old tyme" of the "Auntient whitsun playes") and looked to
the future ("god grunt [we] see theym many A yere"), as though the present
performance of the plays was an assured continuation of past practice. The
Late Banns, however, are silent as to the cycle's future prospects, and focus
instead on the present—the now of "this daye"—as a time period separate
from "that daye and that age":

> So all that doe heare them. we moste humblye praye
> Not to compare this matter or storye
> With the age or tyme wherein we presently staye
> But to the tyme of Ignorance whearein we doe straye
> And then dare I compare that this lande throughout
> None had the like. nor the like durste set out
>
> . . . .
>
> If the same be lykeinge to the commons all
> Then our desyre is satisfied, for that is all oure gayne
> If noe matter or shewe. thereof enye thinge speciall
> Doe not please but mislycke ye moste of the trayne
> Goe backe againe to the firste tyme I saye
> Then shall yow finde the fine witte at this daye aboundinge
> At that daye and that age, had uerye smale beinge[44]

Carefully deploying the categories of old and new, the Late Banns rhetorically divide the history of the Chester mysteries into periods for a strategic
purpose: they avoid responsibility for any lingering superstition by reminding
the audience that the plays were written in the remote "tyme of Ignorance"
(regardless, it seems, of the forward-looking innovations of Ranulf Higden).
A few decades after the composition of the Late Banns, the Chester antiquarian David Rogers would echo their estimation of the "tyme of Ignorance"

or "firste tyme," saying, "we haue all cause to power [pour] out oure prayers before god that neither wee. nor oure posterities after us. maye neuar see the like Abomination of Desolation [as the plays], with suche a Clowde of Ignorance to defile with so highe a hand. the moste sacred scriptures of god. but oh the merscie of oure god. for the tyme of oure Ignorance he regardes it not."[45] Missing from Rogers's account—yet so striking in the above passage from the Banns—is the thinly veiled civic pride that views Chester as an exceptional city even in its darker days: "dare I compare that this lande throughout / None had the like. nor the like durste set out."

Perhaps this sense of civic identity explains why the Banns do not entirely conform to later, more extreme Protestant views—nor to the histories of drama we've seen put forward by Crashaw, Heywood, and others. Adopting the historiographic posture of exemplarity whereby the past is viewed as a ready and reliable storehouse for present rhetorical and material practice, the Late Banns allow a third, more conciliatory attitude to emerge. The post-Reformation Chester plays, they suggest, are not wholesale importations of popery, as Crashaw would have it, nor do they revive pagan antiquity, as Heywood insists. The Late Banns preserve traditional theatrical materials by extracting them from a broadly defined "tyme of Ignorance" (the word "exemplum" derives from the Latin verb *eximere*, "to extract") and holding them up as ancient yet accustomed models for modern performance.[46] Thus, they urge that the traditional appearance of the devil be preserved:

> And nexte to this yow the Butchers of this Cittie
> The storye of Sathan that woulde Criste needes tempte
> Set out as accustomablie vsed haue ye
> The Deuell in his ffeathers. all Rugged and rente[47]

This description is quite literal: Chester REED documents tell us that shredded rags (hence "rugged") of canvas were used to make two "dye menes Covtes" for the *Harrowing of Hell*.[48] The Banns likewise promise that Christ's *Resurrection* will be performed with few alterations from the "olde fashion" or model:

> The Skynners before yow after shall playe
> The storye of the Resurrection
> Howe Criste from deathe arose the thirde daye
> Not altered in menye poyntes from the olde fashion[49]

Making even the smallest details of the past, like devils' costumes, present once more is part of the attraction—and therefore of the advertising—of this production. Ingenious in their historiography, the Chester Banns lay claim to acceptable material by portraying Higden as a man ahead of his own time. Yet they excuse undesirable topics and staging by depicting the plays as products of a witless bygone age that is divided from the "tyme wherein we presently staye." Either way, of course, the Banns argue that the mystery plays are worthy of performance in front of post-Reformation audiences because they are part of Chester's unique historical past.

But how old is the "olde fashion" they promote, and how ancient are the "Auntient whitsun playes"? Whereas pro- and antitheatricalists bolstered their accounts with appeals to classical authorities, whether the early church or pagan Greece and Rome, here local and more recent custom is clearly being brought to bear. Crucially, however, the language of both Early and Late Banns strives to blur the distinction between recent and remote history. Sixteenth-century usage of the word "ancient" could denote that "which existed in, or belonged to, times long past, or early in the world's history."[50] For example, when Holinshed's 1587 *Chronicles of England, Scotland and Ireland* speaks of "ancient" names or religions, it refers to the days of Celtic Albion, before the Roman conquest.[51] For the Banns' audience the word "ancient" could also describe a long-established custom or tradition—not necessarily an originary practice but one that is nonetheless timeworn.[52] A visitor to Chester who heard this proclamation may therefore have come away with the impression that these plays were either initiated by the town's earliest inhabitants or else performed longer than any current citizen could remember.

In 1575, Chester civic leaders gave this very impression when they "voted 33 to 12 in favor of performance" yet in defiance of the archbishop of York and the earl of Huntingdon, lord president of the North.[53] Chester mayor John Savage and his council warranted the plays, "for the dyvers good and great consideracions redoundinge to the comen wealthe, benefite, and profitte of the said citie in assemblie there holden, *according to the auncyente and lawdable usages and customes* there hadd and *used fur above remembraunce*."[54] Mayor Savage and the Chester aldermen were not lying to the archbishop and the earl. As we saw in the previous chapter, it was possible for early modern subjects to view certain highly valued objects anachronically, to revere them as ancient relics even if they were quite aware of the fact that the artifacts had been fabricated in the more recent past.

Faced with ecclesial and state censorship, both the Banns and city officials express genuine anachronic deference toward the antiquity of the stage objects of Chester mystery cycle. In their apologetic yet reverential opening stanzas, the Banns claim that under Mayor Arneway's supervision Higden "abreuiated" stories from the Old and New Testaments and arranged them into "xxiiij partes or playes." Then "this worthie knighte Arnewaye" himself assigned the order of pageants to various trade guilds and directed them to be performed. David Rogers's 1609 gloss on these opening lines fixes a specific date of origin: "Sir Iohn Arnewaye the first maior of Chester first sett oute the whitson playes *anno domini* 1329."[55] Significantly, Rogers and other Chester antiquarians—and therefore probably most late sixteenth-century Cestrians—continued to view Arneway as a founding figure of the city's drama even after they learned that he was neither the first mayor nor mayor during the first years of the mysteries.[56] This was not the result of historical ignorance or apathy. Closer examination of the opening stanzas of the Banns demonstrates the deeper purpose of this historiography. Like hagiographic *inventiones* narratives, they document a long oral tradition discovering the cycle's origins in the precincts of St. Werburgh's. Associating its dramatic relics with the illustrious Higden, they tell the story of how they were translated (*translatio*) into their present form by the revered knight Arnewaye. The citizens of Chester are therefore not merely performing plays; they are asserting their rights and privileges to view the time-honored artifacts of two civic saints.[57]

The Chester cycle was probably moved from Corpus Christi to Whitsuntide before 1521. Sometime after that date, it was significantly extended and began to feature ambulatory performances at more than one location over a three-day period. Plays like the *Fall of Lucifer*—noted by the Late Banns as a pageant "that of Custome olde" has been "trulye sett out" by the tanners—were added in the early sixteenth century, while others, such as the vintners' *Herod* and the Mercers' *Magi,* were expanded and divided. In shape, size, content, technology, and technique, the Chester cycle dates to the early sixteenth century rather than the ancient history of the city's founding.[58] Much of the cycle, in other words, was only a few decades old when both the Early and Late Banns were composed and Mayor Savage and the city council were trying to justify performances based on their antiquity. What is at stake in this rather astonishing example of anachronic historiography is the need to authorize the staging of the plays in the face of growing concerns that they smacked of popery.[59]

The Banns knowingly antiquate dramatic remnants in order to justify their present resurrection and return to the stage. Being old not only conferred a kind of dignity to them ("And then dare I compare that this lande throughout / None had the like") but also, and rather paradoxically, rendered them less important. Though products of the Roman Church's "ignorant" fetishizing of objects, these dramatic spectacles are harmless old toys. Godly

Chester Protestants therefore "with quiett mynde / Can be contented to tarye / . . . on Whitson mondaye" and enjoy the plays.[60] At other times, however, the Banns treat Catholicism not as a superseded religion but as a contemporary fallacy that lamentably continues to influence popular beliefs. The Banns therefore bemoan that people for "manye yeares [were] soe blinded" with ignorance regarding Christ's Passion that even in enlightened modern times Christians for "the moste parte cannot finde" the true and proper understanding of it: many remain in darkness.[61] Whether blatantly relocating the pageants to a remote and ancient past or anticipating the present anxiety stemming from recent creedal shifts, the Banns not only recognize that historical change has occurred, but they perform it. Seemingly sympathetic with Reformation efforts to stamp out residual superstition, the Banns preempt the discourse of those who oppose the Chester pageants. But they are cruel only to be kind; the Late Banns censure—not to censor but to conserve.

Yet it would be inaccurate to view the historiography performed by the Banns as a sixteenth-century version of the periodization that has divided modern academic study. While the Late Banns posit a sophisticated Protestant modernity that has replaced an ignorant Catholic past, it's also true that they view these morally beneficial religious pageants simultaneously as secular civic and commercial investments instituted by a mayor as well as a monk during Chester's earliest days. They celebrate the mutually supporting roles played by both clergy and city officials from the inception of the plays. As Lawrence Clopper argues, the decision to hold the annual performances at Whitsun rather than Corpus Christi was commercially, not doctrinally, motivated. At some point during the early sixteenth century, fiscally minded Chester leaders must have calculated that more people would visit the city, and therefore more revenue would be generated, if their biblical cycle didn't have to compete with the great Coventry plays.[62] And finally, while the Late Banns overtly endorse Protestant doctrines such as the teaching that the Eucharist is only a memorial of the Last Supper, they generally resist dramatic iconoclasm and seek to preserve and excuse traditional stage practices whenever possible.

We can see the bold recusancy of the Late Banns if we look to those passages concerning pageants—based on scriptural as well as apocryphal sources—which flirt with thorny doctrinal issues. These moments attest to the persistent attraction of the "olde" mystery plays, for it is here that the Banns are especially resourceful in their attempt to promote and continue the staging of provocative religious material in a climate of growing animosity. A combination of reassurance, moralizing, and antiquarianism aims to justify much of the incendiary pre-Reformation material. The Banns preach, for instance, that the utterance of Christ's words at the Last Supper should not be misinterpreted as popery:

> And howe Criste our sauioure at his laste supper
> Gaue his bodye and bloode for redemtion of us all
> Yow Bakers see that with the same wordes you vtter
> As Criste himselfe spake them to be a memorall
> Of that deathe & passion within playe after ensue shall[63]

The insistence that the bakers get the words exactly right seems strange until we remind ourselves of the decades of bitter debate over whether the sacrament of Eucharist—in which a priest utters "the same wordes" as Christ at the Last Supper—is an efficacious act summoning God down to the altar or merely a memorial sign of his "once for all time" sacrificial death. To be sure, the Banns pay lip service to the teaching of Reformers like Goodman that the sacrament is merely a commemorative symbol, but in urging the bakers to "cast godes loues [i.e. God's loaves] abroade with *accustomed* cherefull harte" they once again invoke custom as their authority.[64] So the need to be theologically up-to-date is balanced against an antiquarian desire to preserve the past.

We might expect that when the source of a pageant story is apocryphal, the Banns would be particularly cautious. Yet, in fact, they are rather bold—laying out a blanket excuse that, "onely to make sporte," monk Higden felt free to intermingle scripture with

> Some thinges not warranted by anye wrytte
> Which glad the hartes he would men to take hit[65]

This rather blithe passage of the Late Banns is a far cry from the indignant censure of antitheatricalists like Crashaw, as it insists that the audience literally laugh off any unwarrantable material. Besides this "let-out clause of comic relief,"[66] the Late Banns invoke the rhetoric of exemplarity as they assure individual guilds staging apocryphal scenes that this material has the warrant of "Custome":

> Now yow worshipfull Tanner that of Custome olde
> The fall of Lucifer did trulye sett out
> Some writers awarrante your matter therefore be bolde
> Lustelye to playe the same to all the route
> And if anye therefore stande in anye doubte
> your Author his Author hath youre shewe lett be[67]

The Banns are satisfied that continuity with supposedly ancient civic tradition as well as several textual sources (which they feel no obligation to name) is a good reason for the players to "be bolde" with the nonscriptural matter they're performing. Like the tanners, the cooks are also reassured that their *Harrowing of Hell,* though not biblically depicted, is authorized by the traditional Christian prayer, the Apostles' Creed:[68]

> As oure belefe is: that Christe after his passion
> Decended into hell. but what he did in that place
> Though oure author sett forthe after his opynion
> Yet creditt yow the beste lerned. those he dothe not disgrase
> We wishe that of all sortes the beste you imbrace
> Yow koockes with your Cariage see that you doe well
> In Pagiante sett oute the harrowinge of hell[69]

Urging the audience to have an open mind toward "all sortes" of textual sources, the Late Banns have little difficulty promoting nonbiblical material. It is the historical precedent of annual performances that gives them needed leverage against the dictates of *sola Scriptora.* In fact, we'll see momentarily how theatrical representations of Lucifer's fall and Hell's gate are much safer than the fundamental narrative of the Christian scriptures: God's incarnation.

The Late Banns conclude with a serious note of warning about the issue of idolatry, perhaps the most central theme throughout all Reformed polemics against the Church of Rome, and certainly the motivation for the widespread iconoclastic devastation of the English Reformation.[70] Fearing charges of idolatrous representation, the Late Banns remind spectators of the guilds' dramaturgical limitations and insist that it is their thoughts which now must deck the players:

> Of one thinge warne you now I shall
> That not possible it is these matters to be contryued
> In such sorte and cunninge & by suche players of price
> As at this daye good players & fine wittes. coulde deuise
> ffor then shoulde all those persones that as godes doe playe
> In Clowdes come downe with voyce and not be seene
> ffor noe man can proportion that godhead I saye
> To the shape of man face. nose and eyne
> But sethence the face gilte doth disfigure the man that deme
> A Clowdye couering of the man. a Voyce onlye to heare
> And not god in shape or person to appeare[71]

In order to defend the players from the charge of idolatry, the Banns admonish the audience to excuse the embodied representation of God. "If you see a player in a gilt mask playing God, then imagine it's a cloud or that you hear only a voice!" the Banns prescribe. Research into the acoustical effects of theatrical masks may support the Banns' claim; if properly constructed to achieve vocal resonance, wooden masks could "consistently amplify" certain vocal ranges without much effort on the part of the actor: "the mask can sharpen and deepen a scenic illusion by affording the voice previously un-explored possibilities."[72] Consequently, a gilt mask that had previously made God visible could now be supposed to render Him audible—to "disfigure" divinity not in the sense of "deform" but to "un-figure," or remove, God's body.[73]

What is so surprising is not that the Late Banns give a note of warning but to whom that word of caution is spoken: they admonish *the audience* to ad-just its thinking. There is never any question that dubious pre-Reformation material will be staged. The Late Banns are not, as we would expect on such an incendiary religious issue, bowing to pressure from Reformers but in fact urging tolerance of traditional stagecraft.[74] Human flesh would continue to be gilded—deified if you will—as before. Yet if fault is to be found with this staging technique, then, according to the Late Banns, it lies with the audience, not the players, for misinterpreting what is being staged. As with previous subject matter, historical precedent is underscored so as to assuage any discomfort, but so too is historical distance, so that here again the Banns rely on the diachrony they have constructed between the "fine wittes" of "this daye" and the benighted "matter" of "Auntient" times:

> not possible it is these matters to be contryued
> In such sorte and cunninge & by suche players of price
> As at this daye good players & fine wittes. coulde deuise[75]

In other words, since even contemporary craftsmen-actors cannot develop an effective alternative to staging Christ without somehow incarnating him, the traditional technique of painted masks must be adopted. "These matters" were the product of a rude, bygone age, the Late Banns admit, but since there is no present alternative, the audience must appreciate their historicity and excuse them. In David Rogers's paraphrase of the stanza, onlookers are urged "to conceaue of the matter so as it mighte be profitable" and not "offen-ciue."[76] Rogers adopts the Banns' phrase "these matters," and his gloss would be equally at home in the margins of act 5 of *A Midsummer Night's Dream,* where Theseus urges his fellow nobles to use their imagination to amend the "palpable gross play" of the "rude mechanicals."[77] What Rogers's gloss leaves unsaid, however, is the manner in which the Late Banns adopt a Reformist mistrust of the materiality of stagecraft in order to authorize the physical stage presence and costuming of "those persones that as godes doe playe."

"Craftes Men and Meane Men"

The historiography performed by the Late Banns entails assumptions and prejudices (also reminiscent of Theseus's admonitions in *Dream*) about the social status of the players—namely, that they are inferior in social rank as well as acting ability:

> By Craftes men and meane men these Pageanntes are playde
> And to Commons & Contrymen accustomablye before.
> If better men and finer heades now come what canne be sayde
> But of common and countrye players take yow the storye.[78]

In times past, both audiences and players were naive about stage performance, and although more sophisticated audiences attend modern productions, the Banns shrug their shoulders ("what canne be sayde") as they admit that contemporary players remain rude mechanicals. If underselling the acting ability of performers seems a strange way to promote a drama, subsequent lines make clear that the Banns are once again adroitly deflecting criticism. In fact, the insertion of this apology immediately following the warning about idolatry is not accidental. Nor is it merely an abject and "pitiful" expression of "churlish humility" by a blushing provincial speaker "swamped by the idea of a centralized national culture."[79] It is tactically designed to provide further justification for broad-mindedness toward otherwise troubling subject matter. This passage also reiterates the same rhetorical strategy of placing the blame upon the audience rather than the guildsmen-players: the viewers' imaginations must make up for the histrionic limitations of the actors just as they must excuse potentially idolatrous stage practices. If spectators are not up to that task, then they are welcome to pack up and leave at any time: "if anye disdayne then open is the doore / That lett hime in to heare, packe awaye at his pleasure." Those who remain, therefore, should be "contented" and of "quiett mynde." After all, these mean craftsmen who are unable to please the wiser sort are simple dilettantes who shun profit: "Oure playeinge is not to get fame or treasure."[80]

On the other hand, it *is* strange that the Banns remind the audience that "by Craftes men and meane men these Pageanntes are played," for they have done nothing but call attention to the fact that these are craftsmen, not professional actors. Far from offering a dramatis personae, they announce the assignment of each pageant to a particular guild saying, "youe wrightys and slaters wilbe fayne / bryng forth" ; "Paynters glasiars & borderers in fere / Have taken on theym" ; "you barbers & waxe Chandlers of antiente tyme / In the 4th Pageante." ; "Cappers and Lynen Drapers, see that ye forthe bringe."[81] In the Early Banns, exhortations like that addressed to the dyers to "bryng forth A wurthy cariage / That is A thing of grett costage" are typical. With eager anticipation, they "haue no doubt" that the mercers' pageant "with sondry Cullors [] shall shine / of veluit satten & damaske fyne / Taffyta Sersnett of poppyngee grene."[82] The word "carriage" appears so often in the proclamation (no fewer than ten times) that it soon becomes clear that a guild's reputation depends less on the actors' playing ability than on their wealth and material craft. More than the tradesmen, it is the handmade theatrical objects and stage pieces to which the Banns call attention—or rather, that seem to demand acclamation. The guilds are as often instructed to present particular costumes, props, or spectacles as they are to carry out the plot of a given scene. The tanners, for example, are told,

> Bryng forth the heuenly manshion
> Thorders of Angellz and theire creacion
> According done to the best
> And when the thangellz be made so clere
> Then folowyth the falling of lucifere.[83]

The Early Banns' keenness to see artisanry on display was not restricted to the sets or wagons. The goldsmiths, for instance, are encouraged to "magy-fye" their craft to deck out King Herod for the *Slaughter of the Innocents*. The "3 kings Royall" of the *Herod and the Magi* scene must likewise look "worthy to appere."[84] Sometimes the use of specially made props is called for, such as the mappa mundi—probably a large painted cloth map of the world that the drapers would have designed specifically for the Creation story.[85] The pre-Reformation Banns also anticipate the spectacle of "balam on An Asse sytting," the "Toumbe of Lazarey," breakable Hell's gates, and the emission of "precyus blud" from Jesus's wounds—all of which would have required customized designs.[86] For the Early Banns, a mystery pageant never simply presents biblical history; it simultaneously dramatizes a particular guild's present-day affluence and workmanship.

Like the Early Banns, the Late Banns are deeply invested in the artisanship of the various guilds. "Acordinge to your welthe sett oute wealthelye" the story of Cain and Abel, the affluent drapers are told.[87] The carpenters are similarly instructed to "Lustely bringe forth. your well decked Caryage," and if David Mills is correct, then they may have eagerly complied by continuing the pre-Reformation practice of using not one but two platform areas.[88]

Multiple playing spaces would have provided ample opportunities for the wrights to show their woodworking skills. The craftsmanship celebrated by the Late Banns encompasses some props that we might not at first associate with artisanry in the sense of mechanical handicraft. For instance, the Banns specifically ask that the vintners "amplify" the story of Herod and the Magi to include, quite literally, the fruits of their labor, presumably so that the raging tyrant had "plentye of wine" to drink.[89] Even when a prop, carriage, or costume has not been fashioned by the associated guild, the Late Banns don't suppress their enthusiasm for theatrical objects. The previously mentioned "Rugged and rente" feathers of the Devil in the butchers' *The Temptation of Christ* is a good example: the costume was probably manufactured for the butchers by the weavers or other cloth-making guild, and the Banns note the costume's texture and remind the audience of its history as an "accustomablie vsed" garment of the butchers' play.

The attention paid to handicraft in both versions of the Chester Banns makes sense given the considerable labor involved in these civic productions.[90] Yet I do not mean to suggest that we reduce the Chester mysteries to a purely mechanical stage devoid of the literary sophistication so readily attributed to Shakespeare. Through the reflexive figure of the Expositor, for example, the Chester cycle explicitly raises questions about scriptural authenticity and biblical idiom as well as the hermeneutics of signs, tokens, and prophecies.[91] Highlighting the craftsmanship of the Chester cycle, I aim to establish material points of contact and comparison between Shakespeare and the mysteries and not to create a crude medieval foil for Renaissance sophistication. I underscore the materiality of early English drama in order to expose the fallacy that Shakespeare's literary genius transcended it. The need to reconsider the craftsmanship entailed in sixteenth-century English drama is particularly necessary for scholars living in a modern, postindustrial, global economy. Besides needing skills to weave costumes or construct a pageant wagon, guildsmen-actors faced a tremendous variety of material challenges. Rudimentary items like paint and nails could not be purchased. Because guilds closely guarded the "trade secrets" involved in even the most basic processes of manufacture, they had to collaborate and barter with one another during the hectic period leading up to the performance.[92] Such interactions must have fostered cooperation, civic pride, and mutual respect for the abilities of fellow tradesmen. Animosity, resentment, and a keen sense of competition were undoubted byproducts as well. Mystery drama, therefore, required real work and, often, extensive collaborative labor. This central fact explains why, for the Banns, these various plays are *works*—the material manifestations of Cestrian guild labor—as much as they are dramatized stories.

If we regain our sense of playwriting as play-wrighting—the building or making of plays—we become attuned to the fact that the London companies faced the same technological hurdles and collaborative opportunities that their provincial counterparts did. Being housed in permanent playhouse structures and thereby benefiting from the material resources such spaces afforded, they were uniquely poised to pursue their craft in ways that were unthinkable for provincial tradesmen staging occasional mystery plays. But professional London players still needed to manufacture, borrow, adapt, and maintain stage architecture, set pieces, props, costumes, and technologies that had become proven crowd-pleasers (whether on pageant wagons or on their own boards). The Chester Banns demonstrate an awareness of this play-wright perspective as they expressly rely upon the workability and popularity of various material elements of the plays in order to market them to late sixteenth-century urban audiences.

The well-known invectives of Puritan antitheatrical writers, though clearly biased and exaggerated, also remind us of the centrality of material stage properties on the London stages.[93] Gosson famously railed against the "mere trifles" such as "many a terrible monster made of broune paper" that form "the soule of your plays."[94] Fifty years later Prynne would echo Gosson's sentiments by complaining, "In Play-houses . . . people use to learn filthy *things*, to heare dishonest *things*, to see pernicious *things*."[95] He wasn't referring necessarily to theatrical props alone, yet it's clear that these "things" of the theater combine to bombard the senses and imperil the soul.[96] Playwrights themselves considered their dramas to be profoundly material artifacts. Scholars often note the fact that Ben Jonson felt a keen rivalry between his poetic verse and the designers and artisanal manufacturers of stage materials.[97] A quick glance at Henslowe's 1598 inventory of rocks, cages, tombs, Hell mouths, golden fleeces, globes, golden scepters, bay trees, garlands, altars, heads, Cupid's bows, moss banks, and clothes of the Sun and Moon, and many other "*properties for my* Lord Admeralles men" easily substantiates Jonson's fears.[98] As the "English Horace," he styled himself after the poets of antiquity and in supposed contradistinction to modern artisanal practitioners of play-wrighting. Yet (as we will see in the epilogue) Jonson was himself quite skilled at adapting time-honored stage properties and costumes to suit his needs.

A Palimpsestic Proclamation

As we've seen, the Chester Late Banns draw upon the historiographies of exemplarity and anachronic substitution in important ways, but as palimpsests they may also aid our study. Even as the Banns attempt to preserve the sixteenth-century Chester cycle as ancient history dating to the city's founding, the material texts of these proclamations themselves reflect not one moment in time but many. In their palimpsestic polychronicity, they reenact the Banns' rhetorical historiographies at the level of ink and parchment.[99] As annual public decrees, the Banns had to be flexible enough to meet the vicissitudes of performance. Even so, their witness to the flux of history—the consecutive attempts to correct, rewrite, cross out, edit, restore, and even update what constitutes the "custom" that supposedly "ever was"—deserves closer inspection.

The Late Banns, which were revised and transcribed by different authors on several occasions during Shakespeare's lifetime, bear witness to several different moments in the late sixteenth century when the future of the Chester cycle was in jeopardy. According to Clopper, stanzaic shifts in surviving manuscripts correspond to two revisions—sometime between 1561 and 1572—of a text originally composed around the 1550s (1548–61). He proposes that the introductory and concluding material composed in longer rhyme royal stanzas (*ababbcc*) was added to basic four-line stanzas rhyming *abab*. "We should not assume," he further argues, "that the different versions of the Late Banns represent the inaccurate and incomplete transmission of a single document; rather, we should allow the possibility that the Rogers [Harley 1944 and Chester City Archive *Breviary*, both 1609], Bellin [Harley 2013–1600], and Bedford [Bodley 175–1604] copies represent the cycle at, perhaps, three different times or for three different occasions and that the original Late Banns, now lost, represented the cycle at a fourth time."[100] If Clopper's theory that stanzaic shifts correspond to revisions, then it would seem that the historiography performed by the Banns grew bolder and more innovative as opposition to the Whitsun plays grew. The "defensive introductory stanzas" claiming that the plays began in the early fourteenth-century may have been added when the document was first revised (1561–72). The conclusion urging proper interpretation of gilt masks and telling opponents to "packe awaye" was inserted later, probably in the late 1560s or early 1570s.[101]

The materiality of the Early Banns, which survive to us only in Harley 2150, exhibits more visually arresting acts of textual and ideological recalcitrance and recuperation. According to Clopper, the Early Banns were originally composed for performances surrounding the feast of Corpus Christi between 1505 and 1521, then revised by a scribe between 1521 and 1532, after the plays were moved to Whitsun and expanded. They were most likely transcribed in their present form around 1540, for several erasures were made subsequently as a result of Edwardian reforms such as the suppression of Corpus Christi and Marian devotion. Sometime in the late sixteenth century (c. 1570), a scribe copied them onto folios 85v to 88v of Harley 2150.

Their designation as Early Banns is therefore rather misleading, and the story of their emendation doesn't end there by any means. During the period 1630–68, long after any Chester audiences had seen their famous mysteries performed, the Chester antiquarian Randle Holme II collated the Early Banns with other sixteenth-century civic records by adding previously omitted lines and explicitly marking passages that had been "erazed" in the authorized post-Reformation version of the Banns (the Late Banns) during the previous century.[102]

Perhaps most significant, and certainly most striking, are his marginalia. Holme drew black vertical lines to the left of lines 156 through 163 of the Banns with a horizontal line above line 156. He also marked lines 164 through 171 with a vertical line in the left-hand margin, with a horizontal line drawn beneath line 171 (figures 3 and 4). Holme labeled both of these boxed-in passages as "erazed in the booke," presumably referring to the city's official "White Book of the Pentice." These passages describe liturgical and Marian elements of the cycle similar to those that outraged the Protestant clergyman Christopher Goodman. Holme's restoration and notation are meticulous and consistent; finding only a single line of erased material, he follows the same procedure and draws a vertical line to the right of the last word of line 185—"Marie"—and underscores the line as before.[103]

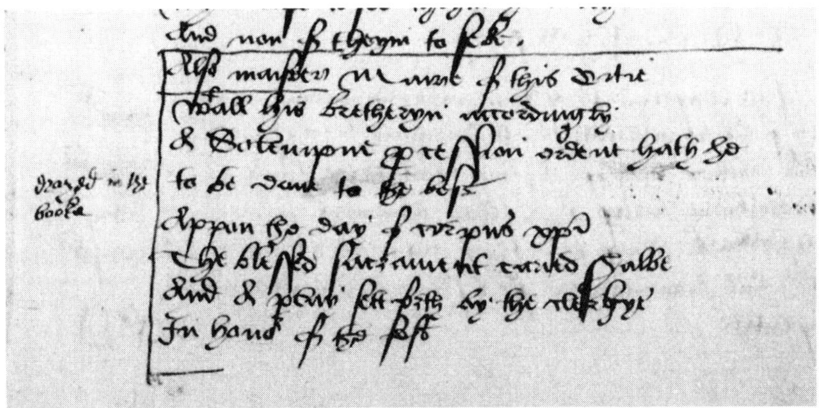

FIGURE 3.   Randle Holme's marginalia in the Chester "Early" Banns. © The British Library Board, MS Harley 2150, fol. 88r, detail.

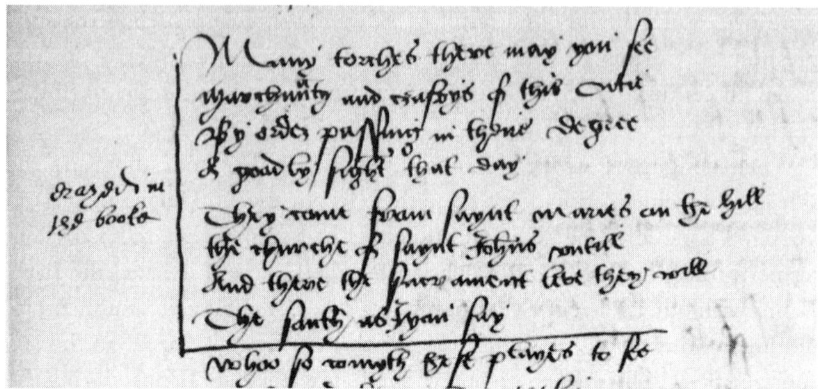

FIGURE 4.   Randle Holme's marginalia in the Chester "Early" Banns. © The British Library Board, MS Harley 2150, fol. 88v, detail.

The bold lines of Holme's marginalia call the reader's attention to censored material and in doing so invite us to consider his purpose in drawing them, particularly in light of the fact that they appear to be unique: as far as I have been able to determine, no other material that he copied into the Harley 2150 manuscript is similarly annotated. These marginal lines may simply reflect Holme's assiduous record keeping; they carefully delineate which passages had been erased in order to make the Banns conform to the suppression of Roman dogmas and devotion. But I want to go further and suggest that they hinge upon the very same historiography that is at work in the Goodman letter with which I began this chapter. Just as the Late Banns attempt to preserve the sixteenth-century Chester cycle as ancient history dating to the city's founding, the ink on folios 88 recto and verso marks particular dramatic material as past, superseded, and indeed "erazed in the booke." We have seen how the Late Banns co-opt the biased historical periodization of Protestants like Goodman in an effort to ensure the cycle's continued performance. Perhaps, therefore, Holme's annotation of erased material similarly preempts an iconoclastic act of erasure in order to retain rather than obliterate the textual record of past Catholic devotion and practice.

We will probably never know the reasons for Randle Holme's collation and emendation of this censored text. He may have carefully recorded the textual permutations of the Banns in response to the ideological upheavals occurring in his own time. Active in his antiquarian pursuits from the 1630s into the 1660s, including the bitter siege years of 1644–45, perhaps he feared iconoclastic outbursts as a result of the civil war. Julie Spraggon has studied numerous instances of iconoclasm performed by parliamentarian armies, and while she acknowledges that much of the destruction may have been the result of the wreckage and looting common to all wars, she contends that these men often saw their army as a godly agent of antipapist reformation. As Canterbury Cathedral was being ransacked, for example, one fervent soldier played a parliamentary song on the organ and sang of his willingness "to fall in battle to maintain / God's worship" and to "extirpate Papacy."[104] Altar rails, organs, sacred images, service books, and vestments obviously suffered their violent disapprobation, but in their zeal to eradicate popery in all its forms, soldiers also targeted books and parish records for destruction. As Spraggon explains, "the suspicion of the written records of the church can be seen at Peterborough, where the soldiers believed the records they destroyed to be papal bulls. Similarly, at Ashover and Derbyshire, soldiers burnt an old parish register because it was written in Latin, and they believed it, therefore, to be 'full of popery and treason.'"[105] They might have viewed the manuscripts of the Chester cycle in a light similar to Christopher Goodman's in the previous century. Goodman represented the texts of "the old Popish plays of Chester," full of manifold "absurdities" that he felt obliged to catalog in a letter to the archbishop of York, as threats to the queen and the common weal.[106]

Holme's antiquarian collections might therefore bear witness to his ideological undertakings. Defiant acts of opposition (perhaps civically rather than doctrinally motivated), they aimed both to restore what had been iconoclastically erased by the predecessors of the Roundheads nearly a century before and, perhaps, to anticipate further acts of erasure. As scholars have noted, Holme was a zealous scribe "who in many cases reproduced the same spellings, abbreviations, contractions, and the like of his manuscript source."[107] Whatever his motives or intentions, Holme does not merely resurrect the Early or Catholic version of the Banns but collates it with the censored, post-Reformation copy that was available to him. As a result, the horizontal and vertical lines he has drawn between accepted and erased passages have a double effect: they preserve the act of censorship but also cordon off and seemingly protect forbidden areas. Antiquarian recuperation therefore blurs strict temporal distinctions between present and past even as it records the effects of historical (and ideological) change.

Holme's ink acts as an open box or reliquary that contains and yet exhibits dangerously idolatrous matter from England's pre-Reformation past. Given Spraggon's scholarship, we might say that his ink forms a siege wall to protect an oppressed, beleaguered Catholic past from present Protestant assault. As reliable a scribe as Holme may have been, however, his antiquarianism did not simply restore old texts but added new meaning by the very act of transcription. As we saw in chapter 1, even the most assiduous recusancy brings new devotional perspectives and purposes to a traditional text.[108] If antiquarian or theatrical recuperation unavoidably inscribes novelty, then strict temporal distinctions between present and past begin to intermingle within the object itself. Whether stage prop or material text, the amalgamated artifact can never indulge our desire for original meaning, but it can help to illustrate how seventeenth-century readers and audiences received and reworked sixteenth-century mystery plays.

Synchronic Diachrony

Careful attention to the palimpsestic properties of texts and objects and the "reworking of the past in the present" guides Jonathan Gil Harris's important study of Renaissance theories of matter. He argues that "English Renaissance writers repeatedly recognize the polychronic dimensions of matter—the many shaping hands, artisanal and textual, that introduce into it multiple traces of different times, rendering the supposedly singular thing plural, both physically and temporally."[109] Harris aims to allow sixteenth- and seventeenth-century conceptions of matter and time—and in particular what he calls the "untimeliness of matter"—to guide contemporary critical methodologies, especially material culture studies. To accomplish this task, he frames the temporal relations he explores—supersession, explosion, and conjunction—in the philosophical traditions of G. W. F. Hegel, Walter Benjamin, and Bruno Latour, respectively. A similar (though much briefer) theoretical contextualization might also be illustrative for our study of the Chester Banns.

With its theory of the ruin, Walter Benjamin's *The Origin of German Tragic Drama* (1928) explores the manner in which past objects, particularly the stage properties of *Trauerspiel*, or baroque mourning-drama, may persist in the present precisely as superseded remnants.[110] Far from celebrating the arrival of a new epoch, Benjamin's ruin represents the stubborn persistence of a past work, though it is no longer culturally in vogue.[111] In the wake of Henrician and Edwardian reforms, the Chester plays were losing their social currency. For this reason, the Banns text was updated, and it begged the pardon of its increasingly Reformed audience for the vestiges of popish ignorance. Yet in doing so the Late Banns give their matter a rebirth, a rebirth as accustomed cultural artifacts of the city's ancient past. They revive the mysteries and prevent them from being swept away in the current tide of Reformation by anchoring them in the city's ancient past, "that age" which seems so remote from "the age or tyme wherein we presently staye"—that time loathed by Goodman because it is buried in "the depth of ignorance" and "Popish policy." In a similar fashion, the Chester antiquarian Randle Holme did not simply recopy the Early Banns with the previously excised material restored to its original place but transposed them with the forbidden material set apart as superseded matter. We might say that Holme, like Benjamin's historical materialist, resurrects shards of Chester's Catholic past that have been "sundered from official [Protestant] history and now presents the possibility of doing and imagining things differently."[112]

Attentive to the lively and comely use of "accustomed" stage properties, the Banns, much like Benjamin's provocative account of the supposedly dead and superseded stage properties of *Trauerspiel,* encourage our study of Shakespeare's playwright craftsmanship: they urge us to explore the afterlives of remnants of the mystery plays on the professional London stage.[113] For, though the Banns speak again and again of "custom old," there is an unmistakable sense of the play cycle's present vitality even in the face of the crisis of Reformation iconoclasm and antitheatricality. The Banns urge the guilds to "wealthily" and "lustily" bring forth their traditional costumes and pageants regardless of how "costly" they are. To the ecclesiastical opponents of the mysteries and to their proponents as well, the annual pageants were still vital enough in the late sixteenth century to expend tremendous legal and political energy.[114]

The Banns demonstrate that this vitality is evidenced not only in the histrionic conventions that Michael O'Connell and others have explored. The memory of the mystery plays, they suggest, remains tethered to dramatic artifacts themselves. They are vital stimulants to playing that carry rich histories—histories that were being erased and rewritten, but also recorded and performed, throughout the sixteenth century: sometimes by amateur actors on stage, sometimes by the craftsmen who repaired or remade them, and sometimes (as in the case of the gilt masks) by the text of the Banns themselves. Adopting the Banns as a hermeneutical paradigm, subsequent chapters will underscore rather than elide the tension between custom and novelty. We will attempt to see the material vestiges of this theatrical tradition as vital remnants: present and past, alive and dead, continuously being reinterpreted and renewed, yet increasingly antiquated and outdated; familiar customs but also forbidden practices; palpable gross play bound up with nuanced philosophical and theological questions that were deeply held and hotly debated.

Following the work of Richard Emmerson, then, my aim is to perform synchronic analysis of early English drama by juxtaposing concurrent theatrical traditions previously separated by disciplinary and period divisions. Emmerson's approach does not reduce sixteenth-century theatrical experience to a homogenous whole but rather highlights similarity and continuity as well as divergence and disjunction. Synchronic study is therefore as much concerned with complexity and range as it is with temporal overlap, as is demonstrated in the case of the Chester play of Antichrist. Over a period of seven decades, this apocalyptic figure represents far more than standardized Christian doctrine about the End Times; to the contrary, he assumes many contemporary guises which polemically interrogate Chester politics during the years of the pre-Reformation, Henrician Reforms, and Elizabethan settlement.[115]

Like Emmerson I am eager to overcome the rigid temporal boundaries that sequester dramatic forms and objects by locking them into their supposedly original historical period. However, the Chester Banns caution us not to take our desire for a synchronous "theatrical era" too far, thus replacing one form of periodization with another.[116] They recognize—indeed, their own material existence has come about as a result of—an unmistakable historical difference between the then of pre-Reformation drama and the now in which the Whitsun plays are under assault. As we've seen, the Late Banns manipulate, and often exaggerate, that temporal difference to their advantage. Yet even though they locate the Whitsun plays in a remote and ignorant time, their diachronic narrative is not reducible to our modern notion of a medieval-Renaissance divide. Rather than temporally isolating dramatic artifacts, the Banns' diachrony creates the possibility of preserving past objects and practices in the present—creates the possibility, paradoxically enough, of synchrony.

This synchrony within (and resulting from) diachrony is significant for two reasons. First, it avoids the construction of an artificial and inflexible period boundary that divorces pre- and post-Reformation dramatic forms. Second, it recognizes historical change and difference but avoids the pitfalls of E. K. Chambers's biological narrative of the growth and evolution of early English drama, a narrative that, as we saw in chapter 1, arises from a post-Enlightenment model of authorship. The Banns, on the other hand, view sixteenth-century theatrical objects, not the Renaissance author, as the source of dramatic inspiration and audience entertainment. True, they attribute the Chester pageants to the famous author of the *Polychronicon,* but they have no desire to see the pageants staged as Higden originally intended. On the contrary, they willingly impose modern interpretations upon traditional stage practices in order to avoid controversy. Literary meaning is jettisoned to guarantee the object's literal stage presence. The Banns invoke Higden for the same reason they invoke Mayor Arneway and repeatedly underscore the authority of ancient custom: to preserve the familiar sights, sounds, and spectacles of the pageant wagons, props, and costumes. Palpable objects—not transcendent subjects, and Shakespeare least of all—shape the historical narrative of the Chester Banns. Far from being dead, superseded precursors, as Chambers would have it, the material elements of the mystery plays are the great attractions that the Banns implore audiences to come and see. Their stated goal is to have the guilds resurrect these treasures of Chester theater history. Material craft thus precedes the author's pen. If Hegelian histories (like that of Chambers) strain arduously toward the telos of freedom for the individual subject, then the Banns, it would seem, narrate a history in which material objects are set free, not by breaking away from the past but by becoming synecdochically tied to it.

In their rhetorical and graphic historiography, the Chester Banns engage in calculated acts of periodization, but if they erect a temporal divide, it is a curious partition that creates the possibility of temporal proximity as well as distance. Presently conspicuous as remnants of the past, the spectacles and sounds of the pageant cycle may inspire creative reinterpretations of their own meaning, and audiences are encouraged to view them in new ways that might even contradict their previous significance. Gilt masks are (must be) new precisely because they are covered, and therefore protected by, the patina of past custom. If the late sixteenth-century apologies of the Late Banns and the seventeenth-century marginalia in the Early Banns manuscript tell us anything, therefore, it is that despite the emendation and eventual suppression of the mysteries, this dramatic material was not entirely superseded. The mysteries had by no means lost their old Catholic signification and therefore belonged to a "past time of monkish ignorance." For many people these plays could not so easily be banished to a previous age. Certainly for Goodman they were not bygone but a present "perill or danger to . . . the common weal."[117]

The Chester Late Banns demonstrate that late sixteenth-century audiences could and did look back across the Reformation divide to the mystery plays—and not past them, as Lodge and Heywood did. Like the Banns, Shakespeare's plays situate volatile material in an ancient past: pre-Christian Athens, eighth-century Denmark, and tenth-century Scotland. Next, Shakespeare underscores the materiality of the mystery play remnants being borrowed. Stage technologies, props, and architecture are not celebrated as the craftsmanship of a particular guild, of course, but the company's possession of them *as theatrical materials* is highlighted in the text of the play. Finally, much as the Late Banns authorize traditional gilt masks to represent the Deity but denigrate their previous signification, Shakespearean drama advertises the ownership of particular stage properties yet mocks, denies, or otherwise ignores their mystery play past.

The ensuing focus of this book will be the plays of Shakespeare but not at the expense of earlier forms of English drama. This chapter, for example, has illustrated how the reclassification of traditional Catholic material—what Stephen Greenblatt calls the "circulation of social energy"—was under way before the first commercial theaters were erected. Subsequent chapters will follow through on this revisionism by suggesting that religious properties did not always migrate directly from the disbanded monasteries to the professional London stage. Rather, the pageant wagons of the mystery plays were also important sites of cultural re-formation.

Having gained a better appreciation of the ongoing agency of supposedly superseded theatrical objects, we can now move away from author-centered narratives boasting of Shakespeare's creative autonomy over the plays we attribute to him. The next three chapters argue that the material elements of the mysteries were present sources of "lyuelye" and "comlye" inspiration and entertainment for the London theater companies and their audiences. In fact, I maintain that three of the plays often cited as evidence of Shakespeare's mastery of the genres of comedy and tragedy owe much of their artistic inspiration to plays performed before England's most famous playwright was even born. We shall consider how, like the gilt masks spoken of in the Chester Late Banns or the erased passages in the Early Banns transcribed by Randle Holme, some of the remarkable remnants of the mysteries seemingly demanded a dramatic rebirth when professional acting companies encountered them. Whether they appeared as dramatic fossils in the new professional playhouses, these artifacts were not dry bones awaiting the breath of Shakespearean genius. Quite the opposite. Exerting their material agency on the stage of the Globe, they were actors in plays that we all too casually label "Renaissance" or "Shakespearean" drama.

 CHAPTER 3

Balaam to Bottom

A Sixteenth-Century Translation

> There is now in vogue that song of the feast of
> Corpus Christi which is patched together from many
> passages of Scripture. . . . It is the dream of a poor
> senseless idiot. Here [Melchizedek's bread and wine,
> Elijah's cake, and the manna of the fathers] have had
> to serve as figures of the sacrament. It is a wonder
> that he did not include Balaam's ass.
>
> —Martin Luther

It has been assumed since at least the nineteenth
century that the rude mechanicals of *A Midsummer Night's Dream* are a comic
rendition of the artisan actors of the provincial mystery plays. In 1898,
for example, Georg Brandes observed that Shakespeare's burlesque scenes
"doubtless drew upon childish memories of the plays he had seen performed
in the market-place at Coventry and elsewhere." In doing so, says Brandes,
Shakespeare was satirizing older forms of English drama.[1] More recently,
Clifford Davidson and Stephen Greenblatt have read the craftsmen-actors of
Dream in the context of the "traditional plays" the boy Shakespeare might
have witnessed in Coventry.[2] Louis Montrose argues that the mechanicals recall not only the civic and artisanal aspects of mystery drama but its religious
context as well. Although the subject matter of the mechanicals' play is nonbiblical, Montrose insists that their performance evokes the Feast of Corpus
Christi with its elaborate ceremonial procession and pageants.[3] John Parker
compares the rude mechanicals' presentation of *Pyramus and Thisbe* with the
"hilarity of earlier artisan-sponsored" scenes in which the craftsmanship of
the guilds was "rendered flamboyantly deficient."[4]

Yet, while the rude mechanicals in *Dream* have long been associated with
late medieval and early modern English provincial drama, the ass's head
"fixed" on Bottom by Robin Goodfellow, or Puck, is generally discussed
in the context of classical sources such as the story of King Midas in Ovid's

Metamorphoses. Kenneth Muir, for example, acknowledges Reginald Scot's 1584 *Discoverie of Witchcraft* as a possible influence but argues that a more likely source of Bottom's transformation is the 1566 translation of Apuleius's *The Golden Ass* by William Adlington.[5] This chapter proposes that the ass's head brought to Shakespeare's stage cultic and material affiliations—especially with sixteenth-century mystery drama—that were likely to have been more culturally pervasive than its classical associations.

I therefore consider Bottom's asinine transformation in the context of the drama, liturgy, festival, and polemic of the sixteenth century. In doing so, however, I explore what Richard Emmerson calls "the great complexity of theatrical experience in the century that spans the traditional medieval/Renaissance divide." Arguing against critical narratives that "trace how a naïve pre-Shakespearean theater flowered into the golden age of Elizabethan drama," Emmerson proposes synchronic analysis that juxtaposes concurrent theatrical traditions previously separated by disciplinary and period divisions. Rather than homogenizing dramatic practices, synchronic study asks how their meaning changes over time; it is as much concerned with complexity and range as it is with temporal overlap.[6] This chapter therefore examines how the meaning of the ass varied and changed from pre-Reformation Chester through the midcentury Reformation to the Elizabethan stage.

As I trace the sixteenth-century provenance of the ass's head, I argue that it is a piece of theatrical artisanry—an artifact, and thus a material link, between the mysteries and the London stage. In chapter 2 the Chester Banns called our attention to the significance of the handiwork of craftsmen-players for provincial mystery pageants. Shakespeare's *Dream,* not unlike the Banns' aspersion of "Craftes men and meane men," mocks the "palpable-gross play" (5.1.350) of the "Hard-handed men that work in Athens here, / Which never laboured in their minds till now" (5.1.72–73). Yet this denigration is strategic: material craft is as central to Shakespeare's shadowy dream as it is to the dramatic performances heralded by the Banns. When Bottom first enters wearing the ass's head, he is greeted with the words, "Bless thee. Thou art translated" (3.1.105). In *Dream,* translation is both a mechanical and a linguistic practice. Prompted by the synchronic diachrony of the Chester Banns, whereby obsolescence holds out the possibility of recovery, I examine how Shakespeare's commercial theater "translates" this manufactured object: how it alters or transforms but also recovers and restores old dramatic material.

Early Sixteenth Century: The Chester Ass

Sometime between 1505 and 1522, a new play was added to the Chester mystery cycle: *Moses and the Law: Balaack and Balaam,* performed by the cappers.[7] It not only tells the story of Moses but also introduces the memorable character of a talking ass. Alarmed by the Israelites' defeat of other pagan kings, Balaack, King of Moab, sends for his prophet and servant, Balaam, whose magical powers he hopes will destroy Moses's people. As Balaam journeys to meet the king, however, an angel blocks the road, and his ass prostrates itself in fear and homage. Balaam is initially unaware of the divine messenger and thinks the beast is being stubborn:

Balaham

What the divell? My asse will not goe.

. . . .

Then Balaam shall beat his ass. And here someone ought to be transformed into the guise of an ass; and when Balaam strikes, the ass shall say:[8]

Asina

Mayster, thow doest ill secerly,
soe good an asse as mee to nye.
Now hast thow beaten mee here thrye,
that bare the thus abowte.

Balaham

Burnell, whye begylest thow mee
when I have most neede to thee?

Asina

That sight that before mee I see
maketh mee downe to lowte [bow].
Am not I, mayster, thy owne asse
to beare thee whyther thow will passe,
and many winter readye was?
To smyte me hyt ys shame.
Thow wottest well, mayster, perdee,
that thow haddest never non like to mee,
ne never yett soe served I thee.
Now am I not to blame.

(217–39)

The exchange between man and beast closely follows the biblical text (Numbers 22:28–30), with the ass proudly—and rather comically—declaring its long-standing record of loyal service. In scripture, furthermore, the ass first veers off into a field to avoid the angel, then runs into a wall and smashes

Balaam's foot, and ultimately lies down in the middle of the road. When the prophet's eyes are finally opened to the angel's presence, his immediate response is to mimic the beast and lie prostrate: "And the Lord opened the eies of Balaám, and... he bowed him selfe and fel flat on his face" (Numbers 22:31 Geneva).[9] Thus even in scripture the passage is humorous, and though no stage directions dictate the stage business of the ass's movements, it is easy to imagine the cappers improvising its meanderings (and Balaam's increasing frustration) in order to delight their audience. The Chester pageant adds to the comedy when Balaam calls his beast by the nonbiblical name Burnell. The name effectively personalizes the female donkey—so much so that the quarrel between man and she-ass recalls the humorous bickering between the impatient Noah and his obstinate wife.

It's not surprising, then, that the Chester Late Banns specifically call for this animated scene to be performed yet again: "Make the Asse to speake and sett hit out lyuelye."[10] Moreover, REED documents confirm that the ass was in demand by Chester audiences as late as 1610: nearly four decades after the Whitsuntide plays had been prohibited, "greate charges" were incurred to furnish a new ass (termed "the beast") for the city's Midsummer celebration.[11] The talking ass must also have been memorable because with the exception of the serpent, it is the only talking beast in the Old Testament. It is rather remarkable that no other surviving mystery play cycle seized upon the talking ass's theatrical potential. York's *Nativity* pageant comes closest, as it recalls Balaam, his prophecy, and his talking beast when Mary observes the star overhead:

> For Balam tolde ful longe beforne,
> How that a sterne shulde rise full hye,
>
> .   .   .   .
>
> Forsuth, it is my sone so free
> Be whame Balam gon meene.
>
> (99–100, 104–5)

As she then lays her child in the manger, Joseph is startled at the behavior of the ox and ass:

> O Marie, beholde thes beestis mylde,
> They make louyng in ther manere
> As thei wer men.
> Forsothe, it semes wele be ther chere
> Thare lord thei ken.
>
> (122–26)

While the babe's parents and the beasts do not exchange dialogue as had Balaam and the ass, Joseph nevertheless observes their human behavior: they possess knowledge ("Thare lord thei ken") and offer praise ("They make louyng . . . / As thei wer men.").

Yet the Chester story of Moses could readily have been staged without this episode, and given that the play already tasks one actor with the role of Expositor, Balaam's backstory is particularly superfluous. Beyond the sheer entertainment value of a talking animal, I want to suggest that the cappers, pinners, and linen drapers may have chosen to manufacture a talking ass for material and economic reasons. According to Lawrence Clopper, the cappers "had been granted sole rights to the retailing of coarse wares by Mayor Thomas Smyth in order that they might 'brynge forthe A playe concernynge the store of kynge balak & Balam the proffet.'"[12] If we more broadly survey mystery pageants, we can further see how these dramatic endeavors were deeply invested in craftsmanship. For instance, a stage direction from the Chester *Noah's Flood* pageant reads: "Then he [Noah] shall send forth a dove; and there shall be in the ship another dove carrying an olive-branch in its beak, which someone shall send from the mast by a rope into Noah's hands."[13] The stage direction makes clear that the ark would have been a massive stage set with multiple levels that could accommodate the movements of at least eight actors, including some means for a stagehand to climb the mast (perhaps secretly) and operate the dove-on-a-rope. Perhaps this person was the actor playing God—deus ex machina—for the play's initial stage direction situates him in the clouds or "some high place."[14]

The ark might have had other mechanisms for the raising of the rainbow when God gives the closing speech:

> The stringe is torned towardes you
> and towardes me is bente the bowe,
> that such wedder shall never showe;
> and this behett [promise] I thee.
> My blessinge nowe I give thee here,
> to thee, Noe, my servante deare.
>
> (321–26)

The ship must also have had portholes or other means of hanging the pictures of animals enumerated by each of the members of Noah's family as they boarded the ark. The stage direction following line 160 reads: "Then Noe shall goe into the arke with all his familye, his wyffe excepte, and the arke muste bee borded rownde aboute. And one the bordes all the beastes and fowles hereafter reahersed muste bee paynted, that ther wordes may agree with the pictures." As Noah's wife speaks, for example, she lists the animals depicted on one of the panels:

> And here are beares, wolves sett,
> apes, owles, maremussett,
> wesills, squerrells, and fyrrett;
> here the eaten there meate.
>
> (173–76)

For obvious reasons live animals were not used; the guildsmen of the Chester *Flood* manufactured painted boards to supplement the descriptive speeches.

In the York mystery cycle, the guilds performing the Noah story went to even greater pains. First, the play was divided in two: *The Building of the Ark* performed, not surprisingly, by the shipwrights, and *The Flood* itself rendered by the fishers and mariners. The shipwrights designed their pageant so as to actually build the ark during the progress of their play. In Chester and in York, therefore, the actors' words are accompanied not only by histrionic gesture but by physical labor (prior to and during the play). In York, moreover, the opening speech of God in *The Building of the Ark* recounts the labors of creating the world and its inhabitants and in doing so mentions the word "work" five times, "make" or "made" four, and the verb "wrought" on five occasions. This theme of the Divine Laborer climaxes with God's command to Noah to be His co-laborer: "I wyll thou wyrke withowten weyn / A warke to saffe thiselfe wythall" (35–36). The construction of the ark then begins accordingly.

It would be an oversimplification to say that mystery drama was merely artisanal: musicians, scribes, clergy, civic officials, and many others played crucial roles. It is equally misguided, however, to overlook the incredible amount of labor that was invested in props, costumes, and staging materials. As we saw in the previous chapter, drama in preindustrial England frequently demanded the cooperation and coordination of various forms of skilled labor using materials and technologies that were often scarce and costly in order to achieve even the most fundamental theatrical costumes, properties, staging, and effects.[15] Mystery pageants not only *required* work but *are* works—the material manifestations of guild labor—as much as they are dramatic stories or expressions of civic pride and religious belief. Shakespeare, as we'll see, is keenly aware of the centrality of craft to mystery playing, and the *Pyramus and Thisbe* scenes in *Dream* comically exploit it.

Beyond the story of Noah, almost every pageant afforded opportunities to showcase workmanship, whether in the bakers' *Last Supper* or the goldsmiths' *Herod and the Magi*.[16] The most powerful example—because the most visceral—is the crucifixion scene wherein the nailers and pinners (not only of York but of Chester as well) botch the construction of the cross so that Christ must be stretched and pulled to fit the premade nail holes. An odd way to advertise craftsmanship perhaps, yet according to John Parker the workers' "staged inadequacy" becomes felicitous insofar as it leads to God's suffering—and therefore their own salvation. In this way, the mysteries see their own failed workmanship as comic, part of the larger *felix culpa* of Christianity's doctrine of original sin.[17] The tile thatchers' conspicuously deficient roof thus allows the miraculous star of *The Nativity* to shine upon the newborn God-child.[18]

When the episode of Balaam's talking ass was added to the Chester mysteries in the early sixteenth century, therefore, it afforded the cappers, pinners, and linen drapers an extraordinary opportunity to showcase their handiwork. The actor playing Moses probably wore a headdress when he returned from Mount Sinai bearing the Ten Commandments, for his resplendent face is surmounted by horns.[19] Wishing, perhaps, to maximize the exhibition of their wares, the cappers might have incorporated the ass's head into a more elaborate two-man costume with the actor playing Balaam donning the rear end and, centaur-like, appearing to ride the stubborn beast. A fellow actor, meanwhile, would wear the front end of the guise and speak Burnell's lines.[20]

I have focused thus far on the material and economic significance of the Chester talking ass from the perspective of the guildsman who staged it, but of course it was a polyvalent theatrical object whose meaning varied over time and among different audience groups. I will consider those variations once we examine how the Reformation received and altered the ass's meaning. But if we are to avoid the reification of the traditional medieval-Renaissance divide, then before turning to the Reformation and to Shakespeare, it must be noted that Balaam's ass was itself a theatrical innovation. As discussed in chapter 2, the first three decades of the sixteenth century witnessed considerable expansion and alteration in the plays of the Chester cycle sequence, particularly those dramatizing stories from the Old Testament. Prior to this time, the city's annual drama was largely a Passion play. During the period of 1505–32—most likely before 1521 but in any case prior to the Reformation—the plays were moved from the feast of Corpus Christi to Whitsuntide and began to be performed over a three-day period on moving wagons that processed through the city. The Chester cycle is therefore largely Tudor in its content, organization, and dramaturgy.[21]

Clopper theorizes that the desire for larger tourist revenue and a strong sense of competition with Coventry prompted Chester city officials to shift their plays to Whitsuntide. Coinciding with this move were efforts to enhance the cycle's pageantry and spectacle by adding more episodes and by performing the plays on mobile platforms.[22] From this perspective, we can see why authorities would have welcomed a new pageant episode featuring a talking ass, and perhaps too why Mayor Smyth subsequently agreed to protect the rights of the cappers' guild: Balaam's ass was a cash cow. Prompted by sacred and secular interests, the addition of the Chester ass supports Theresa Coletti's assertion that the mysteries were continually adapting to meet new dramatic and cultural challenges and opportunities.[23] Commercially implicated upon its arrival, Balaam's ass also illustrates why we must abandon diachronic narratives that starkly divide static, conformist, religious medieval drama from vibrant, diverse, secular Renaissance theater, and why we must further explore the possibility of material connections between these two stages.

Mid-Sixteenth Century: The Popish Ass

Scot's *Discoverie of Witchcraft* (1584) includes the story "Of a man turned into an asse, and returned againe into a man."[24] The man is a sailor transformed into bestial shape by a witch, and, spurned by his shipmates, he eventually finds himself near a church as the consecration of the Mass is about to take place. Not daring to enter the church "least he should have beene beaten and driven out with cudgels," he instead "fell downe in the churchyard, upon the knees of his hinder legs, and did lift his forefeet over his head, as the preest doth hold the sacrament at the elevation." Seeing the "prodigious sight" of an ass "in great devotion," the townspeople gather, discover the witch, and force her to remove the spell. The tale is so outrageous for Scot that his commentary derides more than it refutes: "What lucke was it, that this yoong fellow of *England,* landing so latelie in those parts, and that old woman of *Cyprus . . .* should both understand one anothers communication." "I mervell then what would have become of this asse," he later quips: "whether he should have risen at the daie of judgement in an asses bodie and shape." An ardent Reformer, Scot takes aim not at witchcraft alone but at sorcery as it relates to Catholic teaching on the Eucharist.[25]

Pondering the "the witch, the asse, the masse," he states that he doubts "the miracle of transubstantiation" and jokes "that the asse had no more wit than to kneele downe and hold up his forefeete to a peece of starch or flowre which neither would, nor could, nor did helpe him." The transformations performed by the witch and the priest are indistinguishable for Scot; both are equally preposterous. Witches supposedly transform shipwrecked sailors into beasts, and priests claim to transubstantiate wafers into God. In Scot's account, the ass mimics the priest by "hold[ing] up his forefeete" when he hears "a little saccaring bell ring to the elevation" of the host. Scot then laughs at the futility of the ass's imitation: "I wonder," he says, "that the masse could not reforme that which the witch transformed." The absurdity of the man turned ass thus confirms what Scot already believes about Catholicism: its priests are already asses (they don't need a witch), and its Eucharist is a mere "peece of starch or flowre." His mockery of Roman dogma is so vehement in its attempt to stamp out idolatry that it risks sheer anticlericalism and outright contempt for the sacrament.[26]

When editors and scholars discuss the possible nonclassical sources of Bottom's translation, they most often point to Scot's *Discoverie*. What they fail to note, however, is that Scot's text is merely one example of the ass in Reformation discourse. By the time Scot published his *Discoverie,* the figure of an ass-headed man had long been an icon of Protestant propaganda mocking the wrongheadedness of the Church of Rome.[27] In a German pamphlet first published in 1523 but later translated into English and published in London in 1579, Philipp Melanchthon and Martin Luther warned of *Two VVonderful Popish Monsters,* including a "Popish Asse" (figure 5) and a "Moonkish Calfe." The famous engraver, printmaker, and painter Lucas Cranach was commissioned to provide richly detailed full-page illustrations to reinforce the 1523 pamphlet's incendiary polemic. The *Papstesel,* or "Popish Asse," was endowed with several hybrid features to show the corruption of the Catholic Church: its Griffin-like foot signifies its overweening legal authority; its feminine breasts and belly denote its voluptuousness; its scales represent secular princes who cling to and protect its spiritual and worldly authority; on its buttocks is a dragon's head symbolizing the corrupt books and bulls issued by the pope, while the old man's head signifies the papacy's waning power.

Yet, though the pamphlet considers each element in this fantastic assembly in some detail, it is the ass's head that gives the creature its name, as both the original German and later English title pages bear witness.[28] Melanchthon's interpretation of this feature, moreover, sets the terms by which the rest of the monster will be anatomized:

First of all, the heade of the Asse is a description of the Pope, for the Churche is a spirituall bodye and kingdome, assembled together in spirite. And therefore it cannot nor ought not to have a mannes head, nor a visible Lorde. But onely the LORD JESUS, which formeth the heartes inwardlye, by the holy Ghost. . . . Contrary unto these thinges, the Pope hath made himselfe the visible and outwarde heade of the Churche. (Sig. B1v)[29]

FIGURE 5. Lucas Cranach the Elder, the "Popish Asse," from Melanchthon and Luther, *Of two vvoonderful popish monsters* (London, 1579). Reproduced by permission of the Folger Shakespeare Library.

Citing Exodus 13:13, which stipulates that a firstborn ass, an unclean animal, be redeemed by the sacrifice of a lamb just as God's chosen people are redeemed at Passover, Melanchthon adds, "For the holy Scriptures doe understande by the Asse, the externall and carnall lyfe, and the Elementes of the worlde" (sig. B1v–B2r). Melanchthon crowns the pope with an ass's head, in other words, to signify the fleshiness of the Roman Church, and indeed the Popish Asse is spoken of as if it were a physical object. Like an artifact of the Old Religion, it is said to be "founde at Rome in the Riuer of Tiber" after the flood of 1496 receded (sig. B1r).

In contrast to the spirituality of the Reformers, the pope-ass is a Catholic relic, a monstrous example of Rome's superficiality, its "shewe and appearaunce of truth," not to mention its "craft" and "trumperies" (sig. B1r). But God, writes Melanchthon, brought forth this monster as a "token" of his displeasure with the church of Rome: "God at all times doth liuely represent by certeine tokens and after a wonderfull sort, either his wrath or mercie . . . to the ende that all true faithfull men and Christians should bee admonished in good time, and shoulde take heede" (sig. B1r). For Melanchthon, in other words, the pope-ass is a stage prop in God's "lively representation," or drama, that simultaneously manifests the carnality of Catholicism and refutes it. True Christians, the audience for whom God "hath sette foorth this horrible figure," are admonished to continue the work of reforming their lives and the church (sig. B1r). In the same pamphlet, then, the ass is subject and object, a Catholic agent of Antichrist and a Protestant mouthpiece of God, a relic of the past and a symbol of future wrath.

I will subsequently highlight some of the other features of the pope-ass and situate this image in a brief history of liturgical practices, but I must first underscore its widespread and long-standing popularity and influence. The Popish Asse "was one of the most sensational monsters to appear in the age of the Reformation," according to R. W. Scribner, who also affirms that "it was one of the most heavily used for anti-papal polemic."[30] Julie Crawford contends that Melanchthon and Luther's illustrated pamphlet set the precedent for the use of woodcuts and tales depicting monstrous births as a means of attacking discredited Roman beliefs in sixteenth-century Protestant polemics.[31] The number of editions and translations featuring the papal ass attest to its iconic power. There are nine German editions of the entire pamphlet and five more of the popish ass alone. The 1579 English translation derives from a 1557 French translation to which John Calvin, though estranged from the German Lutherans over the doctrine of the Eucharist, ascribes a commendatory preface. There is also a Dutch translation.

In addition to *Two VVonderful Popish Monsters,* other English publications featuring the pope-ass include John Barthlet's *The pedegrewe of heretiques* (1566) and Pierre Boaistuau's *Certaine secrete wonders of nature* (1569).[32] The prodigy was adopted by other assorted collections, such as Lycosthenes's *Wunderwerck* of 1557. In the seventeenth century, a new image of the papal ass was published in Germany, yet by this time the monster captured less polemical and theological interest than the scientific curiosity of the Italian naturalist Fortunio Liceti and others.[33] The importance of the image for Luther is perhaps best evidenced by its inclusion as the first of only nine woodcuts in his 1545 *Depiction of the Papacy,* a work he was said to have called "his testament," for it summed up his decades of struggles with Rome.[34]

Whatever its extensive post-Reformation popularity, Protestants were not the first to associate the ass with Catholic liturgy and practice. In fact, it was precisely because the ass was such a familiar sight in late medieval liturgical ceremonies that Luther and Melanchthon found it such a suitable objective correlative for popish idolatry. During the late Middle Ages, the church itself brought the ass to the altar during Christmas and Easter celebrations. In thirteenth- and fourteenth-century church pageants known as *Prophetae et Stella,* the figures of Old Testament prophets parade sequentially, each testifying to the forthcoming messianic birth. Last to deliver a monologue was Balaam, who told of the star that shall arise from Jacob (Numbers 24:17). Following his speech, the angel appeared, and the ass began to converse with her rider. For E. K. Chambers, the significance of this "miniature drama" is that it represents an attempt by the church to redirect vital pagan practices toward orthodox ends and "to turn," he says, "the established presence of the ass in the church to purposes of edification rather than of ribaldry." He therefore suggests that Balaam's appearance was merely a pretext "for the sake of his ass."[35]

As Chambers notes, the ass did indeed have an established presence in church ritual and drama dating as far back as the thirteenth century. In Beauvais, France, a Christmastide holiday commonly known as the Feast of the Ass (*asinaria festa*) was held on January fourteenth to celebrate the Virgin's flight into Egypt on a donkey. These festivals were often marked with religious ceremonies, even so-called donkey masses, in which a swaddled infant was placed in a young girl's arms and then the two were mounted on an ass and led in procession to the church. There a special mass was sung praising the ass and urging it to speak as the congregation imitated it with uproarious braying at various times.[36]

As at Christmas, the ass played a prominent role in the other major church season, Eastertide. On the Continent, special hobby-asses, called *Palmesels,* were used to celebrate Christ's entry into Jerusalem on Palm Sunday, the start of Holy Week leading up to Easter. *Palmesels* were commonplace in the streets of many German and Swiss towns every year, and Luther and Melanchthon probably seized upon the image of the popish ass after witnessing the adulation and applause this dramatic property received from thronging crowds.[37] The German word *Palmesel* means "palm ass," yet the term encompasses both man and ass—frequently referring to both the painted wood donkey and the statue of Christ affixed to it. The man-beast *Palmesel* was mounted on wheels for Palm Sunday processions through city streets and churches.[38]

In England, however, a Eucharistic host carried in a monstrance by a priest typically was used instead of a *Palmesel*.[39] The Catholic Rheims New Testament (1582) recalls this practice in a gloss on Christ's entry into Jerusalem (Matthew 21:8): "These offices of honour [strewing of palms, etc.] done to our Saviour extraordinarily, were very acceptable: and for a memory hereof the holy Church maketh a solemne Procession euery yere vpon this day, specially in oure Countrey when it was Catholike, *with the B. Sacrament reuerently caried, as it were Christ vpon the asse.*"[40] The recusant author of the gloss finds the substitution of the sacrament for "Christ vpon the asse" not only acceptable but laudable; he adds, "The like seruice and the like duties done to him [Christ] in al other solemne Processions of the B. Sacrament, and otherwise, be vndoubtedly no lesse gratefull."[41]

The Reformation overturned the teaching on transubstantiation and, as we saw with Scot's *Discoverie of Witchcraft,* mocked the association between the Eucharist and the ass. A 1589 annotated edition of the New Testament printed Reformer William Fulke's responses to the "horrible Idolatrie" of the Catholic Rheims gloss on Christ's entry into Jerusalem by rebuking the "Maygame and pageant play" whereby Catholics celebrate Palm Sunday with "theatricall pompes." "But it is pretty sport," says Fulke, "that you make the Priest that carrieth the idol, to supply the roome of the Asse on which Christ did ride."[42] In Fulke's bitter jest, the priest carrying the monstrance containing the communion host plays the ass. Whereas in Scot's *Discoverie,* the ass had behaved like a priest (raising his arms at the moment of consecration as the priest elevated the host), here we have the priest behaving like an ass, playing the role of the *Palmesel*. Both writers glimpse an inherent theatricality in bestial transformation that transcends witchcraft or the "pompes" of Palm Sunday processions and is, for them, bound up with the hocus pocus of Catholicism in general. This theatrical potential—which both the Chester play and Shakespeare's *Dream* tap for its comedic and commercial value—is what makes the talking ass so worthy of derision for these Reformers. But the Roman Church apparently didn't get the joke. Such "dreams" were repeatedly performed in the liturgical calendar. Pageants like the *Prophetae et Stella* yoked Balaam's speaking ass to the incarnated flesh of the newborn messiah, and Palm Sunday processions tied Jesus and his donkey together into one life-size, though silent, wooden beast.

Luther and Melanchthon sought to desacralize the ass, yet they were also, perhaps unwittingly, translating it from a secular to a religious context. The depiction of the ass-headed pope was previously a political caricature of Alexander VI mocking his aspiration to be "head of the world" as he sought to aggrandize the authority of the Papal States in the wake of the French invasion of 1494.[43] More than a quarter century later, Luther and Melanchthon asked Cranach to re-create the image, yet much of it was left unchanged, including the Roman landmarks associated with Alexander's despotic reign: the tower of the papal prison as well as the castle where he had secluded himself. If we are to grasp Bottom's translation on the London stage, we must first note that the "new" pope-ass did not erase but *incorporated* its antecedent. Adapting the popish ass from political to religious purposes, the two Reformers confer an ambiguous temporality on the "relic." An artifact of recent Roman politics, the pope-ass is adopted by the Reformation and coded as Catholic and therefore a remnant of the Old Faith now superseded by the righteousness of the current Reformation enterprise. But this old object retains present efficacy; it remains a current threat.

Indeed, it is precisely its belatedness that allows the pope-ass to uphold the current claims of the Reformation, to make Protestantism more fashionable, if you will, by performing the difference between past and present.[44] The 1523 pamphlet accomplishes this kind of temporal incorporation when John Crespin's preface reminds "ALL which fear the Lord" that the "Romish Antechrist" can be seen "at this day, yea, in his latter age farre out of modestie" (sig. A3v). And to help readers grasp the immediacy of this threat, the images of the Popish Asse and Monkish Calfe are materialized with full-page illustrations. Anticipating Melancthon's dramatic metaphors, Crespin describes two competing dramas in which the pope-ass and monk-calf are subject and object, actor and prop, present and past: "Now for as much as the Moonkes are the principall proppes of that drunken and enchaunting harlot [the pope], very fitte is happened this other monster, in the likenesse of a Monkish Calfe, hauing on him a coole [cowl], who will playe his part as well as the Popish Asse. Giuing all men to vnderstande what sanctitie hath chiefly blinded the eyes of the world: to wit, the holinesse of a disguised frocke and habite" (sig. A3v). Monks are deceptive props in the pope's grand show of holiness. But this drama is overthrown by God's use of those very same props to admonish present-day believers with a morality play of past depravities. Luther and Melanchthon's translation of the pope-ass urges us to rethink our periodized view of sixteenth-century history. Whereas the traditional, diachachronic model of secularization implies unremitting progressive succession, the Popish Asse performs in a complex theater of temporalities. As Catholic relic it re-presents the past, and as Protestant portent, it forecasts God's impending wrath. "Everyone should shudder as they take it to heart," wrote Luther.[45] The Popish Asse straddles the Reformation divide—and, as we'll see, so too does the ass's head fixed on Bottom.

Before turning to Shakespeare, however, I would first like to return to Chester. In the wake of Reformation polemic, the ass was not only temporally ambivalent but symbolically vexed as well. Chester audiences in the late sixteenth century, therefore, would probably have viewed Balaam's ass quite differently than their grandparents had decades before. Both generations were keenly aware of the urban topography that, according to Robert Barrett, is underscored by the cappers' play as it mediates the city's gradual evolution from monastic to mercantile organizations of time and space.[46] On 7 August 1509, Barrett explains, Henry VIII's royal arbitrators handed the city corporation a jurisdictional victory over St. Werburgh's abbey with the result not only that former tenants of monastic lands became citizens under the corporation's authority but also that agents of that body were at times granted access to the abbey precinct.[47] In the years immediately following this transformation of Chester's topography from monastic to urban space, therefore, it is possible that the rebuke of a religious figure like Balaam by a common, ordinary ass may have stung the monks looking on from the abbey walls. Later sixteenth-century performances of the mystery cycle, as Barrett also demonstrates, reflect the long and vexed yet inevitable shift in discourse from the hagiography and exegesis fostered by the monastic community to the emergent oligarchic ideologies promoted by the city's authorities.[48]

Thus when the archbishop of York refused to allow performance even of an amended text in 1575 because, according to a witness, he continued to associate "the popish plaies of Chester" with the outlawed doctrines and liturgies of the Rome, a recusant audience member may well have grudgingly agreed with the archbishop and recalled (not without bitterness or reverie) when the cappers' pageant was part of the city's Corpus Christi celebrations before that feast was suppressed.[49] Audience response to Balaam's talking ass would have resembled the diverse mixture of delight, satisfaction, alienation, and outrage that, according to Emmerson, characterized feelings of many post-Reformation spectators who witnessed the revision of the Chester play of Antichrist.[50]

Cestrians with Protestant leanings, even if they found much of the vindictive polemic against the papacy distasteful, may have viewed the prophet Balaam as a personification of the contemporary Roman church: a once-faithful servant of God who was now regrettably wayward. In the hands of Reformation writers both on the Continent and in England, Balaam soon became the Old Testament type of Rome's modern-day simony. The Geneva Bible glossed 2 Peter 2's declamation of false prophets who "haue gone astray folowing the way of Balaam, the Sone of Bosor" (15) by claiming that the passage "is evidently sene in the Pope and his Priests, which by lies and flatteries sel mens soules, so that it is certeine that he is not the successour of Simon Peter, but of Simon Magus."[51] Likewise a marginal gloss in John Foxe's *Acts and Monuments* directs readers to a passage, by no means unique in this work, where "the pope [is] well compared to Balaam which was wont [to] curse Gods people for reward of money."[52]

What must be emphasized, however, is that these typological readings of Balaam, like Luther's own commentary on 2 Peter 2, are preceded—and probably, if indirectly, inspired—by Melanchthon's "Declaration of a Popish Asse" in the 1523 *Deuttung der czwo grewlichen Figuren*.[53] It is significant that Melanchthon metonymically tethers the monstrous papal ass to the biblical figure of Balaam. Just as the papal ass displays its naked female breasts and belly, so the unashamed body of churchmen engages in unrestrained prodigality: "[T]he belly and the stomacke, the which do resemble the belly and stomacke of a woeman, signifie the body of the Pope: That is to say the Cardinals, Archbishops, Bishops, Abbots, Moonkes, Priests…these, without any shame, doe lead a dissolute and wanton lyfe, full of all filthinesse and wickednesse" (sig. B4v). Summoning scripture to support his accusation, Melanchthon cites 2 Peter 2:10–19, including the allusion to Balaam (15), which he finds particularly apt as a gloss of the monster's belly: "And truely this [passage] doth liuely sette out the Pope, and paynteth him in his right coloures, and vncouereth fullye the feminine bellye of the Popishe Asse" (sig. C1v).

In sixteenth-century Protestant polemic, therefore, Balaam is a figure of Rome's spiritual disobedience and greed. But he might also be metonymically associated with beastly appetites, as he is in Melanchthon's description of the pope's "bawdes, and fatte hogges, which haue none other care all their lyfe time but to feede and pamper their paunches with delycious wynes and delycate dishes: to seeke their ease and all the allurements and entisements to whoredome" (sig. B4v). So too for John Bale, the modern descendants of Balaam easily lure "carnal idyotes" like a "gorgious glittering whore": "Folowinge hys wayes therefore, they haue always for lucres sake, gloriously garnished theyr… proude sinagoge of Sathan, wyth golde, siluer, pearle, precious stone, veluets, silkes, miters, copes, crosses, cruetes, ceremonies, sensinges, blessinges, bablinges, brawlynges, processions, popetts, and such other madde mastryes."[54]

Like Balaam, the pope-ass could be sexualized in order to criticize the wantonness of the papacy, as in a 1545 work by Luther referring to the papal ass and "attacking the 'hermaphrodites and sodomites' around the pope, and addressing the pope himself as the 'maiden popess.'"[55] Ulinka Rublack notes that the pope-ass's sexual features were enhanced in later Reformation woodcuts where she/he/it now "sported sexy legs, pointed breasts and a firm body."[56] Consequently, a Reformed citizen of Chester may have looked on both characters in the cappers' play as representations of the papacy's "dissolute and wanton lyfe," particularly if the two actors are joined together as ass and rider in the same bestial costume.

Regardless of audience interpretation, the talking ass was so popular that, as previously noted, it long outlived the play in which it first appeared. Popular in 1505 for its novelty, it was undoubtedly beloved by later audiences (Reformed and recusant alike) for its familiarity: nostalgia may have trumped ideology for many onlookers. Beyond its religious polysemy, it must have continued to effectively advertise the handiwork of the cappers' guild. For they still paraded it (without the context of the surrounding biblical narrative) through the streets of Chester in early seventeenth-century Midsummer processions.

Late Sixteenth Century: The Shakespearean Ass

Like the craft guilds of provincial mystery drama, Shakespeare's company also wished to showcase its acting skill as well as its properties. The very existence of careful, exhaustive records such as those in REED documents and Henslowe's *Diary* attest to the fact that both stages were tremendously invested in the storage, care, repair, and economic use of dramatic properties and costumes. In the public playhouses, however, it was the possession, rather than the manufacture, of properties that prompted the theater companies to feature them in plays.[57] The London stages often owned rather everyday items that could nevertheless occasion powerful dramatic scenes: a bed, a simple handkerchief, a ring. Yet the acting companies also possessed more unusual items—thrones, tents, skulls, and Hell mouths—which they valued as well, for these could become the stuff that dramatic dreams were made on. Perhaps none of these was more curious, or offered as much dream potential, as the ass's head.

The 1623 folio specifically calls for the actor playing Bottom to enter "with the Asse head,"[58] and the text of the play repeatedly highlights this prop. Soon after sighting Bottom's monstrous face, Snout exclaims, "O Bottom, thou art changed. What do I see on thee?" Bottom's reply draws attention to his headgear: "What do you see? You see an ass-head of your own, do you?" (3.1.102–4). When Puck later informs Oberon of his mischievous prank, he not only states, "My mistress with a monster is in love" (3.2.6) but underscores the artificiality of the "monster" he has created, saying, "An ass's nole I fixèd on his head" (3.2.17). Finally, when it comes time to "take this transformèd scalp / From off the head of this Athenian swain" (4.1.61–62), the text makes the prop conspicuous as it handles the difficult task of "magically" removing it from the actor's head while the audience looks on.

Modern editions (such as the Norton edition quoted below) resolve this difficulty by editorially inserting a stage direction:

Titania

O, how mine eyes do loathe his visage now!

Oberon

Silence a while.—Robin, take off this head.—
Titania, music call, and strike more dead
Than common sleep of all these five the sense.

Titania

Music, ho—music such as charmeth sleep.
Still music.

Robin

[*taking the ass-head off BOTTOM*] Now when thou wak'st with thine own fool's eyes peep.

(4.1.76–81)

Early editions of the play give no indication of precisely when or how Robin is to remove the ass's head.[59] But the on-stage removal of the headgear (with Puck carrying it off in his hands or on his own head) suggests that the text of *Dream* is trying to call our attention to its artificiality—as though, rather than apologizing for its awkwardness as do the players of *Pyramus and Thisbe,* it is providing an excuse by highlighting the clumsiness of the headgear. It's possible that Bottom wears a simple mask or pair of ears, yet the play's repeated use of words like "head," "nole," and "scalp" suggest a more substantial (and therefore clumsy) piece of headgear. Davidson compares Bottom to the miniature image of a mummer whose head is completely covered or "fixed with an ass's head"—snout, fur, ears and all—in the margin of a fourteenth-century manuscript (Bodley MS 264, fol. 181v).[60]

Quince's famous ejaculation—"Bless thee, Bottom, bless thee. Thou art translated" (3.1.105)—though often glossed by editors as implying simple "transformation," further highlights the materiality of the ass's head. The *OED* notes that while "translate" could mean in Shakespeare's time "to change in form, appearance, or substance," it could also describe the actions of a tailor "to renovate, turn, or cut down" a garment, or "of a cobbler, to make new boots from the remains of (old ones)."[61] The latter definition would come naturally to a craftsman like Quince, but it also glimpses the restorative potential of the professional London stage and offers a clue as to where Shakespeare might have acquired this extraordinary prop. The material translation of the ass from Balaam to Bottom as a form of recycling or renovation is a far cry from textual translation in the sense of interpretation. Yet it does resemble the allusive and acquisitive mechanism of one particular form of textual translation: typology. As quoted in the epigraph to this chapter, Luther mocks the Eucharistic typology of the Roman Breviary as a "dream" "patched together" by a "poor senseless idiot."[62] His intention is to ridicule Catholic exegesis, but he uncovers the essential hermeneutic of typological reading: it creates new narratives by patching together older discursive threads.[63] *Dream,* too, is a patchwork of older material: the textual matter of Ovid and Apuleius as well as the handcrafted matter of the mystery play guilds.

Dream is the only surviving play from the Elizabethan-Jacobean stage (1580–1642) that specifically requires the property of an ass's head.[64] The work of Scott McMillin and Sally-Beth MacLean on the touring of the Queen's Men shows that Chester was a repeated destination for the London company, including the back-to-back seasons of 1590–91 and 1591–92.[65] Their work has prompted Helen Cooper to suggest the possibility that the financially pinched cappers sold the disused ass-head to the touring London actors.[66] If the cappers of Chester resembled their Coventry counterparts, then they retained their stage properties long after the prohibition of the plays. The Coventry cycle had last been performed in 1579, and yet a 1591 "Invitori of the Implments of the company of cappers" includes such sundry items as "pylates dublit," "mary maudlyns goune," and a "hell mowth." Considering the lack of performance opportunities, the guild's preservation of more than a dozen "headpeses"—mostly wigs, but also masks and other headgear—is extraordinary: "one headpese…iij headpeses…pylates

heade[,] fyve maries heades…gods head[,] the spirites heade…The gian-
des head."[67] Moreover, given the late appeal of Balaam's talking ass, it is not
unthinkable that the headgear may still have existed and that a professional
London company might have been inspired by it or acquired it outright from
a craft guild that had once participated in this older and recently outlawed
play tradition. Many of Shakespeare's collaborators and competitors were
first-generation actors—the sons of bricklayers and shoemakers—and many
had been apprentice saddlers, joiners, and dyers with connections to tradesmen in London and the provinces.[68]

Once acquired, this remarkable piece must have demanded a dramatic occasion. As Peter Stallybrass has stated regarding the famous props of *Hamlet,*
"It would be pointless to write a play with a ghost appearing first in armor
and then in a nightgown, with a young man wearing black, with the use of
rapiers, and with a skull, unless the company already owned some of those
props. The props themselves, then, were stimulants to writing."[69] A dramatic
craftsman, or play-wright, Shakespeare translated mystery play remnants into
contemporary commercial stage magic, but to suggest that Shakespeare's
stage may have borrowed, purchased, or imitated Balaam's ass does not imply
that we ignore the innovations separating his theater and that older play tradition. Rather, by surveying the late medieval and early modern history of the
ass—from so-called donkey masses as well as Christmas and Easter interludes
and processions, to the artisanal stages of the York *Nativity* and *Entry into
Jerusalem* and the Chester *Moses and the Law* pageant, and to parodic Reformation discourses—we can better appreciate not only *Dream*'s contact with
these earlier cultural manifestations but also its distance and novelty.

We might compare, for example, the song of the donkey mass at Beauvais,
France, with Bottom's singing in the "flow'ry bed" of Titania. The former
began with a Latin verse and French refrain roughly translated as:

> From the East
> The Ass has come,
> Beautiful and strong,
> Able to bear burdens.
> Hey, sing, Sir Ass!
> Your fair mouth frowns.
> You will have hay enough
> And oats aplenty.[70]

While the ass may not have sung along, the congregation joined in a clamorous braying: "Hinham, hinham, hinham!" In *Dream,* the ass sings and is
similarly attended with great ceremony and promises of plentiful food: "Or

say, sweet love, what thou desir'st to eat. . . . Good hay, sweet hay, hath no fellow" (*Dream,* 4.1.28, 31). Likewise, in both Shakespeare and the Christmas liturgy, the ass is praised for his beauty and urged to sing. The congregation at the donkey mass described him as "belle" and "pulcher" as they coaxed him into song ("Hez, Sire Asnes, car chantez"). Titania says to Bottom, "I pray thee, gentle mortal, sing again. / Mine ear is much enamoured of thy note; / So is mine eye enthrallèd to thy shape" (3.1.121–23). But there are crucial differences as well. What had occasioned the "Song of the Ass" in Beauvais was the celebration of the Flight into Egypt. What prompts Bottom's singing is the flight of his friends, which Puck will later compare to a flock of birds "rising and cawing at the gun's report" (3.2.22). Left alone in the woods, he, like any child, sings in order to calm his fears: "I see their knavery. This is to make an ass of me, to fright me, if they could; but I will not stir from this place, do what they can. I will walk up and down here, and I will sing, that they shall hear I am not afraid" (3.1.106–9).

More important, Shakespeare's lovable ass is not a devotional but a sexual object. During the liturgy, the ass was admired for its service to the infant Jesus. Bottom, however, is the object of Titania's erotic love. She confesses instantaneous love for Bottom "on the first view" of him (3.1.125), but he is more interested in other bodily appetites:

> Monsieur Cobweb, good monsieur, get you your weapons in your hand and kill me a red-hipped humble-bee on the top of a thistle; and, good monsieur, bring me the honeybag. Do not fret yourself too much in the action, monsieur; and, good monsieur, have a care the honeybag break not. I would be loath to have you overflowen with a honeybag, signor. (4.1.10–15)

Sending Titania's fairies off on several errands, Bottom accepts service rather than lending it, as did the ass at Beauvais, which was able to bear the burden of the Virgin and child ("*Pulcher et fortissimus / Sarcinis aptissimus*"). Thus while Bottom's singing is a reincarnation of a liturgical spectacle, it is also remembering with a difference—a commemoration nearly beyond recognition. The Reformation greatly facilitated the ass's translation by unmooring it from its previous cultural and religious affiliations. Melanchthon declared that the popish ass's female breasts and belly symbolized "all the allurements and enticements of whoredome" practiced by cardinals, bishops, monks, and priests. The feminine features of the pope-ass were enhanced in later woodcut illustrations of the monster. Shakespeare, then, is not the first to eroticize the ass or associate it with bodily appetites, but his comic translation is far removed from religious invective. It has more in common with the Chester cappers' subtly misogynist gendering of Balaam's ass, where the female donkey's stubbornness is presented as a kind of shrewish resistance to male authority. In Shakespeare it is not the ass but the fairy queen who is obstinate and wayward. By the late sixteenth century, therefore, the ass's head is remarkable not only for its monstrosity and theatrical potential but also because this old prop is available for new interpretations that highlight, obscure, or merely hint at its religious and dramatic provenance.

Is "secularization" the correct term to describe the translation of the ass from mystery drama and liturgy to the London stage?[71] The answer is, at first, straightforward: Shakespeare "translates," in the sense of "transforms," a cultic object into a commercial one. But "translate" also means to renovate, to make "new" boots or clothes—or props—from "old" ones, in which case previous material is retained and preserved. The pope-ass is, as we've seen, both a relic of the old religion and a present danger. The ass's head in *Dream* is also temporally vexed: it is both the remnant of a bygone play tradition and the means by which Shakespeare's play claims to be innovative and advanced. Jan Kott noted that the ass had long been a complex syncretic object that undermined dogma while simultaneously celebrating it: "In the Feast of Fools, or *festum asinorum,* the low clerics parodied the Holy Offices while disguising themselves with the masks of animals."[72] Of course Kott, like E. K. Chambers, was eager to underscore the importance of ancient folk rituals for the professional London stage. He insisted that Shakespeare's indebtedness to carnival and *serio ludere* renders him not only a secular poet but also—and for that reason—a modern, not a medieval, one: "This encounter of Titania and Bottom, the ass and the mock-king of the carnival, is the very beginning of modern comedy and one of its glorious opening nights."[73]

If, like Kott, we are eager to find "the very beginning of modern comedy" in Shakespeare, we may miss the extent to which *Dream* is looking backward rather than forward—moments such as Bottom's dream, where Shakespeare's play brings the religious history of the ass into closer proximity by retaining previous cultural affinities.[74] Restored to his everyday asininity, Bottom tries to recount his experience in Titania's bower:

I have had a most rare vision. I have had a dream past the wit of man to say what dream it was. Man is but an ass if he go about t'expound this dream. Methought I was—there is no man can tell what. Methought I was, and methought I had—but man is but a patched fool if he will offer to say what methought I had. The eye of man hath not heard, the ear of man hath not seen, man's hand is not able to taste, his tongue to conceive, nor his heart to report what my dream was. (4.1.199–207)

Since the play is set in pagan, pre-Christian Athens, its allusion to the text of 1 Corinthians is extraneous. Yet given the sixteenth-century provenance of the ass, often as prayerful as it was parodic, the syncretism of *Dream* has precedent. Praised by the faithful in Palm Sunday processions, the ass was likewise a symbol for reformers of the crude sorcery and blasphemous materialism of popish liturgy. Melanchthon's derogation of the Popish Asse reads like a paraphrase of this same biblical passage: "For the Churche is a spirituall bodye and kingdome, assembled together in spirite. . . . Contrary vnto these thinges the Pope hath made himselfe the visible and outwarde heade of the Churche" (sig. B1v). In the Chester mystery plays, the talking ass incited laughter even as it served as God's mouthpiece to admonish moral waywardness. Bottom's dream achieves a comic effect, but mixed in with the laughter at Bottom's synesthetic jumbling of the Bible text is the pleasure of recognition: of the familiar passage itself, to be sure, but also perhaps of witnessing a talking ass situated in a biblical context for the first time since the mysteries had staged the story of Balaam a generation before.[75]

At the same time, however, the mangled text of 1 Corinthians is also an opportunity for *Dream* to distinguish itself from the ass's previous religious manifestations. Bottom, after all, "will get Peter Quince to write a ballad of this dream" and he "will sing it in the latter end of a play, before the Duke" (4.1.207–10). His aim is pure profit, not moral instruction. The same can be said for their performance of the "tedious brief scene of young Pyramus / And his love Thisbe" (5.1.56–57): "If our sport had gone forward," laments Snug before Bottom returns, "we had all been made men" (4.2.16–17). Shakespeare overlays Bottom's dream with a biblical passage, but the playful misquoting of 1 Corinthians lacks the didacticism of the cappers' play even as it shares the Chester guild's commercial motives. We can see, then, that there was never a moment when the ass underwent secularization; rather, its sacred and secular manifestations long coexisted.[76] When *Dream* was first performed in the mid-1590s, the ass was still closely tethered to the material "trumperies," "shewes," and "appearances" of pre-Reformation liturgy and drama. Shakespeare may be teasing his audience with aspects of this history in order to differentiate his play from the mysteries.

Lawrence Welborn's study of Paul's epistles suggests that associations between the ass's head, theatrical comedy, and Christianity date from the earliest days of the church and may have inspired Paul to see himself as the "fool of Christ" and the cross as "folly" in 1 Corinthians 2:6–16, the same passage that Shakespeare translates into Bottom's dream. Welborn's historical linguistic argument proposes that Paul draws upon secular, pre-Christian associations of the term "foolishness" that a Corinthian audience would immediately have associated with the mannerisms of the buffoon from the vulgar form of comedy known as mime.[77] The distinguishing features of this theatrical figure at the bottom of the social ladder were his drooping, ass-like ears. The buffoon was also a "patched fool" (4.1.204), who wore a colorful motley tunic called a *centunculus*.[78]

Given this insight, Bottom's translation in Shakespeare's play reverses the Pauline epistle: whereas Paul turned pagan theatrical material to theological ends, Shakespeare applies the language of the sacred text to a laughably asinine Hellenic artisan-actor. Yet Paul had never fully sacralized the ass for, as Welborn also shows, it retained its ability to debase articles of faith. In a graffito from the Palatine Hill in Rome (c. AD 225) depicting a crucified figure with the head of an ass, "the central mystery of the Christian faith is parodied as a scene from the mime, in which the crucified god of the Christians is mocked as a grotesque, much-slapped ass."[79] The misshapen features of the ass-man apparently did as much to caricature Roman Christianity in the third century as they did in the sixteenth century for Reformers like Reginald Scot.

The scholars I alluded to at the beginning of this chapter have offered persuasive reasons for reading the "rude mechanicals" of *Dream* as comic representations of the craftsmen-actors of the mystery tradition.[80] It must be admitted that Bottom & Co. are staging a classical story whose subject matter is far removed from the mystery play tradition. Yet this assertion relies on a historical consciousness, an "ability to detect and avoid anachronism," that fifteenth- and sixteenth-century English culture did not share.[81] As the work of Patricia Parker has shown, the late medieval practice of moralizing Ovid through allegorical commentary complexly interweaves passages of scripture into the story of *Pyramus and Thisbe* from the *Metamorphoses*.[82] Classical and biblical stories are unhesitatingly wedded for moral and theological purposes as Ovid's ancient love story typologically anticipates medieval teachings about Christ's passion. I argued in chapter 1 that the notion that the Renaissance shared modernity's sensitivity toward anachronism is itself anachronistic, and in fact we will see in the next chapter that early modern English drama seems particularly comfortable with temporal anomaly. If this is so, then neither the setting of ancient Athens nor the classical subject matter would necessarily preclude Shakespeare from adding contemporary rustic actors. Chronological difference is respected no more than the genre of Ovid's tragic tale: "*The Most Lamentable Comedy and Most Cruel Death of Pyramus and Thisbe*" (1.2.9–10).

Appealing to a cosmopolitan audience's sense of urbanity and sophistication even as it recycles well-worn dramatic customs, *Dream* presents the guild drama of the previous generation as a bumbling, rustic form of theater preoccupied with material stage properties and Shakespeare's own stage as ethereal and dreamlike.[83] The remainder of this chapter shows how his light-hearted parody of artisanal drama cleverly masks his own indebtedness to the mysteries and his own investment in the power of material props as sites of imaginary creation. Following Michael O'Connell, I believe the mystery play tradition was still vital enough to shape audience perception of later professional drama as well as to influence the practices of the professional London stage.[84] And so, when faced with his profound reliance on material stage props to address fundamental dramaturgical challenges—how indeed do you stage an animal like a lion or an ass? or moonshine? or a wall?—Shakespeare often turned to that older dramatic tradition. He might do so in earnest, as when his tragedy called for a ghost to spur a revenger into action by whispering of his purgatorial sufferings. But he might also turn to the mysteries in jest and laugh at their expense. I do not intend to reduce mystery drama to mechanical craft devoid of literary nuance and skill, yet I want to suggest that Shakespeare sometimes did so, for it is wonderfully entertaining to watch as he showcases a bulky material prop in order to contrast his supposedly airy, fantastic stage with the mechanics of the mysteries. I draw attention to the craftsmanship of the mysteries because I wish to see Shakespeare himself as a homespun play-wright.

It may have been economically and politically urgent that Shakespeare's commercial theater distance itself from an obsolete yet still memorable dramatic tradition. Gone were the days of intermittent, itinerant playing, and the company of the Lord Chamberlain's Men, however successful, was under continual pressure to appear new and up-to-date in a crowded theater market. Whatever its artisanal origins, London's playgoing culture was also strongly influenced by university wits and aristocratic patronage; a successfully published poet as well as a company shareholder, Shakespeare was keenly aware of these pressures and responded to them in his writing.[85] Moreover, the London stages were under attack from antitheatricalists who drew no distinction between their plays and the popish plots of mystery and morality drama. What made the mysteries so objectionable for Puritans was, in part, their "hellish devices," their physical means of representing godly things.[86]

We have noted the importance of handicraft to the craftsmen-actors of the mysteries, such as the cappers of Chester, whose wares and skills were dramatized by the talking ass. Audiences, too, were eager to behold the materiality of mystery play performance; the Chester Banns command the water leaders to see that "all poyntes" of Noah's ark are properly constructed.[87] The carpenters are similarly instructed to bring forth a "well decked Caryage," that may actually have incorporated two richly decorated platform stages that would have to be hauled through the narrow streets of the town.[88] In Shakespeare's parodic translation, mystery drama's fondness for staged crafts is compulsive. Confronted with a story that mentions moonlight and a wall, the mechanicals feel they must provide material analogues:

Bottom

Why, then may you leave a casement of the great
chamber window where we play open, and the moon may
shine in at the casement.

Quince

Ay, or else one must come in with a bush of thorns and
a lantern and say he comes to disfigure, or to present, the
person of Moonshine.

. . . .

Snout

You can never bring in a wall. What say you, Bottom?

Bottom

Some man or other must present Wall; and let him
have some plaster, or some loam, or some rough-cast about
him, to signify 'wall.'

(3.1.48–53, 56–59)

Shakespeare's rude mechanicals are not ignorant of rhetorical solutions to dramatic dilemmas—after all, they compose an apology to reassure their audience that the Lion means no harm.

But these "hard-handed men" who "never laboured in their minds till now" (5.1.72-73) are as captivated by material stage properties as they are linguistically incompetent; they seemingly have no recourse but to props and costumes. Indeed Starveling, as Moonshine, is at a loss for words to explain anything more than his appearance: "All I have to say is to tell you that the lantern is the moon, I the man i'th' moon, this thorn bush my thorn bush, and this dog my dog" (5.1.247–49). The effect of stage properties on Pyramus is not reticence but repetitive loquacity. The wall transfixes him:

O wall, O sweet O lovely wall,
That stand'st between her father's ground and mine,

> Thou wall, O wall, O sweet and lovely wall,
> Show me thy chink
>
> (5.1.172–75).

Later the "gracious, golden, glittering gleams" of the sweet moon's "sunny beams" (5.1.261–63) charm him as well.

The denigration of craftsmen-actors and their material accoutrements is reflected in Theseus's aristocratic perspective on theater. Told that the tradesmen "can do nothing" when it comes to acting, Theseus responds with "noble respect":

> The kinder we, to give them thanks for nothing.
> Our sport shall be to take what they mistake,
> And what poor duty cannot do,
> Noble respect takes it in might, not merit.
>
> (5.1.89–92)

What is important, according to Theseus, is not what actors do with their bodies but what nobles do with their minds. "The best in this kind are but shadows, and the worst are no worse if imagination amend them," he later remonstrates (5.1.208–9). Drama is not entirely played out in the clumsy, grossly material costumes, props, and bodily gestures (often as obscene as the Wall's "chink") of earthy tradesmen—these are "nothing" to him. Invested with "might" (in the sense of *potentia,* or ruling power), the noble spectator distinguishes between "merit" (what actually happens on stage) and "might" (what might have been if the actors were competent). For the mechanicals, on the other hand, dramatized tales must be thoroughly fleshed out with props and costumes that leave little to the imagination. Bottom advises his companions:

> Masters, you ought to consider with yourself, to bring
> in—God shield us—a lion among ladies is a most dreadful
> thing.
>
> . . .
>
> Nay, you must name his name, and half his face must
> be seen through the lion's neck, and he himself must speak
> through, saying thus or to the same defect: "ladies," or "fair
> ladies, I would wish you" or "I would request you" or "I would
> entreat you not to fear, not to tremble."
>
> (3.1.27–29, 32–36)

Theseus, in the words of the same Pauline text that informs Bottom's dream, trusts not to eye or ear but to the imagination in order to grasp "all things, yea, the deep things"—which is to say, the bottom[89]—of "poor" spectacle.

The epilogue of the play is complicit in Theseus's views; it, too, wants the "Gentles" in the audience to give "thanks for nothing" (5.1.89), albeit for commercial purposes:

> If we shadows have offended,
> Think but this, and all is mended:
> That you have but slumbered here,
> While these visions did appear;
> And this weak and idle theme,
> No more yielding but a dream,
> Gentles, do not reprehend.
>
> (Epilogue, 1–7)

A mischievous game is being played here: like the Athenian mechanicals, Shakespeare relies on an apology for his play, and the epilogue undoes its own claim to being a dream of shadows once the actor breaks the illusion of fiction and reminds the spectators that they are an audience watching actors' bodies move about on stage. Bottom and his fellows, who were so eager not to offend that they addressed the audience numerous times, would find this epilogue quite proper. In exchange for a supposedly ethereal, ineffectual experience, spectators must compensate in very material ways: the price of admission and audible applause. "Give me your hands, if we be friends, / And Robin shall restore amends" (15–16).

More important, Puck's excuse that the play is no more than a dreamlike vision conveniently overlooks the extent to which his presence on stage has been defined by material stage properties; his character is important to the play because he must introduce the "little western flower" and the "ass's nole."[90] Indeed, for all his mockery of the hard-handed Athenian craftsmen, the play associates Robin himself with country life and labor. When we first meet him, a fairy inquires about his rustic reputation:

> Are not you he
> That frights the maidens of the villag'ry,
> Skim milk, and sometimes labour in the quern,
> And bootless make the breathless housewife churn,
> And sometime make the drink to bear no barm—
>
> . . . .

Those that 'hobgoblin' call you, and 'sweet puck,'
You do their work, and they shall have good luck.
                              (2.1.34–38, 40–41)

Robin acknowledges this account of his "labour" and "work" and adds, "The wisest aunt telling the saddest tale / Sometime for three-foot stool mistaketh me; / Then slip I from her bum. Down topples she, / And 'tailor' cries" (2.1.51–54). By his own admission, the airy "sprite" (or "spirit") Puck has been transformed into a bottom, a simple wooden stool upon which a rude village woman tries to rest her bum. When we last see him, he bears his traditional emblem, a broom, which he will use, perhaps, to spank a lazy housewife's bum or to help an industrious woman "sweep the dust behind the door" (5.2.20).[91] To have the actor playing Puck leaning on a broom while proclaiming himself and his fellow actors "shadows" in a mere "dream" is perhaps the last joke of all—and one that transports ("translates") the audience back to those middle acts where the play not only exploited an unavoidably material ass's head in the fairy world of the forest but repeatedly called attention to it as a prop.

The views on dramatic imagination espoused by Theseus and the epilogue have been read autobiographically as reflections of Shakespeare the aesthetician. Yet perhaps the Chester Banns can free us from our author-centered narratives by calling our attention to the dramaturgical work that these speeches perform in the play. Like the Athenian duke, the Chester Late Banns offer apologies for the limited abilities of the mean craftsmen staging the city's annual mystery pageant and instruct their audiences on how to interpret their dramatic representations. They translate the gilt masks of actors playing Jesus and Deus into clouds or voices, idolatrous impersonation into harmless ventriloquism. Deem the mask, they say, "A Clowdye coueringe of the man. a Voyce onlye to heare / And not god in shape or person to appeare."[92] In the words of the seventeenth-century antiquarian David Rogers, the Banns urge spectators "to conceaue of the matter so as it mighte be profitable" and not "offenciue." For all his interest in his city's theatrical history, Rogers nevertheless thanked God that future Cestrians would be spared from the "abomination of desolation" and "cloud of ignorance" by which the city's mystery pageants once defiled "with so high a hand the most sacred Scriptures of God."[93]

Yet Rogers's Protestant convictions may have blinded him to the strategy of the Banns' apologies, their effort to co-opt Puritan distrust of material stage properties and theatrical spectacle in order to authorize the continued staging of "those persones that as godes doe playe."[94] For the Banns' disparagement of craftsmen-actors and the obsolescence of props and costumes is aimed at securing the audience's authorization to use pre-Reformation stage materials and practices. It may very well be that Shakespeare begs a similar dispensation from his audience as his play draws to a close. *Dream* enacts structurally as well as thematically Shakespeare's relationship to his sixteenth-century predecessors: acts 3 and 4 borrow a stage property from a mystery play tradition that, in act 5, is derided for its amateurism and perfunctory habit of exhibiting theatrical artifacts. Yet Puck's broom and the ass's head unsettle Theseus's attempt to locate drama in the mind as well as the Athenian audience's mockery of the artisans' compulsive use of props in *Pyramus and Thisbe*.[95]

Overthrowing the Pauline wisdom of 1 Corinthians 2:6–16, which embraces the spirit at the expense of the flesh, as well as Reformation discourses condemning popish trumperies, *Dream* wants to have it all—bodies and minds, props and imagination, old and new.[96] Once metonymic with the Eucharistic transubstantiation of base matter into divine substance as well as the carnal excesses of popery, the ass's head elevates and denigrates Bottom: he rises from the artisanal world of work to the airy world of magic but also descends from dignified human labor to beastly appetites and sexual desires. And it is fitting that Robin Goodfellow, a spirit who "labours" and "works" in the "villag'ry," is the agent of this double translation.

Contrary to Kott's view that sees *Dream* as the "very beginning of modern comedy," Shakespeare's conspicuous use of staged properties like the ass's head underscores the proximity of his stage to the crafts of the mysteries—even as his play pretends to have transcended them. The ass's head of *Dream* no longer serves as a hallmark of the manufacturing skill or economic prestige of a craft guild but as a piece of raw material for the emerging craft of professional acting. Just as Luther and Melanchthon's pope-ass incorporates and therefore re-presents a Catholic past that it supposedly supersedes, Shakespeare's "translated" Bottom is a carryover from sixteenth-century drama, ritual, and craft yet also a means of mocking old-fashioned artisanal performance. The ass's comic and complex reemergence urges us to reevaluate our critical assumptions about the relationship of the professional London stage to that of the mystery cycles. Thus, although the question of where Shakespeare acquired the ass's head is itself intriguing, much more is at stake.

If Balaam's ass inspired Bottom's translation, then we need to rethink the importance of sixteenth-century dramatic objects once sequestered from the preeminent Renaissance subject—William Shakespeare—by being labeled "medieval" and therefore irrelevant. *Dream* derives pleasure not from the foolishness of the rude mechanicals alone but from theater's game of mixing old and new: how, that is, an object like the ass's head can be old yet in fact newly available precisely because it is old. To trace the genealogy of the ass's head is therefore to gain new purchase on the circulation of social energy whereby "a consecrated object is reclassified, assigned a cash value, transferred from a sacred to a profane setting, deemed suitable for the stage."[97] For if *Dream* is, as Theseus and Puck claim, little more than a dream in the minds of the audience, yet those imaginings are transformed into "strange and admirable" (5.1.27) stage properties and given a local habitation within the wooden-O of the playhouse. The comedy relies upon—and may have been written when Shakespeare acquired—a very rude, mechanical prop with a very rich history. The play, therefore, is "bodied forth" not from "airy nothing" but from the material remnants of the mystery stage it has translated.

CHAPTER 4

"Then Is Doomsday Near"

Hamlet, *the* Last Judgment, *and the Place of Purgatory*

> Where, then, I ask, will purgatory be found?
> —Calvin, *Institutes*

"Art thou there, truepenny?" (1.5.152). Hamlet's question, directed at the "old mole" of a ghost in the understage cellarage of the Globe Theater, raises a question of the play: what *is* there, under the stage—Purgatory or Hell? The Ghost says, or rather implies, that he has come from Purgatory, where "the foul crimes done in [his] days of nature / Are burnt and purged away" (1.5.12–13). "It is an honest ghost" (1.5.142), young Hamlet tells Horatio, and later he swears he'll "take the Ghost's word for a thousand pound" (3.2.263–64). But he has also expressed fears that the disturbed spirit is no "truepenny" (or true fellow) at all but may indeed bring with him "blasts from hell" (1.4.22). Perhaps he has: with his father's commands still ringing in his ears, the prince later appears to Ophelia "As if he had been loosèd out of hell / To speak of horrors" (2.1.84–85). Adding to the confusion about the Ghost's origin is its "questionable shape" (1.4.24): on the one hand, he bears "A countenance more / In sorrow than in anger" (1.2.228–29), yet he's dressed in armor and playing the role of an avenging Senecan ghost.[1] And the command to "Revenge his foul and most unnatural murder" (1.5.25) is out of joint with his other enjoinder that his son "Remember" (1.5.91).[2] If there's a *psychomachia,* or soul war, in *Hamlet,* then in light of these ambiguities it seems to take place not within Hamlet but under the stage. The play contests two accounts of the soul of Hamlet's father—as either a "goblin damned" (1.4.21) or else a pitiable "poor ghost" (1.5.4) "Doomed for a certain term" to do penance in Purgatory (1.5.10).

Why bother to have a purgatorial ghost at all? It would seem that by staging a relic of Catholicism—with scant scriptural authorization—Shakespeare risks attack from antitheatrical Reformers, not to mention state censure.[3] Thomas Kyd's *Spanish Tragedy* achieved success without the need for such risks: his ghost leaves Pluto's regions alongside Revenge to "serve for Chorus" to the subsequent events of the play.[4] Even Christopher Marlowe's *Faustus,* which had adapted medieval material such as the procession of the Seven Deadly Sins, has devils emerge from a stage trapdoor to drag Faustus down to an unambiguously hellish fate. The doctor, apparently contrite, pleads for mercy at the last minute:

Faustus

Ugly Hell, gape not! Come not Lucifer!
I'll burn my books!—O, Mephostophilis!
    Exeunt [Devils with Faustus.][5]

But Hell gapes to receive him nonetheless. His desperate wish for Purgatory, a term of punishment with a definite end rather than Hell's "incessant pain," just a few lines earlier is denied:

Faustus

O God,
If thou wilt not have mercy on my soul,
Yet for Christ's sake, whose blood hath ransomed me,
Impose some end to my incessant pain!
Let Faustus live in hell a thousand years,
A hundred thousand, and at last be saved!
No end is limited to damnèd souls![6]

Like the shade of Don Andrea, *Hamlet*'s Ghost bellows for revenge; like Mephostophilis it raises the specter of Hell. Why, then, does Shakespeare shroud the Ghost's origins in ambiguity by suggesting that Purgatory as well as Hell may lie beneath the stage?

Stephen Greenblatt's *Hamlet in Purgatory* offers a history of the idea of Purgatory in England with particular emphasis on the fifteenth and sixteenth centuries and the Reformation. His aim is to explore how this doctrine powerfully manifested and asserted itself both institutionally and intimately for centuries.[7] For, as several studies have demonstrated, Purgatory with its associated "cult of the dead" was not an adjuvant theory but a central tenet of medieval Christianity.[8] The torments of Purgatory were as vivid in the imagination of believers as they were tangibly visible in church architecture and literature across England.

Greenblatt examines various artifacts that bear witness to popular preoccupations and fears concerning the afterlife: devotional prayer books, narrative accounts of dream visions, church furniture and frescoes, personal wills and parish records. He does so always with an eye toward Shakespeare's *Hamlet,* which he sees as "participating in a violent ideological struggle that turned negotiations with the dead from an institutional process governed by the church to a poetic process governed by guilt, projection, and imagination."[9] Though the Reformation had attacked the doctrine of Purgatory, its psychic and institutional energies were not entirely dissipated by the time Shakespeare wrote his most famous play. As a result, says Greenblatt, *Hamlet* "can offer the viewer, in an unforgettably vivid dream of passion, many of the deep imaginative experiences, the tangled longing, guilt, pity, and rage" evoked by the doctrine of Purgatory.[10]

While Protestant tracts and other literature caricatured purgatorial souls, Shakespeare, according to Greenblatt, "was virtually unique in understanding and giving dramatic expression to its tragic potential."[11] Citing many references to Purgatory to bolster a larger claim regarding its vast cultural reach, *Hamlet in Purgatory* dwells only in passing on fifteenth- and sixteenth-century drama. Greenblatt quotes the speech of "Imperator Salvatus" in the Chester *Last Judgment* to illustrate the similarities between the torments of Hell and those of Purgatory according to church teaching.[12] He dedicates only a few more lines to the morality play *Everyman* (c. 1495) to show how Everyman "narrowly escaped one of the worst medieval nightmares," a sudden and unexpected death, the same fate that befalls the Ghost in *Hamlet.*[13]

Yet to say that the cult of the dead was exorcised from medieval religious liturgy, practice, and art only to return later, in "disenchanted" form, on the public stages of London is not quite the full story. Between the medieval church pulpit and the cellarage of Shakespeare's stage there was a middle place for purgatory, a material space that gave theatrical habitation to that "vast piece of poetry," the Doomsday pageants of the mystery plays.[14] Given the incredible investment of material and labor by a city's most prestigious guild in what was surely meant to be a spectacular climactic finish to the biblical pageant cycle, Greenblatt's oversight is not a small one. The wagons often used in these dramas were not simple carts but sophisticated theatrical machines designed to accommodate the three levels of Heaven, Earth, and Hell as well as hoisting mechanisms to lower and raise Christ and, in some cases, angels and saved souls. In addition, the lower part of the wagon may have been decorated with a giant, grotesque hell mouth and its floor featured one or, more probably, two trapdoor graves, one for the blessed and the other for the damned.[15] This chapter calls attention to the speech and appearance of those saved souls and the understage space from which they arose with their sins newly "burnt and purged away" (*Hamlet,* 1.5.13). For Shakespeare was not the first English playwright to stage the "tangled longing, guilt, pity, and rage" associated with the apocryphal place of Purgatory.[16]

Many scholars have noted the carryover of the three-tiered cosmography of medieval drama to the public theaters, but few, if any, highlight the disappearance of Purgatory and how a commercial dramatist might seize upon its foreclosure. I show how Shakespeare profited by the Reformation's prohibition of the theatrical, rather than the theological, space of Purgatory. Underscoring Shakespeare's role as a dramatic craftsman, or play-wright, I call attention to his joining of the material features of his playhouse and the restoration of the understage space of Purgatory to the language of his play and the generic demands of revenge tragedy. My aim is to fill the gap left by Greenblatt's masterful study and pursue Helen Cooper's keen observation that Shakespeare's famous play curiously displaces its most immediate dramatic concerns. "Any anxiety over the ethics of revenge is reworked as anxiety over 'discernment of spirits,'" she writes, adding "once Hamlet is satisfied on that score, he moves swiftly to what he momentarily believes to be the killing of the king, though it turns out to be Polonius."[17]

For Cooper, the discernment of spirits—the medieval practice of *discretio spirituum,* by which a person could formulaically distinguish between good and evil apparitions—illustrates one of the many ways in which the medieval world pervaded Shakespeare's life and work. Prompted by Cooper's insight, I explore its implications, yet as with Greenblatt, I emphasize that the "presence repeatedly felt in . . . detail even as it is being rejected" is not only a cultural indebtedness to "the medieval" but also, more specifically, a physical remnant of the mystery play tradition.[18] For if we momentarily set aside our notion of Purgatory as a medieval institution, we can perhaps begin to appreciate it as a theatrical space, one no longer available to Shakespeare in quite the same way that it was for provincial guildsmen staging the Doom, yet perhaps all the more attractive and accessible for that same reason.

Because souls in the cellarage of *Last Judgment* plays emerged from both Hell and Purgatory, the main action of these scenes may be considered as a kind of grand *discretio spirituum,* not a formal rhetorical inquiry such as the church prescribed to visionaries and clerics but a separation, a sorting of sheep and goats followed by their eternal consignment.[19] Discretion etymologically entails judgment: to discern, separate, or distinguish as well as to pronounce a decision.[20] Only a few fortunate saints proceeded immediately to Heaven upon their death, and plays of the Doom assign long speeches to those who remain, the purged as well as the damned. Dramatically speaking, Purgatory thus complicates the plot of the *Last Judgment* and delays its resolution, its Final Doom. It likewise affords Shakespeare the opportunity to forestall the immediate achievement of Hamlet's revenge by compelling his protagonist to discern the origins of his father's ghost.[21]

Come from the Grave

Before we consider how Purgatory retards the achievement of Hamlet's revenge, we must first understand the dramaturgical conventions and technologies by which the public theaters represented Hell. How, in other words, did Shakespeare's audience come to assume that the understage cellarage was infernal? With its graphic illustration of the theatrical genealogies that informed professional English drama, the title page of Ben Jonson's 1616 *Workes* may help us to begin answering this question (figure 6). The first vernacular dramatist to publish his plays together with poems in a grand folio text, Jonson signals his allegiance to humanist culture by emphasizing the poetic and textual value of his plays. The substantial edifice that fills Gilbert Hole's engraving proclaims Jonson's mastery both of generic variety and of the ancient history of drama: allegorical figures represent the classical dramatic genres of tragedy and comedy as well as the poetic categories of satire and pastoral. Three theatrical venues are also depicted, including the amphitheater (labeled *visorium*) and the theater of classical antiquity.

Added to these is a *plaustrum,* a two-wheeled wain or cart used to transport heavy loads. The wagon may, as in George Puttenham's account, be associated with ancient comedy, and the Latin inscription almost certainly aims to underscore its antique origin.[22] Yet the wagon also glimpses more recent and local English theater history: the pageant or movable platform stage, scenery, and machinery of the mysteries, as well as the troupes of vagabond players who predated the permanent theaters of London.[23] The term *plaustrum* was also used by provincial guildsmen as they prepared for their performances. As REED research has established, entries in the York mercers' account rolls for the years 1509 and 1518 indicate that the tradesmen apparently needed wagonloads of earth, or *plaustratis terre,* for their *Last Judgment* stage ("a le pagyaunt house").[24] Though perhaps used to make plaster mortar, the large quantity of earth suggests the possibility that the floor of the pageant wagon was made to look like a graveyard, complete with mounds of dirt marking tombs that now stood tenantless.

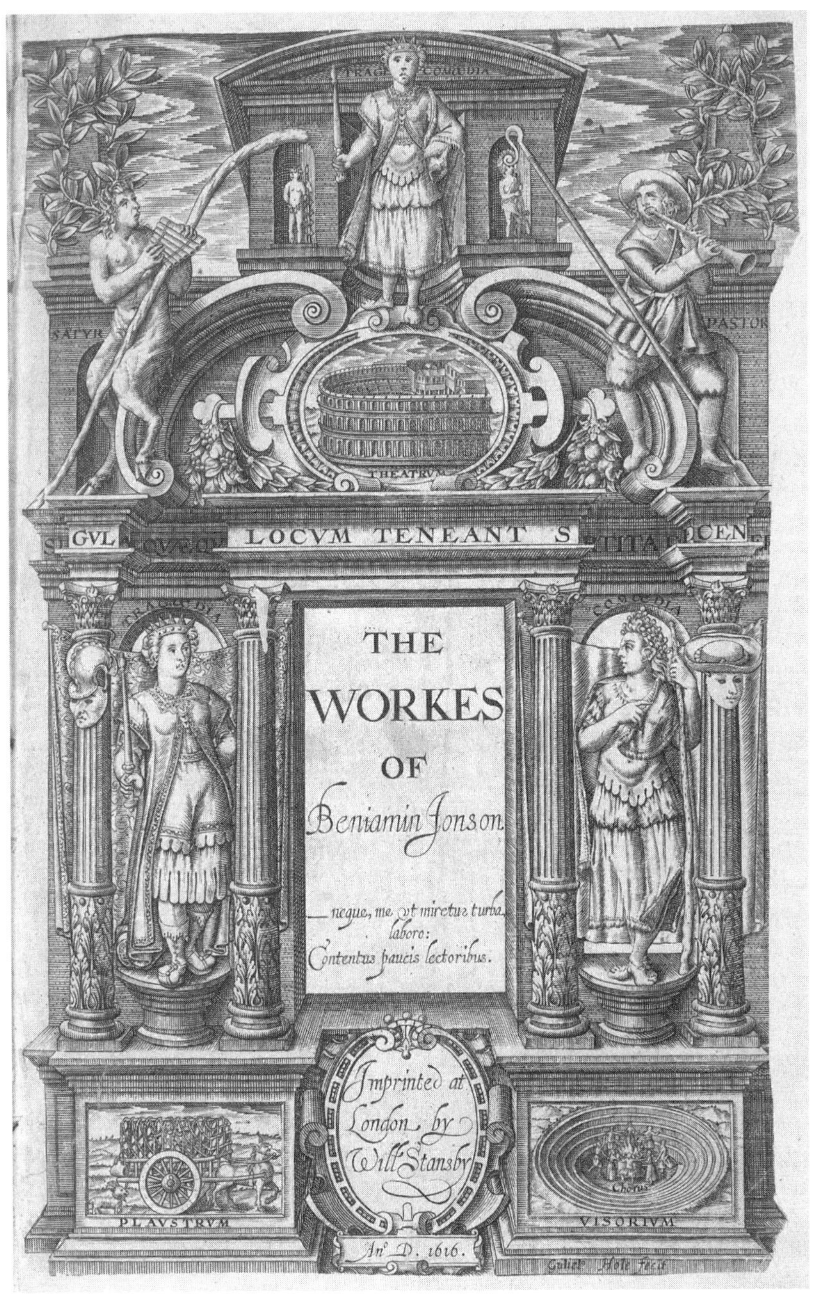

FIGURE 6. Gilbert Hole, title page engraving, *Workes of Benjamin Jonson* (London, 1616). Reproduced by permission of the Furness Memorial Library, Rare Book and Manuscript Library, University of Pennsylvania.

As Stephen Orgel has noted, the *plaustrum* scene depicted in the plinth of Hole's engraving also encompasses Jonson's contemporary theater. For, while we see the legendary founder of tragedy, Thespis, he is not wearing a toga as historical accuracy would require but dresses like a modern Jacobean playwright in doublet and hose (figure 7).[25] The chorus dancing in the round *visorium* at the base of the opposite column on the frontispiece is not antique either. Like Thespis, the figures wear Jacobean attire.[26]

Anachronism, the easy intermixture of objects and costumes from various historical periods, characterizes this graphic representation of the professional stage. It is also evident in the famous 1595 sketch attributed to Henry Peacham of an early performance of Shakespeare's *Titus Andronicus*. Peacham's drawing mixes classical, medieval, and Renaissance costumes and props. Titus's Roman toga shares the stage with soldiers carrying Tudor halberds, while Tamora, Queen of the Goths, looks like a character from medieval romance.[27] Yet anachronism was a well-developed dramatic strategy before it reached the London playhouses. As James Simpson demonstrates, thoughtful and deliberate anachronism afforded the York and Wakefield mysteries a powerful immediacy in their critique of contemporary lords as well as the hardships of domestic life and the brutality of regulated labor.[28]

Like the edifice in Jonson's folio and the costumes and props in Peacham's sketch, early London playhouses were anachronic; they mingled out-of-date classical and medieval theater architecture for the purpose of entertaining a modern audience. While it is true, as Andrew Gurr reminds us, that professional acting companies remained perfectly capable of performing a substantial number of the plays in their repertoire at court or in a patron's manor house without the materials and technologies of

FIGURE 7.   Gilbert Hole, *plaustrum* detail, title page engraving, *Workes of Benjamin Jonson* (London, 1616). Reproduced by permission of the Furness Memorial Library, Rare Book and Manuscript Library, University of Pennsylvania.

their theaters, late sixteenth-century London nonetheless offered a growing number of both indoor and outdoor playhouse structures that reflect this anachronism.[29] James Burbage's successful venue, The Theatre, built in 1576 north of the city, in Shoreditch, was joined in a span of months by the neighboring Curtain (1577); later the Rose and the Swan were constructed in Southwark (in 1587 and 1595, respectively). When Shakespeare's company dismantled The Theatre and used the timber to build the first Globe in 1599, Philip Henslowe erected the Fortune in its former place. That year hardly marked the end of theater building, for it also witnessed the opening of the Red Bull as well as the conversion of the Boar's Head from an inn yard. In 1614 the Globe was rebuilt while Henslowe and Edward Alleyn built the Hope—the last of the traditional playhouse amphitheaters.[30] In addition to these public stages, court hall playhouses sprang up, including the (second) Blackfriars (1596), the Cockpit (1616), and Salisbury Court (1629).

All these early English playhouses shared important common features. They often boasted classical affinities, for example, such as their columns, pillars, and the quasi-circular amphitheater design of most outdoor playhouses. These elements are not surprising considering the conscious cultural reawakening of ancient pagan drama among university and court circles in early sixteenth-century England. Burbage's decision to give his new public establishment a Latinate name signaled the transfer of this "neo-classical enthusiasm" to the commercial stages.[31] But while London playing companies imported classicism from the court, they also adopted the structural iconography of the popular mystery plays both for the outdoor public amphitheaters and for the indoor courtly playing halls. With its trapdoor, stage floor, and star-gilt roof, the London playhouse rematerialized the three-tiered cosmography of Heaven, Earth, and Hell of medieval drama.[32] This "cosmic theatre," as Cooper terms it, afforded the professional theaters a comprehensive field of dramatic possibilities spanning the rustic life of shepherds and the mundane speech and mannerisms of London's inhabitants as well as the intrigues of foreign courts and adventures on the high seas. More important, the immediate physical juxtaposition of these theatrical spaces inspired and encouraged playwrights to incorporate the machinations of demons and the providence of Heaven into the plots of their plays.[33] From this perspective, it is perhaps not surprising that professional acting companies incorporated the moral universe of the mysteries into their playhouse architecture: for as long as anyone could remember, provincial guildsmen staging the *Last Judgment* had ambitiously yet indisputably demonstrated the kind of poignant drama and magnificent pageantry that might be achieved within it.

The Length and Breadth of an Indenture

A 1433 indenture, or official inventory, for the York guild of mercers includes an extensive catalog of materials pertaining to their Doomsday pageant.[34] It lists costumes, wigs, and masks for as many as six devils, four good and bad souls, twelve apostles, and probably ten or more angels. A gilt mask similar to that worn by God the Father in the Creation story symbolizes the divinity of Christ. A leather body suit bearing the wounds of the Crucifixion ("Sirke Wounded") would, by contrast, have represented his naked and vulnerable humanity as it appeared to bleed afresh. Much of the inventory describes the features of the mercers' elaborate pageant wagon. At ground level the audience probably confronted, all too near, the hungry bestial maw of Hell.[35] The platform of the wagon itself may have served as the Earth, complete with thrones of Judgment for Christ and the apostles. As in Chester, functioning trapdoors may have allowed reincorporated souls to rise from their graves. In the upper level of the wagon was Heaven, constructed upon an iron frame with four iron supports ("iiij Irens to bere vppe heuen").

Scholars generally agree that the York mercers' dramatic representations are an attempt to reproduce the visual features of innumerable contemporary paintings and sculptures of the Final Doom.[36] Christ, therefore, would be seated on a rainbow or cloud. The Chester Doomsday directed that he descend as he had ascended at the end of the Gospels, in a cloud (*quasi in nube*). Perhaps the York mercers' inventory describes a similar seat for Christ when it lists "iij peces of rede cloudes with sunne bemes of golde & sternes for the hiest of heuen with a lang small border of the same Wurke." That a locksmith had to be hired at one point (1451–52) to repair Heaven may suggest that this hoisting mechanism was intricate enough to require skills beyond those of the average ironworker.[37] Around Christ were his apostles; seven "grete Aungels" bearing the *Arma Christi,* or implements of the Passion (hammer, nails, crown of thorns, etc.); and two angels bearing great trumpets to sound the general Doom. Heaven incorporated nine mechanical or puppet angels that ran about in a circle like the cherubim and seraphim circumscribing Christ's rainbow throne in the restored west window of the Church of St. Mary in Fairford, Gloucestershire.[38] All these figures stood before painted cloths ("costers") at the back and sides of the pageant, which also featured red and blue clouds, golden sunbeams, and stars spangled on the roof (or "hiest of heuen"), much like the Globe's "majestical roof fretted with golden fire" (*Hamlet,* 2.2.291–92).

The elaborate technologies and dazzling materials of the 1433 mercers' pageant undoubtedly conveyed the wealth and importance of York's most powerful guild.[39] While other craft guilds were probably unable to match the scope and detail of this pageant, the 1433 indenture nevertheless helps us to recognize that the staging of medieval mystery plays was hardly a crude enterprise mounted on bare, flat carts or converted wagons.[40] With a superstructure featuring integral winching gear and "flying" puppet angels, a functional Hell mouth, trapdoors, and costly scenery, mystery pageant wagons were intricate, custom-made performance platforms. As detailed as this scene undoubtedly was, however, it was apparently not enough: in 1501, the mercers abandoned their old wagon for a pageant newly designed by the city's best carver.[41] Of all the scenes in the cycle of biblical stories, the Doomsday pageant, it seems, demanded particular commitment by the guild: a large investment of money, material, and labor, not to mention continual artistic reenvisioning.

Not that pageant wagon staging was uniform or universal. In the previous chapter we noted the singular designs employed in the York and Chester Noah plays. Furthermore, as detailed study has established, processional drama could take many forms, including the arrangement of the Digby *Conversion of St. Paul,* which required the audience to accompany the actors from one performance space to the next. It must be noted, however, that despite the constraints of maneuvering and staging a mobile pageant in the narrow confines of a city street, sixteenth-century provincial guildsmen (in not one but several major play cycles) were not content with simply converting the vehicles of their trades to performance stages. They went to the trouble of building wheeled platforms small enough to navigate crowded streets yet large enough to first, allow reasonably large crowds to see and hear the play; second, substantially showcase their craft skills; and finally, emphasize the incredible scale of the stories they were acting—no less than the history of the world and the creation and destruction of the universe.[42]

The 1433 York mercers' indenture may be the only surviving document of its kind, yet the substantial material investment in *Last Judgment* pageants to which it testifies was very likely common to all the major play cycles. The most wealthy and powerful guilds of Chester and Coventry (arguably the two most important cities besides York for which records of early English drama survive) were also tasked with performing the Doomsday pageant. They, too, would have devoted considerable resources to their productions. In some ways, it's surprising that these prominent groups did not choose a prime-time scene like the *Nativity* or *Crucifixion.*[43] It may be, however, that they were the only guilds that could afford to stage this large-scale pageant. In York, for example, the affluent mercers typically spent nearly twelve shillings a year on repairs alone. This amounted to roughly a month's wages for a common laborer but was not an unusual amount for the mercers during the 1460s.[44] A century later—in 1574, barely a decade after they had completely replaced their old pageant wagon—they spent the large sum of three pounds, four shillings and fourpence for "Reparacions of our pagyant howse," presumably the building where they stored this valuable performance platform.[45] By comparison, the bakers' accounts in 1573 record only twenty-two pence paid for similar repairs.[46]

As with the York mercers' 1433 indenture, REED documents concerning repairs and modifications to Doomsday pageants reflect more than a guild's commercial interests in mystery drama; they manifest a larger cultural interest and participation in another (moneyed) economy: the afterlife and the fate of souls.[47] Living and worshiping near the remains of deceased relatives and friends, most late medieval and early modern English Catholics quite naturally assumed the reciprocal relationship of Purgatory and prayer for the dead. Indeed, the doctrine of Purgatory was to a certain extent the official justification for such offerings and devotions. This shibboleth was reinforced by a great variety of artifacts, including church decorations, funeral monuments, breviaries, and wills.[48] But before and during Shakespeare's boyhood, the teachings, objects, and practices associated with Purgatory underwent a profound repudiation, and the social and cultural upheaval would continue beyond his lifetime. As Chamberlain of Stratford, the playwright's father, in fact, "payd for defasyng ymages in ye chappell" in accordance with the 1559 royal injunctions against "idolatry" and "superstition."[49] The whitewashed images included a wall painting of souls receiving their Final Doom at the *Last Judgment* (figure 8). The chancel arch of the church at Coventry bears the same scene in elaborate detail; in fact, the Doom was one of the most commonly rendered scenes in medieval English parish church painting.[50] These paintings typically represent the figure of Christ seated upon a rainbow with the world as his footstool; beneath him, the dead arise from their graves at the sound of angelic trumpets. Saint Michael often plays a prominent role in the weighing of souls (*psychostasis*), while devils herd the damned off to the gaping bestial maw of Hell and the punishments beyond.[51]

In mystery plays, as in churches, audiences expected to see the climax of history lavishly displayed. The Chester mystery cycle devoted not one or two but three pageants to the events of the Eschaton.[52] In fact, these three plays— *The Prophets of Antichrist, Antichrist,* and *The Last Judgment*—amount to more

FIGURE 8.   *Doomsday,* from Thomas Fisher, *A Series of Ancient Allegorical, Historical, and Legendary Paintings . . . on the Walls of the Chapel of Trinity, at Stratford upon Avon* (1807). © The British Library Board, MS 1899, n. 11, pl. 19.

than seventeen hundred spoken lines, or more than the four plays of the Passion sequence combined.[53] The websters of Chester staged an extravagant performance. Twenty speaking parts were supplemented by an indeterminate number of angels, devils, prophets, and patriarchs. The guild's actors had to be capable of singing, playing instruments, delivering long speeches from high scaffolds, and interacting with the crowds to frighten and amuse both adults and children. The resulting visual spectacle—including Christ's eschatological descent, his bleeding wounds, the exultant pageantry of saints and angels, and the terrifying threats of hellish fiends—must have excited the full range of audience emotions.[54] The play text calls attention to visual display as Deus commands the angels to set up the *Arma Christi,* which serves as both his kingly sigil and the hallmark of his mercy:

Deus

Therefore, my angelles fayre and bright,

. . . .

     Shewe you my crosse appertlye here,
crowne of thorne, sponge and speare,
and nayles to them that wanted nere
to come to this anoye;

and what weede for them I weare,
upon my bodye nowe I beare.
The most stowtest this sight shall steare [daunt]
that standeth by streete or stye.

(13, 17–24)[55]

Gathering and exhibiting these implements, the angels themselves must have put on an impressive display. The "lang small corde" listed in the 1433 York indenture seems to have been used to make the mechanical angels of the York *Last Judgment* flutter or "renne aboute" Heaven. The "ij paire Aungell Wynges with iren in the endes" perhaps enabled the two actors playing these roles to "fly" as well. Chester audiences, like Horatio,[56] expected to see angels soaring down to rescue saved souls, and Jesus expressly gives them this task:

Therfore, my angelles, goe you anon
and twyne my chosen everye one
from them that have benne my foen
and bringe them unto blysse.
On my right hand they shall be sett,
for soe full yore I them beheight
when the dyd withowten lett
my byddinge not amysse.

(493–500)

At this point in the play, the dead have already risen from their graves and received their sentences, so that when the next stage direction reads: "Then all the saved [souls] follow [the angels]," it is likely, as David Mills suggests, that the blessed ascend to Heaven by means of ladders lowered to them by the angels.[57]

The *Last Judgment* was a grand acoustic experience as well. Horatio's final prayer for Hamlet would have been answered in Chester, where "flights of angels" (*Hamlet,* 5.2.302) sang two liturgical hymns, referred to in stage directions as *Laetamini in Domino* and *Salvator mundi, domine,* as they escorted saved souls in procession to the throne of heaven.[58] Among the damned, however, the most common sound was not musical. "Alas, alas, alas, alas," says a corrupt pope, and every unfortunate soul who follows him will echo this word. It will be heard nearly forty times by the end of the play.[59] In fact, every damned soul's speech begins with the word "alas," which is curiously very similar to the first utterance of every good soul ("A, lord . . .") as if eternal fate hangs by the merest aural thread. Devils would enter the scene roaring, "Out out harrow!" In this regard, mystery drama enjoyed a distinct advantage over contemporary paintings of the Doom, whose considerable graphic details attempt to capture the many sounds of the Last Day. The Judgment scene in the nave of the Guild Chapel at Stratford, for example, features angels with trumpets, harps, and other instruments, while devils laugh and growl and blow large curled horns. Many of the damned souls in torment "speak" scrolls from their mouths that declare their sins: *Ira, Avaritia, Gula,* etc.[60]

But the most arresting sounds in the mystery plays came from musical instruments. The dramatic action of the scene began when the angels let forth a trumpet peal that must have been heard for a great distance and signaled (even to townspeople watching earlier scenes at other stations within the city) that the Promised End was drawing near. The angels' loud blast would have conjured images of, in Laertes's words, "minist'ring angel[s]" and "howling" souls (*Hamlet,* 5.1.224–25). As the first Bad Soul of the York *Judgment* states:

> Allas, allas, that we were borne,
> So may we synfull kaytiffis say;
> I here wele be this hydous horne
> Itt drawes full nere to domesday.
>
> (113–16)[61]

Richard Rastall's study of the music of the Chester cycle calls attention to the trumpet's special, and perhaps exclusive, presence in the *Last Judgment*. The use of trumpets was a royal prerogative associated with kingship in general but especially with the kingly role of adjudicator. The blaring sound of these instruments in the Chester *Last Judgment* would of course inform the audience of the Almighty Ruler's imminent approach, yet even the sight of a heraldic *buisine* (elongated trumpet) would signal that a king was about to sit upon the Judgment seat.[62] As the wall painting in the Stratford Guild Chapel once depicted, devils herding the wicked through the gates of Hell sounded their own horns in mockery of the angelic trumpets. The Primus Devil of the Wakefield *Judgment* shouts, "Oute, haro, out, out! / Harkyn to this horne."[63] Possibly made from an animal horn, this short instrument would have been as bestial as his demon costume and quite distinct from the long, elegant trumpets of the angels.[64]

Commercial plays from the 1580s through to the closing of the theaters in 1642 exploited the pageantry and stage architecture formerly showcased in plays of the Doom. Around 1588 Marlowe's Faustus is dragged down to Hell by demons (most likely at The Theatre); in 1601 Hamlet's old mole shouts from the Globe's cellarage; that same year the figure of Envie (itself a leftover of morality drama) arises from the center-stage trapdoor at the Blackfriars to begin Jonson's *Poetaster.* If, as John Cox has established, the devil enjoyed a long and healthy stage career in early English drama, so too did his place of origin—the understage space of Hell—as well as his trapdoor access to the Middle Earth of the main stage.[65] Henslowe's accounts of the Rose repertory lists "i Hell mought," which may, as Andrew Gurr has suggested, be the same stage property that is "discovered" in the 1616 text of *Faustus.* He also cites the English Wagner Book of 1594 for its glimpse into a performance of the same play: "there might you see the ground-worke at the one end of the Stage whereout the personated divels should enter in their fiery ornaments, made like the broad wide mouth of an huge Dragon . . . the teeth of this Hels-mouth far out stretching."[66] That a commercial theater owned "i Hell mought" is not so surprising if we consider that the Reformation accepted, for the most part, the orthodox view of the universe: it retained Heaven, Earth, and Hell, and disputed only the basis for a soul's salvation (faith vs. works), not its final destinations. And if the material base of theater culture changed very little between the 1570s and 1640s, then acting companies would have continued with tried-and-true stage designs.[67]

With their visual and aural power and ceremony, *Last Judgment* scenes would have made—were materially crafted to make—a profound and long-lasting impression on their English audiences. This impression endured long after the demise of the mysteries. To see this, we must first address specifically the representation of Purgatory in pageants of the Doom. Whereas Greenblatt implies that Shakespeare was unique in his recognition of the theatrical potential of Purgatory, I explore how Purgatory was materially incorporated in traditional mystery play staging of the *Last Judgment.* Like its spectral double, Hell, it was often located underneath the stage, yet whereas the location of the former was often marked with a Hell mouth, Purgatory was typically manifested through the speech and appearance of souls who rose from it. Despite these corporeal signifiers, however, the theatrical presence of Purgatory was rather ghostly—perceptible in effect but unseen beneath the pageant floor—though it is possible that guildsmen staging this pageant may have attempted to give its apocryphal entrance a local habitation by a specifically assigned tomb or trap.

As ideology, Purgatory was explosive, and Reformers of various stripes stamped out any precepts associated with it. As theater, however, it could be easily disguised through its association with Hell. The Chester Late Banns preserved the gilt masks of Jesus and the Deity by interpreting them as clouds rather than as vain attempts to incarnate divinity. The preservation of Purgatory would have been much simpler and less audacious for both a Chester guild and a London playwright. With relative ease—by depicting, say, an armored, vengeance-seeking Senecan ghost rather than a penitent soul—Purgatory might remain under the very noses of Puritan antitheatricalists, beneath the boards of the professional London playhouses.[68]

Purgatory Affirmed

The Chester Puritan Christopher Goodman was as persistent in his letter writing as he was forthright in his opposition to the city's mystery cycle, and in addition to the 1572 letter to the earl of Huntingdon discussed in chapter 2, he and his supporters wrote numerous times that year to the archbishop of York. To one of those letters Goodman attached "Notes of the absurdities &c in the Chester plays," or as he calls them in the body of the letter, "the old Popish plays of Chester."

Concerning the final play in the cycle, the *Last Judgment,* Goodman noted several offensive topics, including the "preaching of merits of man," "The divell speaking Latin," and the "invocation of Saints." Topping Goodman's list of absurdities for the Doomsday pageant was that he found "Purgatory affirmed."[69] Goodman was undoubtedly correct in his allegations. When staging the Doom, Chester guildsmen, like their counterparts in York and Wakefield, chose not to stage the relatively safe, and certainly spectacular, events in the Book of Revelation. They instead extrapolated the text of chapter 25 of the Gospel of Matthew, which emphasized good works that could earn salvation and, according to church teaching, free souls from Purgatory.[70]

In the evangelist's account, Christ "and all the holy Angels with hym sitte vpon the throne of his glorie," where he pronounces Final Judgment on the souls of the dead whom he has divided between the saved and the damned "as a shepeheard deuideth the shepe from the goates." Each group comes forward and is told that their sentencing depends on the performance of deeds of charity: "Then shal he aunswere [the damned], saying: Ueryly I say vnto you, in as much as ye did it not to one of the least of these, ye did it not to me. And these shall go into euerlasting payne: the ryghteous into life eternall."[71] As Jesus says in the York Doomsday pageant, souls "far and near" are judged "Aftir ther werkyng, wronge or right" (192). In the Chester play, good works are part of a larger economy of salvation that includes contrition for sins and the fires of Purgatory. In fact, all four saved souls who speak in the Chester *Last Judgment* acknowledge their lack of sufficient good deeds but express gratitude that Purgatory, though harsh, has prepared them to be with God. A saved queen, for example, admits that she "neyther prayed" nor

fasted on earth, yet "almes-deedes" as well as "great repentance at the laste"
allowed her to suffer Purgatory's temporary ordeals rather than Hell's unend-
ing torments (153–60). And so, she says,

> Sythe I have suffred woe and teene
> in purgatorye longe too benne,
> lett never my synne be on me seene
> but, lord, thou hit forgett.
>
> (169–72)

Deus does forget her purged sins, as he does those of Papa Salvatus, whose
"fleshlye will that wicked was" during his lifetime, now "purged yt ys with
paynes yll / in purgatorye that sore can gryll" (61, 69–70).

The York Doom is less explicit when it comes to Purgatory, but the same
economy of good works, contrition, and postmortem cleansing is clearly in
place. The first Good Soul comes forward in gratitude, saying,

> Loued be thou, lorde, that is so schene [radiant],
> That on this manere made vs to rise,
> Body and sawle togedir, clene,
> To come before the high justise.
> Of oure ill dedis, lorde, thou not mene [speak]
>
> (97–101)

In both York and Chester, the pageant did more than elaborate a scriptural
passage about good works to include beliefs about purgatorial purification;
the guildsmen invested their wealth and reputation in this controversial scene.
Building upon scripture, the mystery pageants of York, Chester, Coventry,
and other towns added exchanges between God and his apostles and angels,
representative speeches by redeemed and damned souls, and the raucous behavior of stage devils. They also added elaborate sets, costumes, and devices
that demanded significant artistic detail, labor, and material cost—all gauges
of the kind of "cultural energy" Greenblatt explores.[72] Little wonder, then,
that the mysteries faced increasing opposition from Reformers or that this
busy, often dazzling, and somewhat unsettling stage business was assigned to
a premier guild that could assemble a group of actors and artisans equal to it.

In the manuscript illustrations studied by Greenblatt, the torments of Purgatory and Hell can be distinguished in the event only by a "single differentiating feature," that is, by an intervention of heavenly powers, such as
a hovering angel whose outstretched arms are shown in the act of rescuing
purged souls while, in a juxtaposed panel, hounding demons check all means

of escape for the damned.[73] In *Last Judgment* scenes of the mystery cycles, the uncertain distinction between Purgatory and Hell is resolved over the course of the play by dramatic action. The resurrected souls who emerge on stage are already aware of their final destination. In York, Good and Bad Souls alike ask for explanations of their Judgment. Souls in the Chester Doomsday pageant are more forthright about their guilt and God's mercy and justice. The purpose of the *Last Judgment*—its stage business, costumes, props, and settings—is therefore to achieve a certain and final *discretio spirituum,* or separation of the saved and the damned. Theologically this division of souls entails the erasure of Middle Earth's ambiguities, the end of Purgatory, and the achievement of the New Jerusalem once and for all. Theatrically, as the dead emerge from graves in the stage floor, several stage practices help the audience perform the necessary *discretio* simultaneously with Deus or Jesus: costumes, speeches, and the orchestrated movement of actors.

First, black and white leather costumes and face paint allowed audiences viewing the *Last Judgment* to tell the damned from the redeemed. Coventry REED documents contain numerous references to these costumes, which "suggest that the Souls (they are always called that, even though strictly speaking they are body and soul reunited) wore closefitting top and tights to represent the naked resurrected body familiar from the iconography of Doomsday."[74] Meg Twycross argues that these costumes are both emblematic—reflecting the soul's spiritual health and ultimate destination—and quite literal. According to popular belief, the risen flesh restored to souls at the Final Doom would manifest their corruption or cleanliness.[75] This popular religious belief was made visible in the "blacckyng of the Sowles facys" year after year in the Coventry Doomsday pageant.[76] In York, the bad souls' sins were literalized as weighty backpacks—"Oure wikkid werkis may we not hide, / But on oure bakkis vs muste them bere" (154–55)—that Twycross imagines as "a haversack" or as their sins "written on rolls pinned to their backs."[77] In Chester, a devil objects to having to bear the weighty load of sins committed by the damned.[78] Meanwhile a damned merchant points to the corrupted flesh and soul of his costume and descants on his own deformity:

> Alas, alas, now woe is me!
> My foul body, that rotten hath be,
> And soul together now I see.
> All stinketh, full of sin.
>
> (325–28)

Mercator Damnatus's speech and costume lay bare his "inmost part" (*Hamlet,* 3.4.20), and thus the Chester audience could turn their eyes to his "very soul" and see there "such black and grainèd spots / As will not leave their tinct" (*Hamlet*, 3.4.79–81). Though his bosom is as "black as death" (*Hamlet,* 3.3.67), he's presumably not so decayed as to be unrecognizable as a merchant; in fact, the costumes of all of the Chester souls feature some badge of earthly rank or occupation, as do many in the Stratford Guild Chapel wall painting.[79] In the N-Town pageant, Twycross explains, the bodies of saved souls undergo purgative metamorphosis before the audience's eyes:[80]

Deus

Venite, benedicti, my bretheryn all,

.   .   .   .

All tho fowle wyrmys from yow falle.
With my ryght hand I blysse yow here.
My blyssynge burnyschith yow as bryght as berall;
As crystall clene it clensyth yow clere,
All fylth from yow fade.[81]

In N-town, therefore, Purgatory is "affirmed" through an onstage costume change, a transformation designed to exhibit its cleansing effects.

"Let the devil wear black, for I'll have a suit of sables" (3.2.117–18), says Hamlet, alluding to the traditional garments of stage devils.[82] Like the souls of various Doomsday scenes, loyal and fallen angels were also clothed in white and black. The costumes of the cosmic powers don't simply tell the audience what team they play for; they materially record their history. The Chester Late Banns demand to see the figure of Satan whose blackened feathers and shredded rags tell us that he is, as Milton would later have it, "Late fallen himself from heaven" into hell fire.[83] These expensive costumes would have feathers intricately woven onto leather suits with grotesque, and sometimes enormous, "damnable faces" (*Hamlet,* 3.2.231), heads or masks.[84] The rebel angels of the York *Fall of the Angels* rapidly change their attire during the performance: after "falling" through the pageant wagon's trapdoor, they charge from a smoking Hell mouth with blackened faces or masks and charred wings that exhibit their degeneracy.[85]

Next, the testimonies of the newly arisen souls in *Last Judgment* pageants help to determine their netherworld origin. The redeemed souls all share two preoccupations: they are understandably overjoyed at having been saved, yet rather than dwell upon the blessings to come, their speeches remain preoccupied with what *Hamlet*'s Ghost calls "the secrets of [his] prison house," that is, with their recent experiences of Purgatory (1.5.14). The very first soul to appear in the Chester pageant states,

Hit is three hundredth yeares and three
Synce I was put in grave.
Nowe through thy might and postye
Thy beames blast hath raysed mee—
I, flesh and blood as I nowe see—
My judgment for to have.
. . . thy commandment to fulfill
I was full neglygent.
But purged yt ys with paynes yll
In purgatorye that sore can gryll.
Yett thy grace I hope to come tyll
After my great torment.

(43–48, 67–72)

Like this character of a good pope, Papa Salvatus, other saved souls talk of being raked across the coals in the "gryll" of Purgatory until "the foul crimes done in [their] days of nature / [were] burnt and purged away" (*Hamlet,* 1.5.12–13). All of them emphasize both the intensity and the duration of their experience; Imperator Salvatus states, for example,

In Purgatorye my soule hath binne
a thousand yeares in woe and teene.
Nowe ys noe synne upon mee seene,
for purged I am of pyne.

. . . .

As hard payne, I darre well saye,
in purgatorye are night and daye
as are in hell, save by on waye—
that one shall have an end.

(89–92, 97–100)

His final point, that Hell and Purgatory are distinguishable only by their duration, is reinforced by the fact that he has a damned doppelgänger: Imperator Damnatus. This evil twin declares similar torments but holds out no hope for redemption, and indeed is shortly returned to hellfire.

In addition to costumes and speeches, the eventual assignment of souls to a particular tier of the pageant stage—Heaven for the redeemed, Hell for the damned—allowed for the final differentiation between the sheep and the goats. In Chester, it is not only Jesus who demands this separation but also the devils, who, eager to drag away their victims, address their suits to the "righteous Judge":

Demon Primus

Yea, this thou sayd, verament,
that when thou came to judgment
thy angelles from thee should be sent
to put the evyll from the good

. . . .

which wordes to clearkes here present
I wyll rehearse.
"Sic erit in consumatione seculi: exibunt angeli et [separabunt]
malos de medio justorum, et mittent eos in caminum ignis, ubi
erit fletus et stridor dentium."

(573–80)

Successfully quoting scripture (specifically Matthew 13:49–50) to suit his purpose, Demon Primus then carries off, among others, a lecherous queen and a king who died "withowt amendment" (595). Following the stage direction at line 676 consigning the unrepentant to the fiery furnace of Hell ("Tunc demones exportabunt eos"), the devils and the damned may descend through a stage trap or may reach the understage space through a Hell mouth decorated on the front of the wagon. While the sinners go down, the blessed ascend, probably, as Mills suggests, by ladders rather than by the lifting mechanism needed to lower Jesus from Heaven, which perhaps resembled the "cloud & ij peces of Rainbow of tymber" in the 1433 York indenture.[86] The stage direction associated with this machinery underscores the guildsmen's attention to the placement of actors in the vertical scale of the pageant wagon: "Jesus shall come down as if in a cloud, if it can be contrived, because, according to the opinions of scholars, the Son of God shall give judgement in the air close to the Earth."[87]

In the York *Last Judgment* the separation of the sheep and goats taking place on the set of the pageant wagon is reiterated by the poetry of the play's final lines:

Jesus

Nowe is fulfillid all my forthoght,
For endid is all erthely thyng.
All worldly wightis that I haue wroght
Aftir ther werkis haue nowe wonnyng.
Thei that wolde synne, and sessid noght,
Of sorowes sere now shall thei sing;

And thei that mended thame whils thei moght
Shall belde and bide my blissing.

(373–80)

The passage stresses that souls will now remain permanently in Heaven or Hell. To "belde" (or "dwell") with God is to have his blessing; to "bide" is both to await and to continue in the state of that blessing—the verb effectively stretches out the act of dwelling to suggest the endlessness of eternity.[88] Emphasizing "fulfillment," these closing lines imply that the entire cycle of plays can end only when every actor occupies his proper "wonnyng," or "dwelling place," in the binary universe of the Apocalypse, where a middle place of purgation is no longer required.

Although the wall paintings of the *Last Judgment* in churches throughout England apparently never represented Purgatory, it is possible that Doomsday pageants wanted to indicate its entrance by assigning specific trapdoor graves to saved souls. Both plays and murals depict three major locations. Heaven contains Christ enthroned as well as apostles, angels, and saints who greet newly arrived souls. Hell's gaping maw spews "sulph'rous and tormenting flames" (*Hamlet,* 1.5.3) as it receives the damned, and in Doom paintings it is the only subterranean space represented. In the middle is Earth, where the dead emerge from graves, learn their fate, and encounter either "a spirit of health" or "goblin damned" (*Hamlet,* 1.4.21), who carries them off to their eternal destination. "Where, then, I ask, will purgatory be found?" writes John Calvin in the third book of his *Institutes of the Christian Religion* (1559). As he considers Rome's "alleged proofs of Purgatory from the Gospel," he is not looking for a literal response, of course, but seeks to deride the legendary accounts of Purgatory as he insists that not "so much as a single syllable" of "the entire law and gospel" mentions Purgatory or condones prayers for the dead.[89]

Calvin's polemic takes aim at the popular fascination with the geographical location of Purgatory, which as Peter Marshall notes, was the subject of much debate and speculation. Though commonly positioned in a subterranean region adjacent to Hell, it might be locally identified with a particular well-known cave or volcano. Or it might, as in Dante, be assigned to a mountainous area neighboring Heaven if not floating in the air.[90] The broad circulation of the twelfth-century Latin prose treatise *Saint Patrick's Purgatory* reflects this widespread curiosity on the part of Christians across Europe.[91] The book underwent numerous translations, including Middle English dream visions purporting to tell of the adventures of Owayne Miles, a knight who came upon the entrance to Purgatory in county Donegal and demanded admittance despite its terrifying resemblance to Hell and the warnings of Saint Patrick, who had first discovered it.[92]

Perhaps Doomsday pageants appealed to the desire to locate this famous portal. A stage direction at line 40 in the Chester Doomsday pageant states that at the sound of the trumpet *omnes mortui de sepulchris surgent*. If the term *sepulchris* is plural, it may suggest that more than one stage property resembling a tomb or grave was used. If David Mills is correct in his proposal that the stage featured two trapdoors, one for the redeemed and one for the damned, then as all saved souls in Chester allude explicitly to the postmortem removal of their sins, we may assume that one of the sepulchres effectively marked the entrance to Purgatory.[93] The conventions of *Last Judgment* iconography might also have offered precedent for the mystery stage to provide two traps—left and right. As Pamela Sheingorn and David Bevington have argued, horizontal symmetry was a particularly important concern in Doomsday scenes and may have influenced the Chester *Last Judgment,* where good and bad souls are, with the exception of one Damned Merchant, paired (a good and a bad pope, etc.). In various church paintings, they further note, the souls on Christ's right are escorted through Heaven's gates while those on the left are forced through Hell's mouth.[94] For Richard Beadle, the "stark symmetry" of the York Judgment play is a result of the scriptural narrative in Matthew's Gospel, which carefully delineates those on the right and left of God's throne.[95] Quite possibly, then, plays of the Doom extended this careful balance to the trapdoors in the pageant floor.

Surviving records in York may indirectly support a stage design involving a special wagon for souls to rise out of, including a trapdoor specifically assigned to purged souls. According to REED entries for 1463, the mercers constructed a "now [new] pagand that was mayd for ye sallys to ryse owtof."[96] The emphasis on rising here implies that the souls are coming from graves or similar "underground" places, much like those souls described in a surviving fragment of the N-town Doom who arise from underneath the earth, *subtus terram*.[97] In light of the N-town fragment and the York REED evidence for a separate souls' wagon, the use of real dirt (*plaustratis terre*) by the York mercers does not seem so strange: long before Hamlet matched wits with the Gravedigger, provincial craftsmen-actors had staged a graveyard scene for the *Last Judgment*.[98] Though small, the extra wagon would have been unnecessary if only one trapdoor was needed.[99] Said another way, it's difficult to see why the York mercers would go to the trouble of building a separate stage platform for souls to rise out of and then outfit that space with only one trapdoor. Relying on existing documentary evidence as well as expert conjecture, modern productions of the mysteries have re-created the *Last Judgment* pageants featuring two trapdoors. The York Doomsday play directed by Meg Twycross at the 1988 York festival featured a separate souls' wagon with two traps, one on either side of the sword Michael uses to part the sheep and goats when he commands "parte you in two! / All sam schall ye noght be in blisse" (169–70).[100]

Grounds More Relative

The mere suggestion by *Hamlet*'s Ghost of a "most horrible" interlude whose "secrets" would supposedly give the hearer pause, harrowing the soul and freezing the blood (1.5.16), introduces the uncertain distinction between Hell and Purgatory with which I began this chapter. For it was commonly believed that a demonic agent could assume the appearance of a deceased loved one suffering the agonies of Purgatory.[101] Dramaturgically speaking, *Hamlet* lacks the theatrical strategies by which Doomsday pageants achieved the absolute resolution of good and evil. Shakespeare's tragedy opens in a morally tangled, postlapsarian "unweeded garden" (1.2.135), and with its allusions to last trumpets, ministers of grace, flights of singing angels, souls damned and black as hell, eternal audits, and so forth, the play eagerly anticipates the Last Judgment. "Then is doomsday near" (2.2.234), but its final resolution is continually deferred, and the play remains poised "as against the doom" (3.4.48).[102] In this way, the play-wright Shakespeare joins the material remnants and thematic language of *Last Judgment* pageants in order to, on the one hand, create an atmosphere of impending tragedy and, on the other hand, defer Hamlet's revenge.

Hamlet, when facing the Ghost for the first time, cries out for an act of angelic rescue—"Angels and ministers of grace defend us!"—and then ponders whether the apparition is a heavenly power or a demon:

> Be thou a spirit of health or goblin damned,
> Bring with thee airs from heaven or blasts from hell,
> Be thy intents wicked or charitable,
> Thou com'st in such a questionable shape
> That I will speak to thee.
>
> (1.4.20–25)

Instead of the "questionable shape," vague origin, and uncertain audit of his father's purgatorial Ghost, Hamlet would have the stark black-and-white certainty of the *Last Judgment*. But the spirit he sees is too ambiguous, it seems, for the prescribed *discretio spirituum*. Old King Hamlet hints at his purgatorial sufferings, and it's perhaps fitting that, in a play filled with "compulsive remembrance," the Ghost should be dressed "in his habit as he lived" (3.4.126).[103] Yet from the standpoint of the *Last Judgment* mystery pageants, he's wearing the wrong costume. According to Davidson, only angelic powers like the archangel Michael wore armor in dramatic and illustrated representations of the Doom.[104] In the York pageant, for example, Michael draws his sword to part the saved and the damned and leads the former off to heaven.[105] When Hamlet first sees his father's spirit, he asks whether the Ghost might in fact be a "spirit of health" like Michael, but Old Hamlet's clothes say more about his deeds in his earthly life than about his fate in the next: "Such was the very armour he had on / When he . . . / Did slay this Fortinbras" (1.1.59–60, 85). Moreover, as we've seen, his armor might also place him in the older Senecan tradition of infernal spirits sent to do Hell's bidding in the bloody business of revenge. Nor does the "eternal blazon" of a "dear murderèd" (1.5.21, 2.2.561) entirely reassure young Hamlet of the "honest" Ghost's true intentions.

When the Ghost returns to the cellarage in 1.5, Hamlet speaks to it as if he believes its story of purgatorial fires.[106] When we next see Hamlet two scenes later, however, he mistrusts that previous assumption and hits upon a scheme to resolve the uncertainty of the Ghost's origin. He devises the Mousetrap play to test Claudius's guilt, which is to say, to test whether the old mole arose from Purgatory as claimed or from Hell:

> The spirit I have seen
> May be the devil, and the devil hath power
> T'assume a pleasing shape; yea, and perhaps,
> Out of my weakness and my melancholy—
> As he is very potent with such spirits—
> Abuses me to damn me. I'll have grounds
> More relative than this. The play's the thing
> Wherein I'll catch the conscience of the King.
>   (2.2.575–82)

"Once Hamlet is satisfied on that score," Cooper explains, "he moves swiftly to what he momentarily believes to be the killing of the king, though it turns out to be Polonius."[107] In the first half of the play, therefore, Shakespeare borrows the understage space of Purgatory from Doomsday pageants to forestall the inevitable revenge of his protagonist. The Mousetrap play snares Claudius's conscience in 3.2, and while Cooper is undoubtedly correct that the pace of the plot quickens noticeably after Polonius's death, Hamlet's "swift" and sudden murder of Polonius creates further obstacles—chiefly his banishment—to the achievement of his goal. The revenger's vow is far from attained, but with the problem of Purgatory removed by the assurance of Claudius's guilt, Shakespeare must find other sources of dramatic delay to hinder Hamlet's revenge.

We might expect Hamlet's voyage to England to serve the purpose quite well, yet that journey and his "sudden and more strange return" (4.7.45) are handled briskly with a letter to the king and the dialogue between Hamlet and Horatio at the beginning of 5.2. More significant to the further delay of Hamlet's revenge than the fifty or so lines dealing with Hamlet's aborted voyage are the nearly three hundred lines of the graveyard scene that intervene between Hamlet's promise of a "more horrid" course of action (3.3.88) and the final destruction of the Danish royal family.[108] Here again, the material remnants of Doomsday plays take center stage. But Shakespeare conspicuously recycles the cellarage and stage trap of Purgatory to mark his departure from the old plays of the Doom.

Remembrances Redelivered

The problem of final judgment and the eternal fate of souls returns immediately after the Mousetrap play as Hamlet ponders killing the king while he is praying. He contrasts the uncertainty of his father's "audit," or spiritual account in Purgatory, against the assured fate of Claudius "now a is praying":

And now I'll do't,
    [He draws his sword.]
       and so a goes to heaven,
And so am I revenged. That would be scanned.
A villain kills my father, and for that
I, his sole son, do this same villain send
To heaven.
O, this is hire and salary, not revenge!
A took my father grossly, full of bread,
With all his crimes broad blown, as flush as May;
And how his audit stands who knows save heaven?
But in our circumstance and course of thought
'Tis heavy with him. And am I then revenged
To take him in the purging of his soul,
When he is fit and seasoned for his passage?
No.
[He sheathes his sword.]
             (3.3.74–87)

Considering the matter further, Hamlet seeks not only to murder his father's killer but, like the stage devils of the *Last Judgment,* to send his soul off to Hell:[109]

> Then trip him that his heels may kick at heaven,
> And that his soul may be as damned and black
> As hell whereto it goes.
>
> (3.4.88–95)

Fiendlike, he imagines tossing Claudius's soul into the gaping maw of Hell, but in place of this infernal portal, the play, unlike Marlowe's *Faustus,* offers Ophelia's newly dug grave.

"What ceremony else?" (5.1.207), Laertes asks the "churlish priest" (223) performing Ophelia's "maimèd rites" (202) beside the stage pit. Outraged by the question, the clergyman declares that he has "enlarged" her funeral ceremony too much already; her body must lie as it is until rejoined with her soul when the last trumpet signals the Day of Doom:

Priest

> Her obsequies have been as far enlarged
> As we have warrantise. Her death was doubtful,
> And but that great command o'ersways the order
> She should in ground unsanctified have lodged
> Till the last trumpet.
>
> (5.1.208–12)

The Priest's reply depends on the same metonymic relationship between trumpets and the Apocalypse found in the *Last Judgment.* In light of the mystery stage practice of restricting trumpet playing to Doomsday pageants, the metonymy would have encouraged Globe audiences to recall the final episode in the mystery cycles as well as imagine the Second Coming. Less metonymic yet still resonant with the Doom is the play's attention to dirt.

The graveyard scenes in *Hamlet* and the York mercers' *Last Judgment* share a preoccupation with dirt. Shakespeare's repeated jokes and musings on the decomposition of bodies into mud, earth, clay, and loam recall the cartloads of dirt tradesmen possibly heaped in mounds to give their Doomsday pageant wagon the look of a graveyard. In order to make room for Ophelia's body, "the remains of the dead are removed in a material form closer to dust than flesh."[110] Goodman Delver exaggerates this fact when he informs Hamlet, "We have many pocky corpses nowadays, that will scarce hold the laying in" (5.1.152–54). And, though not a reference to the *Judgment* play, his comic pun, "The Scripture says Adam digged. Could he dig without arms?" (5.1.34–35), likewise reminds the audience of the traditional prop that

Adam carried in the mysteries as a sign of his punishment and toil after the Fall: a spade.[111] The clownish sexton may even raise his own shovel when he declares that grave makers "hold up Adam's profession" (5.1.29).

If the comedy of the scene seems a far cry from the earnestness of Doomsday pageants, we must also note the manner in which, as we saw with Bottom's dream in the previous chapter, these jokes bring the mysteries into closer proximity even as they transform the significance of accustomed stage properties and practices. Delver's humorous boast that "the houses that he makes lasts till doomsday" (5.1.54–55), is a direct reminder to the audience that one day those "houses" will collapse or break open just as they did upon the mystery stage. Besides such comic moments, many serious passages in the play also draw upon yet depart from scenes of the *Last Judgment*. In Q1, Hamlet finds "joyful hope" in the fact that the "dreame of death" does in fact have an end "when wee awake / And [are] borne before an everlasting Iudge."[112] But the hope is ironically uttered in a moment of suicidal despair that risks the eternal ire of that judge. "The devil take thy soul," shrieks Laertes at his father's murderer as they grapple in Ophelia's grave (5.1.243). The sentiment echoes the divine imperatives of the Doom: "Go to the fire" (Chester, 644) and "sit by Satanas the fiend" (York, 372). And yet his words surely would have sounded out of place to Shakespeare's audience for the precise reason that they are a divine prerogative.

Above all, however, it is the material remnant of the understage space of Purgatory that undergoes the most significant transformation. Having incorporated Purgatory in order to rework the play's anxiety over revenge into an anxiety over the discernment of spirits, Shakespeare returns to the *Last Judgment* pageants in 5.1. He re-creates the grave, but instead of serving as the former resting place for resurrecting souls, it frames descending bodies, one dead and two grappling to kill each other. The graveside is no longer a place where eternal destinies are proclaimed but one where questions are debated about the undiscovered country and the fate of souls in it: "Is she to be buried in Christian burial that willfully seeks her own salvation?" (5.1.1–2). We have noted how the Chester Banns endorse traditional stage practices and properties yet simultaneously denigrate and transform their previous dramatic signification. In the same way, Shakespeare resurrects Purgatory as the origin of Hamlet's Ghost in act 1, but in act 5 he forgoes this interpretation when the stage floor opens again as the grave for a young maid who suffers "muddy death" (4.7.154) and whose eternal fate is wryly and fervently debated.

Whereas the opening of graves in the *Last Judgment* heralded the arrival of the heavenly kingdom, the opening of Ophelia's grave and the grapple between Hamlet and Laertes portends the doom of the Danish realm. The play turns from eschatology to topography and taphonomy:

Hamlet

This fellow might in 's time be a great buyer of land, with his statutes, his recognizances, his fines, his double vouchers, his recoveries. Is this the fine of his fines and the recovery of his recoveries, to have his fine pate full of fine dirt?... The very conveyances of his lands will hardly lie in this box; and must th'inheritor himself have no more, ha? (5.1.94–98, 100–102)

The bodies of great emperors may patch a wall (5.1.199) or stop a beer barrel (5.1.195), but they do not, it seems, rise again. The Doomsday that looms in the following and final scene of the play is not the Christian Apocalypse but the "eruption" (1.1.68) and collapse of the Danish state. If we recall that the play opened with allusions to Christ's Incarnation and now moves to a close in the shadow of the Second Coming, then we will appreciate Shakespeare's subtle echo of a frequent refrain in *Last Judgment* plays—namely, the vanity of all earthly power in the face of eternity. With a glance at the burgeoning colonial aspirations of his own country, he renders Denmark's proud history of empire as brittle and transient as the dynasties of Caesar and Alexander.[113]

In comparison with Kyd's *Spanish Tragedy,* which concludes with Revenge and the ghost of Don Andrea declaring eternal punishments for many, Shakespeare's *Hamlet* is far less Senecan and perhaps more ambiguous yet still preoccupied with the final audit of souls.[114] Considering himself "more an antique Roman than a Dane," Horatio momentarily ponders suicide, but this consummation is denied when Hamlet intervenes (5.2.283). Laertes pronounces the king "justly served" before he and the prince make assurances of forgiveness so that, at the Final Judgment, their souls will not be accountable for each other's murder (5.2.269–74). In Q1, Hamlet's final speech ends in a prayer common among saved souls in plays of the Doom: "heauen receiue my soule" (I3v).[115] Fortinbras's first glimpse of the scene prompts an eschatological apostrophe: "O proud death, / What feast is toward in thine eternal cell / That thou so many princes at a shot / So bloodily hast struck!" (5.2.308–11). Horatio's final wish is that his friend's soul be taken beyond the fiend's clutches to the *requiem aeternum* of peace-parted souls. His farewell may have prompted Globe audiences to recall the familiar spectacle of the Doomsday pageants: "Good night, sweet prince, / And flights of angels sing thee to thy rest" (5.2. 302–3).

All these passages evoke commonplaces from the *Last Judgment:* the ultimate reckoning of souls (among whom kings, queens, and other nobility are prominent), the devil's "eternal cell," a gaping Hell mouth, heavenly music, and angelic choirs. As if in final acknowledgment of these once-lavish pageants, Shakespeare delivers, through language, what the mystery plays had achieved through costumes, musical instruments, ladders, wooden trusses, and hoisting mechanisms—as well as gorgeous poetry. Perhaps we should read this versifying of material elements of the *Last Judgment* as a rejection of the mechanical stagecraft of that older dramatic tradition. According to this reading, *Hamlet* simply and rather opportunistically re-creates the theatrical space of Purgatory in the cellarage of the Globe but ultimately denies the audience an account of what the prince's revenge has supposedly achieved. After all—and in further disparity to plays of the Doom—Hamlet's father does not arise to declare his gratitude for God's mercy or to enjoin his son to perform works of charity such as alms deeds, prayers, or fasting. To the contrary, the prince is commanded only to kill the king.[116] Yet the lyrical poignancy of Horatio's farewell, the immediacy with which its imagery evokes the costly and long-awaited final moment of the great mystery cycles, seems to encourage the audience to recollect rather than reject the antecedents of the London stage. More tributary more than triumphalist, Horatio's prayer is a paean to the mystery play tradition that redelivers the remembrance of Doomsday pageants with one last metatheatrical note of grief and loss and thus frees the play to end with the more earthly concerns of conquest and succession that are its premise.

Staging a Senecan ghost from a medieval Purgatory, Shakespeare further intermingles medieval and classical conventions in an already polychronic English dramatic tradition. The Chester Banns help us to see the synchronic diachrony that enables Shakespeare to borrow Purgatory from the *Last Judgment* scenes of the mysteries. Supersession secures preservation. Shakespeare antiquates the purgatorial ghost in an already outdated play: his source, the so-called *Ur-Hamlet,* was considered unfashionable; the story is set in a pre-Norman era of English history; and it relied heavily on hackneyed stage conventions and ancient Senecan formulas. But above all, as Margreta de Grazia explains, "It retained the most archaic feature of all—a ghost returning from an old-faith Purgatory, enjoining the retaliative ('an eye for an eye') revenge of the Old Testament."[117]

Just as the Chester Banns avoid responsibility for any lingering superstition by reminding the audience that the plays were written in the remote "tyme of Ignorance," Shakespeare may have rendered the Ghost conspicuously obsolete to blunt the evocation of Purgatory and avoid censure. Associating the old mole of a Ghost with what is past and outdated, Shakespeare acquires an innovative source of delay for his revenge tragedy. *Gorboduc* (1561), *The Spanish Tragedy* (c. 1587), and even *The Jew of Malta* (1590) and *The Misfortunes of Arthur* (1588) evoke a classical Hades or present effectively Senecan ghosts without any hint of Purgatory. But Shakespeare spied in the *discretio spirituum* of Doomsday plays a means of delaying Hamlet's inevitable achievement of his vow of revenge.[118] The elaborate Doomsday pageants that had demanded great artistic effort and material expense were finally banned, but not before the professional London stages preserved their three-tiered architecture of Heaven, Earth, and Hell and, in *Hamlet,* merged the trapdoors of Hell and Purgatory to create the understage portal for a hellishly purgatorial Ghost who would enjoy an eternal theatrical life.

CHAPTER 5

"Here's a Knocking Indeed!"
Macbeth *and the* Harrowing of Hell

Batter my heart, three-personed God; for you
As yet but knock...
That I may rise and stand, o'erthrow me, and bend
Your force, to break, blow, burn, and make me new.

—John Donne, Holy Sonnet 14

Knock. Knock. Who's there? In the *Harrowing of Hell* scenes of English mystery plays, the answer to that question was no joke. The *Harrowing* marks the climax of the battle between God and Satan for the fate of humanity. After the Crucifixion, Christ descends into Hell and lays siege to its battlements in order to "harrow," or plunder, the souls in Limbo.[1] It was commonly believed that these imprisoned souls did not experience Hell's many torments, but were, as Macbeth would say, "cabined, cribbed, confined" (3.4.23) in the darkness of Limbo, where they suffered the absence of God. "Foure thowsande and sex hundereth yere, / Haue we bene heere in this stedde" (39–40), says Adam in the York play. Medieval theologians accepted the apocryphal story from the Gospel of Nicodemus because it addressed an important conundrum, namely, the fate of righteous souls during the long expanse of time between the Fall of Adam and the birth of Christ.[2] Yet, after the Reformation, the legendary tale retained its appeal, perhaps in part for its inherent typology. The Fall in Genesis is reversed as Christ (the "New Adam") rescues Adam and Eve from Limbo and restores them to Paradise.[3]

Though typology might excuse the *Harrowing* for many readers, Reformers like the acrimonious Cestrian preacher Christopher Goodman neverthe-less found fault with stage performances. Indeed, few of the pageants in the

1572 production of the Chester cycle warrant as many notations in his list of "absurdities &c" as the *Harrowing* play, a fact that has led Paul Whitfield White to speculate that the Late Banns may have been commissioned to respond specifically to Goodman's criticisms.[4] Goodman objects to "Michael bringing the fathers out of hell with the cross hanging upon the [redeemed] theef's back," "Enoch & Elias living in paradise in the flesh," and "a fable of Seth begging oyl in paradise to anoint Adam when he was sick." Most interestingly, he condemns the "deliverance of Adam &c out of hell & [Christ's] bringing these words to affirm his purpose Attollite portas."[5] With their scriptural authority, the words *Attollite portas* would seem one of the least objectionable elements in this apocryphal legend. They are taken from verses 7 and 9 of Psalm 23 (AV 24): "Attollite portas, principes, vestras, et elevamini, portae aeternales, et introibit rex gloriae" (Vulg.) (Lift up your heads, O ye gates, and be ye lift up, ye everlasting doors, and the King of Glory shall come in [AV]). As we will see, however, they conjured up a long history of pre-Reformation liturgical rites, teachings, and dramatic performances.

Why did the legend appeal to Shakespeare as he was writing the forty lines of the Porter scene (2.3) in *Macbeth* that are most often described as comic relief? For many years, literary critics denied that he did write them and that the episode had any bearing on the rest of the play. Pope shoved the scene of drunkenness and bawdy humor into the margins of his edition; Rowe severely cut the Porter's lines on the grounds that "too many meretricious weeds grow upon the banks of Avon." Coleridge believed that except for the single sentence at lines 16–18 ("I had thought to have let in some of all professions that go the primrose way to th' everlasting bonfire"), "not one syllable has the ever-present being of Shakespeare."[6] While recognizing later additions of songs and passages from Thomas Middleton in the scenes of the witches and Hecate, literary historians of the twentieth century have generally accepted the Porter scene as authentic Shakespeare.[7] In recent years, moreover, critics have begun to explore connections between this scene, the legend of Christ's Descent into Hell, and *Macbeth* more generally.[8]

More than forty years ago, Glynne Wickham noted that Shakespeare's play relies upon his audience's familiarity with mystery drama and that *Macbeth* draws from the dialogue, action, and setting of *Harrowing of Hell* pageants.[9] Wickham's research set an important precedent. Scholars such as Michael O'Connell, Helen Cooper, and Beatrice Groves, for example, have made important claims about the histrionic conventions and incarnational aesthetics that Shakespeare inherited from the mystery plays like the *Harrowing*.[10] This chapter, though clearly indebted to Wickham's scholarship and sympathetic to O'Connell and others, makes a different claim: I argue that a sound effect borrowed from mystery drama catalyzes dialogue and action in a Shakespeare play. Sounds are not objects in the traditional sense of material culture studies, yet it may be helpful to think about the acoustic affinity between *Macbeth* and the *Harrowing* in terms of material stage properties—as if Shakespeare had borrowed an aural prop, rather than a Hell mouth or devil's costume, to momentarily suggest the setting of Hell.[11]

The knocking at the gate of Inverness castle prompts the Porter of *Macbeth* to tell jokes and ask questions in the manner of traditional devil-porter behavior in the mysteries. In this way, the re-creation of a sound from an outlawed stage tradition brings the pre-Reformation theatrical past into the present. It is, therefore, not a neutral dramaturgical choice but a potentially subversive bit of stage business that has two important implications for Shakespeare's play. First, by inviting but then denying affinities with Christ's climactic battle with Satan, the Porter scene exposes the inadequacy of Jacobean political theology. When Wickham's essay was published, it joined John Harcourt's "I Pray You, Remember the Porter" in arguing that Shakespeare, pressured by royal patronage, wrote *Macbeth* in support of James's views on kingship and godly rule.[12] Later scholarship, however, has stressed the play's potential involvement in resistance theory.[13]

My own contribution to this critical conversation will be to suggest that the Porter scene, once the cornerstone of pro-Jacobean readings of Macbeth's reign as an "awful parenthesis," is in fact an elaborate joke that undermines the crown's claims to sacred authority. Second, by borrowing from the seemingly outdated dramaturgy of pre-Reformation plays, the Porter scene mocks religious opponents of the London playhouses. At the time that *Macbeth* was being performed, antitheatricalists like the Protestant preacher William Crashaw were calling upon James I to extirpate "the vngodly Playes and Enterludes so rife in this nation."[14] Critics of the theater condemned the public stages as the theatrical progeny of popish mystery drama, and I suggest that the knocking at the gates provokes and unprovokes such desires to link commercial drama with its Catholic antecedents.

Hearing and Remembering

Bruce Smith's work *The Acoustic World of Early Modern England* explores how early modern audiences experienced sound—both inside and outside the Globe theater. According to Smith, sound and other extraverbal aspects of drama require us to adopt a more expansive approach to Shakespeare's plays than textual study has traditionally permitted. His "historical phenomenology" therefore aims to situate the study of human hearing in the historical context of early modern England.[15] How, in other words, did Shakespeare's audiences experience sound, and how did they understand it? Two aspects of Smith's study are important for this discussion of the knocking in *Macbeth:* first, both sound and memory were viewed as material remnants of past experience, and second, extraverbal sounds were often crucial to a Globe performance. With regard to the former, late sixteenth- and early seventeenth-century studies of the brain's faculties understood memory as a "densely material" trace of speech. As Smith explains, "Early modern physiology invited people to think of their memory as something physical and graphic: a trace in the brain tissues that could practically be seen and touched."[16]

Renaissance theorists of memory drew upon the writings of Plato and Aristotle, which, among other metaphors, compared human memory to wax that retains the impression of a seal or other object no longer present.[17] According to Smith, this material understanding of memory implies that the brain must re-create the experience of hearing a word when it recalls that word and transforms it into a sound. "Because words have semantic meanings," he writes, "we forget that they also encode bodily experience—at the very least the expulsion of air, the adjustments of muscle, the shaping of tongue that it takes to pronounce those words." And so, "memory transforms air waves into embodied action. It *re*members sound in various parts of the human body: in the other ventricles of the brain, in the ears, in the hands, in the eyes, in the body as a kinaesthetic whole."[18] In early modern accounts, therefore, the recollection of sound is more than a cognitive phenomenon: it is a somatic experience. Guided by the ear, the mental faculties re-member, or re-embody, "traces of sound that were already lodged in the [hearer's] brain, lungs, larynx, and mouth."[19] The Chester Banns help us to further explore the importance of Smith's work with respect to the history of early English theater: sounds have an inherent synchronic diachrony. When a sound effect was produced on the London stage, it triggered a person's previous bodily experience of that noise, so that an auditor was, in effect, standing simultaneously in a present and past theatrical moment. The hearer may not only have perceived a synchronous connection between the remembered and re-membered sounds but may also have experienced the temporal difference between them, particularly if encouraged to do so by an actor onstage.

Like the human body, the London playhouses were "instruments for producing, shaping, and propagating sound." The timbers, plaster, lath, and joists effectively transformed the stage into a "gigantic sounding board." Far from being acoustically restrictive, the 1599 Globe "offered a volumetric listening space per auditor that actually surpasses that of modern theaters."[20] Sound effects were therefore often crucial to an early modern audience's experience of a play. As Smith shows with regard to the thunder heard during the opening scenes of *Macbeth* and *The Tempest,* plays had "soundscapes," or auditory fields, that were often purposefully defined at the outset of the play.[21] Yet the Globe not only produced, shaped, and propagated sound—it remembered it. Moreover, following Smith's insight, the London playhouses re-member sounds. The opening peal of thunder "through the fog and filthy air" (1.1.11) surrounding the weird sisters and the hellish pounding din we hear later at the Porter's "Hell gate" were, as we'll see, prominent features in the soundscape of *Harrowing of Hell* plays. In fact, the noises produced on or behind the stage were so similar to the older plays—and so familiar to audiences—as to allow the professional theater to play upon the previous significance and context of these sounds.[22] The clown playing the Porter of Macbeth's castle does just that.

A History of Hard Knocks

"Here's a knocking indeed! If a man were porter of hell-gate, he should have old turning the key" (2.3.1–2). When the actor playing the Porter enters saying these words, he is alone on stage. There is no dialogue that prompts him to compare himself to a devil guarding Hell's gates. There is only a noise—which the 1623 First Folio records as a stage direction repeated ten times—"Knocke within."—and which the Porter himself repeatedly mimics.[23] It is that knocking, too, that would have encouraged the audience to play along with his imagination. They have heard, as the Porter has not, Macbeth's final line in the previous scene: "Wake Duncan with thy knocking. I would thou couldst." (2.2.72). After the Reformation, as before, a knock that could wake the dead from their sleep in a dark castle recalled the popular apocryphal legend of Christ's *Descensus ad Inferos.* Christians in Europe and England had been reading about—and enacting—the legendary knocking of the *Descensus* for centuries. The story excerpted from the Gospel of Nicodemus probably came to the pageants of the late medieval mysteries from the *Legenda Aurea* and *A Stanzaic Life of Christ.*[24]

The Nicodemus account, moreover, turns on the famous *Attollite portas* verse from Psalm 23[24] that would later arouse Christopher Goodman's contempt. The command is spoken with a "hideous" voice like thunder ("A voice spak than full hydusly, / Als it war thonours blast"), before finally "Ihesus strake so fast, / the yhates in sonder yhede / And Iren bandes all brast."[25] Traditionally sung on Holy Saturday, the phrase, according to

E. K. Chambers, was also used in the dedication of a new church (*Ordo Dedicationis Ecclesiae*) as early as the ninth century. In this dramatic exorcism:

> The bishop and his procession approach the closed doors of the church from without, but one of the clergy, *quasi latens,* is placed inside. Three blows with a staff are given on the doors, and the anthem is raised *Tollite portas, principes, vestras et elevamini, portae aeternales, et introibit Rex gloriae.* From within comes the question *Quis est iste rex gloriae?* and the reply is given *Dominus virtutum ipse est Rex gloriae.* Then the doors are opened.[26]

In the fourteenth century, a liturgical drama enacting the *Harrowing of Hell* commissioned by Lady Katherine of Sutton, abbess of Barking Abbey, similarly required that the officiating priest and two deacons process through the church with a *labarum,* or cross surmounted by Christ's standard.[27] As they approach the door or gates, they

> shall begin three times this antiphon: *Tollite portas.* This priest indeed shall represent [*representabit*] the person of Christ about to descend to hell and break down the gates of hell. And the aforesaid antiphon shall be begun at each repetition in a higher or louder voice [*altiori uoce*], which the clerks repeat the same number of times, and at the beginning each time he shall beat with the cross at the aforesaid door signifying [*figurans*] the breaking down of the gates of hell. And at the third knock, the door shall open.[28]

The sound of knocking in the Descent into Hell predates the mystery plays, yet whether on stage or in poems, sermons, and liturgies, the climax of the story always occurs at the suspenseful moment when the gates of Hell echo with blows yet seem unbreakable.[29]

In its varied textual forms, the *Harrowing* often borrowed the tropes of other genres, such as the heroic joust of a medieval romance, yet when performed as a mystery pageant, it seems to have remained a relatively simple and straightforward demonstration of divine power.[30] The *Harrowing* plays in York, Chester, Wakefield and N-town repeat the *Attollite portas* or similar lines as many as three times, with the gates crashing down on the final injunction. The gates of Hell cannot prevail and the knocking of Anima Christi therefore becomes central to the play—because of it, guildsmen were obliged to construct a Hell mouth with gates that would appear to collapse.[31] The Chester cooks, for example, constructed a huge bestial maw tall enough to contain gates and a "dungeon" emitting smoke and sulphurous stench.[32] REED documents for the city of Coventry list payments to those hired "for kepying of the wynde [i.e. windlass]," "for kepying of hell mowthe & the fyer," and "for opening & shutting of the doores."[33] These records as well as stage directions in the plays themselves make clear that Hell was represented not as a barren wasteland or fiery pit but as a dark-walled fortress or castle.[34]

Mystery play adaptations of the *Descensus ad Inferos* from the Gospel of Nicodemus and other sources also reproduce the hideous "thonours blast" that accompanies Christ's approach to Hell's gate. A stage direction in the Chester play calls for great clamor and noise: *Tunc venit Jesus et fiat clamor, vel sonitus magnus materialis.*[35] The precise meaning of the "material noise" remains a crux for scholars. Wickham interprets this stage direction as "trumpets and knocking." Mills is less specific in his modernized translation: "Then Jesus shall come, and there shall be a cry, or a great physical din." Richard Rastall points out that if the word *materialis* is a noun rather than an adjective then it's quite possible that the stage direction is telling the cooks who are performing the play to make "a great sound of material," namely, by banging together the pots and pans of their trade. This interpretation, says Rastall, activates a medieval conceptualization of Hell that "we understand only imperfectly: the idea of Hell as a kitchen."[36]

Whether kitchen or torture chamber, Hell is confusion's masterpiece, and yet the devils in the *Harrowing of Hell* are, like Macbeth, appalled by noise: "How is't with me when every noise appals me?" (2.2.56). They cannot abide either the knocking or the commotion it arouses among their prisoners. In the Chester play, the din at the gates prompts Sathanas to cry, "Owt, alas, what is this?" (161). In York, the pounding precipitates further noises as the devil-porter Rebalde runs to warn Belsabub of the great commotion among the souls in Limbo:

I Diabolus

Helpe, Belsabub, to bynde ther boyes—
Such harrowe was neuer are herde in helle.

II Diabolus

Why rooris thou soo, Rebalde? Thou royis [talk nonsense]—
What is betidde, canne thou ought telle?

I Diabolus

What, heris thou nought this vggely noyse?
Thes lurdans [wretches] that in Lymbo dwelle,
Thei make menyng of many joies
And musteres grete mirthe thame emell.

(97–104)

The stage devils are quite disturbed by noise, for it heralds the arrival of Christ. In Chester Sathanas forebodes the loss of his "soveryntie" in Hell when he learns who is threatening to crash his gates: "Owt, alas, I am shent! / My might fayles, verament. / This prynce that ys nowe present / will pull from me my praye" (177–80). "Telle me what boyes dare be so bolde / For drede to make so mekill draye" (145–46), says the York Sattan when he hears the clamor ("draye"). The Wakefield Sathanas, much like Shakespeare's Porter, mockingly imitates the repeated knocking he hears—commanding his devils not to be abashed ("abaste") by Christ's presence and to "ding," or knock, "that dastard downe!"[37] Roaring "Owte, harrowe!" (184, 195, 343), the York demons raise a clamor of their own. Yelling, complaining, and mimicry of the knocking were commonplaces among devils in the *Harrowing,* and so it is fitting that Macbeth's Porter should act in a similar manner.

Shakespeare's stage, in fact, utilized many of the same technologies as the mysteries, including those used to make thunderous noises.[38] In 1584, a man named "starche" was paid "to make the storme in the pagente" for the Coventry Doomsday and Destruction of the World play. Perhaps Starche made use of the "baryll for the yerthe quake" listed in the records and was aided by "Christofer Dyglyne... [with] hys ij drummes."[39] In a similar way, the London playhouses vigorously pounded drums or rolled cannonballs on metal sheets to create the noise of thunder.[40] If a drum or barrel had been pounded steadily, rather than tempestuously, it might have produced the kind of din that irritates the Porter ("Knock, knock. Never at quiet." [2.3.15]), not to mention Macbeth ("Whence is that knocking?" [2.2.55])—the noise evidently so loud that he can't tell where it's coming from. Indeed, if Smith is correct, the Globe's twenty-sided polygonal architecture and building materials would have propagated the sound all through the theater.[41] Macduff's response to Macbeth's prompt entrance ("Our knocking has awaked him" [2.3.38]) would then seem as humorous as it is ironic. Who *wouldn't* have been awakened?

As in previous chapters, I argue that the remnants of mystery drama have literary as well as material agency in Shakespeare's plays. In the case of *Macbeth,* therefore, the knocking in 2.3 resonates throughout the play text as well as the theater space, and its vibrations are felt in the abstractions of character, action, theme, imagery, and wordplay. Our present consideration of the knocking's textual resonance within the Porter scene itself therefore requires us to listen for echoes of the *Harrowing* throughout the play, to resurrect problems and preoccupations that have long interested critics, and to query elements of the play long assumed to be unique to this late Shakespearean tragedy.

Sound and Fury

An early modern audience's kinesthetic experience of thunder and knocking in the "volumetric listening space" of the Globe would have been profound, and hearing an actor describe sounds through linguistic "imagery" is substantially different from hearing those noises emanate from the "hut" above the canopied roof of Heaven. Yet the language of Shakespeare's play also contributes significantly to the aura of Hell, just as the repeated intonation of the *Attollite portas* verses did in the *Harrowing*. After all, without the Porter's verbal commentary, the knocking at the gate may be reminiscent of *Harrowing* plays but would not necessarily signify Hell. Instead, a bell "invites" Macbeth to commit the murder, and he imagines that it is Duncan's death knell, summoning him "to heaven or to hell" (2.1.62–64). While "he is about it" (2.2.4), Lady Macbeth imagines an owl shriek as if it were a funeral bell tolling: "Hark, peace!—/ It was the owl that shrieked, the fatal bellman / Which gives the stern'st good-night" (2.2.2–4). "Hark!" she cries again a few lines later (2.2.11). After the murder, the two again hear noises:

Macbeth

I have done the deed. Didst thou not hear a noise?

Lady Macbeth

I heard the owl scream and the crickets cry.
Did you not speak?

Macbeth

      When?

Lady Macbeth

      Now.

Macbeth

      As I descended?

Lady Macbeth

      Ay.

Macbeth

      Hark!—

            (2.2.14–16)

They volley words in rapid succession—an aural ping-pong match of monosyllables. But the Macbeths are not the only ones hearing strange sounds. Lennox later tells Macbeth of "Lamentings heard i'th' air, strange screams of death, / And prophesying with accents terrible" (2.3.52–53). The clamor in nature that he describes is soon matched by the confused cries of Duncan's subjects as Macduff returns from the chamber and compares the scene to the Final Doom. "Awake, awake! / Ring the alarum bell," he cries, adding: "Up, up, and see / The great doom's image. Malcolm, Banquo, / As from your graves rise up, and walk like sprites / To countenance this horror" (2.3.70–71, 74–77).

In *Last Judgment* pageants, where "the great doom's image" was performed, there was an earthquake as the angels blew their trumpets to awake the dead. Macbeth is reminded of it when he feels his reign circumscribed by the never-ending line of Banquo's issue: "What, will the line stretch out to th' crack of doom?" he asks the witches (4.1.133). As the *OED* explains, the word "crack" refers to the blaring trumpets of the angels sent by God to summon the dead: "A sudden sharp and loud noise as of something breaking or bursting," including the "thunder-peal" or "archangel's trump" on the Day of Judgment. Macbeth's use of the term in act 4 underscores the broader linguistic and extraverbal soundscape of the play. It anticipates his impending doom, when Macduff will command, "Make all our trumpets speak, give them all breath, / Those clamorous harbingers of blood and death" (5.6.9–10). "Crack" also reminds the audience of the play's opening: *"Thunder and Lightning. Enter three Witches"* (1.1.1, s.d.).[42] Macbeth himself, when struggling to carry out Duncan's murder, had compared the death of the king to apocalyptic "blasts" and "trumpet-tongued" angels (1.7.18–25).

The thunderous knocking of the Porter scene thus resonates with the many cracks, blasts, trumpets, bells, howls, and shrieks of the play's hellish cacophony of sound and fury. When we last see Lady Macbeth, she is still haunted by the knock at the gate, and her final monosyllabic words are a repetitious staccato reminiscent of the knocking she still fears: "No more o' that, my lord, no more o' that. . . . To bed, to bed. There's knocking at the gate. Come, come, come, come, give me your hand. What's done cannot be undone. To bed, to bed, to bed" (5.1.37–38, 56–58).

Who Art Thou?

If the knocking at the gate cues Macbeth's gatekeeper to imagine himself a stage-devil in a *Harrowing* play, he imitates much more than just the outcry and complaints of devil-porters. As he makes his way across the courtyard, he entertains the audience by recounting the sins of those he expects to find at the door: "'Faith, here's an English tailor come hither for stealing out of a French hose. Come in, tailor. Here you may roast your goose" (2.3.12–14). But then, ostensibly awakened by the cold, he suddenly decides, "this place is too cold for hell. I'll devil-porter it no further" (2.3.15–16). Here "devil-porter" is a verb, not a noun, and the gatekeeper assumes that the role entails certain actions.

What does it mean to "devil-porter" other than to "let in some of all professions that go the primrose way to th'everlasting bonfire" (2.3.17–18)? First, devils traditionally ask questions and mock those bound for Hell's flames. The repeated question of "Who's there?" may be traced to the apocryphal source text of many of the mystery pageants, the Gospel of Nicodemus, which I now cite at length to underscore the centrality of the interrogative mood to demonic speech:

When Hell and death and their wicked ministers saw that, they were stricken with fear, they and their cruel officers, at the sight of the brightness of so great light in their own realm, seeing Christ of a sudden in their abode, and they cried out, saying: We are overcome by thee. Who art thou that art sent by the Lord for our confusion? Who art thou that without all damage of corruption, and with the signs (?) of thy majesty unblemished, dost in wrath condemn our power? Who art thou that art so great and so small, both humble and exalted, both soldier and commander, a marvelous warrior in the shape of a bondsman, and a King of glory dead and living, whom the cross bare slain upon it? Thou that didst lie dead in the sepulchre hast come down unto us living and at thy death all creation quaked and all the stars were shaken and thou hast become free among the dead and dost rout our legions. Who art thou that settest free the prisoners that are held bound by original sin and restorest them into their former liberty? Who art thou that sheddest thy divine and bright light upon them that were blinded with the darkness of their sins? After the same manner all the legions of devils were stricken with like fear and cried out all together in the terror of their confusion, saying: Whence art thou, Jesus, a man so mighty and bright in majesty, so excellent without spot and clean from sin? For that world of earth which hath been always subject unto us until now, and did pay tribute to our profit, hath never sent unto us a dead man like thee, nor ever dispatched such a gift unto Hell. Who then art thou that so fearlessly enterest our borders, and not only fearest not our torments, but besides essayest to bear away all men out of our bonds? Peradventure thou art that Jesus, of whom Satan our prince said that by thy death of the cross thou shouldest receive the dominion of the whole world.[43]

As John D. Cox has noted, devils repeatedly ask insolent questions in medieval rituals and liturgical plays on the Continent, including a thirteenth-century *Ordo Paschalis* from Klosterneuburg and a sixteenth-century service in Bamberg.[44] In the Wakefield mystery play, Sathanas asks, "Why, who durst be so bold for drede to make on us a fray?" (148–49). His porter, Ribald, questions Jesus's authority: "What devil is he / That callys him king over us all?" (116–17). His counterpart in York puts this question to Jesus: "With al thy booste and bere, / . . . telle to me this tyde / What maistries make thou here?" (214–16). And in Chester: "What, what ys hee, that kinge of blys?" (197). With these questions, the devils refuse to recognize God's majesty and in doing so stage a rebellion. Hell becomes a rebel stronghold where divine order and the lawful rule of God's anointed are mocked and rejected. The impertinence of challenging questions is entirely in keeping with the anarchic, burlesque "social background and function" of stage devils, which, according to Robert Weimann, connects them to the folk fool.[45]

And, like fools, they mock the folly of others. The gatekeeper at Inverness amuses himself with the transgressions of sinners bound for Hell: "Here's a farmer that hanged himself on th'expectation of plenty. Come in time! Have napkins enough about you; here you'll sweat for it" (2.3.4–6). Devils of the *Harrowing, Antichrist,* and *Last Judgment* pageants enjoyed the same sport of baiting sinners with their crimes. In the Chester play *The Coming of Antichrist,* the archangel Michael eventually kills Antichrist and as he is dying, devils appear to haul him off to Hell. As they do so, they thank him for all of the mischief he has caused:

Secundus Demon

Of mee shall come thy last doome,
for thou hast well deserved.
And through my might and my postee [power]
Thou hast lyved in dignitie
and many a soule deceyved.

. . . .

Manye a fatt morsell wee had for his sake
of soules that should have bine saved—in hell be the hydd!

(662–66, 677–78)

The devils' jibes were not reserved for apocryphal figures like Antichrist but often struck much closer to home by naming certain estates or occupations. In the Chester *Judgment,* for example, Primus Demon declares,

This popelard pope here present
with covetousenes was aye fullye bent.
This emperour also, verament,
to all synne did enclyne.
This kinge also all righteouse men shent,
damned them through false judgment
and dyed so withowt amendment;
therefore I hould him myne.

(589–96)

A corrupt judge and dishonest merchant also have their sins told. "This justice, lord, was ever thy foe, / but falsehood to further he was ever throo [eager]" (665–66), says Secundus Demon. He adds, "This marchant also that standeth here, / . . . / As oft-times he him forsware / as seeds be in my seck [sack]" (669–72). Some of all professions and estates "go the primrose way to th'everlasting bonfire" (*Macbeth,* 2.3.17–18).[46]

The recitation of sins could be as amusing as it was admonitory. After Christ has freed the patriarchs from Limbo and all have left the stage of the Chester *Harrowing,* an entertaining coda is included in one version of the play that involves an alewife who has cheated her customers.[47] Two demons, appropriately played by tradesmen of the cooks' and innkeepers' guilds, "welcome" her to Hell by taunting her with her "sins," which include encouraging her patrons to drink and carouse like "any beast":

Secundus Demon

Welcome, sweete ladye! I will thee wedd,
For manye a heavye and drunken head
cause of thy ale were brougt to bedd
farre worse then anye beaste.

Tertius Demon

Welcome, deare darlinge, to endles bale.
Usynge cardes, dyce, and cuppes smale,
with many false othes to sell thy ale—
nowe thou shall have a feaste!

(329–36)

The alewife confesses herself a liar and equivocator: she overpriced her drinks ("My cuppes I sould at my pleasure, / deceaving manye a creature" [290–91]);

pretended to pour full measures ("I kept no trewe measure" [289]); and added hops, ashes, and herbs to make her poor ale seem strong ("with hoppes I made my alle stronge; / esshes and hearbes I blend amonge / and marred so good malt" [294–96]).[48] In this comic addendum to the Chester *Harrowing* where cooks and innkeepers play the roles of devils, Hell is a place of drinking, feasting, and carousing in which Shakespeare's Porter might have felt right at home.

Palter in a Double Sense

In return for the alewife's many false oaths, the demons promise that she "shall have a feaste!" (336), but they "palter…in a double sense" (*Macbeth*, 5.10.20): they mean that she will be the feast, just as Sathan had boasted to his legions (in a mocking allusion to the Eucharist) that they would soon have "Jesu that ys Godes Sonne" as a "noble morsell" (101–2).[49] Medieval stage devils characteristically equivocated in speech and appearance, a point often overlooked by modern editors, who see the Porter's reference to equivocators simply as a topical allusion to the Jesuits implicated in the Gunpowder Plot.[50] Satan's envy of the human race leads to guile and subterfuge in the early episodes of the mystery cycles, particularly the temptation of Eve.[51] The battle of wits between God and the devil continues throughout the cycle, including the climactic encounter of good and evil during Christ's Descent into Hell. In the York Saddlers' *Harrowing,* the devil confronts Jesus not, as in some illustrations, dressed for battle but like a shrewd attorney who jealously defends his property claims through sophistry.[52] Aiming to forestall the liberation of the souls in Limbo, Sattan countermands Christ's assertion of divinity by juggling with the identity of Jesus's "fadir":

Jesus

Now is the tyme certayne
Mi fadir ordand before,
That they schulde passé fro payne
And wonne in mirthe euer more.

Sattan

Thy fadir knewe I wele be sight,
He was a write [carpenter] his mette [meat] to wynne,
And Marie me menys thi modir hight

(225–31)

When Jesus again asserts himself as God's "awne sone" (236), Sattan continues to quibble—this time not with the word "fadir" but with the word "sonne," which he construes to mean "a ladde" (242), that is, a "symple knave" (243) or lowborn person.

The dialogue, or rather debate, that ensues moves to questions about the proper interpretation of God's word.[53] Quoting scripture to suit his purpose, Sattan casuistically argues that the writings of Solomon and Job show that Hell was intended by God to be a place of never-ending torment, not temporary detention:

> Nowe sen the liste allegge the lawes,
> Thou schalte be atteynted or we twynne,
> For tho that thou to wittenesse drawes
> Full even agaynste the will begynne.
> Salamon saide in his sawes
> That whoso enteres helle withynne
> Shall neuer come oute, thus clerkis knawes-
> And therfore felowe, leue thi dynne.
> Job, thi seruaunte, also
> Thus in his tyme gune telle
> That nowthir frende nor foo
> Shulde fynde reles in helle.
>
> (276–87)

Sattan's argument here is so masterfully cunning that he seemingly has no stake in the case whatsoever. He's merely following God's word as if he has been a loyal subject all along. The Porter's account of the equivocator suits him perfectly: the devil did not rebel, he "committed treason enough for God's sake" (*Macbeth,* 2.3.9). He will say anything, "swear in both the scales against either scale" (2.3.8–9), to keep his kingdom.

Jesus must outmaneuver Sattan with equivocation rather than the force of truth. Job, he says, was ignorant of Limbo, so his use of the word "helle" should not be interpreted to include that place. Arguing for a distinction between damned souls assigned to the proper precincts of Hell and those being held in Limbo, Jesus states,

> He saide full soth, that schall thou see,
> That in helle may be no reles,
> But of that place than preched he
> Where synffull care schall euere encrees.
> And in that bale ay schall thou be
> Whare sorowes sere schall neuer sesse,
> And for my folke therfro wer free,
> Nowe schall thei passe to the place of pees.

Thai were here with my wille,
And so schall thei fourthe wende,
And thiselue schall fulfille
Ther wooe withouten ende.

(289–300)

Jesus's guile here is part of a larger pattern of "divine duplicity" that Beadle, Cox, and others have noted in the various cycle plays.[54] Satan ensnares Adam and Eve by disguising himself as a serpent; God counteracts this dissimulation by taking on the guise of human flesh. Sacred history thereby becomes a masquerade as the devil struggles futilely to uncover Christ's divine nature until it's too late. Thus, in the end, God defeats the Father of Lies at his own game of tricks and deceits.[55]

Beginning with Satan's transformation into serpent form in the Garden of Eden, devils often disguised their appearance. Lady Macbeth's advice to her husband to "look like the innocent flower, / But be the serpent under't" (1.5.63–64) is, according to Glynne Wickham, an allusion with many demonic antecedents in the medieval mysteries, above all *Creation* pageants in which Lucifer assumes a transvestite costume, "an adder's coat topped by a woman's face, a flaxen wig and falsetto voice." Satan's disguise so perfectly wedded envy and betrayal to assurance and charm that it became a theatrical trope culminating, more than a century and a half later, in Lady Macbeth's famous counsel.[56]

Yet in some mystery pageants, demons do not simply disguise their appearance; rather, they have dual identities. Named Lucifer and Lightborne before their fall from grace, they emerge from Hell's fires as characters like Primus and Secundus Demon. It is possible that different actors may have been used in some cases, and indeed the Chester *Fall of Lucifer* highlights this double identity as well as the porous boundary between theatrical and demonic illusion when the devil Lightborne is renamed Ruffyn to suit the gruff and ill-mannered behavior he now displays.[57] Long before Macbeth's "false face" was mocking the time "with fairest show" and hiding his "false heart" (1.7.81–82), devils were believed to be (and actors playing devils certainly were) creating the illusion of transformation.[58]

Remembering and Re-membering the Porter

Using similar dramaturgical technologies to create thunderous sound effects, *Macbeth* reproduces the knocking of the *Harrowing of Hell*. What must be emphasized, however, is that Shakespeare adapts and transforms these acoustic sounds without entirely erasing the previous significance of the knocking.[59] Rather, past theatrical material is brought into the present *as past material.* "Sound in early modern theater," Smith writes, "is important not so much for what it *is* as for what it *signifies.* What audiences actually heard in the theater and what they *imagined* they heard may not always have been the same thing." Drawing from Stephen Handel's work on sound perception, he notes three distinct levels of sound experience. The audience would first of all have perceived certain *physical* phenomena (the noise of trumpets, hautboys, and drums, for instance) as well as elusive *perceptual* phenomena conveyed by these physical sounds ("brightness" in the trumpet, for example, or "pointedness" in the hautboys).

Most important for our discussion of the knocking in *Macbeth* is what Smith describes as "certain imaginative phenomena" that a sound effect, musical instrument, or an actor's speech can "invite" the audience to hear. "By a process of metonymy," Smith explains, "what the audience hears, in the last analysis, is not just physical properties of sound, nor even psychological effects, but the acoustic equivalent of a visual scene—an 'aura,' perhaps."[60] Brass instruments, he suggests, might aurally create a royal or "power scene" while those same instruments coupled with drums and gunfire might suggest combat.

In the previous chapter we noted that the trumpet blasts of buisines signified the impending Doom of the Last Judgment. I am suggesting that Hell, too, had an "aural scene" that Shakespeare's audience would readily have recognized from its experience of provincial mystery drama.[61] Playgoers familiar with the Coventry mystery pageants would have experienced particularly powerful resonances between the castle porter in *Macbeth* and the devil-porter of Hell in the *Harrowing.*[62] Hamlet's warning to the players not to overact (to "out-Herod[ ] Herod," 3.2.12) and the description of Master Slender's "Cain-coloured beard" in *The Merry Wives of Windsor* (1.4.20) are two verbal echoes of the theatrical practices of the mysteries that likewise presuppose audience familiarity with this older dramatic form. Applying Smith's analysis of sound phenomena in the Globe to the knocking at Macbeth's castle gate, therefore, we might say that the acoustics of the Porter scene are temporally ambivalent or double. The audience hears a "perceptual" knocking that it associates with the present action of the play, presumably the arrival of one of the play's characters at the gate. Simultaneously, they experience an "imaginative" knocking or "acoustic equivalent of a visual scene" that would have resonated with the *Harrowing* plays of the recent past. Thus, as the walls of the Globe and the listeners' ears and brains re-member the physical phenomena of the knocking, they are also remembering the aura of Hell from the mysteries. Like the historiography performed by the Chester Banns, the knocking at the gate is diachronic (remembered) as well as synchronic (re-membered).

The actor playing the Porter encourages dramatic remembrance. He opens the gate with the request that Macduff pay him for his services: "I pray you remember the porter" (2.3.20). The line is often delivered so as to amuse the audience with the clown's sudden politeness and propriety. But it is also possible that the Porter addresses this line to the audience. Certainly it was not unusual for stage devils to interrupt the action of the play—particularly at crucial moments—to ask for money from the audience.[63] But what if the Porter is not begging but simply putting the question to them: "Do you remember the porter?" That is, "Do you recall the devil-porters of the mystery plays whom I have just imitated?" Wickham first noted this possibility that the Porter's request "is in two worlds at once; that of Macbeth's castle and that of another scene from another play [namely, the *Harrowing of Hell*] which has just been recalled for the audience and which the author wants them to remember."[64]

The Porter scene derives much of its power—and its comedy—from its temporal ambivalence.[65] Cued by the sound of knocking, the Porter performs a bit of old devil-like behavior from the mysteries. He doesn't simply answer the gate—he "devil-porters" the gate by telling jokes at the expense of Hell's inmates and repeatedly asking "Who's there?" in the manner of the *Attollite portas* rituals. The devils of the *Harrowing* are made present again through the performance of the actor playing the Porter. Yet they are not fully present, for, like Iago, the gatekeeper wears no cloven feet; he is not really a devil but a clown pretending to be a devil.[66] In *Macbeth,* devilish behavior has become a dramatic custom, a stylized role that can be remembered, performed, and then discarded: "I'll devil-porter it no further" (2.3.16).[67]

The Porter scene is a moment in which the Shakespearean stage borrows acoustic stage properties and customary practices from the mysteries, disowns them as not really relevant ("this place is too cold for hell" [2.3.15–16]), and then asks the audience if they recall the old plays. In Smith's terms, the *Harrowing* plays are re-membered and remembered. First, they are made theatrically present again—re-membered—as the thunderous knocks reverberate throughout the Globe and the gatekeeper embodies (by "the expulsion of air, the adjustments of muscle, the shaping of tongue") the traditional behavior of stage devils. But then Shakespeare's play treats the mystery plays as a thing of the past; they are superseded insofar as the actor playing the Porter can ask his audience if they remember them. And in a play where even the slightest imagined hum triggers subsequent dramatic action—"The shard-borne beetle with his drowsy hums / Hath rung night's yawning peal, there shall be done / A deed of dreadful note." (3.2.43–45)—it is a sound, a "Knocke within," that prompts the remembering/re-membering of mystery drama. But I would now like to consider why, following the synchronic re-creation of knocking of the *Harrowing of Hell,* Shakespeare underscores the historical distance of his play from the mysteries—why, like the Banns, he disowns the theatrical past of the mysteries even as he restages a material remnant from that history.

Giving Them the Lie

Having argued that both the sound of knocking in *Macbeth* and its dramatic provenance have material as well as literary significance for the play, I suggest that the Porter scene is a knock-knock joke at the expense of both Shakespeare's royal patron and the religious opponents of the theaters.[68] A knock-knock joke, after all, is a homonymic equivocation that plays upon what Smith calls the "perceptual" and "imaginative" hearing of the audience. For the joke to work, there must be a double hearing: the listener must initially "misidentify" the sound of the knocker's name until the punch line reveals the "mistake." But in fact it is the joke teller (Shakespeare in this case) who punningly misuses sound. He playfully encourages the audience to "hear" Christ at the gate before opening the door to two Scottish lords.

Recent criticism on *Macbeth* has been marked by considerable dispute as to the play's views on Jacobean ideologies and mythologies of kingship. Perhaps the most important contribution to this debate has been Rebecca Lemon's study of the sociopolitical impact of English treason legislation up to and beyond the 1605 Gunpowder Plot. According to Lemon, Shakespeare's responses to treason in *Macbeth* prove more complicated than has traditionally been allowed by critics who believe he courted favor with his royal patron. It is the representation of Malcolm, she argues, through which the play challenges the rhetoric of divine-right kingship with a more "negotiable model" whereby equivocation and other forms of verbal deception so often attributed to traitors prove essential to monarchical rule. Analyzing the rhetorical strategies of scaffold speeches as well as accounts of the Gunpowder Plot, Lemon argues that Shakespeare, after initially contrasting the demonic Macbeths with sacred Scottish kingship, lays bare the fiction of the latter. Both Malcolm and the audience are increasingly implicated in the rhetoric of treason as the play unfolds.[69]

In no scene of the Scottish play are the "demonic Macbeths" more at odds with "sanctified kingship" than when the gate of their castle is imagined as a Hell mouth. And yet the Porter scene has been largely overlooked in this critical debate. If the scene is mentioned, it is usually for its topical reference to the infamous equivocating Jesuit in the Gunpowder Plot, Father Henry Garnet. Alvin Kernan, for example, cites Shakespeare's treatment of Garnet's prevarication as evidence of the playwright's shrewd understanding of royal patronage. The Porter's joke—"an equivocator that could swear in both the scales against either scale, who committed treason enough for God's sake, yet could not equivocate to heaven" (2.3.8–10)—is accordingly a cold and heartless jest calculated to please James, just as the play's borrowings from Holinshed endorse the king's political mythology regarding his divinely ordained prerogative.[70]

Perhaps another reason that the Porter scene is now overlooked when arguing for the play's engagement with resistance theory is that, for nearly two hundred years, it has been read in support of the rhetoric of sacred kingship. The eighteenth century found the Porter too bawdy for "our Poet" and marginalized the scene in print and cut it from performance.[71] In the nineteenth century, however, the Porter scene underwent a stunning reevaluation. No longer superfluous, it became the linchpin of the play's tragic action. Thomas De Quincey's famous essay "On the Knocking at the Gate in *Macbeth*" (1823) is largely responsible for this critical reconsideration. In De Quincey's account, the knocking in the Porter scene closes an "awful parenthesis" of demonic evil following the murder of Duncan. The regicide performed, Macbeth and Lady Macbeth are, he says, "transfigured: Lady Macbeth is 'unsexed'; Macbeth has forgot that he was born of woman; both are conformed to the image of devils; and the world of devils is suddenly revealed." But then comes that "Knocke within," and, De Quincey explains, "when the deed is done, when the work of darkness is perfect, then the world of darkness passes away like a pageantry in the clouds: the knocking at the gate is heard, and it makes known audibly that the reaction has commenced; the human has made its reflux upon the fiendish."[72] De Quincey's reading of the knocking in *Macbeth* as a kind of apotropaic ritual is seductive, particularly in that, like Shakespeare's play itself, it compares Macbeth and Lady Macbeth to hellish fiends.[73]

When, more than a century later, Wickham argued for the scene's indebtedness to medieval *Harrowing* pageants and liturgies, he left De Quincey's "awful parenthesis" largely intact. Although he claims there was "no attempt" by Shakespeare to write *Macbeth* as a "direct parallel" of the *Harrowing,* Wickham nevertheless contends, "Thunder, cacophony, screams and groans were the audible emblems of Lucifer and hell on the medieval stage [and] their relevance to the moral meaning of [*Macbeth*] could scarcely have escaped the notice of its first audiences."[74] For Wickham, as for De Quincey, *Macbeth* is the beneficiary of the *Harrowing*'s black-and-white moral universe such that, by act 5, "Scotland has been purged of a devil who, like Lucifer, aspired to a throne that was not his…and was finally crushed within the refuge of his own castle by a saviour-avenger accompanied by armed archangels. Hell has been harrowed: 'the time is free.'"[75]

According to Wickham, therefore, the play didactically replicates the moral absolutes of the *Harrowing:* Macbeth and his queen are demonic fiends; Macduff and Malcolm are agents of divine recompense; Inverness represents Hell Castle; fair is fair and foul is foul. Not surprisingly, therefore, the import of the line "I pray you remember the porter" (2.3.20) for Wickham is not its retrospection on the *Harrowing* plays per se but its foreshadowing. If the audience interprets the request to remember the porter as referring to the devil-porters of mystery drama, then, he says, they cannot fail to "recollect that it was Jesus who with a loud knocking entered Hell-castle in search of Satan." The play, therefore, though barely into its second act and in the middle of a seemingly insignificant comic interlude, already signals its resolution.[76] As with De Quincey, then, the Porter scene in Wickham's account anticipates the conclusion of the play when good triumphs over evil and "the time is free" (5.11.21).

This morally straightforward reading of the play echoes the views King James espoused in *Basilikon Doron,* the 1599 treatise on government written in the form of a private letter to his eldest son and heir, Henry, but published in London after his accession to the throne. James asserts that the way to tell a good king from a tyrant is not only how he conducts himself in life but how he leaves it. "A good Kinge," he writes, "dyeth in peace, lamented by his subjectes, admyred by his Neighbours," whereas

> a Tyrantes miserable and in-famous life, armeth in ende his owne subjectes to become his burreaux: And although that rebellion bee euer vnlawfull on their parte, yet is the worlde so wearied of him, that his fall is little meaned by the reste of his subjectes, and but smyled at by his neighboures.[77]

Whereas Wickham reads the Porter scene (and indeed the entire play) as an earnest endorsement of Jacobean claims to sacred authority, I believe that it is an elaborate knock-knock joke. The Porter scene first offers a tantalizingly straightforward reading of history in which a "saviour-avenger accompanied by armed archangels" rescues and guards the Scottish crown. But this is like the first response to "Who's there?" in a knock-knock joke. A double hearing is required. Shakespeare's audience is invited to hear not only the past context of the knocking but also its present significance. If they listen carefully, in fact, they hear the Porter overturn the association with the *Harrowing*: "this place is too cold for hell" (2.3.14–15). And the aura of the *Harrowing* is shattered when the flawed Macduff knocks and enters, not the Christ-like Malcolm—and certainly not James's ancestor, the "true, worthy Banquo" (1.4.54).

Contrary to Wickham's account, the conspicuous absence of a Christ-like savior reemerges at the conclusion of the play, which brings not the utter defeat of evil and the establishment of godly rule but moral and political uncertainty. Its ending eerily resembles its opening: a supposedly pious and virtuous yet still untested king sits on the throne of Scotland, backed by a deadly and determined military leader, while the three witches presumably continue to "meet again" (1.1.1) and brew mischief and destruction. More disturbingly, the whereabouts and intentions of the greatest threat to this fragile state, Banquo's heir, are unknown. These uncertainties, and their resemblance to the events in act 1, cast doubt on De Quincey's awful parenthesis as it seems that Scottish history is thoroughly dark with ambition, intrigue, murder, and war.[78] Shakespeare's play dramatizes flawed heroes and regretful villains with acute moral awareness. Macbeth himself is not exempt from the "violent sorrow" Ross describes (4.3.170).[79] Overcome with guilt from the murders she has abetted, Lady Macbeth fears the dark as if she were in Hell[80] and clings to the merest taper that will "peep through the blanket of the dark" (1.5.51):

Doctor

How came she by that light?

Gentlewoman

Why, it stood by her. She has light by her
continually. 'Tis her command.

(5.1.18–20)

The play equivocates: it creates a murky, ambiguous world that refuses the moral antinomies of the *Harrowing* scenes it simultaneously invites its audience to remember.[81]

Indeed, it is quite possible that the *Harrowing* inspired the theme of a ceaseless and unresolved confrontation between good and evil. Though it is one of the last episodes in the cycle, this mystery pageant performed the restraint of Satan's rule, not his absolute destruction. As souls are being freed from Limbo, Jesus or Saint Michael often puts the devil in chains. In the Chester *Harrowing* Sathanas groans,

Owt, alas! Nowe goes awaye
all my prisoners and my praye [prey];
and I myselfe may not starte awaye,
I am so stretyle tyed.

(221–24)

Satan undergoes a similar fate in the *Harrowing of Hell* in York's cycle:

Jesus

Mighill [Michael], myne aungell, make the boune
And feste yone fende that he noght flitte.
And, Deuyll, I comaunde the go doune
Into thy selle, where thou schalte sitte.

Sattan

Owt! Ay, herrowe! Helpe, Mahounde!
Now wex I woode oute of my witte.

. . . .

Allas, for dole and care,
I synke into helle pitte.

(339–44, 347–48)

The restraint of the devil anticipates his eternal imprisonment in Hell at the Last Judgment, but he is still free to send his agents—"murd'ring ministers" (1.5.46) like the weird sisters—into the world to cause harm. In fact, the premise of the subsequent *Antichrist* play is that the *Harrowing of Hell* did not complete the story of humanity's salvation. Who knows when Christ will return or what demonic hurly-burly will be done in the long interim until the Final Doom?

Scotland is not Hell, and the murky chronicle histories of its kings are not quite so fair as James would have them. As with the punning use of sound in a knock-knock joke, Shakespeare's mocking of Jacobean political theology relies on an acoustic gap or distance between *Macbeth* and the mysteries as much as on their aural resonance. I am not making an argument for Shakespearean sophistication at the expense of medieval simplicity, for, as scholars have shown, stage devilry in the mysteries was itself highly nuanced and politically subversive. Cox, for example, sees a "political pattern" running through all the major mystery play cycles, a pattern that joins disobedience and pride with social clout, affluence, and authority.[82] Responding to this "feudal reading," Robert Barrett suggests that the Chester *Fall of Lucifer* is less "a palace revolt" than it is an engagement with the city's political ideologies and institutions in which Lucifer's power grab is self-consciously analogous to civic oligarchy.[83] These brief examples of the politics of demonic performance further illustrate why Shakespeare may have borrowed from the mysteries in order to engage in resistance theory: by the time *Macbeth* is written, devils had long been used to stage "abuses of power by the powerful."[84]

Only if the re-membered knocking brings the theatrical past into the imaginative present can the play provoke and unprovoke the king's fantasy of godly rule. Once we appreciate the scene's moral—and temporal—ambivalence, the Porter's assertion "But this place is too cold for hell" (2.3.15–16) does more than simply mark the transition from comedy back to tragedy; it becomes an ideological refutation of James's *Basilikon Doron* insofar as it denies that "this place" (Scotland) is a realm where "the true difference betuixt a lawfull good King, & a vsurping Tyrant" can be so easily delineated.[85] That is not to deny the "structural antithesis" that, as Peter Stallybrass argues, so strikingly distinguishes Shakespeare's play from Holinshed's account.[86] It is to note, in fact, that the knocking-at-the-gate scene is an important source of antithesis. And second, it is to suggest that the play may structure itself antithetically but still expose the untenability of moral and political absolutism. *Macbeth,* as Lemon argues, initially opposes the evil plots and sedition of the Macbeths with sacred kingship but subsequently exposes the fiction of such triumphalist narratives by implicating Macduff, and indeed the audience itself, in treasonous conspiracies against the crown.[87]

Popish Progeny

Aside from these political considerations, Shakespeare may have had more self-interested reasons for first evoking and then disavowing the *Harrowing.* Recalling from chapter 2 the manner in which antitheatricalists repeatedly compared the London stages to popery and pre-Reformation Catholic drama, then perhaps the Porter scene is a joke at their expense as well. In his *Playes Confuted in Five Actions* (1582), Stephen Gosson admits that Gregory Naziancen, one of the fathers of the church, wrote a Passion play, yet he claims that it was merely an edifying closet drama, not a blasphemous stage production:

> For Naziancen detesting the corruption of the Corpus Christi Playes
> that were set out by the Papistes, and inueighing against them, thought
> it better to write the passion of Christ in numbers himselfe, that all
> such as delight in numerositie of speach might read it, not beholde
> it vpon the Stage, where some base fellowe that plaide Christe, should
> bring the person of Christ into contempt.[88]

Gosson not only projects Corpus Christi drama back to the fourth century but, more important, makes no effort to distinguish between ancient and modern, pagan and papist theatrical forms. In fact, he eagerly yokes them together on account of their fleshly idolatry—all are the "pompe, the plaies, the inuetions of the Diuell"—in order to call for the eradication of contemporary English theater. "Haue we sinned with the Gentiles in representinge of theire Playes?" he asks, admonishing: "Let vs learne with true Christians to abolish them."[89] Gosson's historical account of English theater was commonplace, as Cooper notes regarding the polemics of John Northbrooke and Henry Crosse, who also condemned stage performance whether sacred or secular.[90]

Macbeth seems to enjoy arousing antitheatricalist desires to tie the public playhouses to pre-Reformation drama, a point that may help to advance current critical conversations about Shakespeare's response to Reformation fears concerning theater and idolatry. Whereas, for example, the famous statue scene in *The Winter's Tale* is often said to realize the worst nightmares of Puritan opponents to the professional stage, Huston Diehl argues that the theatricality of Hermione's statue may have less to do with Roman Catholic idolatry than with Pauline texts, which would have been lately rediscovered and reclaimed by Protestant theologians.[91] Nevertheless, she does agree with O'Connell and others that Shakespeare willfully flirts with dangerous religious topics in order to arouse suspicions that his dramatic spectacles are forbidden Roman idols.[92]

Whether or not the statue of Hermione is Pauline or popish, it shares with the knocking in *Macbeth* a sense of Shakespeare's noticeable boldness toward puritanical opposition in his late career. And here I think the Chester Banns may help us to see that perhaps we too eagerly anticipate the 1642 closure of the theaters and thus overestimate the Puritan threat to the London stage in the early decades of the seventeenth century. Radical religious opposition to early English drama was not necessarily met with anxious timidity and polite acquiescence. Faced with theological opposition from preachers like Christopher Goodman, the Late Banns nonetheless embraced the monastic authorship of their civic pageants. As the early seventeenth-century gloss of the Banns' second stanza reads: "This moncke was of the most esteimed a godly man and religeose in those dayes." The Banns are also untroubled by the fact that some dramatic elements, like the *Harrowing,* lacked strict biblical authority. The author-monk, they say,

> Intermminglinge therewithe onely to make sporte
> Some thinges not warranted by anye wrytte
> Which glad the hartes he woulde men to take hit.

Chester audiences are further encouraged to supply the deficiencies of the plays with "noe wante of good will."[93] Shakespeare's attitude toward religious antitheatricalists mirrors the self-assurance and good humor of the Chester Banns. Both *Macbeth* and *The Winter's Tale* (written within a few years of each other, around 1606 and 1609, respectively) flaunt their proximity to pre-Reformation drama and religious practice. In fact, with its comic transformation of the *Harrowing* into a series of jokes about drunkenness and lechery, the Porter scene seems quite guilty of the charge leveled at the theater in Philip Stubbes's *Anatomie of Abuses* (1583): "they [are] most intollerable, or rather Sacrilegious, for… the price of Christ his bloud, & the merits of his passion, were not giuen, to be derided, and iested at as they be in these filthie playes and enterluds."[94] Like the Banns, the Porter scene would have us "make sporte" of this sacrilege.

The Porter scene is no ordinary jest but, as we noted with regard to the Jacobean politics of the play, a homonymic pun that toys with the audience's interpretation of the knocking. When the "Knocke within" is first heard at 2.2.54, the Macbeths are still on stage, and the audience naturally assumes that one of the play's characters is at the gate. But as the Porter enters and says, "If a man were porter of hell-gate," the knocking and the action of devil-portering begin to confirm the worst fears of the theater's religious opponents by suggesting that the mystery plays are not, in fact, superseded after all. Like the two role-players in a knock-knock joke, the Porter and the audience are, in Wickham's words, "in two worlds at once; that of Macbeth's castle and that of another scene from another play [the *Harrowing*]." Line 2.3.20 ("remember the porter") is the punch line, for as he says these words, the Porter opens the gate and Macduff and Lennox enter. The temporal ambivalence catalyzed by the re-membered sound reverberating around the Globe now ends, and as the noise fades, the audience gets the joke: "Who did you think it was—Christ?"

Whereas Heywood's *Apology* (discussed in chapter 2) is at pains to distance professional theater from pre-Reformation religious drama, the anticlimactic entrance of Macduff and Lennox laughs off the dangerous proximity of *Macbeth* to the mystery plays. Shakespeare lets his audience believe what they want about the relationship between the two forms of drama as the scene knavishly makes and mars the polemical narratives of the theater's most vituperative enemies. From this perspective it becomes clear that pre-Reformation dramatic material was not entirely feared or spurned but rather quite attractive to theater companies always eager for new material. True, they were prohibited from staging some volatile religious topics, yet the iconoclasm and censorship introduced by the Reformation were in some ways a boon for the London playhouses. Besides the liturgies and dogmas that, according to Greenblatt, were "emptied out" and reimagined for commercial theater, religious upheaval led to the prohibition of mystery drama and thereby provided more direct—and more material—dramatic resources. As a craftsman of plays, the playwright Shakespeare could recycle the stage properties, costumes, and sound effects of the mystery play pageant wagons and refashion them to suit his purposes.

Critical discussion of the Porter scene in *Macbeth* has suffered from historical bifurcation: either the scene is significant for its topical allusions to Garner's equivocation, or else the medieval antecedent of the *Harrowing of Hell* is discussed. I have argued for the synchronic diachrony of the knocking at the gate in order to suggest that the play exploits the past to gain present political leverage. Or rather (if we put aside our tendency to privilege the modern at the expense of the medieval) the past, by virtue of its obsolescence, asserts its topicality.

Epilogue

Riding the Banns beyond Shakespeare

> What matter who's speaking?
> —Foucault

To appreciate Shakespeare's stagecraft we must first undermine his authorial immortality and question his originality. To the extent that we continue to view Shakespeare not only as *the* author—the pinnacle figure of English letters—but even *an* author or originator, we will continue to buttress the medieval-Renaissance divide and abstract him from medieval dramatic artifacts. For, as Michel Foucault explains, "The name of the author remains at the contours of texts—separating one from the other, defining their form, and characterizing their mode of existence."[1] The Chester Banns help to free us from this "author function" by conceiving a history of early English drama, including Shakespearean drama, as a genealogy of theatrical objects and practices produced and re-created through the cooperative crafts of actor and playwright. This displacement of the subjective self-reflexivity of individual authors has significant consequences, for it aids current scholarly efforts to view the professional plays of the London stage as more deeply intertwined with pre- and post-Reformation drama. And it becomes possible to seek further material links between Shakespeare and the mysteries—and between other forms of sixteenth-century drama and the plays of other commercial playwrights. This epilogue therefore sketches some of those possibilities in an effort to suggest further lines of critical inquiry. More than simply gesturing beyond Shakespeare, I propose that the Banns can guide us in areas of study where their unique perspective on early drama might seem least promising. I will briefly assay three such improbable points: not John Bale's tragedy of *King John* but Shakespeare's history plays, a genre ostensibly far removed from biblical pageants and morality tales; not the hellish fall of Doctor Faustus but a city comedy by the devout humanist Ben Jonson whom, unlike Marlowe, we might expect to shun any dramatic material smacking of "the medieval"; and not material remnants of the mysteries found in the contemporaneous plays of Bale and Marlowe but stage properties used by acting companies well into the seventeenth century, even as late as 1640, not long before the professional theaters would be banned—and long, long after we might expect to find any influence of the mysteries.

A Game of Thrones

Previous chapters explored material remnants of mystery drama in Shakespearean comedy and tragedy, but the catalog of plays in the 1623 First Folio included another genre: the histories. The stories told in these plays originated from medieval chronicles, yet their props, costumes, settings, and stagecraft seem far removed from the salvation history of the mystery cycles. Setting aside the Vice figure Richard III and the succuba Joan la Pucelle, it is tempting to remove this entire group of plays from any further consideration. Moreover, some of the material remnants of mystery drama we have explored have been rather exotic, not to mention controversial, and we might not expect that mundane objects peculiar to the secular politics of the histories could have been drawn from biblical drama. But the royal throne in Shakespeare's *Henry VI, Part 3* begs closer examination. No single stage property, with the exception of the crown, could be said to encapsulate the protracted power struggles of both tetralogies.

But many decades before the throne became the locus point of Shakespeare's War of the Roses, it was the centerpiece of another civil war. In the Chester *Fall of Lucifer,* God, or Deus, appoints Lucifer as governor over the nine orders of angels and in doing so places the chief angel's seat next to his own—"here I set you nexte my cheare" (88). Before withdrawing to survey the realm he has recently created, however, God forbids Lucifer from touching or even approaching the throne of the Godhead:

> I have forbid that ye neare shoulde;
> but keepe you well in that stature.
>
> . . . .

> For I will wende and take my trace
> and see this blesse in every tower.
>
> (106–7, 110–11)

No sooner does God disappear "To be revisible in shorte space" (124), than Lucifer is drawn to the seat of divine knowledge and power: "All in this throne yf that I were, / then shoulde I be as wise as hee" (130–31). After a debate between the loyal and rebellious angels, the throne again becomes the focus of dramatic action as Lucifer declares, "Though God come, I will not hense, / but sitt righte here before his face" (212–13). The very instant that he seats himself upon the throne, Deus reappears and demands to know "Lucifer, who set thee here when I was goe?" (222). Having once sat "so nighe [God's] majesty" (227), the trespasser now falls "into the deepe pitt of hell ever to bee" (229). As a stage direction in the Chester *Harrowing of Hell* indicates, Satan later acquires a chair of his own in the castle of Hell.[2]

Aside from its religious significance, the scene simultaneously explores earthly power dynamics. As Robert Barrett argues, the Heaven described in the Chester *Fall of Lucifer* is a chartered borough, and the play spatially works out the social tensions created within its precincts. At the center of this fraught political space, it must be emphasized, is the throne, which Barrett's reading uncovers as a seat of both divine and civic authority.[3] Lucifer's attempt to occupy this material space catalyzes the plot of the Chester tanners' pageant—and indeed the entire three-day cycle. In the York *Fall of the Angels,* God's throne is also the conspicuous object of Lucifer's pride, and the moment he seats himself upon it and proclaims that he is "worthy and exalted" ("derworth and defte"), he and his fellow rebels fall into perdition:

> Ther sall I set myselfe full semely to seyghte,
> To ressayue [receive] my reuerence thorowe righte o renowne;
> I sall be lyke vnto hym that es hyeste on heghte.
> Owe, what I am derworth and defte—Owe! Dewes [Deus]! All goes downe!
> My mighte and my mayne es all marrande—
> Helpe, felawes! In faythe, I am fallande.
>
> (90–95)

The throne scenes of Shakespeare's *3 Henry VI* do not secularize the mystery plays so much as admire and share their shrewd insight. With his craftsman's eye, Shakespeare could spy the dramatic potential built into stage properties, and in *The Fall of Lucifer,* he found a powerful catalyst proven to instantly awaken dramatic tension and drive the plot of a play. Neither the 1595 octavo text of *The True Tragedy of Richard Duke of York* nor the folio text of *The Third Part of King Henry the Sixth* mentions the chair of state in the stage directions, but this does not diminish its importance. For one thing, as Alan Dessen and Leslie Thomson have established, stage directions mention seats of royalty much less often than they were used onstage; in fact, the only time that a Shakespearean stage direction specifies the word "throne" is when Richard III "ascendeth the throne" (*Richard III,* 4.2.3 s.d.).[4]

As the opening scene of *3 Henry VI* unfolds, we hardly need stage directions to appreciate the central importance of the chair of state. Warwick's address to Richard explicitly points out "the regal seat":

> Before I see thee seated in that throne
> Which now the house of Lancaster usurps,
> I vow by heaven these eyes shall never close.
> This is the palace of the fearful King,
> And this [*pointing to the chair of state*], the regal seat—possess it, York,
> For this is thine, and not King Henry's heirs'.
>
> (1.1.22–27)

Shakespeare uses several notable stage properties at the beginning of the play, including bloody swords and a severed head. These props help to bring the audience up-to-date by symbolically recapitulating the action of the previous play, *The First Part of the Contention betwixt the Two Famous Houses of York and Lancaster* (*2 Henry VI*). The chair of state, however, is another matter. Introduced by Warwick's ominous vow, it redirects the audience's attention toward impending tragic action. They immediately recognize that his "is" ("For this is thine") is precipitous, and the subsequent action of the scene—the initial verbal clash of the two rival factions in the play—bears out the irony of his statement.

Both *The Fall of Lucifer* and *3 Henry VI* conspicuously stage a vacant throne, as if the spectacle of the empty chair itself tempts or beckons would-be usurpers. Moreover, just as the heavenly throne had divided the angelic choirs, so the chair of state in act 1, scene 1 of *3 Henry VI* sparks debate, divides factions, inspires encomium, and prompts rebuke and censure. The seat used by the Lord Chamberlain's Men is more than a material metonym for English sovereignty or the current political upheaval: like an actor, it plays a role on stage by commanding the attention of both competing parties, York and Lancaster, who allude directly to it no fewer than seven times in the opening scene alone. Shakespeare directly imitates the action of the mysteries by having conflict erupt at the precise moment that the ambitious claimant seats himself on the unoccupied throne:

Warwick

Resolve thee, Richard—claim the English crown.
[York sits in the chair. Flourish. Enter King Henry, Clifford, Northumberland, Westmoreland, and the rest.]

King Henry

My lords, look where the sturdy rebel sits—
Even in the chair of state! Belike he means,
Backed by the power of Warwick, that false peer,
To aspire unto the crown and reign as king.

(1.1.49–53)

It is peculiar that Henry calls his companions' attention not to the person of Richard Plantagenet per se but to "where the sturdy rebel sits— / Even in the chair of state!" His objection would have seemed even stranger to a Globe audience governed by treason laws that encompassed not merely the act but the intent to depose the monarch. Both the Chester *Fall of Lucifer* and the York *Fall of the Angels* serve as dramatic precedents for the king's indignant response to York's self-enthronement. In both mystery plays Lucifer proudly boasts of his beauty and rank and expresses his desire to rule over his peers, but God does not banish him for his sin of pride or ambitious intentions—until he physically seizes the throne.

But Shakespeare goes further. As in *The Fall of Lucifer*, the entire action of the play is premised upon the seat of majesty; we may also say that by bracketing the play with throne scenes in act 1, scene 1 and act 5, scene 7, he imitates the mystery cycles: the plot is set in motion with a dethronement and culminates with a figure seated in majesty and declaring,

Once more we sit in England's royal throne,
Repurchased with the blood of enemies.
What valiant foemen, like to autumn's corn,
Have we mowed down in tops of all their pride!

. . . .

Thus have we swept suspicion from our seat
And made our footstool of security.

(5.7.1–4, 13–14)

King Edward's words are more than a descriptive statement of fact; they summarize the events of the play as a struggle for the chair on which he sits.

Though he reigns over his enemies, who, like Lucifer, are punished for their pride, he will not achieve the final surety and fulfillment of the *Last Judgment*. In fact, his brother Richard of Gloucester's asides redirect the audience to other well-known scenes from the mystery plays, including the blasted harvests of Egypt and the treachery of Judas: "To say the truth, so Judas kissed his master, / And cried 'All hail!' whenas he meant all harm" (5.7.33–34). Richard's comments forebode that the throne will continue to inspire rebellion and division, and even when he "ascendeth the throne" to become Richard III, he confides to Buckingham his fear that his high seat will not prove everlasting:

> Thus high by thy advice
> And thy assistance is King Richard seated.
> But shall we wear these glories for a day?
> Or shall they last, and we rejoice in them?
>
> *(Richard III,* 4.2.4–7)

Shakespeare was undoubtedly an innovator of the emergent dramatic form of history, but the throne in *3 Henry VI* illustrates how he worked as a craftsman of plays. Faced with the challenge of quickly resuming the feud begun in *The First Part of the Contention* (*2 Henry VI*), he draws upon *The Fall of Lucifer* as an exemplary model and in fact borrows the essential theatrical set piece of that pageant as a material framework upon which to build his scene. The raw material of Holinshed's *Chronicles* is then cut, shaped, and molded onto this prototype. We've seen how exotic pieces like the ass's head inspired Shakespeare's dramatic craft, but the throne in *3 Henry VI* asks us to consider the possibility that supposedly commonplace, secular stage objects might have extraordinary theatrical provenances that include pre-Reformation religious drama.

Jonson's "New Play"

The popular London city comedies had been abundantly lucrative for the various professional companies for nearly two decades[5] when, in 1616, the prologue of Ben Jonson's latest contribution to the genre boldly announced:

> 'The Devil is an Ass.' That is, today,
> The name of what you are met for, a new play.
>
> . . . .
>
>   If you'll come
> To see new plays, pray you afford us room,
> And show this but the same face you have done
> Your dear delight, 'The Devil of Edmonton.'
>
> . . . .

> And when six times you ha' seen 't,
> If this play do not like, the devil is in 't.
>
> (1–2, 19–23, 25–26)[6]

Wishing to present *Devil* as new and fashionable, Jonson is keenly aware of theatrical history. He hopes, for example, that audiences will greet the play with the same enthusiasm afforded to the anonymous *Devil of Edmonton,* which had been periodically performed since 1602. And he alludes playfully to the less successful *If This Be Not a Good Play, the Devil Is in It* (1611) by Thomas Dekker. Beyond these two brief topical allusions, the novelty that Jonson claims for *Devil* is achieved—throughout the play—at the expense of much older dramatic forms, particularly plays in the morality tradition. The play's first scene is set in Hell, where Satan tells an ambitious young devil named Pug that his strategy for carrying a Vice with him to London to tempt its inhabitants is hopelessly out-of-date:

> Remember
> What number it is: six hundred and sixteen.
> Had it been but five hundred—though some sixty
> Above, that's fifty years agone, and six—
> When every great man had his Vice stand by him
> In his long coat, shaking his wooden dagger,
> I could consent that then this your grave choice
> Might have done that with his lord chief, the which
> Most of his chamber can do now.
>
> (1.1.80–88)

Satan, like the play itself, dismisses the "old Iniquities" (118) typically found in Tudor moral interludes. As in the Chester Banns, the identity of a play, or in this case an entire genre of plays, is represented by its accustomed stage properties: the long coat and wooden dagger of the Vice.

But for all his laughter at outdated dramatic conventions, Jonson nevertheless borrows a number of them, or at least alludes to them. Though Satan and Pug are undoubtedly dressed as conventional stage devils, Jonson later satirizes the traditional feature of these costumes, cloven feet:

Fitzdottrel

> I looked o' your feet afore; you cannot cozen me,
> Your shoe's not cloven, sir, you are whole hoofed.
> *He views his feet again.*

Pug

Sir, that's a popular error, deceives many.
But I am that I tell you.

Fitzdottrel

What's your name?

Pug

My name is Devil, sir.

(1.3.28–32)

Pug not only fails miserably to outfox London's deceitful inhabitants, but he is arrested for the possession of stolen goods and taken to Newgate Prison. Satan and the Vice Iniquity arrive in act 5, scene 6 to set the young imp free:

Satan

But up, away with him—
Iniquity takes [Pug] on his back.

Iniquity

Mount, darling of darkness, my shoulders are broad:
He that carries the fiend is sure of his load.
The devil was wont to carry away the evil;
But now the evil out-carries the devil.

(5.6.73–77)

In Tudor moralities, the Vice often rode offstage on the devil's shoulders, but Jonson reverses these roles. His announcement "But now the evil out-carries the devil" once again proclaims the play's novelty to the audience: its departure from outmoded stage practices that they were "wont" to see is underscored.

But the historical break that the play accomplishes rhetorically is mitigated by its material practices. For the scene of Pug's rescue not only recalls morality play conventions but is a hilarious inversion of the *Harrowing of Hell* from the mysteries, and the King's Men would have relied upon stage technologies from that dramatic tradition to achieve the sights, sounds, and smells of Hell dungeon:

*A great noise is heard in Newgate. [Enter Shackles and] the
Keepers, affrighted.*

Shackles

Oh me!

1 Keeper

   What's this?

2 Keeper

          A piece of Justice Hall

Is broken down.

3 Keeper

          Faugh! What a steam of brimstone

Is here!

 . . .

4 Keeper

This's strange!

3 Keeper

   And savours of the devil strongly!

2 Keeper

I ha' the sulphur of hell-coal i' my nose.

(5.7.1–3, 9–10)

Devil's repeated claims to novelty are conspicuous and often noted by editors and critics. But the synchronic diachrony of the Chester Banns helps us to see that Jonson's ascription of novelty to his play may be generically driven. For the Banns have taught us that obsolete theatrical materials may inspire new dramatic creation by virtue of their very obsolescence.

By 1615–16 Jonson may have been looking for a fresh approach to the relatively new but popular and increasingly familiar genre of city comedy. He found it, oddly enough, in the old genres of morality and mystery drama. Even the old allegorical personifications are thinly disguised with modern names. Instead of encountering Vice figures named Ambidexter, Subtle Shift, or Myscheff, we meet the "projector" Merecraft and the broker Engine, schemers who profit from royal monopolies and other deceptions familiar to Jonson's seventeenth-century audience. Other names join a character's profession, rank, or gender to his or her moral reputation, including the lawyer Sir Paul Eitherside, Fitzdottrel the Norfolk squire, and the projectress Lady

Tailbush and her female attendant, Pitfall. Encouraged by the deft historiography of the Banns, which ascribe novel interpretations to accustomed stage practices borrowed from a past time of supposed ignorance and superstition, we might venture a more controversial claim: in spite of its recognizable citizens, familiar London locations (e.g., Newgate Prison), and awareness of recent popular plays (e.g., *Devil of Edmonton*), city comedy is not entirely a new genre; it is traditional morality playing that has been dressed in topical, metropolitan attire.

The Theatrical Resurrection of Tombs

With their attention to accustomed stage properties and practices rather than canonical authors, the Chester Banns urge us to take a fundamentally different approach to the history of early English drama. And yet, as this book has demonstrated, their sixteenth-century perspective also reaffirms and supports the recent cross-period engagements of other scholars, medievalists and early modernists alike. Elizabeth Williamson's *The Materiality of Religion in Early Modern English Drama* offers one such opportunity to show how the synchronic diachrony of the Banns may reinforce our understanding of commercial stagecraft well into the seventeenth century. Williamson's chapter entitled "'Things Newly Performed': Tomb Properties and the Survival of the Dramatic Tradition" examines the commercial theater's interest in the popular trope of stage resurrections. Taking her cue from Shakespeare's description of Hermione's statue in *The Winter's Tale* (1610) as a "piece many years in doing, and now newly performed" (5.2.86–87), she argues that this play and Webster's *The Duchess of Malfi* (1614) represent, among others, "plays that inherited a powerful material technology from their medieval predecessors which they endowed with a new type of emotional charge."[7] In chapter 3, I termed this process of inheritance and innovation "translation," and in chapter 5 I discussed the London commercial theater's unique ability to re-member and re-member mystery drama.

For Williamson, however, what is most striking about Shakespeare's and Webster's use of resurrection tropes is "their ability to tap into this tradition without directly importing the material technology."[8] We have observed a similar phenomenon with regard to the absent and out-of-date (yet still quite familiar) cloven-footed stage devil costume referred to in *Macbeth, Othello,* and Jonson's *Devil.* We have also noted the opposite phenomenon, in particular the Late Banns' incredibly deft, and rather stunning, reinterpretation of the gilt masks worn by Deus and Christ as signifiers of divine absence rather than physical presence. If the Banns demonstrate the remarkable resiliency of certain material remnants, then Williamson's study of tomb properties on the commercial London stage further suggests that, even in their absence, material technologies shaped dramatic production. Yet the King's Men remained materially invested in tomb properties and recuperated that investment in a series of plays beginning in the first decade of the seventeenth century until late into the third. It may very well be that the successful reworking of "resurrection affect" in *The Winter's Tale* and elsewhere relied substantially upon the continued (if periodic) exhibition of this stage prop.[9] Here, too, early modern subjective emotions and the stage conventions that give rise to them remain tethered to supposedly bygone medieval artifacts.

I would add to Williamson's fascinating study the point that the influence of mystery pageant technologies on the resurrection topos may extend beyond pageant scenes depicting either tombs or resurrections. *Harrowing of Hell* pageants celebrate that moment when Christ suddenly appears, often with an angel bearing heavenly light, to free the languishing souls over whom Satan presides from his throne.[10] The Chester play opens with an intriguing stage direction calling for a kind of special-effect lighting: "First let some cunning device be used to make a visible light appear in Hell, and then Adam shall speak."[11] As with a performance of *Macbeth* at Shakespeare's Globe, the *Harrowing of Hell* was a daytime performance, and therefore the play must combine props, language, and gesture to convey the blackness of Hell's smoky dungeon. The light produced by "some cunning device" would also signify surrounding darkness to the audience. The speech of the Prophet Isaiah reiterates the visual spectacle of *lux in inferno*:

> Yea, secerlye, this ilke light
> comys from Goddes Sonne almight,
> for so I prophecyed aright
> whyle that I was livinge.
> Then I to all men beheight,
> As I goostlye sawe in sight,
> these wordes that I shall to might
> rehearse withowt tarienge:
> *Populus qui ambulabat in tenebris vidit lucem magnam.* [The people who walked in darkness have seen a great light (Isaiah 9:2)]
>
> (25–32)

As Clifford Davidson notes, many of the surviving manuscripts of *Harrowing* plays indicate that Isaiah's prophecy was accompanied by some sort of "glorious gleme" to "make glad those who have waited in darkness in the prisonhouse of limbo."[12]

Recollection of the important stage business from the *Harrowing* allows us to make two important observations. First, *Harrowing* plays performed the kinds of tombless resurrections that Williamson finds in *The Winter's Tale*. The deliverance of souls from Limbo was certainly quite different from Hermione's reanimation, but the *Descensus ad Inferos* achieved the kind of "resurrection affect" that interests Williamson and may have inspired Shakespeare to create a similar theatrical experience without the need for a tomb. Second, as the Banns have demonstrated throughout this book, traditional objects and practices do not calcify dramatic performance into what E. K. Chambers called "dry bones" awaiting an authorial genius; rather, they themselves inspire innovation. Commercial companies might choose, for example, to combine remnants of the *Harrowing* with materials from other mystery pageants, such as a tomb used for resurrection plays. *Harrowing* plays often featured two important stage technologies that signified the liberation of souls: some sort of *lux in inferno* and gates that would open or collapse from the force of Christ's thunderous knocking. Just as professional London playhouses housed tombs, Hell mouths, and other material remnants of the mysteries, it appears that they also preserved and modified the special lighting effects and crashing gates once used in the *Harrowing*.

A detailed stage direction in Thomas Middleton's 1611 *The Maiden's Tragedy* (sometimes referred to as *The Second Maiden's Tragedy*) seems to suggest that the King's Men combined the stage business of the *Harrowing* with a tomb resurrection: "On a sudden in a kind of noise like a wind, the doors clattering, the tombstone flies open and a great light appears in the midst of the tomb. Enter the Ghost of the Lady, as she was last seen, standing just before him all in white."[13] The possession of this technology would seem to indicate the company's familiarity with *Harrowing of Hell* scenes and the mysteries in general. Change "the Lady" to "Anima Christi," and the stage direction from *The Maiden's Tragedy* might describe the climactic moment in a *Harrowing* play. The fact that the Lady appears to be standing motionless "as she was last seen" suggests that she was raised onto the stage from the trapdoor, like *Hamlet*'s ghost but also in a manner reminiscent of the souls in the *Last Judgment* or the *Raising of Lazarus* or even *The Coming of Antichrist*. The King's Men may also have found other uses for some of this machinery, including the harrowing of Pug from Newgate Prison in Jonson's *Devil*.

According to John Russell Brown, the fascinating stage direction from *The Maiden's Tragedy* suggests that a similar device is used in act 5, scene 3 of *The Duchess of Malfi* (1614) when Antonio thinks he sees the Duchess speaking from her grave (5.3.44–45).[14] It may be true that Webster's use of the incorporeal echo proves more innovative insofar as it commands a powerful audience response without the spectacle of a miraculous resurrection from a tomb, yet I would argue that the empty tomb property itself remains as essential to the scene as the ethereal voice of the Duchess.[15] Indeed, to appreciate Webster's achievement here, we need to take the vacant sepulchre into account: for *The Duchess of Malfi* fully and successfully exploits the emotional affect long conditioned in audiences by resurrection plays while nimbly eluding the censor's pen and the charge of mocking the scriptures with a lewd woman's return from the dead.

Throughout this book I have argued against teleological models and secularization theories (however revised, localized, or vexed), not only because they have their origins in the reification of the Renaissance and its authorial subjects, but also because they are incomplete: they tell only part of the story. For if Webster's *Duchess* participates in a long tradition of resurrection scenes dating from the mysteries *but also including plays by Shakespeare and Middleton,* then attempts to explain Webster's stagecraft as the theater's desire to assert itself as a social practice independent of religion are inadequate. Teleology and secularization may appear to help us talk about the historical differences brought about by the English Reformation (though I do not believe that they do), but they cannot account for post-Reformation theatrical borrowing among professional playwrights themselves, particularly metatheatrically charged appropriations like the staging of "Hieronymo's old cloak, ruff, and hat" in Jonson's *Alchemist* (4.7.71).[16] The Banns, on the other hand, do offer a better purchase on post-Reformation theatrical recuperation. They call our attention to the long afterlives of dramatic objects and technologies. And their interest in traditional stage objects and practices is carefully balanced against a profound and urgent awareness of the present and the need to appear up-to-date. In this way, they open exciting new possibilities by encouraging us to consider the vagrancy of theatrical clothing as well as of a wide variety of theatrical objects and technologies.[17] With their palimpsestic textures, their anachronic temporality, and their rhetorical synchronic diachrony, the Chester Banns show how strict temporal distinctions of "present" and "past" intermingle and overwrite one another upon theatrically reclaimed stage objects—and therefore why temporally vectored narratives are incomplete and unsatisfactory.

Diverse Times

When researching this book, I often encountered the objection that although the mysteries and other "medieval" dramatic forms may have influenced London drama far more than they've ever been given credit for, it seems obvious that since at least at the end of the sixteenth century, when the commercial playhouses were in their heyday, the demise of the traditional religious drama was all but complete. Even if a few professional playwrights, like Shakespeare, could have witnessed mystery plays as children, this remains a matter of conjecture lacking evidence. I addressed this problem in the introduction in terms of population migration to London from the provinces, but in closing I would like to suggest that perhaps it is not the lack of evidence but our reification of Shakespeare—the "peerless representative of a transcendent dramatic literature . . . [who] disdains vulgar physical accoutrements"—and his professional contemporaries that has rendered existing evidence inscrutable.[18] Since the eighteenth century we have imagined the London stage as a humanist enterprise undertaken by metropolitan Renaissance poets, when much of the dramatic material worked on by those play-wrights was borrowed or inspired by provincial guild-sponsored craftsmen-actors. The plays themselves testify again and again to the lingering influence of mystery and morality antecedents. As late as 1616, Jonson can take for granted his audience's familiarity with the conventional costumes and stage practices of moral interludes so as to premise much of the comedy in *The Devil Is an Ass* on that supposedly outmoded dramatic tradition. Perhaps, too, we have ignored preprofessional dramatic influences because we accept, even now, the claims to urbanity and modish taste often expressed by London plays. The Chester Banns challenge us to reevaluate these assumptions. Exposing the fiction of the Renaissance's claim not to *re*birth but to birth (that is, to fashionableness and originality), they show how obsolescence may become the guarantor of novelty, the *dernier cri*.

As late as 1640, the title page illustration of Nathanael Richards's *Messallina* records the trace of the mystery plays in the "clearly marked" trapdoor in the center of a hall playhouse (figure 9).[19] The stage trap features prominently in the play. It allows for the entrance of Furies who "dance an Anticke and depart," then "gapes and swallowes" three murderers, and finally issues the ghosts of Messallina's victims, who bid her to despair and die.[20] The trapdoor is so heavily trafficked (by more than a dozen spirits!) that it was perhaps the play's most memorable feature, which may explain why the printer, Thomas Cotes, might have chosen to add this illustration to the title page: it is a mnemonic of performances "divers times, by the Company of his Majesties Revells."[21] The fact that the playbook repeatedly advertises this history would support the view that the trap illustration is meant to recall stage performance.

The second title page, moreover, boasts of the "generall applause" the play received from audiences, and Richards's dedicatory epistle to Viscount Rochford reiterates, "This play upon the Stage, passed the general applause

FIGURE 9.   Stage trapdoor, detail from the title page of Nathanael Richards, *The tragedy of Messallina the Roman emperesse*... (London, 1640). Reproduced by permission of the Folger Shakespeare Library.

as well of Honorable Personages as others." "Two passages are past," he adds, "the Stage and the Presse; nothing is absent now but the gentle approbation of your Lordship's clemency."[22] If Andrew Gurr, following John Astington, is correct that the vignette illustration is an inaccurate rendering of a playhouse stage, then it would seem all the more likely that the image was chosen solely for its clearly marked trapdoor—no other stage feature would then be either faithful to or apropos of Richards's play.[23]

Though set in ancient Rome, this late play, one of the last written before the professional theaters were closed, draws heavily from native English dramatic sources. The Furies' "Anticke round" recalls the Hecate scenes of *Macbeth* and, like Middleton's additions to that play, called for singing and dancing. Messallina's behavior, which includes summoning demonic powers, creating mischief, and so forth, recalls the traditional stage Vice. Not surprisingly, therefore, it is also reminiscent of another post-Reformation character derived from that tradition: Richard III. But Messallina's address to the Ghosts who have emerged from the stage trap also recalls Faustus's "Ugly Hell, gape not!" (5.2.196)[24] and Hamlet's "*Hic et ubique?*" (1.5.158):

> Swallow me earth, gape gape and swallow
> Hide me from sight of this sad spectacle,
> No? why then doe state till you burst agen
> 'Tis true, I was your deaths chiefe Actor
> Mischiefes chiefe Engine, ruine of you all
> *Quid faciam? ubi fugiam, hic, & illic,*
> *Ubinam nescio, O dira Fata.*
> > *Exeunt Ghosts.*
> Close eyes and never open, all's vanisht now.
> T'was but the perturbation of my minde
> So let it passe—what agen.[25]

Messallina's stage trap thereby activates the sixteenth-century theatrical space of Hell beneath the scaffolding and in doing so also resurrects the ghosts of the London professional stage from the plays of Marlowe and Shakespeare. More than a century's worth of spirits linger behind that trace outline of the stage trap in the title page illustration of Richards's play.

Yet what is most interesting is how Richards characterizes his work in his dedication: "the sole Ayme of my discovery herein, no otherwise tends then to separate Soules from the discovered Evill, the suppression of Vice, and exhaltation of Vertue, flight from sinne for feare of Iudgement."[26] Much of this explanation is no doubt commonplace dedicatory rhetoric made urgent by Messallina's infamous promiscuity. But if we read Richards's apology in terms of genre rather than character, we may plausibly say that he has written a morality play. Jonson had dressed the old-fashioned Tudor moral interlude in the modern garb of London city comedy, and now Richards costumes it in an ancient Roman toga. No more than two years before religious radicals will close the theaters, the preface of a play attempts to find a sympathetic audience by extolling its antiquity and underscoring its material affiliation with an obsolescent pre-Reformation dramatic tradition.

 # Notes

Introduction

1. "These plays," Alexandra Johnston explains, "could be prophet plays, plays on Old Testament themes, Passion plays, Resurrection plays, 'Creation to Doomsday' sequences, plays on the Creed or the Pater Noster (as at York, Lincoln, and Beverly), or plays on the sacrament itself, such as the *Croxton Play of the Sacrament*. They could have protestant leanings or be staunchly Catholic. They could be lavish and complex, multi-parish plays, like the Passion play at New Romney, or simple, single-parish plays, like the Genesis sequence mounted over several years in St Laurence, Reading." Johnston, "The Feast of Corpus Christi in the West Country," *Early Theatre* 6, no. 1 (2003): 18. In addition, "there were also saints plays, morality plays, and folk plays, particularly the ubiquitous Robin Hood plays. Any of these could be and were played on Corpus Christi Day, as they were on Whitsun, May Day, or Midsummer" (18).

2. For an excellent account of this diverse culture and its relevance to (early) modernity, see Lawrence Clopper, *Drama, Play, and Game: English Festive Culture in the Medieval and Early Modern Period* (Chicago: University of Chicago Press, 2001).

3. See David Matthews and Gordon McMullan, "Introduction: Reading the Medieval in Early Modern England," in *Reading the Medieval in Early Modern England,* ed. McMullan and Matthews (Cambridge: Cambridge University Press, 2007), 5. Several other important books and essay collections address Shakespeare's medieval inheritance, including Curtis Perry and John Watkins, eds., *Shakespeare and the Middle Ages* (Oxford: Oxford University Press, 2009), and Helen Cooper, *Shakespeare and the Medieval World* (New York: Arden Shakespeare, 2010). Brian Cummings and James Simpson strategically deploy the essays of their contributors across the standard boundaries of the medieval and early modern, arguing that "both 'periods' look different when set into dialogue with each other." See Cummings and Simpson, introduction to *Cultural Reformations: Medieval and Renaissance in Literary History,* ed. Cummings and Simpson, Oxford Twenty-First Century Approaches to Literature (Oxford: Oxford University Press, 2010), 5. John Watkins, too, bedevils traditional periodization by highlighting our "new sense of the persistence of 'medieval' conventions of acting, thinking, arguing, and believing well into the so-called early modern world." Watkins, "Bedevilling the Histories of Medieval and Early Modern Drama," *Modern Philology* 101 (2003): 69–70. For an insightful account of what the "incipient cohabitation" of medieval and early modern scholars might mean for future scholarship, see David Wallace, afterword to McMullan and Matthews, *Reading the Medieval in Early Modern England,* 220–27.

4. See the work of Theresa Coletti, including, "The Chester Cycle in Sixteenth-Century Religious Culture," *JMEMS* 37, no. 3 (2007): 531–47, as well as her essay with

Gail McMurray Gibson, "The Tudor Origins of Medieval Drama," in *A Companion to Tudor Literature,* ed. Kent Cartwright (Malden, MA: Wiley-Blackwell, 2010), 228–45.

5. See Scott McMillin and Sally-Beth MacLean, *The Queen's Men and Their Plays* (Cambridge: Cambridge University Press, 1998); Helen Ostovich, Holger Schott Syme, and Andrew Griffin, eds., *Locating the Queen's Men: 1583–1603* (Burlington, VT: Ashgate, 2009); and Richard Dutton, Alison Findlay, and Richard Wilson, eds., *Region, Religion, and Patronage: Lancastrian Shakespeare,* (Manchester, UK: Manchester University Press, 2003).

6. My project owes a great debt to Jonathan Gil Harris's *Untimely Matter in the Time of Shakespeare* (Philadelphia: University of Pennsylvania Press, 2009), which follows the work of Michel Serres in order to explore early modern theories of matter. Harris identifies palimpsests as polychronic materials whose past meanings both live on in the present and, more important, actively influence the manner in which present and past matter are perceived and related. Regarding the concept of the polychronic object, see Michel Serres with Bruno Latour, *Conversations on Science, Culture, and Time,* trans. Roxanne Lapidus (Ann Arbor: University of Michigan Press, 1995).

7. "Object biography" follows the lead of cultural anthropologists Arjun Appadurai and Igor Kopytoff in the seminal essay collection *The Social Life of Things: Commodities in Cultural Perspective,* ed. Arjun Appadurai (Cambridge: Cambridge University Press, 1986). See especially Appadurai, "Introduction: Commodities and the Politics of Value," 3–63, as well as Kopytoff, "The Cultural Biography of Things: Commoditization as Process," 64–94. Archaeologists have been drawn to this approach, Philip Schwyzer explains, "as a way of resisting their discipline's traditional fixation on origins; the archaeologist as object-biographer will not 'privilege the moment of origin' but rather 'interrogate the specific moments of crafting, forging, exchanging, installing, using and discarding.'" Yet as he argues, "an approach to the lives of objects that privileges ceaseless transformation and recycling over origin and essence is not without its own pitfalls." Schwyzer, "Trophies, Traces, Relics, and Props: The Untimely Objects of *Richard III,*" *SQ* 63, no. 3 (2012): 303.

8. For a critique of this synchronic approach as constituting objects "within the freeze-frame of a historical moment," see Harris, "The New New Historicism's *Wunderkammer* of Objects," *European Journal of English Studies* 4, no. 2 (2000): 111–23, as well as *Untimely Matter,* 5–9.

9. As Jonathan Gil Harris and Natasha Korda have noted, literary criticism has long positioned Shakespeare as the "peerless representative of a transcendent dramatic literature whose native habitat, the individual imagination, disdains vulgar physical accoutrements." Harris and Korda, "Introduction: Towards a Materialist Account of Stage Properties," in *Staged Properties in Early Modern English Drama,* ed. Harris and Korda (Cambridge: Cambridge University Press, 2002), 7.

10. Andrew Gurr, "The Shakespearean Stage," in *The Norton Shakespeare: Based on the Oxford Edition,* ed. Stephen Greenblatt et al. (New York: Norton, 1997), 3291, 3294.

11. As Watkins suggests, "medievalists and early modernists alike stand to learn [much] from a greater attention to the artistry of tinkers, joiners, and weavers. Watkins, "Bedevilling the Histories of Medieval and Early Modern Drama," 78.

12. Margreta de Grazia, Maureen Quilligan, and Peter Stallybrass, introduction to *Subject and Object in Renaissance Culture,* ed. de Grazia, Quilligan, and Stallybrass (Cambridge: Cambridge University Press, 1996), 6.

13. As was the case with Bernard Spivack's commendable effort to break free from romanticized notions of Shakespeare's art. See Spivack, *Shakespeare and the Allegory of Evil: The History of a Metaphor in Relation to His Major Villains* (New York: Columbia University Press, 1958). As discussed below in chapter 1, the source of this evolutionary model is E. K. Chambers, *The Mediaeval Stage* (Oxford: Oxford Clarendon Press, 1903). Following Spivack, David Bevington's important *From "Mankind" to Marlowe: Growth of Structure in the Popular Drama of Tudor England* (Cambridge, MA: Harvard University Press, 1962), employed the phrase "hybrid morality" (or "hybrid drama") to refer to plays "not properly belonging to the canon of the orthodox morality because they deal with historical or romantic material and . . . set abstractions and concrete figures side by side in the same play, and are of considerable importance to the development of the popular theater in its transition from the medieval drama of allegory to the later Renaissance drama of secular concern" (10).

14. Paul Whitfield White argues that past studies of sixteenth-century religious drama "have failed sufficiently to recognize that the Reformation produced a range of religious subjectivities which varied with local circumstance and the passage of time" and therefore "we should look for signs of this complex interaction not merely in the events and political maneuvers surrounding performances but within the plays themselves, many of which exhibited an uneasy mixing of traditional and reformed elements." See White, "Reforming Mysteries' End: A New Look at Protestant Intervention in English Provincial Drama," *JMEMS* 29, no. 1 (1999): 140.

15. On the tendency of early modernists to attribute complexity to the texts of their own field at the expense of a monolithic Middle Ages, see David Aers, "A Whisper in the Ear of Early Modernists; or, Reflections on Literary Critics Writing the 'History of the Subject,'" in *Culture and History 1350–1600: Essays on English Communities, Identities and Writing,* ed. David Aers (Detroit: Wayne State University Press, 1992), 177–202. Two important studies that approach medieval culture, including the mystery play tradition, not as a singular edifice but as a complex set of texts, issues, and questions with often conflicting regional responses are Sarah Beckwith, *Signifying God: Social Relation and Symbolic Act in the York Corpus Christi Plays* (Chicago: University of Chicago Press, 2001), and Robert Barrett, *Against All England: Regional Identity and Cheshire Writing, 1195–1656* (Notre Dame, IN: University of Notre Dame Press, 2009).

16. As Helen Cooper argues, we need to remind ourselves that the mystery cycles survived the Reformation "long enough to become part of the cultural memory of Shakespeare and his audiences." And whether they had a direct experience of those plays or merely a generalized familiarity, "what is certain is that the kind of dramaturgy such plays embodied was taken for granted by playwrights and spectators alike: that even if the subject matter had changed from salvation history to the world, the ambition and the stagecraft were continuous." Cooper, *Shakespeare and the Medieval World,* 55–56, 71. Also see Michael O'Connell, "Vital Cultural Practices: Shakespeare and the Mysteries," *JMEMS* 29, no. 1 (1999): 149–68.

17. As Alison Findlay and Richard Dutton explain, "the players emerged from different parts of the country and different occupations, and had distinctive artisan-like ways of relating to each other, often apparently modelled on those of the trade guilds." It was unusual, they also note, that the two greatest actors of the time, Edward Alleyn and Richard Burbage, "seem, in effect, to have been born to the stage and in London." For "even Londoners toured," they argue, and cite Ben Jonson and Richard

Tarleton as examples. See Findlay and Dutton, introduction to Dutton, Findlay, and Wilson, *Region, Religion, and Patronage,* 24.

18. Even Glynne Wickham, for whom "the public theatres of Elizabethan London were the crowning glory of the medieval experiment," argued that the commercialization of theater was an early sign of the cultural decay leading to the "cushioned, conveyor-belted, and cellophane-wrapped" depravities of modernity. Wickham, *Early English Stages, 1300 to 1660* (New York: Columbia University Press, 1963), 1:xxvii, 1:xxv). As Margreta de Grazia has noted, Wickham viewed the 1576 opening of the professional London playhouses as a pivotal moment, the "principal point of demarcation," separating theatrical vitality and dissipation. De Grazia, "World Pictures, Modern Periods, and the Early Stage," in *A New History of Early English Drama,* ed. John D. Cox and David Scott Kastan (New York: Columbia University Press, 1997), 17.

19. REED: *Cheshire,* 1:332–40.

20. Richard Emmerson's call for the synchronic study of sixteenth-century English drama has been an invaluable guide for this book. See Emmerson, "Dramatic History: On the Diachronic and Synchronic in the Study of Early English Drama," *JMEMS* 35, no. 1 (2005): 54–55; as well as "Contextualizing Performance: The Reception of the Chester *Antichrist,*" *JMEMS* 29, no. 1 (1999): 97.

21. "If Shakespeare's vocabulary is rich," Tiffany Stern observes, "that is partly because 'words' were what his audience were paying for." She argues that language was one of the important ways in which the theater competed for audiences with surrounding Bankside attractions. See Stern, *Making Shakespeare: From Stage to Page* (New York: Routledge, 2004), 20–22. As Harris and Korda note, "the public stage was populated not just by extravagant costumes, but by other eye-catching objects as well." Those stage properties "were often intended not merely to catch, but to overwhelm the eye by means of their real or apparent costliness, motion, and capacity to surprise." In fact, "the public playhouse supplemented the visual impact of its costumes and props with its spectacular architecture." Harris and Korda, "Towards a Materialist Account of Stage Properties," 4.

22. The evidence surrounding the "William Shakeshafte" of Alexander Houghton's 1581 will is, as Richard Dutton argues, "cumulatively suggestive." Dutton, "Shakespeare and Lancaster," in Dutton, Findlay, and Wilson, *Region, Religion, and Patronage,* 153. I am content that Shakespeare's knowledge of the west came secondhand from the touring experiences of his professional associates. Theresa Coletti and Gail McMurray Gibson offer a very intriguing connection between London and Chester. Citing Anthony Munday's homage to the Stanleys as well as Chester's dramatic past in a 1590 play written for the Lord Strange's Men, they argue that "memories of Chester's medieval ritual performance, and perhaps even of the already-Tudor biblical plays themselves, momentarily brush elbows with" the professional London stage. See Coletti and Gibson, "The Tudor Origins of Medieval Drama," in *A Companion to Tudor Literature,* ed. Kent Cartwright (Malden, MA: Wiley-Blackwell, 2010), 234–35. Moreover, the notion of a "Lancastrian Shakespeare" is, in Richard Wilson's words, attractive for its scholarly wish fulfillment, "the intellectual break with the xenophobe, misogynistic and imperialist 'Royal Shakespeare' of Hollywood cliché." Wilson, "Introduction: A Torturing Hour—Shakespeare and the Martyrs," in *Theatre and Religion: Lancastrian Shakespeare,* ed. Richard Dutton, Alison Findlay, and Richard Wilson (Manchester, UK: Manchester University Press, 2003), 31–32.

23. See Harris, "The Smell of Gunpowder: *Macbeth* and the Palimpsests of Olfaction," in *Untimely Matter*, 119–39. Also see Holly Dugan, *The Ephemeral History of Perfume: Scent and Sense in Early Modern England* (Baltimore: Johns Hopkins University Press, 2011).

24. Stephen Greenblatt has often used this term; see, for example, Greenblatt, "Remnants of the Sacred in Early Modern England," in de Grazia, Quilligan, and Stallybrass, *Subject and Object in Renaissance Culture*, 337–48.

25. See O'Connell, "Vital Cultural Practices," 149–68.

26. De Grazia, "World Pictures," 13.

27. Compare Alexander Davis's account of the first act of *The Two Noble Kinsmen,* in which "the play is rife with images of unburied bodies, of unquiet bones, and of the half alive, weirdly intertwined with a contrary strain of allusion that emphasizes new life and marriage. The effect may seem macabre . . . but on the terms established by the prologue, we can see that their association is entirely logical: each describes the same process of literary creation, or re-creation. Even as the play urges itself on toward generation, it is necessarily consumed by the vision of a past that refuses to stay dead." Davis, "Living in the Past: Thebes, Periodization, and *The Two Noble Kinsmen," JMEMS* 40, no. 1 (2010): 177.

28. For a fascinating account of the cultural memory of Shakespeare as well as the mnemonic force of theatrical objects in modern productions of his plays, see the collection *Shakespeare, Memory, and Performance,* ed. Peter Holland (Cambridge: Cambridge University Press, 2006), particularly Barbara Hodgdon's contribution, "Shopping in the Archives: Material Memories," 135–67.

29. For a discussion of the etymology of the term "mystery," see the introduction to David Mills, *The Chester Mystery Cycle: A New Edition with Modernised Spelling* (East Lansing, MI: Colleagues Press, 1992), xi–xiii.

30. Edmund Malone writes, for example, that "the Mysteries appear to have originated among the ecclesiasticks; and were most probably first acted with any degree of form by the monks." Malone, ed., *Plays and Poems of William Shakspeare, in Ten Volumes; Collated Verbatim with the Most Authentick Copies, and Revised: With the Corrections and Illustrations of Various Commentators; to Which Are Added, an Essay on the Chronological Order of His Plays* (1790; repr., New York: AMS Press, 1968), 8.

31. The date of Corpus Christi could be as early as May 21 or as late as June 24. To be clear, I agree with Johnston that "Corpus Christi drama as a genre simply did not and does not exist except as a scholarly construct as old as the first commentators on English biblical drama." Johnston, "Feast of Corpus Christi," 16.

32. Yet a "pageant" need not refer to a wheeled vehicle; as in Bristol, it might be carried like a bier on the shoulders of the guildsmen. See Mark Pilkinton, ed., *Bristol,* Records of Early English Drama (Toronto: University of Toronto Press, 1997), xxix; and Johnston, "Feast of Corpus Christi," 19.

1. Toward a Renaissance Culture of Medieval Artifacts

1. Thomas Warton, *The History of English Poetry,* 4 vols. (London, 1774–81), 1:240–41. Warton is quoting from the entry under "Wytney" in Lambarde's *Dictionarium Angliæ topographicum & historicum* (London, 1730), 459 (sig. Nnn2r).

2. Lambarde held various official positions during Elizabeth's reign, and his Reformed religious convictions are readily perceivable throughout his *A Perambulation in Kent* (London, 1576).

3. Warton, *History of English Poetry,* 1:236–37.

4. John T. Lynch, *The Age of Elizabeth in the Age of Johnson* (Cambridge: Cambridge University Press, 2003), 120.

5. Warton elsewhere uses the term "mechanical" in association with manual craft when he notes "that Germany's 'mechanical genius' was responsible for 'an admirable invention,' which was of the most singular utility in facilitating the diffusion of the antient writers over every part of Europe: I mean the art of printing." Quoted from Lynch, *Age of Elizabeth,* 47.

6. Warton, *History of English Poetry,* 1:242.

7. On the common use of darkness and light as a metaphor to describe the transition from the Middle Ages to the Renaissance, see Lynch, *Age of Elizabeth,* 21–28. He cites specific examples from Warton on pages 27 and 28.

8. On Warton's sense of the Middle Ages as a period lacking in historical awareness, see Alex Davis, "Living in the Past: Thebes, Periodization, and *The Two Noble Kinsmen," JMEMS* 40, no. 1 (2010): 173–75.

9. Warton, *History of English Poetry,* 3:361–62.

10. Ibid., 3:496.

11. Ibid., 3:496.

12. Jacob Burckhardt, *The Civilization of the Renaissance in Italy,* trans. S. G. C. Middlemore (New York: Modern Library, 2002), 122–23.

13. Ibid., 93.

14. "Burckhardt's exemplary individuals are often set apart from objects," Margreta de Grazia explains, adding, "like Descartes who begins his *Meditations* by abstracting himself from objects—from the winter cloak he is wearing, from the paper on which he is writing—the subject must remove himself from the world of objects in order to be fully conscious and capable." See de Grazia, "The Ideology of Superfluous Things: *King Lear* as Period Piece," in *Subject and Object in Renaissance Culture,* ed. Margreta de Grazia, Maureen Quilligan, and Peter Stallybrass (Cambridge: Cambridge University Press, 1996), 18.

15. Burckhardt, *Civilization of the Renaissance in Italy,* 129–30.

16. On the English *inventiones* and their provenance dating back to the fifth-century *Revelatio Sancti Stephani,* see Monika Otter, *Inventiones: Fiction and Referentiality in Twelfth-Century English Historical Writing* (Chapel Hill: University of North Carolina Press, 1996), 26–29.

17. "These plot elements," Otter explains,

remain fairly constant for centuries, although there is some flexibility to accommodate local circumstances. The relics are found either by coincidence, usually in connection with some construction or renovation project, or by divine guidance, through dreams or visions. The search for the right place and the digging itself are usually much emphasized; it is stressed that the community "earned" the relic through its intense desire and hard work. There must be an audience present, minimally represented by the bishop or other high clerics in charge, but often described as a large crowd of clergy and laity. There will be some confirmation that the relic is genuine: the body may be incorrupt, or at least emit a pleasant fragrance; sometimes there is an inscription or some identifying artifact. The *inventio* is followed by a *translatio,* that is, the body is brought to a more worthy shrine, and its authenticity is further confirmed by miracles. (Otter, *Inventiones,* 28–29)

18. Ibid., 22.

19. Matter's chronological significance can also be seen in Burckhardt's account of Renaissance melancholy, the subjective corollary that arises from the historical difference it imposes on objects. He writes, "The ruins within and outside Rome awakened not only archaeological zeal and patriotic enthusiasm, but an elegiac or sentimental melancholy." Burckhardt, *Civilization of the Renaissance in Italy,* 131. On melancholia as the "period illness" of the Renaissance as well as the "subjective correlative" of our own disciplinary knowledge, see Margreta de Grazia, "Anachronism," in *Cultural Reformations: Medieval and Renaissance in Literary History,* ed. Brian Cummings and James Simpson (Oxford: Oxford University Press, 2010), 31.

20. For a concise account of the author/work dynamic as one of lordship and bondage, see de Grazia, Quilligan, and Stallybrass, *Subject and Object in Renaissance Culture,* 2–5.

21. Erwin Panofsky, *Renaissance and Renascences in Western Art* (New York: Harper and Row, 1972), 108.

22. Ibid., 36.

23. Alexander Nagel and Christopher S. Wood, "Interventions: Toward a New Model of Renaissance Anachronism," *Art Bulletin* 87, no. 3 (2005): 409.

24. Panofsky, *Renaissance and Renascences,* 108.

25. "It is an indication of the extent to which we remain within this way of thinking," Alex Davis reminds us, "that its governing metaphor is likely to strike us as both natural and compelling." Davis, *Renaissance Historical Fiction: Sidney, Deloney, Nashe* (Cambridge: D. S. Brewer, 2011), 13. Compare Nagel and Wood on the self-interest of modern theorists who "preserve the image of a prosaically historicist Renaissance" as well as "the confusion and irrationalism of medieval thought." Nagel and Wood, "Interventions," 411. Also see Margreta de Grazia's observation regarding "the need to retain the 'cognitive distance' that is the very basis of our disciplinary knowledge." De Grazia, "Anachronism," 31.

26. Panofsky, *Renaissance and Renascences,* 6, 40.

27. Ibid., 30n2.

28. Ibid., 32.

29. Panofsky makes a point of repeating this sneering condemnation of the Middle Ages. See ibid., 205, 113.

30. Ibid., 113. Recalling the story of a sixteenth-century Venetian forger who was able to fool the world with a supposedly ancient Greek relief that, in fact, combined figures borrowed from an authentic Attic stele with those modeled on two famous statues by Michelangelo, Panofsky concludes, "The Venetian forger relied on the fact that in his age no basic difference was felt between the *buona maniera greca antica* of an Attic relief and Michelangelo's *moderno si glorioso.*" Ibid., 41.

31. E. K. Chambers, *The Mediaeval Stage* (Oxford: Oxford Clarendon Press, 1903). As to the significance of the study of medieval drama, not even the Early English Text Society (EETS), founded in 1864, published the first printed editions of medieval drama texts until more than thirty years after its founding. An edition of *The Digby Plays* was issued in 1896, and Hardin Craig's *Two Coventry Corpus-Christi*

Plays appeared in 1902. See *Early English Text Society: Lists of Publications* (London: Oxford University Press, 1936), 46–47. On the society's early publication policies and objectives, see Antony Singleton, "The Early English Text Society in the Nineteenth Century: An Organizational History," *Review of English Studies* 56 (2005): 90–118.

32. Chambers, *Mediaeval Stage* 2:225.

33. Yet John Parker argues that we should embrace rather than eschew Chambers's evolutionary model for its Nietzschean resistance to positivist historicism. See Parker, "Who's Afraid of Darwin? Revisiting Chambers and Hardison . . . and Nietzsche," *JMEMS* 40, no. 1 (2010): 7–35. On the nineteenth-century and especially the Arnoldian influences on Chambers's *Mediaeval Stage,* see Kathleen Ashley, "Edmund Kerchever Chambers (1866–1954)," in *Medieval Scholarship: Biographical Studies on the Formation of a Discipline, Literature and Philology,* ed. Helen Damico and Joseph B. Zavadil (New York: Garland, 1998), 2:313–24.

34. Chambers's historiography is suffused with Hegelian dialectic, though of course his secularism is not identical with Hegel's post-Reformation spiritualism. For Hegel there are never clean breaks from the past. History, in its dialectical progress, retains something of the previous era. Like a seed that grows into a plant or a phoenix rising from the flames (two of his favorite analogies), Spirit negates itself yet gains "a comprehension of the universal element which it involves, and thereby gives new form to its inherent principal." Georg W. F. Hegel, *The Philosophy of History,* trans. J. Sibree (Amherst, NY: Prometheus Books, 1991), 78.

35. In Chambers's words:

> I have indeed shown, I hope, in the course of this imperfect summary, that the variety of medieval theatrical organization was somewhat greater than a too exclusive attention to the craft-cycles of the great towns has always allowed scholars to recognize. But, with all qualifications and exceptions, it is none the less true that what began as a mere spectacle, devised by ecclesiastics for the edification of the laity, came in time to appeal to a deep-rooted native instinct of drama in the folk and to continue as an essentially popular thing, a *ludus* maintained by the people itself for its own inexhaustible wonder and delight. (Chambers, *Mediaeval Stage* 2:147)

36. The expression "palmy days" comes from Chambers, *The Elizabethan Stage* (Oxford: Oxford University Press, 1923), 1:307.

37. Compare de Grazia, Quilligan, and Stallybrass, who argue that "from the moment of its mid-nineteenth-century inception as subject-oriented, the Renaissance as Early Modern has given short and limited shrift to the object." De Grazia, Quilligan, and Stallybrass, *Subject and Object,* 5.

38. In Philip Schwyzer's words, objects have "the capacity . . . to both bridge and testify to" temporal difference; see his fascinating account of the untimely objects, dramatic and otherwise, associated with Richard III: Schwyzer, "Trophies, Traces, Relics, and Props: The Untimely Objects of *Richard III,*" *SQ* 63, no. 3 (2012): 300.

39. As Alex Davis states, exemplarity is a theory of history "premised on a notion of the repeatability of the past." Davis, *Renaissance Historical Fiction,* 22. Compare Timothy Hampton, who writes: "Past and present are linked through a relationship of similitude. . . . The words, deeds, and even the bodies of the illustrious ancients were seen as signs of excellence and patterns of behavior. Without them, and without

the theory of history as repetition, the very notion of a cultural rebirth or re-naissance is unthinkable." Hampton, *Writing from History: The Rhetoric of Exemplarity in Renaissance Literature* (Ithaca: Cornell University Press, 1990), 9.

40. The agonistic model I have in mind here is Harold Bloom's *Anxiety of Influence* (1973). Although Bloom excluded Shakespeare from the first edition, his preface to the 1997 edition discusses the "unhappy freedom" the poet experienced. See Bloom, "Preface: The Anguish of Contamination," in *The Anxiety of Influence: A Theory of Poetry,* 2nd ed. (Oxford: Oxford University Press, 1997), xi–xlvii. Popular English translations of Cicero and Seneca include Arthur Golding's 1578 translation of Seneca's *De Beneficiis* and John Harrington's 1550 translation of Cicero's *Laelius.*

41. By invoking Ciceronian friendship as an analogy, I do not mean to suggest that exemplarity fosters uncritical conformity to past authority. Exemplarity urges contact and exchange, but not necessarily agreement. Rather, it challenges modern readers by laying bare historical and circumstantial differences. J. Allan Mitchell has written definitively on the tendency, especially on the part of early modernists, to view medieval exemplary writing as the unsophisticated application of past history to present concerns. See Mitchell, *Ethics and Exemplary Narrative in Chaucer and Gower* (Cambridge: D. S. Brewer, 2004).

42. Only under a modern regime of originality with its corollary notion of intellectual property would indebtedness to a previous source demand open acknowledgment.

43. Hampton, for example, sees a "close relationship between exemplarity and Renaissance humanism." As he explains, "not only did the humanists most systematically articulate the central role of ancient history in promoting ideals of public virtue, but so too in the fifteenth and sixteenth centuries the ideological tenets of humanist pedagogy spread to every corner of Europe." Hampton, *Writing from History,* 6–7.

44. Larry Scanlon, *Narrative, Authority, and Power: The Medieval Exemplum and the Chaucerian Tradition* (Cambridge: Cambridge University Press, 1994), 3.

45. Ibid., 344.

46. As opposed to a binary structure of the exemplum, "which involves the simple deference of present to the past," Scanlon proposes instead "that we think of authority as triangulated. For it involves not just deference to the past but a claim of identification with it and a representation of that identity made by one part of the present to another. In this way the constraint of authority can also be empowering." Ibid., 38.

47. "The past was valued," Davis explains, "for its ability to meet contemporary circumstances, not only in the sense of offering ethical inspiration and concrete advice, but also as a resource for contingent argumentation, for or against a given position." Davis, *Renaissance Historical Fiction,* 23. Davis is not here thinking primarily of dramatic writing, but his insight is apt.

48. Glynne Wickham, *Early English Stages, 1300 to 1660* (New York: Columbia University Press, 1963), 1:xxvii. In Wickham's view, "while common sense tells us that Shakespeare and his contemporaries reaped the harvest of the seed, tilth and growth of preceding centuries, most modern dramatic criticism, with its heavy literary bias, has in fact severed Elizabethan drama from its roots" (1:xxiii).

49. In *Shakespeare and the Popular Tradition in the Theater: Studies in the Social Dimension of Dramatic Form and Function* (Baltimore: Johns Hopkins University Press, 1978), Weimann builds the case for Shakespeare's singular ability "to relate the dramatic

vitality of a still living past to the drama of contemporary life" (xvii). Weimann challenges traditional literary-centered approaches to early English performance and broadly characterizes the late Middle Ages as a time devoted to popular performance ("the theatrical" or "the actor's voice"). The Renaissance, by contrast, is an emergent period of elite literary humanism ("the poetic" or "the author's pen"). See Weimann, *Author's Pen and Actor's Voice: Playing and Writing in Shakespeare's Theatre* (Cambridge, Cambridge University Press, 2000).

50. As Weimann states, "The rise of the Elizabethan theatre was unthinkable without this conjunction of largely oral, physical, spectacular, body-centered practices of performance and display *and* the availability, in the early modern marketplace, of literary 'endeavors of art' derived from a university or grammar school education in rhetoric and composition." Weimann, *Author's Pen and Actor's Voice,* 55.

51. Cooper, *Shakespeare and the Medieval World* (New York: Arden Shakespeare, 2010), 49.

52. Ibid., 44.

53. While "act[ing] its action," Cooper explains, "may seem to us post-Shakespeareans the obvious thing to do with a play," it was in fact not at all obvious to humanists familiar with Seneca, whose rhetorical drama displaced action with carefully constructed speech. Ibid., 48–49.

54. Cooper argues, "Shakespeare's unique alertness to those elements, whether through acceptance, elaboration, or overt rejection, is indispensable both to his [dramatic] vision and how he gives it shape and body on the stage." Ibid., 169.

55. Michael O'Connell, "Vital Cultural Practices: Shakespeare and the Mysteries," *JMEMS* 29, no. 1 (1999): 160.

56. "The background presence of the pageant of Joseph's jealousy may be felt in something of the same way that Herod and Pilate stand as dramatic avatars of figures who tyrannically abuse power and who, like Macbeth, lose their humanity." Ibid., 161–62.

57. O'Connell, "*King Lear* and the Summons of Death," in *Shakespeare and the Middle Ages,* ed. Curtis Perry and John Watkins (Oxford: Oxford University Press, 2009), 199–216. It is gratifying to find that my book harmonizes with his most recent work, and I am grateful to him for sharing it prior to publication: O'Connell, "Blood Begetting Blood: Shakespeare and the Mysteries," in *Medieval Shakespeare: Pasts and Presents,* ed. Ruth Morse, Helen Cooper, and Peter Holland (Cambridge: Cambridge University Press, 2013), 177–89.

58. John D. Cox, *The Devil and the Sacred in English Drama, 1350–1642* (Cambridge: Cambridge University Press, 2000), 5. According to Cox, the influence of Chambers long blinded twentieth-century criticism to this indebtedness to medieval drama.

59. See Perry and Watkins, *Shakespeare and the Middle Ages,* 4. With this collection Perry and Watkins aim to "resist the lure of a neo-Burckhardtian idea of early modernity" by asking, "To what extent do [Shakespeare's] poems and plays bear the impress not only of Hall and Holinshed—the Tudor chronicles that mediated his knowledge of pre-Elizabethan events—but of written and oral sources and cultural practices that now strike us as quintessentially medieval?" (3).

60. As Karen Sawyer Marsalek argues concerning *1 Henry IV,* this borrowed dramaturgy "interacts with elements of the Oldcastle myth to create a clever response to Puritan antitheatrical prejudices." Marsalek, "Marvels and Counterfeits:

False Resurrections in the Chester *Antichrist* and *1 Henry IV*," in Perry and Watkins, *Shakespeare and the Middle Ages,* 232. The editors use the terms "image" and "motif" to summarize the borrowing she describes, but I think Marsalek's insightful essay is pointing to a much more substantial exemplar.

61. Like the broader essay collection referenced above, Marsalek seeks to counterpoise the notion that Shakespeare invented the Middle Ages through his history plays with "the seemingly antithetical question of the medieval invention of Shakespeare," as Perry and Watkins phrase it in *Shakespeare and the Middle Ages* (3). "For Shakespeare and his contemporaries," the editors state, "the Middle Ages had a present, binding reality that is hard for us to imagine four centuries later." However, as they also point out, "as tangible and powerful as that past might have seemed, it was also subject to continual revision and ultimately reinvention" (14).

62. As Scanlon explains, "the power to define the past is also the power to control the constraint the past exerts in the present. Authority, then, is an enabling past reproduced in the present." Scanlon, *Narrative, Authority, and Power,* 38.

63. The waning of "New Historicism" has allowed a surge of recent scholarship, often termed "New Formalism," to reconsider the significance of literary form. See Stephen Cohen, ed., *Shakespeare and Historical Formalism* (Burlington, VT: Ashgate, 2007), and Mark David Rasmussen, ed., *Renaissance Literature and Its Formal Engagements* (New York: Palgrave Macmillan, 2002). Christopher Cobb, in fact, argues that by attending to the manner in which romance topoi were adopted as "major theatrical expressions of royal, aristocratic, and civic power" in the early modern period we can "extend the study of the theatricality of politics," once the purview of New Historicism. See Cobb, "Storm versus Story: Form and Affective Power in Shakespeare's Romances," in Cohen, *Shakespeare and Historical Formalism,* 96.

64. This is not to argue that genre is reducible to textual features. As Amy J. Devitt argues in her study of rhetorical (versus literary) genre: "At most . . . genres are associated with but not defined by textual form. . . . The fact that genre is reflected in formal features does not mean that genre *is* those formal features." Devitt, *Writing Genres* (Carbondale, IL: Southern Illinois University Press, 2004), 11.

65. Julia Reinhard Lupton, *Afterlives of the Saints: Hagiography, Typology, and Renaissance Literature* (Stanford, CA: Stanford University Press, 1996), xxi, xxv.

66. In Lupton's words, "*The Winter's Tale* picks out the paganism residual in Catholicism and the Catholicism residual in Reformed England, iconographies that, in their very bankrupting by the Protestant historical vision, together underwrite the hagiographic scheme informing the play." Ibid., 177. Her point is not to argue that Shakespeare's play "is at heart either a Christian or a pagan play" but rather "to show how *The Winter's Tale* constitutes 'secular drama' as the reanimation of fragments left over by the repeated breaking of idols in the history of the West" (178).

67. Ibid., 218.

68. "In opting for the romance version of comedy," Helen Cooper writes, "Shakespeare was writing from deep within a vernacular tradition, and one that came with its popular appeal already established. His audiences grew up with narrative romances, many of them medieval ones available in cheap printed editions that came to form the bulk of early Tudor popular reading, the pulp fiction of the age." Cooper, *Shakespeare and the Medieval World,* 176.

69. Ibid., 178–79.

70. Ibid., 171.

71. Ibid., 179. Also see her chapter "Women on Trial," 269–323, in *The English Romance in Time: Transforming Motifs from Geoffrey of Monmouth to the Death of Shakespeare* (Oxford: Oxford University Press, 2004), where she studies the frequency of accusations made against heroines in both medieval and early modern romances and brings into her discussion acute readings of several Shakespeare plays, including *Othello, The Winter's Tale,* and *All Is True.*

72. Cyrus Mulready, *Romance on the Early Modern Stage: English Expansion Before and After Shakespeare* (New York: Palgrave Macmillan, 2013). Remarkably, he identifies more than forty plays sharing this generic kinship that, largely because we have rigidly ascribed the genre to a biographical phase in Shakespeare's career, have gone unnoticed. I am grateful that he has shared portions of his manuscript prior to publication.

73. Mercator's 1569 world map includes an inset along with a narrative cartouche in which Mercator cites a lost account of Arthurian knights as explorers he calls *Gestis Arthuri Britanni* (*The Deeds of Arthur*). Ibid., 3–7.

74. Andrew King, *The Faerie Queene and Middle English Romance: The Matter of Just Memory* (Oxford: Clarendon Press, 2000), 9–10.

75. Ibid., 11. King subsequently explains, "Just as *The Shepheardes Calendar* presents the sense of being an earlier, 'edited' text, so too *The Faerie Queene* might be likened to a [fifteenth-century] manuscript-anthology, particularly in terms of its structure" (38–39).

76. Ibid., vii. "The historian who most powerfully enabled the Elizabethan resuscitation of earlier native literature on the grounds of its proto-Reformation spirit is John Foxe," King argues, adding that "like Eumnestes, Foxe has historical records which prove the legitimacy of the ancient British Church . . . [and his] arguments allow medieval texts and monuments to be 'reformed' to justify the present position, even in the case of a writer as remote as Ælfric." Ibid., 8.

77. "If we look at the anti-romance polemic in terms of its indexes and argumentative strategies, as opposed to the alleged doctrinal allegiance," Tiffany Jo Werth explains, "they can appear surprisingly similar." She adds, "Protestants borrowed heavily from a Catholic legacy of antiromance writings. In other words, the indexes, like the genre they survey, were hybrid composites. Old rhetoric was repurposed for a new context." Werth, *The Fabulous Dark Cloister: Romance in England after the Reformation* (Baltimore: Johns Hopkins University Press, 2011), 12.

78. On Chaucer as an "antique" exemplar for Tudor poets who feel comparatively "unable to reach the heights of pure poetry," see Deanne Williams, "Medievalism in English Renaissance Literature," in *A Companion to Tudor Literature,* ed. Kent Cartwright (Malden, MA: Wiley-Blackwell, 2010), 214–19.

79. Both Yates and Harris draw inspiration from the work of sociologist Bruno Latour and philosopher Michel Serres, especially Latour's *We Have Never Been Modern* (Harvard University Press, 1991) and *Reassembling the Social: An Introduction to Actor-Network-Theory* (Oxford University Press, 2005), and Serres's *Angels, A Modern Myth* (Flammarion, 1995), and their coauthored *Conversations on Science, Culture, and Time* (Ann Arbor: University of Michigan Press, 1995). In Harris's account,

> the palimpsest is more than a collation of diverse inscriptions that accrue over time. It is also a complex, polychronic assemblage of material *agents:* it includes a writing surface, whether parchment or vellum, that enables, even

as it is transformed by, the writing on it. And this network of agency, of course, presumes yet more actors—specifically, writers and readers from different times who work upon the palimpsest surface, transforming it but also exposing themselves in the process to the possibility of transformation. (Harris, *Untimely Matter in the Time of Shakespeare* [Philadelphia: University of Pennsylvania Press, 2009], 17)

According to Yates, Marxist/materialist literary approaches tend to conserve the terms "subject" and "object" even as they challenge this traditional hierarchy. "Network-based models," by contrast, "understand the range of beings that populate its networks" so that "subject" and "object" are merely "grammatical terms that describe momentary positions in the life cycle of a person or thing." Yates further states, "what network-based models of description enable us to recognize is that the crucial discovery in the turn back to 'things' is not the potential 'priority' of the 'object' but the notion of the 'turn' itself, the role that movement, mobility, transportation, animation, and metaphor play in the production of things and persons." Yates, "Accidental Shakespeare," *Shakespeare Studies* 34 (2006): 92–93. Also see his *Error, Misuse, Failure: Object Lessons from the English Renaissance* (Minneapolis: University of Minnesota Press, 2003).

80. Jennifer Summit, *Memory's Library: Medieval Books in Early Modern England* (Chicago: University of Chicago Press, 2008), 9.

81. Ibid., 6.

82. Ibid., 106.

83. William H. Sherman, *Used Books: Marking Readers in Renaissance England* (Philadelphia: University of Pennsylvania Press, 2008), 108.

84. Ibid., 87. This "uncommon" Book of Common Prayer is item 354 in the Huntington Library's Page Collection.

85. Ibid., 105.

86. Ibid., 106–8.

87. As Siân Echard explains, "By the early seventeenth century . . . while 'Gothic' still has a neutral, merely descriptive sense, there are signals that the later seventeenth-century usage (barbarous, rude) is already in play, particularly in the form 'Gothish.'" Echard, *Printing the Middle Ages* (Philadelphia: University of Pennsylvania Press, 2008), 25.

88. Ibid., 29–30.

89. As Alison Shell explains, "Most of these small collections [of folktales] are preserved in polemical writing. But others survive—and many more must have been thrown away—among the papers of government officials whose task it was to gauge levels of Catholic survivalism and anti-Protestant reaction." Shell, *Oral Culture and Catholicism in Early Modern England* (Cambridge: Cambridge University Press, 2007), 64.

90. Shell writes,

But popish words, like idols, could be thought to have an autonomous malign power, which was why even the hostile reporting of popish rhymes could be criticised. In the 1650s Thomas Larkham, the puritan vicar of Tavistock, was accused of bringing in 'many ridiculous rimes, and impertinent stories in his Sermons, very unbefitting the seriousness which becomes one that hath to deal in the name of God.' . . . [The anonymous writers of the complaint] admit that

Larkham was not using the rhymes seriously, but their terms reveal an uneasiness about the act of saying them at all: 'True it is . . . he reproved them when he reported them, but whither charming might not be reproved without all this Gibble-gabble, let wise men judge. (Ibid., 67)

91. As Summit states, "If marginal annotation like [John] Bale's or [Stephen] Batman's is meant to 'purify' the recovered monastic library books by separating the fabulous from the true, it also testifies to the persistence of the one alongside, and indeed within, the other." Summit, *Memory's Library,* 118.

92. Jensen, "'Honest Mirth & Merriment': Christmas and Catholicism in Early Modern England," in *Redrawing the Map of Early Modern English Catholicism,* ed. Lowell Gallagher (Toronto: University of Toronto Press, 2012), 214.

93. Ibid., 227–28.

94. Ibid., 224. She further demonstrates that carols may have been ideologically charged not only in their content but in their context, such as their composition by a priest or physical proximity to a pre-Reformation carol (226–27).

95. Ibid., 234.

96. Ibid., 235. For neither confession was monolithic; in fact, late medieval forms of holiday revelry also occasioned disputes within Catholic and Reformed factions. Puritanical opposition to Christmas probably fostered mainstream attachment to traditional practices, while "members of the English Catholic mission did not themselves agree on the degree to which festive mirth that included gaming, hobbyhorses, and other secular pastimes should be encouraged" (233).

97. See Harris, *Untimely Matter,* as follows: on the urban palimpsest of London, 100–101; regarding histrionicism, passim, but especially 67–81.

98. Shell, *Oral Culture and Catholicism,* 68–69, follows the work of Daniel Woolf, *The Social Circulation of the Past* (Oxford: Oxford University Press, 2003). Regarding the concept of "sites of memory," see Pierre Nora, "Between Memory and History: Les Lieux de Mémoire," *Representations* 26 (1989): 7–24, as well as his *Les Lieux de Mémoire,* 3 vols. (Paris: Gallimard, 1984–92).

99. Shell, *Oral Culture and Catholicism,* 73. She also qualifies Keith Thomas's claim that Protestant caution led to wholesale attempts "to cut the associational links between popular botany and religion" (73).

100. Ibid., 23–24 (emphasis added). Shell is more interested in ghosts and ghost stories, but I wish to call attention to their "attachment" to medieval artifacts in the examples she cites.

101. Ibid., 28. In his 1642 *Noli me Tangere,* Udall writes,

I could therefore wish, That all our Gentry that would preserve their Inheritances, without ruine to their prosperity; would beware they bring not any spoiles of the Church into their Houses, lest they be spoyled by them. . . . And to preserve them from this sin, That they would have a Tablet hung up always in the Dining Roome, where they ordinarily take their repast; in which should be drawne an Altar with Flesh and Fire on it, for Sacrifice, with an Eagle ready to take wing, having in her Talons a piece of Flesh, with a burning coale at it . . . and . . . a tall Tree, with an Eagles Nest in it, [*sic*] and the Heads of her young ones discovered above the Nest, and the Nest flaming with a light fire about them, with this Inscription over the Altar, *Noli me Tangere, ne te & tuos perdam:* For things belonging to the Altar, will certainely prove a snare to the devourers of them. (Quoted from Shell, *Oral Culture and Catholicism,* 28)

102. Shell, *Oral Culture and Catholicism,* 30. She also offers an insightful reading of Andrew Marvell's "Upon Appleton House" as a similar instance of polemical inscription (31–32).

103. Summit, *Memory's Library,* 4.

104. Cooper, *Shakespeare and the Medieval World,* 83.

105. For accounts of these various positions, see H. J. Schroeder, *Canons and Decrees of the Council of Trent* (Rockford, IL: Tan Books, 1978); Martin Luther, "Against the Fanatics," in *Luther's Works,* American ed., vol. 36, *Word and Sacrament II,* trans. Frederick C. Ahrens, ed. Helmut T. Lehmann and Abdel Ross Wentz (Philadelphia: Fortress Press, 1959), 329–61; John Calvin, "Short Treatise on the Holy Supper of our Lord and Only Saviour Jesus Christ," in *Calvin: Theological Treatises,* trans., J. K. S. Reid, The Library of Christian Classics 22 (Philadelphia: Westminster Press, 1954), 140–66; Ulrich Zwingli, "On the Lord's Supper," in *Zwingli and Bullinger,* ed. and trans. G. W. Bromiley, The Library of Christian Classics 24 (Philadelphia: Westminster Press, 1953), 185–238.

106. Greenblatt, *Shakespearean Negotiations* (Berkeley: University of California Press, 1988), 113; "The Mousetrap," in *Practicing New Historicism,* ed. Stephen Greenblatt and Catherine Gallagher (Chicago: University of Chicago Press, 2000), 151.

107. Greenblatt, *Shakespearean Negotiations,* 126.

108. Greenblatt, *Hamlet in Purgatory* (Princeton: Princeton University Press, 2001), 10–46. For all his interest in medieval culture broadly speaking, Greenblatt rarely addresses the early English stage itself, and particularly the famous Corpus Christi dramas that bear the name of the sacrament that so fascinates him. Instead of juxtaposing the ghost of Hamlet's father with any of a number of mystery pageants depicting the *Harrowing of Hell* or *Last Judgment,* his *Hamlet in Purgatory* briefly notes the English morality play *Everyman* (c. 1495). In his more recent *Will in the World: How Shakespeare Became Shakespeare* (New York: Norton, 2004), Greenblatt remains ambivalent about the extent of medieval drama's significance for Shakespeare. On the one hand, it inspired him and provided a repertoire of technical strategies. On the other hand, Shakespeare matured beyond the limits of medieval drama, as evidenced by his mockery of the rude mechanicals in *A Midsummer Night's Dream.*

109. According to Beckwith, "Shakespeare's theater does not represent the supercession and succession of religion, purgatory, and ritual action by a disenchanted theater, but the persistence of its historical concerns in the incarnation of performance." Beckwith, "*Hamlet* and the Forms of Oblivion," *JMEMS* 33, no. 2 (2003): 275. What is omitted in Greenblatt's account, furthermore, "is any sense of presence of the body of Christ in anything other than the terms of physical availability, visibility, and access or lack of it to the senses. But the notion of the Eucharist, especially as it is linked either to the medieval understanding of sacramental penance, or to a reformed notion of penance, was profoundly about the presence of Christians to each other in the body of Christ." Ibid., 267. But whereas Greenblatt reifies the communion host, Beckwith leaves her readers wondering if the physical act of eating is important at all. For an authoritative account of Roman Catholic teaching on this sacrament, see

Matthew Levering, *Sacrifice and Community: Jewish Offering and Christian Eucharist* (Malden, MA: Blackwell, 2005).

110. Beckwith, "Forms of Oblivion," 264.

111. Thomas Cranmer, "Defense of the True and Catholic Doctrine of the Sacrament of the Body and Blood of Our Saviour Jesus Christ," in *The Work of Thomas Cranmer*, ed. G. E. Duffield (Philadelphia: Fortress Press, 1965), 71. See Beckwith, "Forms of Oblivion," 265-67.

112. Calvin, "Treatise on the Holy Supper," 166.

113. John Calvin, *Institutes of the Christian Religion,* trans. Ford Lewis Battles (Philadelphia: Westminster Press, 1960), 1367 (bk. 4, chap. 17, sec. 11). For an insightful explanation of Calvin's position on the efficacy of the sacraments see B. A. Gerrish, *Grace and Gratitude: The Eucharistic Theology of John Calvin* (Minneapolis: Fortress Press, 1993). Also see Randall C. Zachman, *The Assurance of Faith: Conscience in the Theology of Martin Luther and John Calvin* (Minneapolis: Fortress Press, 1993), and David Steinmetz, *Calvin in Context* (Oxford: Oxford University Press, 1995), especially 172–83.

114. See Calvin, *Institutes,* 4.17.31.

115. On Calvin's use of medieval sources like Bernard and even Gregory the Great, see Anthony N. S. Lane, *John Calvin: Student of the Church Fathers* (Edinburgh: T&T Clark, 1999).

116. Studies of the sacramental link between late medieval culture and early modern theater include Thomas Bishop, *Shakespeare and the Theater of Wonder* (Cambridge: Cambridge University Press, 1996); Huston Diehl, *Staging Reform, Reforming the Stage: Protestantism and Popular Theater in Early Modern England* (Ithaca: Cornell University Press, 1997); Anthony Dawson and Paul Yachnin, *The Culture of Playgoing in Shakespeare's England: A Collaborative Debate* (Cambridge: Cambridge University Press, 2001); Jeffrey Knapp, *Shakespeare's Tribe: Church, Nation, and Theater in Renaissance England* (Chicago: University of Chicago Press, 2002); David Coleman, *Drama and the Sacraments in Sixteenth-Century England* (New York: Palgrave, 2007); Regina Schwarz, *Sacramental Poetics at the Dawn of Secularism: When God Left the World* (Stanford: Stanford University Press, 2008); and Elizabeth Williamson, *The Materiality of Religion in Early Modern English Drama* (Burlington, VT: Ashgate, 2009). For an important study of early English theater's sustained relationship with the established religion (Catholic and Protestant) more broadly, see Paul Whitfield White, *Drama and Religion in English Provincial Society, 1485–1660* (Cambridge: Cambridge University Press, 2008).

117. Beckwith, "Forms of Oblivion," 271. On the imbrication and articulation of Christian scriptures and sacraments in early English communities, see her *Signifying God: Social Relation and Symbolic Act in the York Corpus Christi Plays* (Chicago: University of Chicago Press, 2001).

118. See Jennifer Rust, "Political Theologies of the *Corpus Mysticum:* Schmitt, Kantorowicz and de Lubac," in *Political Theology and Early Modernity,* ed. Graham Hammill and Julia Reinhard Lupton (Chicago: University of Chicago Press, 2012), 102–23, as well as her monograph, *The Body in Mystery: The Political Theology of the Corpus Mysticum in Post-Reformation English Literature* (Evanston, IL: Northwestern University Press, 2013).

119. In *Shakespeare and the Grammar of Forgiveness* (Ithaca: Cornell University Press, 2011), Beckwith "traces the fortunes of the component parts of the

sacrament of penance—contrition, confession, and absolution in the Church of England's liturgy and theology (Catholic and Reformed), and in Shakespeare's late plays" (3).

120. De Grazia, "Anachronism," 19. Also see Lynch, *Age of Elizabeth,* passim.

121. Rather than crediting the Renaissance "with having first grasped the fundamental concept of cognitive distance," de Grazia argues, "that sensitivity to anachronism is a later phenomenon more closely coinciding with the formation of the disciplinary divisions under whose aegis we still mainly work. To speak of anachronism *avant la lettre,* then, would itself be an anachronism." De Grazia, "Anachronism," 32.

122. De Grazia cites Nagel and Wood's "Interventions," calling it "an overdue critique of Panofsky's association of the Renaissance with a grasp of historical distance that introduces the anachronistic category of temporal 'instantiation.'" De Grazia, "Anachronism," 29n77.

123. In their challenge to the developmental, "biomorphic" models of art history and endorsement of anachronism, Nagel and Wood are inspired by the work of, among others, Georges Didi-Huberman, including his *L'Image survivante: Histoire de l'art et temps des fantômes selon Aby Warburg,* trans. Jane-Marie Todd (Paris: Minuit, 2002), and *Confronting Images: Questioning the Ends of a Certain History of Art,* trans. John Goodman (University Park: Pennsylvania State University Press, 2005), a translation of the 1990 *Devant l'image.* They seek to update and extend the thesis of substitution, which Richard Krautheimer first proposed in 1942 with respect to the "iconography" of medieval buildings. Nagel and Wood also cite the work of Patricia Fortini Brown, in *Venice in Antiquity* (New Haven: Yale University Press, 1996), on spolia and other artifacts used to fill in gaps in the edifices of monuments.

124. Nagel and Wood further describe the "authorial" or "performative" model of artifacts: "Behind the idea of historical style stands a theory about the origins of formed artifacts. According to this theory, the circumstances of an artifact's fabrication, its originary context, are registered in its physical features. . . . One can characterize this theory of the origin of the artifact . . . as *performative.* The artifact or the work, according to this theory, was the product of a singular historical performance. Any subsequent repetitions of that performance, for example, copies of the work, will be alienated from the original scene of making." Nagel and Wood, "Interventions," 403–4.

125. Ibid., 405–7.

126. Ibid. In their subsequent monograph they emphasize that the substitutional model was not a "moment" in the history of art, for "such an argument would reproduce a traditional account of Renaissance art as an emancipation of the artist from mindless submission to custom." Rather, "the two models were coevolutionary" and, they further explain, competitively responsive to one another. Nagel and Wood, *Anachronic Renaissance* (New York: ZONE Books, 2010), 16.

127. Nagel and Wood, *Anachronic Renaissance,* 14. They subsequently explain that to relegate a work of art to the status of an anachronism, as Panofsky does, "is to say that the work is best grasped not as art, but rather as a witness to its times, or as an inalienable trace of history; it tries to tell us what the artwork *really is.* To describe the work of art as 'anachronic,' by contrast, is to say what the artwork *does,* qua art" (14).

128. Nagel and Wood, "Interventions," 405.

129. In addition to those subsequently cited, see Susan Foister, Ashok Roy, and Martin Wyld, *Holbein's Ambassadors* (New Haven: Yale University Press, 1997), as well as John North's provocative *The Ambassadors' Secret: Holbein and the World of the Renaissance* (New York: Hambledon, 2002).

130. Jessica Wolfe observes, for example, "both formally and thematically, Holbein's canvas attunes us to the inevitability of discord. The distended skull merely accentuates the disunity and distortion that is the subtle yet pervasive theme of the painting as a whole." Wolfe, *Humanism, Machinery, and Renaissance Literature* (Cambridge: Cambridge University Press, 2004), 100.

131. Kenneth Charlton, "Holbein's *Ambassadors* and Sixteenth-Century Education," *Journal of the History of Ideas* 21, no. 1 (1960): 109.

132. Greenblatt, *Renaissance Self-Fashioning: More to Shakespeare* (Chicago: University of Chicago Press, 1980), 17, 18. Though arguing for the importance of objects to the making of identity, Ann Rosalind Jones and Peter Stallybrass also emphasize the novelty of the anamorphosis as an instantiation of the artist's skill. It "brilliantly demonstrates another new element in the repertoire of the modern painter" and "is a representation of Holbein's own skill." Jones and Stallybrass, *Renaissance Clothing and the Materials of Memory* (Cambridge: Cambridge University Press, 2001), 49.

133. See Greenblatt, *Renaissance Self-Fashioning,* 24. "One might argue," Greenblatt further states, "that Holbein's painting signals the *decay* of such [medieval] methods, a loss of intensity that can only be partially recuperated through illusionist tricks, but if so, one must conclude that this decay released a magnificent aesthetic byproduct" (24).

134. In North's account, it is the abbot Richard de Ware who directs the installation of the pavement after a recent trip to Italy, yet, he says, "the abbot's new pavement has to be seen in the context of Henry III's lavishly funded programme of rebuilding and redecorating Westminster abbey. The vast sums being spent there were in preparation for the transfer of the body of Edward the Confessor to the abbey, which took place in 1269." North, *Ambassadors' Secret,* 154.

135. Not until the sixteenth century did Julius II have a neo-cosmatesque floor installed in his private library. For other sacred and profane examples, see Nagel and Wood, *Anachronic Renaissance,* 185–94.

136. By the late thirteenth century, Westminster Abbey had "acquired a peculiar status and a special place in English history. It owed allegiance—as it has done ever since—to the crown rather than to Canterbury." North, *Ambassadors' Secret,* 154.

137. As Echard explains, "This commitment to the authentic representation of Old English text required that special fonts be commissioned and used. This was no simple or cheap undertaking . . . models had to be found, matrices made, punches cut—and the provision of a whole new font would require a considerable outlay of both time and money." Echard, *Printing the Middle Ages,* 27.

138. Richard W. Clement, "The Beginnings of Printing in Anglo-Saxon, 1565–1630," *Papers of the Bibliographical Society of America* 91, no. 2 (1997): 206. Quoted from Echard, *Printing the Middle Ages,* 28.

139. See Zachary Lesser, "Typographic Nostalgia: Play-Reading, Popularity, and Black Letter," in *The Book of the Play: Playwrights, Stationers, and Readers in Early Modern England,* ed. Marta Straznicky (Boston: University of Amherst Press, 2006), 99–126. Lesser provides a helpful caution that we may apply to all forms of anachronism: "We cannot reduce black-letter print to an index to a single group of 'popular' consumers

nor to a single reading based on a common, consensual culture. The nostalgic politics of typeface . . . function differently for different readers" (120).

140. On Richard Pynson's construction of Chaucer as a humanist in the *Proheme* to his 1526 publication of the poet's works and William Thynne's proto-Protestant Chaucer in *Workes of Geffray Chaucer* (1532), see Williams, "Medievalism in English Renaissance Literature," 216–17.

141. King, *The Faerie Queene and Middle English Romance,* 3.

142. See ibid., 3–4n8. Also see Ruth Samson Luborsky, "The Illustrations to *The Shepheardes Calender,*" *Spenser Studies* 2 (1981): 3–53.

143. Nagel and Wood, *Anachronic Renaissance,* 116. Despite the fact that modern methods of dating confirm the roundel's mid-fourteenth-century origin, some scholars are skeptical as to whether Botticelli inserted the icon. Like the influential Roberto Longhi, Keith Christiansen believes it to be a modern (read "anachronistic") insertion, perhaps as late as the nineteenth century. See Longhi, "Uno sguardo alle fotografie della Mostra 'Italian Art and Britain' alla Royal Academy di Londra," *Paragone* 11, no. 125 (1960): 60, and Christiansen, letter in *Burlington Magazine* 129 (November 1987), 744. Ulrich Pfisterer finds it more likely that the roundel once held an image of the youth's beloved. *Lysippus und seine Freunde. Liebesgaben und Gedächtnis im Rom der Renaissance oder: Das erste Jahrhundert der Medaille* (Berlin: Akademie, 2008), 34–35. Nagel and Wood, however, "are not persuaded by these arguments and see no reason not to date the marriage of the icon and the portrait to the 1480s. The venerable icon, or the altarpiece it came from, may have had some significance to the family of the sitter. Or perhaps the sitter was a precocious antiquarian and collector." They further argue that the historical context of icon collecting in late fifteenth-century Italy provides sufficient grounds for the Botticelli panel's assemblage. Nagel and Wood, *Anachronic Renaissance,* 116.

144. As Nagel and Wood argue, "In this period, icons were understood primarily as examples of ancient portraiture, visual records that brought one face to face with the earliest personalities of Christian history." Nagel and Wood, *Anachronic Renaissance,* 119.

145. As Nagel and Wood explain, "The objectification of the old panel, its reframing and presentation as a relic, releases in it an uncanny quality of animation. The saint looks up in the direction of the light, as if in this newly mobile condition his image must maintain, compass-like, an active relation to this immutable source . . . and seems to say, 'I am real, the rest is fiction.'" Ibid., 122.

146. Quoted from ibid., 33.

147. On the medieval/modern divide as a "massive value judgment," see Margreta de Grazia, "The Modern Divide: From Either Side," *JMEMS* 37, no. 3 (2007): 453–67.

148. Nagel and Wood, *Anachronic Renaissance,* 28.

2. The Chester Banns

1. As Paul Whitfield White states, "One is tempted to dismiss Goodman as a mere puritan zealot, but this native Cestrian . . . was an eminent Oxford scholar, Marian exile, political pamphleteer, Bible translator, and chaplain to the nobility, before returning to Chester around 1568, when he was nominated to the Ecclesiastical Commission for the diocese . . . and [by 1570] secured appointment as Archdeacon of Richmond." White, *Drama and Religion in English Provincial Society, 1485–1660* (Cambridge: Cambridge University Press, 2008), 98–99.

2. Goodman's letter is quoted from REED: *Cheshire,* 1:143.

3. See Margreta de Grazia, "World Pictures, Modern Periods, and the Early Stage," in *A New History of Early English Drama,* ed. John D. Cox and David Scott Kastan (New York, Columbia University Press, 1997), 17–21.

4. REED: *Cheshire,* 1:144.

5. William Crashaw, "The sermon preached at the Crosse" (London, 1607), Z1r.

6. Stephen Gosson, *Schoole of Abuse* (London, 1579), sig. B8r–C1r.

7. Munday, *A second and third blast of retrait from plaies and Theaters* (London, 1580), sig. A2v–A3r.

8. Stubbes, *Anatomie of Abuses* (London, 1583), sig. L6r. According to Peter Lake, Stubbes "took up where Gosson had left off" by offering "an intense distillation of what were emerging as the stock arguments against the stage." Lake, with Michael Questier, *The Antichrist's Lewd Hat: Protestants, Papists and Players in Post-Reformation England* (New Haven, CT: Yale University Press, 2002), 435.

9. Stubbes, *Anatomie of Abuses,* sig. L6v.

10. As Paul Whitfield White explains, "The Reformation, during its first fifty years in England, did not impose radical changes on English attitudes towards drama," yet "by 1580 or so, the old consensus of opinion among Protestant leaders and writers in supporting or at least tolerating the theatre was over." White, *Theatre and Reformation: Protestantism, Patronage, and Playing in Tudor England* (Cambridge: Cambridge University Press, 1993), 163–64. Also see his *Drama and Religion* as well as Phebe Jensen, *Religion and Revelry in Shakespeare's Festive World* (Cambridge: Cambridge University Press, 2008), and Lawrence Clopper, *Drama, Play, and Game* (Chicago: University of Chicago Press, 2001).

11. "By the late medieval period," Jensen explains, "plays were clearly associated with other cyclical celebrations—liturgical celebrations on one side, and secular pastimes on the other. Whether performed by parish guilds or other local amateur groups or by travelers, plays were identified with particular moments in the calendar—Christmas, Easter and Whitsuntide, and above all, Corpus Christi." Yet, she adds, "the Protestant Reformation explicitly identified the joining of the sacred and profane with Catholic practice." Jensen, *Religion and Revelry in Shakespeare's Festive World,* 28. Clopper's admonishment against reading "Puritan attacks on the [London] stage as the culmination of an anticipatory antitheatricalism from earlier in the [sixteenth] century" is nevertheless equally important to bear in mind. Clopper, *Drama, Play, and Game,* 24.

12. Having gathered "ancient and moderne testimonies," Prynne declares that "the most of our present English Actors (as I am credibly informed) being professed Papists . . . the Playes which issue from them must needs resemble these their Actors, the fruit being never better than the tree that beares it." Prynne, *Histrio-Mastix: The Players Scourge, or Actors Tragedie* (London, 1633), fol. 142; sig. T3v.

13. Ibid., fol. 112; sig. P4v. Yet as Michael O'Connell notes, "There is, to be sure, a degree of rhetorical play in this defining of theater as false religion; the writers do not appear to mean to make secular theater equivalent to the Mass" and yet "Prynne goes furthest in this direction." O'Connell, *The Idolatrous Eye: Iconoclasm and Theater in Early-Modern England* (Oxford: Oxford University Press, 2000), 33.

14. I borrow this cautionary note from Cathy Shrank's essay, "John Bale and Reconfiguring the 'Medieval' in Reformation England," in *Reading the Medieval in*

Early Modern England, ed. David Matthews and Gordon McMullan (Cambridge: Cambridge University Press, 2007), 179–92.

15. Thomas Lodge, *Defence of Poetry, Music, and Stage Plays* in *Elizabethan Critical Essays,* ed. George Gregory Smith (Oxford: Clarendon Press, 1904), 1:69. This slight or omission becomes most striking when Lodge offers a theological etymology for the word "tragedy":

> For tragedies and comedies, Donate the grammarian sayth, they wer inuented by lerned father of the old time to no other purpose but to yeelde prayse vnto God for a happy haruest or plentiful yeere. And that thys is trewe the name of Tragedye doth importe, for, if you consider whence it came, you shall per- ceiue (as Iodocus Badius reporteth) that it drewe his original of *Tragos, Hircus, et Ode, Cantus* (so called), for that the actors thereof had in rewarde for theyre labour a gotes skynne fylled with wyne. You see then that the fyrste matter of Tragedies was to giue thankes and praises to God, and a gratefull prayer of the countrymen for a happye haruest, and this I hope was not discommendable." (Ibid., 1:80)

16. Ibid., 1:83.

17. Thomas Heywood, *Apology for Actors* (London, 1612), G2v–G3r.

18. Ibid., E4r.

19. REED: *Cheshire,* 1:332. The *Breviary* was written by Robert Rogers, archdea- con of Werburgh Cathedral in the late 1500s (he died in 1595), and completed by his son David, who produced five copies of four versions between 1609 and about 1637. See ibid., 1:cxcvi.

20. As David Mills explains, "The defense of the plays suggests the strength both of support for them and of the opposition to them which the Banns seek to address." He also points out that the plays were performed during the following years of Eliza- beth's reign: 1561, 1567, 1568, 1572, 1575. See Mills, *Recycling the Cycle: The City of Chester and Its Whitsun Plays* (Toronto: University of Toronto Press, 1999), 145–46.

21. See REED: *Chester,* xxiii–l. Also see *REED: Cheshire,* 1:cxciv–cxcviii.

22. "The four Randle Holmes are," according to Clopper, "Chester's greatest transmitters of antiquarian material" who have bequeathed more than two hundred volumes of records. REED: *Chester,* 1:xxiv.

23. The term "antiquary" was available in the mid-sixteenth century as referring to "an official custodian or recorder of antiquities" and the *OED* cites the term being used as early as 1563 to refer to, among others, the writers of local English history such as John Leyland and then later (in 1602) to William Camden, presumably for his *Brittania.* In other words, the term included not only what we would call "clas- sical" historians but "medievalists" as well. See *OED Online,* s.v. "antiquary," defins. 2 and 3, http://www.oed.com.

24. My brief history of the Chester mysteries here is indebted to accounts in REED: *Chester,* liii–lv; REED: *Cheshire,* 1:xxxiii–xxxix; David Mills, *The Chester Mys- tery Cycle: A New Edition with Modernised Spelling* (East Lansing, MI: Colleagues Press, 1992), xiii–xvi; as well as R. M. Lumiansky and David Mills, *The Chester Mystery Cycle: Essays and Documents* (Chapel Hill: University of North Carolina Press, 1983), 205–6.

25. Whitsunday was a movable feast that could be held as early as May 10 or as late as June 13. Apparently the Chester clergy continued to perform a Passion play

on Corpus Christi, though the guilds—for whatever reason—now chose Whitsun. As Mills explains,

> We have no evidence to explain why the guild-play was separated from the Feast. It may have something to do with the great extension of the city's privileges by the royal charter granted to it in 1506. It may reflect an organisational problem, such as certainly occurred at York, in accommodating both play and procession in a single day. It may even suggest a desire to give the play more prominence and expand its scope. Some support is given to this last possibility by a development, attested in a revision of the pre-1539 Banns—the expansion of the play from a one-day to a three-day production, on the Monday, Tuesday, and Wednesday of Whitsun week. (Mills, *Chester Mystery Cycle*, xiv)

26. REED: *Chester,* liv, and REED: *Cheshire,* 1:xxxvi–xxxviii.

27. REED: *Cheshire,* 1:lxx–lxxi.

28. The *OED* lists the first usage of the term "banns" around the year AD 1200, when it was used to describe the announcement of an intended marriage. As referring to a "proclamation or prologue of a play," it was apparently first used around 1440. Etymologically, the word stems from both the medieval Latin word *bannum* and the French *ban,* both connoting edict or legal proclamation. For an explanation of how the Chester Banns "were both read and ridden," see REED: *Cheshire,* 1:xxxiv–xxxv.

29. According to Mills, the Harley manuscript most likely smoothed out an earlier working document spanning a series of revisions made at different times. See Mills, *Chester Mystery Cycle,* 3. In *Essays and Documents,* Lumiansky and Mills note that the first signs of religious censoring of the plays do not begin after Henry's Act of Supremacy as we might expect but following Edward's repeal of the *Six Articles* and the publication of the *First Prayer Book* (190).

30. "Obviously," write Lumiansky and Mills, "the Protestant Late Banns were written to replace the revised Catholic Early Banns, but just when the original Late Banns were composed is not clear because of the scarcity of evidence." Lumiansky and Mills, *Essays and Documents,* 190. Yet they later conjecture more closely as to the date; see ibid., 192. The Late Banns survive in four copies—two are prefixed to surviving copies of the plays (Harley 2013 and Bodley 175), while two were copied by Rogers into his *Breviary* (Harley 1944 and Chester Archive CX/3).

31. REED: *Cheshire,* 1:85, 86.

32. As David Mills reminds us, "The Later Banns are an attempt to defend the plays publicly against criticisms of them as theologically unsound and dramatically blasphemous. . . . [The Late Banns urge] their continuation as a worthwhile but harmless local custom." Mills, *Chester Mystery Cycle,* xix. Or as Paul Whitfield White observes, the Late Banns "announce the plays as a fully Protestantized cycle" but "do not fully deliver on their promise of reformed theater." White, *Drama and Religion,* 90. In *Drama and Religion,* White in fact revisits his earlier account of the Chester cycle in his essay "Reforming Mysteries' End: A New Look at Protestant Intervention in English Provincial Drama," *Journal of Medieval and Early Modern Studies* 29, no. 1 (1999): 121–47, saying, "I now think it was a much more conservative cycle than earlier surmised." White, *Drama and Religion,* 90n81.

33. REED: *Cheshire,* 1:79, 86.

34. Mills, *Chester Mystery Cycle,* 4n7. On the reception of the *Polychronicon* in late medieval England, see Emily Steiner, "Radical Historiography: Langland, Trevisa, and

the *Polychronicon,*" *Studies in the Age of Chaucer: The Yearbook of the New Chaucer Society* 27 (2005): 171–211.

35. In 1594, antiquarians studying the List of Mayors determined that Arneway was not the city's first mayor but served consecutively from 1268 to 1276 (see Mills, *Chester Mystery Cycle,* 4n5); yet the mythical account of his ties to the cycle plays remained unquestioned until the twentieth century. For a discussion of the pertinent dates and the long-standing fabrication of the cycle's early history, see REED: *Chester,* xxv–vi, as well as REED: *Cheshire,* 1:xxxix–xl.

36. REED: *Cheshire,* 1:81 (emphasis added).

37. Ibid., 1:87.

38. Ibid., 1:337.

39. Ibid., 1:332–33.

40. I'm indebted to Mills for this insight into the depiction of Higden as a progressive figure. Mills, *Chester Mystery Cycle,* xvii–xviii.

41. REED: *Cheshire,* 1:333.

42. Ibid., 1:333.

43. Ibid., 1:334. Mills interprets this difficult passage to mean "Do not condemn our subject-matter wherever you hear uncouth words which impart at this day little sense or meaning, such as on occasion 'posty' (power), 'lewty' (loyalty, faith), 'in good manner' (fittingly), or 'in fere' (together)—utterances of that sort will be spoken in delivering their speeches. At that time those speeches were well received. Then if you at this present time take them as if they were being spoken at that former time, then all is well, subject-matter as well as words!" Mills, *Chester Mystery Cycle,* 6, note on lines 50–56.

44. REED: *Cheshire,* 1:334. Mills paraphrases the second stanza as "If any subject-matter or performance in it, anything specific, does not please but displeases the majority of the people following, think back again to the first occasion of their performance, I say." Mills, *Chester Mystery Cycle,* 6.

45. REED: *Cheshire,* 1:345.

46. Compare Meg Twycross and Sarah Carpenter, who write, "The new Banns comment extensively on the plays, showing a rather defensively apologetic attitude towards their 'old-fashioned' drama." Twycross, and Carpenter, *Masks and Masking in Medieval and Early Tudor England* (Burlington, VT: Ashgate, 2002), 194.

47. REED: *Cheshire,* 1:337.

48. Ibid., 1:261. See also Meg Twycross, "The Chester Cycle Wardrobe," in *Staging the Chester Cycle,* ed. David Mills (Leeds, UK: University of Leeds School of English, 1985), 121.

49. *REED: Cheshire,* 1:338.

50. *OED,* s.v. "ancient," definition 2 *esp.*

51. Raphael Holinshed, *The Chronicles of England, Scotland and Ireland. London: Printed by Henry Denham, at the Expenses of Iohn Harison, George Bishop, Rafe Newberie, Henrie Denham, and Thomas Woodcocke* (1587), A1r (folio page 3) and C3r (folio page 19). In Horace Howard Furness Memorial (Shakespeare) Library, University of Pennsylvania. Accessed via Schoenberg Center for Electronic Text and Image (SCETI), http://dewey.lib.upenn.edu/sceti/.

52. *OED,* s.v. "ancient," defin. 5a.

53. The Chester mayor was summoned before the Privy Council in London but apparently went unpunished. See Lumiansky and Mills, *Essays and Documents,* 193.

54. Quoted from Lumiansky and Mills, *Essays and Documents,* 193 (emphasis added). "Used fur above remembraunce" means "practiced for time beyond memory," according to Lumiansky and Mills. Ibid., 193n19. REED: *Cheshire,* 1:173, transcribes this phrase as "far above."

55. REED: *Cheshire,* 1:333, 335, 332.

56. Lawrence Clopper, "The History and Development of the Chester Cycle," *Modern Philology* 75 (1978): 219.

57. "What could be more reasonable," F. M. Salter writes, "than to ascribe them to the man whom all the local antiquaries of the sixteenth century honoured as the first Mayor of Chester?" Salter, *Medieval Drama in Chester* (Toronto: University of Toronto Press, 1955), 36. On the historiography at work in *inventiones* narratives, see Monika Otter, *Inventiones: Fiction and Referentiality in Twelfth-Century English Historical Writing* (Chapel Hill: University of North Carolina Press, 1996).

58. Clopper, "History and Development," 221, 231.

59. Misreading this anachronic historiography, modern scholars have themselves antiquated a mystery cycle that is largely of Tudor origin. "The historians of English literature," Clopper explains,

> seem to imagine that the medieval cycle at Chester was complete in the early fifteenth century, that it was elaborated and enlarged by the end of the century, but that it continued more or less unchanged from the late fifteenth century until its demise in 1575. To the contrary, the sparse evidence of the fifteenth century suggests that the Corpus Christi play was more a Passion play than a cycle; the evidence of the sixteenth century is that the cycle as we know it was largely an invention of Tudor times and that the extant texts are versions performed in the final decades of the cycle's existence." Ibid., 219–20)

60. REED: *Cheshire,* 1:340.

61. Ibid., 1:338.

62. Clopper, "History and Development," 245–46.

63. REED: *Cheshire,* 1:338.

64. REED: *Cheshire,* 1:338 (emphasis added). Mills translates this line as saying, "'Therefore distribute God's loaves around with your usual happy heart.' Evidently the Bakers tossed small loaves to the crowds during the performance." (Mills, *Chester Mystery Cycle,* 9, note on line 138). Yet I am claiming that, given the antiquarian activities in Chester at this time and the repeated language of custom and tradition in both the Early and Late Banns, the word "accustomed" takes on greater significance than the word "usual" would seem to convey.

65. REED: *Cheshire,* 1:333.

66. Mills, *Recycling,* 141.

67. REED: Cheshire, 1:335. Mills paraphrases this passage as "Some writers provide authority for your subject-matter; therefore be confident to play the same enthusiastically to all the people." Mills, *Chester Mystery Cycle,* 7.

68. Mills understands "oure belefe" to refer to the Apostles' Creed: see Mills, *Chester Mystery Cycle,* 10, note on lines 147–51, as well as *Recycling,* 141.

69. REED: *Cheshire,* 1:338. Mills paraphrases this passage as follows: "As it is our Creed that Christ went down into hell after his Passion—but though our author

sets out what he did in that place according to his own opinion, nevertheless you may believe what the most learned men say; he does not fail to do justice to them. We would like you to comprehend the best opinions from all kinds of sources." Mills then goes on to say (though I am not sure that I share his view of the Banns' earnestness): "The creedal article claiming that Christ descended into hell rests upon uncertain scriptural foundation. The Banns accordingly attempt to reassure performers and audience that what they will witness is doctrinally sound." Mills, *Chester Mystery Cycle,* 10).

70. As Michael O'Connell writes, "In a series of steps England would move toward a position of total iconoclasm by the middle of the sixteenth century. . . . In some respects the royal directive of iconoclasm [by Edward VI in 1547] went beyond Zwingli's Zurich." O'Connell, *Idolatrous Eye,* 56. See also Eamon Duffy, *The Stripping of the Altars: Traditional Religion in England, 1400–1580* (New Haven, CT: Yale University Press, 1992), as well as Clifford Davidson, "'The Devil's Guts': Allegations of Superstition and Fraud in Religious Drama and Art during the Reformation," in *Iconoclasm vs. Art and Drama,* ed. Clifford Davidson and Ann Eljenholm Nichols, Early Drama, Art, and Music Monograph Series 11 (Kalamazoo: Medieval Institute Publications, 1989), 92–144.

71. REED: *Cheshire,* 1:340. I read the beginning of this passage as "Since it's impossible even for our talented, present-day actors to devise an alternative means of staging, I must caution you that you will see God impersonated by an actor in a gilt mask." Mills paraphrases the end of this passage as "But since the gold paint on the face does conceal the human features, understand that to be a covering for the man— understand that you hear only a voice, and not God appearing in shape or person." Mills, *Chester Mystery Cycle,* 12. Compare Twycross and Carpenter, who explain, "It is wrong, the passage suggests, for any man to try to 'act' or imitate God, because no human being can 'proportion' the Divinity. But the problem can be averted if we think of the golden face as equivalent to a modern cloud machine which effectively conceals the actor, allowing a 'voice of God' to speak. Twycross and Carpenter, *Masks and Masking,* 195.

72. Torbjörn Alström, "The Voice in the Mask," *Drama Review* 48, no. 2 (2004): 135, 138.

73. See Twycross and Carpenter's discussion of the word "disfigure" in this Banns passage in *Masks and Masking,* 194–95. In addition, they write, "This comparison urges that the mask, like a cloud machine, must be thought of as completely abolishing the man, the actor. We do not see him representing or pretending to *be* God, but only hear the voice in the golden face speaking God's words" (195). Yet the Late Banns' cautious apologies seem beside the point: why pretend gold face paint to be a covering of clouds when, as REED documents show, "clouds" of manufactured cloth were often used as scenery and machinery? The Late Banns themselves describe the "gloriose bodye [of Christ] in Clowdes moste ardente / Is taken vppto the heauens" in the Taylors' *Ascension* pageant. REED: *Cheshire,* 1:339. The use of artificial clouds is also mentioned regarding the annual Midsummer Show in 1610 (1:259). Twycross points out, however, that the Banns are not addressing simply those rare eschatological scenes like the *Creation* story or *Last Judgment* but also many New Testament pageants in which the figure of Christ was also performed behind a gilt mask. So the Banns' curious precaution touches many scenes of the

cycle production and underscores how volatile the mystery plays could be in post-Reformation England.

74. Compare Twycross and Carpenter, who write, "[The Late Banns'] patent uneasiness about the appearance of God on the stage seems foreign to the mysteries, and in fact to almost all medieval drama. In spite of obvious problems of performing divinity, a sense of impropriety in human actors playing God seems to be largely a post-Reformation development." They later add, "Nor does this change overnight with the Reformation. John Bale's mid-sixteenth-century plays, though violently anti-Catholic, introduce Pater Coelestis, Deus Pater, and Christ as characters, without apparent qualms, Christ even addressing the audience to invoke their devotion to himself." Twycross and Carpenter, *Masks and Masking,* 195, 196.

75. REED: *Cheshire,* 1:340.

76. Ibid., 1:340.

77. At 5.1.208–9 (and elsewhere), Theseus instructs, "The best in this kind are but shadows, and the worst are no worse if imagination amend them."

78. REED: *Cheshire,* 1:340.

79. Peter Womack, "Imagining Communities: Theatres and the English Nation in the Sixteenth Century," in *Culture and History, 1350–1600: Essays on English Communities, Identities and Writing,* ed. David Aers (Detroit, MI: Wayne State University Press, 1992), 107. Robert Barrett resists Womack's account in *Against All England: Regional Identity and Cheshire Writing, 1195–1656* (Notre Dame, IN: University of Notre Dame Press, 2009), 128–29.

80. *REED: Cheshire,* 1:340.

81. Ibid., 1:82–83, 335–36.

82. Ibid., 1:85, 83.

83. Ibid., 1:82.

84. Ibid., 1:83.

85. Ibid., 1:82.

86. Ibid., 1:82, 84. The weavers charged with the Chester *Last Judgment* would have designed a special leather costume that appeared to bleed profusely when Christ descended from Heaven and revealed himself to the damned and saved souls (s.d. following lines 426–28). It might have resembled the "Sirke" (shirt) specified by the York mercers for their *Last Judgment* pageant. As Clifford Davidson writes: "[In York] the wounded shirt (possibly indicating a full body stocking of leather) would have allowed for a painted wound, possibly wet in appearance, though the theatrical effect of having blood squirting out of the wound at the appropriate moment, as in Chester, is not recorded." See Davidson, *Technology, Guilds, and Early English Drama,* Early Drama, Art, and Music Monograph Series 23 (Kalamazoo, MI: Medieval Institute Publications, 1996), 90. Also see Michael O'Connell, "Blood Begetting Blood: Shakespeare and the Mysteries," in *Medieval Shakespeare: Pasts and Presents,* ed. Ruth Morse, Helen Cooper, and Peter Holland (Cambridge: Cambridge University Press, 2013), 177–89.

87. REED: *Cheshire,* 1:335.

88. Ibid., 1:336. "The 'well-decked carriage' of the Post-Reformation Banns may have carried two sets in close juxtaposition—the stable [of the Nativity] and the court [of the emperor Octavian]—since the Pre-Reformation Banns speak of 'your cariage of Marie, myld quene, and of Octavian.'" Mills, *Chester Mystery Cycle,* 101.

89. REED: *Cheshire,* 1:336. See also Mills, *Chester Mystery Cycle,* 151.

90. In fact, mystery drama did not always celebrate material labor. As James Simpson notes, the mysteries often complain about the physical exhaustion and brutal danger involved in various crafts; see Simpson, *Reform and Cultural Revolution, 1350–1547* (Oxford: Oxford University Press, 2002), 502–57.

91. Coletti studies the presence of the Expositor, who appears in five of the pageants, as evidence of the cycle's discursive complexity. See Coletti, "The Chester Cycle in Sixteenth-Century Religious Culture," *JMEMS* 37, no. 3 (2007): 531–47.

92. As Clifford Davidson explains, "The performance of drama in pre-industrial England was an activity that demanded much which we in modern times take for granted but which involved the use of scarce technology and expensive commodities for the construction and preparation of the stage, the creation of appropriate costumes and properties, and the arranging of theatrical effects." Davidson illustrates the efforts involved in even the most basic aspects of stage presentation: "It was not a time when one could go to the corner hardware stor[e] to purchase a gallon of paint for one's own use; the guild retained the formula for the paint as a trade secret, and also held an exclusive right to apply it. Even the design to be painted on the pageant would seem to have been a collaboration between the painter's guild and the sponsoring company that owned the wagon." See Davidson, *Technology,* 1–2.

93. The authoritative work on antitheatrical writers remains Jonas Barish, *The Antitheatrical Prejudice* (Berkeley: University of California Press, 1978). Jonathan Gil Harris and Natasha Korda examine the long history of "the widespread erasure of the visual dimensions of the public stage in modern theatre criticism" beginning in the late sixteenth century. Harris and Korda, "Introduction: Towards a Materialist Account of Stage Properties," in *Staged Properties in Early Modern English Drama,* ed. Harris and Korda (Cambridge: Cambridge University Press, 4–5. A more recent contribution is Elizabeth Williamson, *The Materiality of Religion in Early English Drama,* Studies in Performance and Early Modern Drama (Burlington, VT: Ashgate, 2009).

94. Stephen Gossen, *Playes confuted in five actions* (London, 1582), C6r.

95. William Prynne, *Histrio-Mastix,* 346 (sig. Yy1v, emphasis added).

96. Prynne, according to Elizabeth Williamson, "is aware of the affective power of theatrical performance. He even reproduces an early defense of Catholic drama, Lindanus's assertion that 'Stage-playes have a certaine shape of Images; and oft times move the pious affections of Christians, more than prayer it selfe.'" Williamson, *Materiality of Religion,* 19.

97. Harris and Korda, "Towards a Materialist Account," 6.

98. Harris and Korda reproduce Henslowe's inventory in the appendix of *Staged Properties* (pages 335–36), and I quote from it here.

99. My subsequent discussion of the materiality of the Chester Banns is indebted to Jonathan Gil Harris's fascinating work on Renaissance theories of matter and "palimpsested time" in *Untimely Matter in the Time of Shakespeare* (Philadelphia: University of Pennsylvania Press, 2009).

100. Clopper, "History and Development," 236. Yet see Lumiansky and Mills, who express reservations about Clopper's theory about stanzaic shifts. Lumiansky and Mills, *Essays and Documents,* 273.

101. Clopper, "History and Development," 236.

102. Ibid.,231. Lumiansky and Mills, *Essays and Documents,* 273.

103. Lumiansky and Mills, *Essays and Documents,* 299–301; also see REED: *Chester,* 38–39, as well as Clopper's essay "History and Development," 225–33.

104. Julie Spraggon, *Puritan Iconoclasm during the English Civil War* (London: Boydell Press, 2003), 202.

105. Ibid., 209.

106. For Goodman's account of "absurdities" in "the old Popish plays of Chester" see REED: *Cheshire,* 1:146–48; for the perceived "peril" and "danger to Her Majesty" etc., see 1:144.

107. REED editors believe that even when Holme made minor variations in spelling and the like, we can be confident in the accuracy of the large quantity of records that he was responsible for transmitting. REED: *Cheshire,* 1:cxcvi.

108. As Coletti reminds us, "Efforts to recuperate the past nonetheless inevitably inscribed the city's medieval heritage with new religious understandings and possibly even new devotional purposes." Coletti, "Chester Cycle," 538.

109. Harris, *Untimely Matter,* 20.

110. See Walter Benjamin, *The Origin of German Tragic Drama,* trans. John Osborne (London: Verso, 1977). Yet coalescing sixteenth-century narratives and seventeenth-century textual practices with twentieth-century theory risks losing sight of the virtue of the Banns—namely, their temporal proximity to both the mysteries and the professional London playhouses. The Banns, unlike Benjamin, narrate a history of early English drama free from any consideration of Burckhardt's *Kulturgeschichte* and Hegel's dialectics. Thus although I hold up Benjamin's ruin as an illustrative point of comparison, overstating the relevance of his work may unwittingly lead us to dwell upon, rather than to work around, the language of vestiges, precursors, and leftovers—and, perhaps, to a tacit recapitulation of Chambers's secularization thesis (itself derived from a Hegelian scholastic tradition).

111. "Rather than signaling the advent of another epoch's renewal," Benjamin's ruin, writes Julia Reinhard Lupton, "itself constitutes a kind of rebirth, a rebirth as ruin—namely, the survival of a work beyond the period of its cultural currency." Lupton, *Afterlives of the Saints: Hagiography, Typology, and Renaissance Literature* (Stanford: Stanford University Press, 1996), 28.

112. Harris, *Untimely Matter,* 94.

113. Compare Harris and Korda, who suggest that Benjamin's "sympathetic account of how 'the life of [the] apparently dead' prop of *Trauerspiel*" may provide "a potentially fruitful starting point for theorizing the social as well as dramatic lives of stage properties." Harris and Korda, "Towards a Materialist Account," 13.

114. O'Connell, "Vital Cultural Practices: Shakespeare and the Mysteries," *JMEMS* 29, no. 1 (1999): 152–53.

115. Emmerson, "Dramatic History: On the Diachronic and Synchronic in the Study of Early English Drama," *JMEMS* 35, no. 1 (2005): 56.

116. My cautionary note is aimed at my own analysis, and I do not mean to imply that Emmerson's careful essay is deficient in this regard; his aim is to uncover "the similar as well as the dissimilar and to highlight continuities as well as discontinuities." Ibid., 55.

117. REED: *Cheshire,* 1:144.

3. Balaam to Bottom

1. Brandes, "The Airy Dream," in *A Midsummer Night's Dream,* ed., Judith M. and Richard F. Kennedy (New Brunswick, NJ: Athlone Press, 1999), 341.

2. Davidson, "'What Hempen Home-Spuns Have We Swagg'ring Here?' Amateur Actors in *A Midsummer Night's Dream* and the Coventry Civic Plays and Pageants," *Shakespeare Studies* 19 (1987): 87–99; Greenblatt, *Will in the World: How Shakespeare Became Shakespeare* (New York: Norton, 2004), 36.

3. Montrose, *The Purpose of Playing: Shakespeare and the Cultural Politics of the Elizabethan Theatre* (Chicago: University of Chicago Press, 1996), 180, 185. Montrose subsequently argues that Shakespeare "parodies antecedent dramatic forms and performance styles" (190). Responding to Montrose, Michael O'Connell, "Vital Cultural Practices: Shakespeare and the Mysteries," *JMEMS* 29, no. 1 (1999): 149–68, defends the sophistication of the medieval stage.

4. Parker, "What a Piece of Work Is Man: Shakespearean Drama as Marxian Fetish, the Fetish as Sacramental Sublime," *JMEMS* 34, no. 3 (2004): 662–63.

5. Muir, *The Sources of Shakespeare's Plays* (London: Methuen, 1977), 68. Geoffrey Bullough is more open to Scot yet first mentions various classical sources: "The setting of an ass's head on Bottom recalls Circe's charms. It is a piece of poetic justice like the well-known story of Phoebus's revenge on King Midas which I give from Cooper's *Thesaurus Linguae*. . . . Midas has only his ears changed. Bottom's assification is more like that of the amorous Apuleius in *The Golden Asse,* translated by Adlington in 1566, but nearer still to Shakespeare is a version of witches' spells found in Scot." Bullough, *Narrative and Dramatic Sources of Shakespeare* (New York: Columbia University Press, 1957), 1:372. Joseph Rosenblum notes an intriguing affinity between Titania's obstinacy and the figure of "Ostinatione" carrying an ass's head in her hands in CesareRipa's 1593 *Iconologia;* see "Why an Ass? Cesare Ripa's *Iconologia* as a Source for Bottom's Translation," *SQ* 32, no. 3 (1981): 357–59.

6. Emmerson, "Dramatic History: On the Diachronic and Synchronic in the Study of Early English Drama," *JMEMS* 35, no. 1 (2005): 40, 54–57.

7. According to Lawrence Clopper, "The History and Development of the Chester Cycle," *Modern Philology* 75 (1978): 228, "The cappers must have gotten their play . . . sometime between 1505 and 1522."

8. Translation from David Mills in *The Chester Mystery Cycle: A New Edition with Modernised Spelling* (East Lansing, MI: Colleagues Press, 1992), 91. The Latin stage direction reads: "Tunc percutiet Balaham asinam suam. Et hic oportet aliquis transformiari in speciem asinae; et quando Balaham percutit, dicat asina."

9. *The Bible and Holy Scriptures conteyned in the Olde and Newe Testament* (London, 1560), fol. 72 (sig. s4v).

10. REED: *Cheshire,* 1:336.

11. See ibid., 1:lxxi, 356.

12. Clopper, "History and Development," 228.

13. Translation from Mills, *Chester Mystery Cycle,* 60; the Latin stage direction reads: "Tunc emittet columbam; et erit in nave aliam columbam ferens olivam in ore, quam dimittet aliquis ex malo per funem in manibus Noe." Lumiansky and Mills consider this stage direction (quoted in Appendix IA/15+SD of *The Chester Mystery Cycle,* EETS Supplementary Series 3 and 9 [Oxford: Oxford University Press, 1974; repr., 1986], 1:464) essential to the *Noah* play, though it is found only in Harley MS 2124 (1607).

14. Quoted from the stage direction in Mills, *Chester Mystery Cycle,* 50.

15. Clifford Davidson, *Technology, Guilds, and Early English Drama,* Early Drama, Art, and Music Monograph Series 23 (Kalamazoo, MI: Medieval Institute Publications, 1996), 1–2.

16. As Davidson states, "The sponsorship of the guild seems to have meant that whenever possible the craft involved would show off its workmanship." He then continues: "While in the case of the Smiths' pageant at Coventry it is hard to know exactly how their use and display of metalwork was effected except in a few aspects such as the use of gold leaf, the evidence nevertheless suggests high visibility for the products produced by means of their technology. Blacksmiths had very good reason to want to improve their 'image'…since there appears to have been some suspicion about their way of life and also about the quality of their product." Ibid., 38. Scholars have debated the extent and purpose of commercialism in the mysteries. John C. Coldewey argues that the handicraft exhibited by the pageants constitutes a kind of advertising; see "Some Economic Aspects of the Late Medieval Drama," in *Contexts for Early English Drama,* ed. Marianne G. Briscoe and John C. Coldewey (Bloomington: Indiana University Press, 1989), 87. J. W. Robinson critiques this account in *Studies in Fifteenth-Century Stagecraft* (Kalamazoo, MI: Medieval Institute Publications, 1991), 63–64.

17. "On stage," Parker writes, "the vanity that appeared in likening their work to God's gave them hope that all would be repaired." Parker, "What a Piece of Work Is Man," 663.

18. Ibid., 662–63.

19. As Mills states, "The 1607 version of the play also calls for Moses to return from the mountain with 'horns' and a shining face, and possibly we should assume a similar head-dress here." Mills, *Chester Mystery Cycle,* 84.

20. Mills notes the recent use of a two-man costume; see ibid., 84.

21. Clopper, "History and Development," 231.

22. Ibid., 245–46.

23. In her study of "early modern remakings of medieval religious ideas and practices," Theresa Coletti has shown how the Tudor Chester cycle is "neither stabilized as text nor fixed in time or topography as performance." Coletti, "The Chester Cycle in Sixteenth-Century Religious Culture," *JMEMS* 37, no. 3 (2007): 543, 533.

24. Reginald Scot, *The Discoverie of Witchcraft* (New York: Dover, 1989), 54–57.

25. Gail Kern Paster and Skiles Howard characterize Scot as a "vigorous defender" of the Reformation; see William Shakespeare, *A Midsummer Night's Dream,* ed. Gail Kern Paster and Skiles Howard (New York: Bedford/St. Martin's, 1999), 287.

26. As Stephen Greenblatt states, "These contemptuous sallies come close to ridiculing the sacrament itself, even as they attempt to ridicule only the Papists. Yet the Reformers were driven to take the risk in order to counter what they regarded as the still greater risk of idolatry." See Greenblatt, "Remnants of the Sacred in Early Modern England," in *Subject and Object in Renaissance Culture,* ed. Margreta de Grazia, Maureen Quilligan, and Peter Stallybrass (Cambridge: Cambridge University Press, 1996), 343.

27. Ulinka Rublack, *Reformation Europe* (Cambridge: Cambridge University Press, 2005), 1–3.

28. Those titles are, respectively, *Deuttung der czwo grewlichen Figuren, Pabstesels zu Rom und Munchkalbs zu Frieberg in Meissen funden* and *Of Two VVoonderful Popish Monsters to wyt, of a Popish Asse which was found at Rome in the riuer of Tyber, and of a Moonkish Calfe, calued at Friberge in Misne.* See *D. Martin Luthers Werke: Kritische Gesamtausgabe, Schriften,* vol. 11 (Weimar: H. Böhlau, 1900; Unveränderter Abdruck, 1966), 357–86.

29. Melanchthon and Luther, *Of two vvoonderful popish monsters* (London, 1579), sig. B1v. Cited parenthetically hereafter by page signature.

30. R. W. Scribner, *Popular Culture and Popular Movements in Reformation Germany* (London: Hambledon Press, 1987), 284.

31. The first chapter of Crawford's *Marvelous Protestantism: Monstrous Births in Post-Reformation England* (Baltimore: Johns Hopkins University Press, 2005) "takes as its subject the complicated genealogy of the monk calf in the English popular press and imagination." Crawford argues that the success of these monstrous tales and images often "relied on the use of discredited Catholic beliefs, particularly in the relationship between the material and divine" (28).

32. Barthlet, *The pedegrewe of heretiques* (London, 1566), sig. Y1v; Boaistuau, *Certaine secrete wonders of nature* (London, 1569), sig. Mm4r. Barthlet merely discusses the papal-ass; Boaistuau adds a large woodcut illustration that differs in several minor details from that used in the 1579 pamphlet.

33. R. W. Scribner, *For the Sake of Simple Folk: Popular Propaganda for the German Reformation* (Oxford: Oxford Clarendon Press, 1994), 132. Also *Luthers Werke*, 11:361–65. And Konrad Lange, *Der Papstesel: Ein BeitragzurKultur- und Kunstgeschichte des Reformationszeitalters* (Göttingen: Vandenhoeck and Ruprecht, 1891), 92–93.

34. Scribner, *Popular Culture*, 278. Scribner notes that some editions of the *Depiction* contain ten illustrations.

35. Chambers, *The Mediaeval Stage* (Oxford: Oxford Clarendon Press, 1903), 2:57. And so, as in Chambers's broader account, attempts by Christianity to squelch pagan folk culture ultimately translate into drama's "spontaneous growth" and evolution. "Miniature drama" is a term that E. K. Chambers used to distinguish this scene from the previous monologues. Ibid., 2:54.

36. There are several sources for the *asinaria feste* at Beauvais. Chambers cites modern editions of the *Glossarium mediae et infimae Latinitatis,* by Charles de Fresne, sieur du Cange (1610-88). Ducange (as Chambers refers to him) drew from a section of a thirteenth-century *Officium* with the heading *Conductus quando asinus adducitur* (see Chambers, *Mediaeval Stage*, 1:331). The name "donkey mass" is a seventeenth-century term cited by Henry Copley Greene, "The Song of the Ass," *Speculum* 6, no. 4 (1931): 534n5, and comes from a 1697 letter from Foy de Saint-Hilaire, a canon in Beauvais, to M. de Francastel, assistant librarian of the Bibliothèque Mazarien in Paris. According to Greene, Foy de Saint-Hilaire writes, "See what I heard said by my late father, who had seen the whole Donkey Mass, [of] which [the MS] was kept in our parish church of St. Stephen, and which a clerk of the Curé's seized and cruelly burned because of conscientious scruples."

37. Just how irksome Luther found the palm ass is illustrated by his repeated reference to it as a childish innovation that is "contrary to faith" in his 1530 *Exhortation to All Clergy Assembled at Augsburg. Selected Writings of Martin Luther,* ed. Theodore G. Tappert (Minneapolis: Fortress Press, 1967), 108, 111.

38. The *Palmesels* referenced by Chambers seem only to be those that include affixed statues. Chambers, *Mediaeval Stage,* 1:334.

39. See Eamon Duffy, *The Stripping of the Altars: Traditional Religion in England c. 1400–1580* (New Haven: Yale University Press, 1992), 26–27. Also see Chambers, *Mediaeval Stage,* 1:334n2.

40. *The Nevv Testament of Iesus Christ, translated faithfully into English, out of the authentical Latin* (Rheims, 1582), sig. H3r (emphasis added).

41. Ibid. The word "gratefull" here is to be understood in the sense of "pleasing . . . agreeable, acceptable, welcome." *OED Online*, s.v. "grateful," defin. 1, http://www.oed.com.

42. *The text of the New Testament . . . with a confutation of all such arguments, glosses, and annotations, as conteine manifest impietie, of heresie, treason and slander, against the catholike Church of God* (London, 1589), sig. K6v, L1r. Chambers cites the 1633 edition of this text and believes that because Fulke "was evidently unaware that there was an ass as well as the priest in the procession . . . the custom was not known in England." Chambers, *Mediaeval Stage,* 1:334. Yet the Rheims gloss cited above to which Fulke is responding seems to make it clear that Palm Sunday rituals in England are being discussed.

43. Scribner, *Popular Culture,* 285.

44. As Jonathan Gil Harris explains in his discussion of Renaissance theories of "untimely matter," often "in order to perform the very difference between past and present, the matter of the past must be incorporated into the present." Harris, *Untimely Matter in the Time of Shakespeare* (Philadelphia: University of Pennsylvania Press, 2009), 31.

45. Scribner, *Popular Culture,* 285.

46. Barrett, *Against All England: Regional Identity and Cheshire Writing, 1195–1656* (Notre Dame, IN: University of Notre Dame Press, 2009), 61.

47. See Barrett's first chapter, "From Cloister to Corporation," especially pages 47–49, in *Against All England.*

48. Ibid., 61–62.

49. Clopper, "History and Development," 235. Also see REED: *Cheshire,* 1:161.

50. I am not making a specific claim that play 5 was revised after the manner of the Antichrist play but simply observing that (whether or not it was) it was certainly received and interpreted differently following the period of Edwardian reform. Emmerson writes, "Although many in the audience probably still enjoyed the dramatization of the legend and others probably relished the newly explicit condemnation of the papacy and Catholicism as Antichrists, others were probably offended by the introduction of such polemics into their civic celebrations, and any Catholics in the audience, who must have felt like foreigners in their own country, probably were appalled"; see Emmerson, "Contextualizing Performance: The Reception of the Chester Antichrist," *JMEMS* 29, no. 1 (1999): 110.

51. *The Bible and holy scriptures conteined in the Olde and Nevve Testament* (London, 1576), sig. Sssss2r–v. Curiously, this commentary is reiterated graphically in the 1576 edition by the fact that the decorative initial *S* in the name Simon Peter at the beginning of the epistle depicts a figure wearing a miter or triple tiara seated beneath a canopy with his arms raised in benediction. Like Luther and Melanchthon's papal ass, this pope seemingly wears large ass's ears that give him a rather Puckish appearance. Printer Christopher Barker does not appear to have reused the woodcut in subsequent editions of either the Geneva New Testament or the complete Bible.

52. Foxe, *Actes and monuments* (London, 1583), sig. Gg3v.

53. Luther's commentary on 2 Peter 2, published in a 1581 English translation, agrees with the Geneva Bible's interpretation: "Of this matter doeth sainct Peter now here speake, meanyng that our greased Popelynges and Romishe route, with all their

Disciples, Fauourers, Abetters, and Sectaries, are the verie children of this Balaam." He then glosses the meaning of the prophet's name: "Balaam, in the Hebrue tongue signifieth a Deuourer, or a Sweepestake, or a Supper vp, who with open mouthe deuoureth and gulleth vp all that commeth to hand. . . . The Sirname of this Prophete, is the Sonne of Bosor, whiche signifith Fleshe, or as Moses calleth hym Beor, whiche signifieth Foolishe." Luther, *A commentarie or exposition vppon the twoo Epistles generall of Sainct Peter, and that of Sainct Jude* (London, 1581), sig. Pp1r–v. First published in German the same year as the pamphlet depicting the papal ass (1523), Luther's commentary on the epistles of Peter and Jude draws upon the themes of Melanchthon's interpretation of that monster, most significantly the ass's association with the fleshy Roman idolatry as opposed to the godly spirituality of the Reformers.

54. Bale, *The image of both Churches* (London, 1570), sig. A8v.

55. Scribner, *Popular Culture,* 285.

56. Rublack, *Reformation Europe,* 1–2.

57. For a discussion of stage properties as "tangible assets to a play-acting company," their construction, storage, and expense, see Andrew Gurr, *The Shakespearean Stage,* 3rd ed. (Cambridge: Cambridge University Press, 1992), 187–93. While noting the relatively small number of large properties required by Shakespeare's plays (as well as the fact that "stages themselves were colorful yet essentially bare"), Gurr nevertheless states that "given storage space, the wealthier and longer-lived companies could accumulate a good many standard properties." If Henslowe's 1598 diary entry is any indication, several of these items would have been false (mostly bestial) heads and entire animals including "I lyone, ii lyone heads," "i blacke dogge," "i bulles head," "owld Mahemetes head," "I lyone skin; I beares skyne," and "Argosses head." *Henslowe's Diary,* 2nd ed., ed. R. A. Foakes (Cambridge: Cambridge University Press, 2002), 319–21.

58. See *The Norton Facsimile of the First Folio of Shakespeare,* 2nd ed., ed. Charlton Hinman (New York: Norton, 1996), 170. Neither the first nor the second quarto (London, 1600, STC (2nd ed.)/22302 and London, 1600 [i.e. 1619], STC (2nd ed.)/22303, respectively) includes this stage direction—or many others, for that matter. In fact, this paucity has often encouraged editors to say that the folio was most likely the closest of the three to "a theatrical manuscript, probably a promptbook in the possession of Shakespeare's company." See Greenblatt's introduction to the play in *The Norton Shakespeare: Based on the Oxford Edition,* ed. Stephen Greenblatt et al. (New York: Norton, 1997), 812.

59. See Q1, sig. F4r, and Q2, sig. F4r.

60. Davidson, "'What Hempen Home-Spuns Have We Swagg'ring Here?,'" 94.

61. *OED,* s.v. "translate," III.4. On clothing and translation see Peter Stallybrass and Ann Rosalind Jones, *Renaissance Clothing and the Materials of Memory* (Cambridge: Cambridge University Press, 2000), 220–44.

62. Martin Luther, "The Misuse of the Mass," in *Luther's Works,* American ed., vol. 36, *Word and Sacrament II,* trans. Frederick C. Ahrens, ed. Helmut T. Lehmann and Abdel Ross Wentz (Philadelphia: Fortress Press, 1959), 182; original, *D. Martin Luthers Werke: Kritische Gesamtausgabe, Schriften,* vol. 8 (Weimar: H. Böhlau, 1889; UnveränderterAbdruck, 1966), 523.

63. On the temporality of typology, see Harris, *Untimely Matter,* 36–39.

64. *A Dictionary of Stage Directions in English Drama, 1580–1642* (Cambridge: Cambridge University Press, 1999), Alan Dessen and Leslie Thomson's invaluable

study of terms found in the stage directions of English professional plays, lists—under the entry for "head"—only the folio text of *Dream* as calling for the head of an ass (112), though of course many other bestial heads were used, including those of a bull, a stag, a bear, a lion, and a dragon. According to the entry for "ass, mule," real asses appear onstage no more than five times in about sixty years (16). In addition, the entry for "ear" (as in Midas's ass's ears) produces similarly scarce entries—three, to be exact. Two caveats to the study of stage directions of which Dessen has kindly reminded me are, first, that a play might stage an ass's head though its stage directions make no mention of it, and, second, that the texts which survive are deficient.

65. McMillin and MacLean, *The Queen's Men and their Plays* (Cambridge: Cambridge University Press, 1998), 180, 182.

66. Cooper writes, "It is possible that the cash-strapped [cappers] guild sold them the ass-head to raise a little money, or just to dispose of it, since the suppression of the cycle plays had rendered it redundant." Cooper, *Shakespeare and the Medieval World* (New York: Arden Shakespeare, 2010), 220. Yet as I have noted, REED documents testify that as late as 1610, the ass's head was by no means redundant but rather so popular as to be newly made for the city's annual Midsummer show.

67. REED: *Coventry,* 334. On the ambiguity of the word "heade" in early English drama records, see Meg Twycross and Sarah Carpenter, "Masks in Medieval English Theatre," *Medieval English Theatre,* 3 (1981): 7–44, 69–113, as well as their *Masks and Masking in Medieval and Early Tudor England* (Burlington, VT: Ashgate, 2002).

68. See Richard Helgerson, *Forms of Nationhood: The Elizabethan Writing of England* (Chicago: University of Chicago Press, 1992), 197.

69. Stallybrass, "Shakespeare's Desk: The Materiality of Authorship" (paper presented at the Shakespeare Association of America conference in Philadelphia, 15 April 2006). In a similar way, Cooper speculates that its acquisition by the Chamberlain's Men gave "the cue to Shakespeare to work it into a play," and concludes, "It shows the ease with which he himself could negotiate the two theatrical worlds, and turn one into the other." Cooper, *Shakespeare and the Medieval World,* 220.

70. Translation mine; the original reads: "*Orientis partibus / Adventavit Asinus / Pulcher et fortissimus / Sarcinis aptissimus.* / Hez, Sire Asnes, car chantez, / Belle bouche rechignez, / Vous aurez du foinassez / Et de l'avoine a plantez." Quoted from Greene, "The Song of the Ass," 535.

71. Compare Greenblatt, who raises the question of secularization regarding the cult of Purgatory: "Does this mean that Shakespeare was participating in a secularization process . . .? Perhaps. But the palpable effect is something like the reverse: *Hamlet* immeasurably intensifies a sense of the weirdness of the theater, its proximity to certain experiences that had been organized and exploited by religious institutions and rituals." He adds, "Plays can borrow, imitate, and reflect much of what passes for everyday reality without necessarily evacuating this reality or exposing it as made-up." Greenblatt, *Hamlet in Purgatory* (Princeton: Princeton University Press, 2001), 253.

72. Kott, *The Bottom Translation: Marlowe and Shakespeare and the Carnival Tradition,* trans. Daniela Miedzyrzecka and Lillian Vallee (Evanstan, IL: Northwestern University Press, 1987), 50.

73. Ibid., 52. Kott notes the importance of Paul's letter to the Corinthians to Shakespeare's play, yet it is not significant for him as a residue of Bible drama or even Christianity per se but only as part of a larger "tradition, a system of interpretation, and a 'language'" of Neoplatonic or hermetic metaphysics that complements but contradicts the "code of carnival" or tradition of *serio ludere* that also informs the play (32–33). "Shakespeare," he later adds, "is a legatee of all myths" (61).

74. Most recently, Hugh Grady argues that Shakespeare's *Dream* anticipates modernity with its "prescient" aesthetic theories, and in fact the play, he says, displays a rather postmodern ability to deconstruct those theories itself: "It is a play that presciently constructs a modern concept of the aesthetic and at the same time shows us the constructedness of this concept, its relation not only to imagination and the artistic past, but to desire and labor as well." "Shakespeare and Impure Aesthetics: The Case of *A Midsummer Night's Dream,*" *SQ* 59, no. 3 (Fall 2008): 301.

75. For a profound study of the synesthesia in *Dream,* particularly as it impinges upon post-Reformation discourses concerning the body and bodily praxis, see Jennifer Waldron, "'The Eye of Man Hath Not Heard': Shakespeare, Synaesthesia, and Post-Reformation Phenomenology," *Criticism* 54 (2012): 403–17.

76. I agree, moreover, with James Simpson, who eloquently explains that the mysteries were neither ecclesiastically instructional nor wholly secular but rather expressions of "many spiritually sophisticated lay figures in the fourteenth and fifteenth centuries [who] clearly felt the inevitable strains and compromises of the active life, and wished for retirement to the contemplative life of monastic discipline." The plays, then, may be said to "emerge from that sophisticated lay culture, a culture that shaped its own theology of mercy out of its immersion in and knowledge of the rigours of domestic and civic life." Simpson, *Reform and Cultural Revolution, 1350–1547* (Oxford: Oxford University Press, 2002), 509.

77. Welborn, *Paul, the Fool of Christ: A Study of 1 Corinthians 1–4 in the Comic-Philosophic Tradition* (New York: T and T Clark, Ltd., 2005), 32–33. For another insightful book-length study of the centrality of playacting to Christianity, see John Parker, *The Aesthetics of Antichrist* (Ithaca, NY: Cornell University Press, 2007).

78. Welborn, *Paul,* 89, n318; 39. A. Nicoll notes that a first-century AD fragment from a bronze relief "unquestionably" shows an ass-headed actor from "an animal scene of the mimic type." See Nicoll, *Masks, Mimes, and Miracles: Studies in the Popular Theatre* (New York: Harcourt, Brace, 1931), 74–75.

79. Welborn, *Paul,* 142.

80. Other important works that have argued for the indebtedness of the London playhouses to the mystery pageants include Glynne Wickham, *Early English Stages, 1300 to 1660* (New York: Columbia University Press, 1963); John D. Cox, *The Devil and the Sacred in English Drama: 1350–1642* (Cambridge: Cambridge University Press, 2000); and Helen Cooper, *Shakespeare and the Medieval World.*

81. On the aversion of anachronism as "the need to retain the 'cognitive distance' that is the very basis of our disciplinary knowledge," see Margreta de Grazia, "Anachronism," in *Cultural Reformations: Medieval and Renaissance in Literary History,* ed. Brian Cummings and James Simpson (Oxford: Oxford University Press, 2010), 13–32.

82. Parker, "Teaching and Wordplay: The 'Wall' of *A Midsummer Night's Dream,*" in *Teaching with Shakespeare: Critics in the Classroom,* ed. Bruce McIver and Ruth Stevenson

(Newark: University of Delaware Press, 1994), 209. Also see Robert Glendinning's insightful "Pyramus and Thisbe in the Medieval Classroom," *Speculum* 61, no. 1 (1986): 51–78.

83. Shakespeare's parodies of provincial drama discomfort contemporary scholars, as, for example, when Davidson explains, "Shakespeare's negative view of such plays and players in provincial cities and towns is probably misleading in the extreme, for the spectacles . . . were surely not so rough and 'amateurish' as we might imagine." Nevertheless, Davidson argues, *Dream*'s representation of provincial players "serves by its burlesque of amateur actors to set apart their play-within-a-play from the main actions of *A Midsummer Night's Dream* and hence to provide a comment on the role of imagination in the theater itself." Davidson, "'What Hempen Home-Spuns Have We Swagg'ring Here?,'" 94.

84. O'Connell, "Vital Cultural Practices," 159.

85. "By associating his own aesthetic standards with the aristocrats who comment on the absurdity of the mechanicals' entertainment," John Watkins explains, "Shakespeare distinguished himself from an older social order in which the same men who wove, brewed, built, and smelted were deemed simultaneously capable of dramatic excellence." Watkins, "Bedeviling the Histories of Medieval and Early Modern Drama," *Modern Philology* 101 (2003): 68.

86. William Crashaw, "The sermon preached at the Crosse" (London, 1609), sig. Z1r.

87. See REED: *Cheshire,* 335.

88. See ibid., 336. As David Mills writes, "The 'well-decked carriage' of the Post-Reformation Banns may have carried two sets in close juxtaposition—the stable [of the *Nativity*] and the court [of the emperor Octavian]—since the Pre-Reformation Banns speak of 'your cariage of Marie, myld quene, and of Octavian.'" Mills, *Chester Mystery Cycle,* 101.

89. As Beatrice Groves has shown, the Tyndale and 1557 edition of the Geneva Bible use the word "bottome" rather than the phrase "deepe thinges" at 1 Corinthians 2:9. Groves also notes several other interesting connections between Bottom's speech and the Pauline Epistles. Groves, "'The Wittiest Partition': Bottom, Paul, and Comedic Resurrection," *Notes and Queries* 54, no. 3 (2007): 277–82.

90. According to Greenblatt, in *Dream* Shakespeare "split the theater between a magical, virtually nonhuman element, which he associated with the power of the imagination to lift itself away from the constraints of reality, and an all-too-human element, which he associated with the artisans' trades that actually made the material structures" and costumes of the stage. Greenblatt, *Will in the World,* 53. In the discussion that follows, I am suggesting that this Cartesian split is not absolute—that the magical and material worlds in the play overlap in significant ways.

91. As the note for 5.2.20 in the *Norton Shakespeare* explains, Robin traditionally "helped good housekeepers and punished lazy ones."

92. REED: *Cheshire,* 1:340.

93. Quoted from R. M. Lumiansky and David Mills, *The Chester Mystery Cycle: Essays and Documents* (Chapel Hill, NC: University of North Carolina Press, 1983), 194.

94. REED: *Cheshire,* 1:340.

95. As Hugh Grady states, "In the travesty that is the mechanicals' play, [Shakespeare] presents us with the final truth of his own masterpiece—its made-ness, its materiality, its resistance to the artist's shaping fantasies." Grady, "Shakespeare and Impure Aesthetics," 301.

96. In Greenblatt's words, Shakespeare wanted his audience to grasp that "the theater had to have both, both the visionary flight and the solid ordinary earthiness." Greenblatt, *Will in the World,* 53.

97. Stephen Greenblatt, *Shakespearean Negotiations: The Circulation of Social Energy in Renaissance England* (Berkeley: University of California Press, 1988), 113.

4. "Then Is Doomsday Near"

1. In *Renaissance Clothing and the Materials of Memory* (Cambridge: Cambridge University Press, 2000), 255, Ann Rosalind Jones and Peter Stallybrass point out that ghosts in classical Greek tragedy could be depicted as armored but were most often shrouded.

2. On the tension caused by the Ghost's injunctions to revenge and to remember, see Stephen Greenblatt, *Hamlet in Purgatory* (Princeton: Princeton University Press, 2001), 205ff. "Such a call for vengeance," he writes, "could only come from the place in the afterlife where Seneca's ghosts reside: Hell" (237).

3. On "Protestant iconoclasm [that] resulted in the suppression of actual representations of divine mysteries," see Cecile Cary, "'It Circumscribes Us Here': Hell on the Renaissance Stage," in *The Iconography of Hell,* ed. Clifford Davidson and Thomas H. Seiler, Early Drama, Art, and Music Monograph Series 17 (Kalamazoo, MI: Medieval Institute Publications, 1992), 187. See also Greenblatt, who states, "Purgatory could be represented as a sly jest, a confidence trick, a mistake. . . . But it could not be represented as a frightening reality. *Hamlet* comes closer to doing so than any other play of this period." Greenblatt, *Hamlet in Purgatory,* 236.

4. Kyd, *The Spanish Tragedy,* ed. David Bevington. Revels Student Editions (Manchester, UK: Manchester University Press, 1996), 1.1.91.

5. Marlowe, *Doctor Faustus,* ed. Sylvan Barnet (New York: Signet Classic, 2001), 5.2.196–97.

6. Marlowe, *Doctor Faustus,* 5.2.172–78.

7. Greenblatt, *Hamlet in Purgatory,* 102.

8. For a particularly engaging account of the presence of the dead and the affinity between Purgatory and late medieval English religious culture, see Peter Marshall, *Beliefs and the Dead in Reformation England* (Oxford: Oxford University Press, 2002).

9. Greenblatt, *Hamlet in Purgatory,* 252.

10. Ibid., 253.

11. Ibid., 240.

12. Ibid., 230.

13. Ibid., 231.

14. On Purgatory as a "piece of poetry," see ibid., esp. 47–101.

15. David Mills, *The Chester Mystery Cycle: A New Edition with Modernised Spelling* (East Lansing, MI: Colleagues Press, 1992), 414–15.

16. Greenblatt, *Hamlet in Purgatory,* 253.

17. Cooper, *Shakespeare and the Medieval World* (New York: Arden Shakespeare, 2010), 159.

18. "Although the play denounces such outmoded stage practices as out-Heroding Herod (3.2.14)," Cooper explains, "the medieval makes it presence repeatedly felt in this kind of detail even as it is being rejected." Cooper, *Shakespeare and the Medieval World,* 159.

19. Strictly speaking, the term *discretio spirituum* is the ability to discern, or judge, between good and evil earthly apparitions, and it has never, to my knowledge, been applied to the judgment and separation of spirits at the Final Doom. Yet, as I hope will become clear in this chapter, it is helpful to emphasize the kinship between these two moments of judgment as they pertain to *Hamlet.* I wish to follow an insight that Shakespeare himself seems to have pursued: the play, in other words, associates Hamlet's discernment of the ghost and the major action of Final Doom plays, the time-consuming business of separating good and evil souls. For a discussion of the ecclesiastical doctrine of the *discretio spirituum* and of its development into a discourse central to the empowerment and articulation of late medieval visionaries, see Rosalynn Voaden, *God's Words, Women's Voices: The Discernment of Spirits in Late-Medieval Women's Visionary Writing* (Woodbridge, UK: York Medieval Press, 1999), especially chapter 2. On the relation of *discretio spirituum* to Purgatory, see Greenblatt, *Hamlet in Purgatory,* 103–5.

20. See *OED Online,* s.v. "discretion," http://www.oed.com. Also see "discern, "defin. 4.c, and "decern"; the latter remains a technical term in Scottish juridicature meaning "to decree by judicial sentence." Ibid., defin. 2. These intertwined English etymolygies have Latin antecedents. Augustine's paraphrase of 1 Corinthians 12:10 (concerning spiritual gifts) bears witness to the verbal overlap between the discerning and judging of spirits that informs my reading of *Hamlet.* Augustine translates this verse as *alii dijudicatio spirituum,* whereas the Vulgate reads *alii discretio spirituum.* See Augustine, *Patrologia Latina* 34, ed. Jasques Paul Migne (Paris, 1844–64), 465. Quoted from Voaden, *God's Words, Women's Voices,* 46.

21. The subsequent discussion of Hamlet's famous delay presumes that it is a dramaturgical, not a psychological phenomenon. Dilatory elements, whether long-winded soliloquies about inaction and indecision, the antics of clowns, or the insertion of a play-within-the-play, are as constitutive of a revenge plot as madness and murder. See Margreta de Grazia, *"Hamlet" without Hamlet* (Cambridge: Cambridge University Press, 2007), 158–204, esp. 164–71.

22. George Puttenham's *Arte of English Poesie* (London, 1589) references various ancient playing spaces including the semicircular "scaffolds or stages of timber" that the Greeks erected for tragedies. At times, however, it is not clear whether Puttenham is imagining ancient Greek drama or more contemporary English mystery plays: "The old comedies," he writes, "were played in the broad streets upon wagons or carts uncovered." Puttenham, *Arte of English Poesie,* sig. F3r.

23. The term "pageant," then, could refer both to a play or scene in a medieval mystery cycle and to the platform staging. *OED Online,* defins. 1.a and 2.a. Pageant wagons varied in their design, and because historical data are scarce, critics continue to wrangle over their essential features. As David Mills explains, "the only account of the Chester pageant-waggons surviving comes from Archdeacon Rogers, who

describes them as 'a high place made like a howse with 2 rowmes beinge open on the tope the lower rowme theie. Appareled and dressed them selues. And the higher rowme, theie played.' [*REED: Chester,* 239]. Modern critics doubt the necessity for a lower dressing-room, debate the variation between six and four wheels on each waggon which occurs in David Rogers's different versions, and speculate whether, though open at the top, the waggon would not have had some sort of cover or canopy to protect the set. . . . Rogers gives no clear indication of size, but a recent estimate based on carriage-house sites, street-sizes and logistics suggests that a waggon may have measured twelve feet in length, five feet six inches in width, and stood up to twelve feet in height." Mills, *Chester Mystery Cycle,* xxv. For a careful study of the sophistication of pageant wagon technology—including an in-depth response to the long-standing claim that "the pageant wagons had fixed axles and no steering mechanism," see Clifford Davidson, *Technology, Guilds, and Early English Drama,* Early Drama, Art, and Music Monograph Series 23 (Kalamazoo, MI: Medieval Institute Publications, 1996), 17–31.

24. REED: *York,* 1:208. The 1518 entry states that the mercers paid iiij d to "Iohanno Clynt . . . pro ij lode terre" (219). The REED volume also includes *plaustratum* in its Latin glossary, and from this it is clear that the York mercers distinguished between a cart used for day-to-day labor and a wheeled platform built for the sole purpose of acting.

25. Orgel, "Shakespeare Imagines a Theater," *Poetics Today* 5:3 (1984): 552.

26. Orgel reinforces this reading with a linguistic point: "*Visorium* is not the Roman word for amphitheater. It is not a Roman word at all. It exists in no classical or medieval source, but . . . is a pure Renaissance coinage." Ibid., 561.

27. "Roman general, medieval queen, Elizabethan guardsman are grouped together in an integral though anachronistic stage picture," writes Orgel in "Shakespeare Imagines a Theater," 552. Yet June Schleuter has disputed whether this sketch is of Shakespeare's *Titus;* see her "Rereading the Peacham Drawing," *SQ* 50 (1999): 171–84.

28. See Simpson, *Reform and Cultural Revolution, 1350–1547* (Oxford: Oxford University Press, 2002), 514, 518–19. In his chapter "The Smell of Gunpowder: *Macbeth* and the Palimpsests of Olfaction" in *Untimely Matter in the Time of Shakespeare* (Philadelphia: University of Pennsylvania Press, 2009), 119–40, Jonathan Gil Harris explores the complex "anachronic" smell of gunpowder in the early modern theater, as it blends old Catholic olfactory rituals with the contemporary Gunpowder Plot.

29. Gurr, *The Shakespearean Stage: 1574–1642,* 3rd ed. (Cambridge: Cambridge University Press, 1992), 115. I have relied here upon Gurr's work—in *The Shakespearean Stage* as well as *Playgoing in Shakespeare's London* (Cambridge: Cambridge University Press, 1996), and *The Shakespeare Company, 1594–1642* (Cambridge: Cambridge University Press, 2004)—as well as the work of John Orrell in *The Human Stage: English Theatre Design, 1567–1640* (Cambridge: Cambridge University Press, 1988).

30. Gurr, *Shakespearean Stage,* 117–18.

31. As Glynne Wickham observes, "In the fifty-odd years of neo-classical enthusiasm which preceded Henry VIII's first divorce and break with Rome, enough research had been undertaken in Italy and had percolated to England for the notion of a raised platform stage, set up in a hall adjacent to a screen equipped with two or

more doors, to have established itself as something approaching a Roman style of theater." Wickham, *Early English Stages: 1300–1660* (New York: Columbia University Press, 1963), 2:201. For his argument regarding the genealogy of English playhouses from the remains of Roman theaters in Cornwall see pages 164–72.

32. Classical theater also featured a Heaven, of course, but as John Orrell states, "soon after the Heavens first appeared at the Rose and the Globe we find Heywood and Cotgrave identifying its starry decorations with features of the Roman stage, but the playwrights soon charged it with unclassical, Christian meaning. In *Dr Faustus* a refulgent throne descends while music plays to conceal the sound of the ropes, and the Good Angel speaks of sad ironies from the tiring house door: 'Faustus behold, / In what resplendent glory thou hadst set / In yonder throne, like those bright shining Saints, / And triumpht ouer hell.'" Yet Orrell is not comfortable with making too strong a connection to the medieval stage (at least as far as Heaven is concerned); he writes, "But it would be unwise to conclude from such uses as this that the Heavens was a further Gothic addition to the theatre. It was never a place from which God speaks, as He does in medieval pageants." Orrell, *The Human Stage: English Theatre Design, 1567–1640* (Cambridge: Cambridge University Press, 1988), 89.

33. "Early-modern dramatists," writes Cooper, "literally had the world as their subject, and they made the most of it." Cosmic theater, she explains, was an "idea derived directly from the cycle plays." It brought "the totality of human experience" to the English stage and "offered huge opportunities, and challenges, to playwrights both medieval and early modern." Cooper, *Shakespeare and the Medieval World,* 54.

34. The York indenture reads:

ffirst a Pagent with iiij Wheles helle mouthe iij garmentes for iij devels vi deuelles faces in iij Vsernes [masks] Array for ij euell saules that is to say ij Sirkes [shirts] ij paire hoses ij vesenes & ij Chauelers [wigs] Array for ij go[o]de saules that is to say ij Sirkes, ij paire hoses ij vesernes & ij cheuelers ij paire Aungell Wynges with iren in the endes ij trumpes [trumpets] of White plate & ij redes iiij Aubes [albs] for iiij Appostels iij diademes [haloes] with iij vesernes for iij Appostels iiij diademes with iiij Cheuelers of yalow for iiij Appostels A cloud & ij peces of Rainbow of tymber Array for god that ys to say a Sirke Wounded a diademe With a veserne gilted A grete coster [hanging] of rede damaske payntid for the bakke syde of the pagent ij other lesse costers for ij sydes of the Pagent iij other costers of lewent brede [broad linen cloth] for the sides of the Pagent A litel coster iiij squared to hang at the bakke of god iiij Irens to bere vppe heuen iiij [small] coterelles [cotter pins] & a Iren pynne A brandreth of Iren that God sall sitte vppon when he sall sty vppe to heuen, With iiij rapes [ropes] at iiij corners A heuen of Iren with a naffe of tre [wooden hub] ij peces of rede cloudes & sternes of gold langing [belonging] to heuen ij peces of blu cloudes payntid on bothe sydes iij peces of rede cloudes with sunne bemes of golde & sternes for the hiest of heuen with a lang small border of the same Wurke vii grete Aungels halding the passion of god Ane of thame has a fane of latoun [brass vein] & a crosse of Iren in his hede giltid iiij smaller Aungels gilted holding the passion ix smaller Aungels payntid rede to renne [run] aboute in the heuen A lang small [thin] corde to gerre [make] the Aungels renne aboute ii shorte rolls of tre [wooden rollers] to putte forthe the pageant. (REED: *York,* 1:55–56)

For a helpful description of the 1433 indenture, see Greg Walker, ed., *Medieval Drama: An Anthology* (Malden, MA: Blackwell, 2000), 159.

35. As Greg Walker states, "The indenture reveals that, in keeping with iconographic convention, the entrance to Hell was depicted as the mouth of a great beast, probably situated on the front or side of the wagon at ground level." Ibid., 159. For an in-depth study of the construction and configuration of Hell mouths in the mysteries, see Peter Meredith, "The Iconography of Hell in the English Cycles: A Practical Perspective," in *The Iconography of Hell,* ed. Clifford Davidson and Thomas H. Seiler, Early Drama, Art, and Music Monograph Series 17 (Kalamazoo, MI: Medieval Institute Publications, 1992), 158–86.

36. Richard Beadle, *York Mystery Plays: A Selection in Modern Spelling* (Oxford: Clarendon Press, 1984), 67.

37. Davidson, *Technology*, 31.

38. Ibid., 89. The glass is a nineteenth-century reproduction of the original, which had been destroyed by a severe storm during the previous century.

39. See ibid., 30.

40. Alan Nelson argues that multistoried wagons were rare; see Nelson, "Some Configurations of Staging in Medieval English Drama," in *Medieval English Drama: Essays Critical and Contextual,* ed. Jerome Taylor and Alan H. Nelson (Chicago: University of Chicago Press, 1972), 118. Davidson expresses a different view in *Technology,* 17–31.

41. On the history of the York mercers' pageant wagon, see Beadle, *York Mystery Plays,* xx–xxii.

42. As Davidson shows, this critical interpretation extends back to at least the early twentieth-century views of critics such as Maud Sellers but can be glimpsed more recently in John Coldewey's "Some Economic Aspects of Late Medieval Drama," in *Contexts for Early English Drama,* ed. Marianne G. Briscoe and John C. Coldewey (Bloomington: Indiana University Press, 1989). See Davidson, *Technology,* 17; also see his more recent article on the history of this critical debate: "York Guilds and the Corpus Christi Plays: Unwilling Participants?," *Early Theatre* 9, no. 2 (2006): 11–33. I enter this long-standing debate by resisting the view that guildsmen begrudged the "unwanted chore and expense" of staging their individual pageants. Like Mervyn James, I contend that a guild's honor and reputation were at stake in its "painted and gaily decorated pageant wagons, as well as in the wealth of costume, accessories . . . all giving proof of its vitality, and of the surplus resources among its members which could be put to communal use." James, "Ritual, Drama, and Social Body in the Late Medieval Town," *Past and Present* 98 (1983): 17. Yet, as I discuss above, there were larger cultural forces at work beyond the guildsmen's commercialism. As Lawrence Clopper has stated, the mysteries were "an expression of civic control, civic pride, and civic concern for the religious education of the townspeople." Clopper, *Drama, Play, and Game: English Festive Culture in the Medieval and Early Modern Period* [Chicago: University of Chicago Press, 2001), 142.

43. Performing the last scene in the cycle might mean that the mercers didn't perform at all, as was the case in Coventry in 1457 when Margaret of Anjou was visiting and "alle the Pagentes pleyde saue domes day which myght not be pleyde for lak of day." See REED: *Coventry,* 37.

44. REED: *York,* 1:95–97.

45. Ibid., 1:376–77.

46. Ibid., 1:374.

47. As Greenblatt explains, "The whole social and economic importance of Purgatory in Catholic Europe rested on the belief that prayers, fasts, almsgiving, and masses constituted a valuable commodity—'suffrages' as they were termed—that could in effect be purchased, directly or indirectly, on behalf of specific dead persons." Greenblatt, *Hamlet in Purgatory,* 19. On the material and monetary provisions that English Christians made for the afterlife, see especially pages 21–30.

48. On Purgatory as the rationale and shibboleth for prayers for the dead, see Marshall, *Beliefs and the Dead in Reformation England,* 4, 142 passim. "Ordinary men and women, including those quite uninterested in theological niceties, worshiped in close proximity to the mortal remains of those whose souls had passed on to their reward or punishment," explains Greenblatt, adding, "The wall paintings, carved doors and capitals, altarpieces, stained-glass windows, and funeral monuments further reinforced the deep link between Christianity and the fate of the dead." Greenblatt, *Hamlet in Purgatory,* 18.

49. Clifford Davidson, *The Guild Chapel Wall Paintings at Stratford-upon-Avon* (New York: AMS Press, 1988), 10. Also see de Grazia, *"Hamlet" without Hamlet,* 188–89, 241n104.

50. For illustrations of the Coventry Doom, see Davidson, *Technology,* 87–88. As de Grazia has noted in *"Hamlet" without Hamlet,* 241n103, a growing (and wonderfully diverting) catalog of medieval English church art is being restored and made available online at http://www.paintedchurch.org/conpage.htm

51. On the conventionality of Doomsday paintings in medieval England, see Davidson, *Guild Chapel Wall Paintings,* 32.

52. Peter Travis was the first scholar to note the significance of this point; see his *Dramatic Design in the Chester Cycle* (Chicago: University of Chicago Press, 1982), 224.

53. See table 2.1 in Travis, *Dramatic Design,* 52. The four plays of the Passion sequence I'm referring to here include the bakers' *Last Supper and Betrayal,* the coopers' *Trial and Flagellation,* the ironmongers' *Crucifixion,* and the skinners' *Resurrection.* Even if we add the cooks' *Harrowing of Hell,* then these five plays barely exceed the three Eschaton plays by about two hundred lines.

54. As indeed they did centuries later at the Chester 2010 performance held 22–24 May 2010, at Victoria College, University of Toronto, which I was fortunate to attend.

55. Mills translates the word "steare" as "daunt." Mills, *Chester Mystery Cycle,* 416.

56. Commenting on Horatio's famous farewell to Hamlet ("Good night, sweet prince, / And flights of angels sing thee to thy rest." [5.2.302–3]), Greenblatt observes, "The flying of the angels here is as important as their singing. Angels in flight figure in many images of Purgatory and clearly constitute one of the central ways in which the faithful imagined that assistance would come to them in their distress." Greenblatt, *Hamlet in Purgatory,* 51.

57. This is my translation of the stage direction following line 508, which reads: *omnes salvati eos sequentur.* On the use of ladders, see Mills, *Chester Mystery Cycle,* 415.

58. Regarding these hymns, Mills writes, "The first, Psalms 31 (AV 32). 11, 'Be glad in the Lord and rejoice,' is from the Offertory for the Common of Martyrs.

The second, 'Saviour of the world, Lord,' is a verse hymn." Mills, *Chester Mystery Cycle,* 431–32.

59. Thirty-seven times, to be exact. In York, the word occurs thirteen times, which is also considerable given that the pageant is about half as long as that of Chester. In *Hamlet,* it is Claudius who responds "alas, alas" when he learns of Polonius's doom and is reminded of "the end" of his own mortal body (4.3.25–26). Perhaps his "alas, alas" reminds Hamlet of the damned who are bound for hell, for he says a few lines later that Polonius is "in heaven" and that if Claudius's messenger cannot find him there, the king should "seek him i'th' other place" himself (4.3.33–34).

60. Davidson, *Guild Chapel Wall Paintings,* illus. 17.

61. The metonymic association between trumpets and Doomsday (discussed below) is based not only on the seven trumpets mentioned in Revelation 11 but also on the text of 1 Corinthians 15 (verse 51ff), where Paul writes, "Behold, I shew you a mystery. We shall not slepe, but we shall all be changed, and that in a moment, in the twinkeling of an eye by the last trompe. For the trompe shall blow and the dead shall rise incorruptible, & we shall be changed." Quoted from *The Newe Testament in Englishe translated oute of the Greke, according to the translation of the greate Bible, whiche is appointed to be red in churches* (London, 1569), sig. DD6v.

62. Richard Rastall, "Music in the Cycle," in *The Chester Mystery Cycle: Essays and Documents,* ed. R. M. Lumiansky and David Mills (Chapel Hill: University of North Carolina Press, 1983), 117. Rastall explains the various terms (like *buisine*) for trumpets used in the cycle plays. He subsequently shows why earlier instances of music in the pageant courts of Kings Balaack and Herod would not have called for trumpets—arguing specifically that "the use of trumpets for royalty, even at this [earlier] stage in the cycle, would detract from the impact of the Last Trumpet in Play 24," the *Last Judgment* (117–18).

63. Quoted from Mary Remnant, "Musical Instruments in Early English Drama," in *Material Culture and Medieval Drama,* ed. Clifford Davidson, Early Drama, Art, and Music Monograph Series 25 (Kalamazoo, MI: Medieval Institute Publications, 1999), 176.

64. As Remnant explains, "Representations of the Last Judgment in English Romanesque art normally show both angels and devils to be blowing horns, but after the arrival of long metal trumpets in the thirteenth century these instruments were more often given to angels." Ibid., 175.

65. See Cox, *The Devil and the Sacred in English Drama: 1350–1642* (Cambridge: Cambridge University Press, 2000).

66. Quoted from Gurr, *The Shakespearean Stage: 1574–1642,* 3rd ed. (Cambridge: Cambridge University Press, 1992), 185.

67. On the material conservatism of early English drama, see Cox, *The Devil and the Sacred,* 5, who makes a point about the relative lack of variation in devils' costumes between the medieval and early modern stage that is similar to the one I am proposing regarding stage construction and design.

68. Compare Greenblatt's statement that "this reality [of Purgatory in *Hamlet*] is theatrical rather than theological; it can accommodate elements, such as a Senecan call for revenge, that would radically undermine church doctrine." Greenblatt, *Hamlet in Purgatory,* 253.

69. Quoted from REED: *Cheshire,* 1:148. See also David Mills, "Some Theological Issues in Chester's Plays," in *"Bring furth the pagants": Essays in Early English Drama*

Presented to Alexandra Johnston, ed. David N. Klausner and Karen Sawyer Marsalek (Toronto: University of Toronto Press, 2007), 217.

70. For a "comparative chart of the actions of the three surviving texts of Last Judgment pageants" at Chester, York, and Towneley, see Peter Meredith, "The Iconography of Hell in the English Cycles: A Practical Perspective," in *The Iconography of Hell,* ed. Clifford Davidson and Thomas H. Seiler, Early Drama, Art, and Music Monograph Series 17 (Kalamazoo: Medieval Institute Publications, 1992), 170–71.

71. Quoted from *The Newe Testament in Englishe translated oute of the Greke, according to the translation of the greate Bible, whiche is appointed to be red [sic] in churches* (London, 1569), sig. D8v–E1r. As Mills explains regarding the Chester *Last Judgment,* "Christ explains that the criterion for salvation is the performance of acts of charity based upon knowledge of his teachings and his sacrifice, while damnation results from willful disregard of such acts." Mills, *Chester Mystery Cycle,* 414.

72. As Anthony Low states regarding medieval English "investment" in the doctrine of Purgatory, Shakespeare "understood very well that the abrupt and, to a large degree, forcible dismantling of Purgatory at mid-century, together with its deep psychic resonances among the common people, its elaborate cultural associations, and its extensive institutional supports, had drastic consequences for society and for the individuals who formed and were formed by society. Before the Reformation, few countries had a deeper investment (financial, cultural, and spiritual) in Purgatory and in commemoration of the dead than England. After the Reformation, few countries turned their backs more abruptly on Purgatory and, with it, on their own dead." Low, "Hamlet and the Ghost of Purgatory: Intimations of Killing the Father," *English Literary Renaissance* 29 (1999): 447.

73. Greenblatt, *Hamlet in Purgatory,* 52. Though the pictorial difference is slight, the consequences cannot be overstated; as de Grazia observes, "Between the two destinations there is a world of difference." De Grazia, *"Hamlet" without Hamlet,* 192.

74. Meg Twycross, "'With What Body Shall They Come?' Black and White Souls in the English Mystery Plays," in *Langland, the Mystics, and the Medieval English Religious Tradition,* ed. H. Phillips (Cambridge: Cambridge University Press, 1990), 272. For more on this iconography as it is illustrated in MS Douce 134 in the Bodleian Library, see her "More Black and White Souls," *Medieval English Theatre* 13 (1991): 52–63.

75. The costume, writes Twycross, "was not purely symbolic: popular belief seems to have held that the sins of the Damned would be reflected in the corruption of their risen flesh, whereas the Saved would share the *claritas* of Christ revealed in the Transfiguration." Twycross and Sarah Carpenter, *Masks and Masking in Medieval and Early Tudor England* (Burlington, VT: Ashgate, 2002, 195. Elsewhere Twycross explains, "It may well be that the citizens of Coventry, and very possibly of York and Chester, saw it more literally than that. In at least three late medieval English works of popular religious instruction, the *Cursor Mundi,* the *Pricke of Conscience,* and *The Mirour of Man's Salvation,* the English translation of the *Speculum Humanae Salvationis,* and it may well be in others, we are told that though we will all be raised body and soul together at the Last Judgment, there will be a visible distinction between the saved and the damned." Twycross, "'With What Body Shall They Come?,'" 273.

76. REED: *Coventry,* 230 passim.

77. Twycross, "'With What Body Shall They Come?,'" 286.

78. See lines 671–76 and Mills's corresponding note in *Chester Mystery Cycle,* 437.

79. See Mills, *Chester Mystery Cycle,* 414. Contrast the specific titles given to the Chester souls ("Imperator Salvatus," "Justiciarius Damnatus," etc.) with the generic names in the York pageant ("Anima Mala" and "Anima Bona"). The wall painting in the Stratford Guild Chapel depicts both unexceptional naked souls and those set apart by rank and station. Interestingly, none of the damned stand out according to occupation. None wear costumes (hats, veils, crowns), nor are any tonsured.

80. Twycross, "'With What Body Shall They Come?,'" 285.

81. N-Town Cycle, play 42, lines 40, 44–48. Quoted from Stephen Spector, ed., *The N-Town Play: Cotton MS Vespasian D. 8,* EETS Supplementary Series 11 (Oxford: Oxford University Press, 1991),1:411.

82. As de Grazia states, "In the attiring-house, Hamlet's 'inky cloak' or 'customary suits of solemn black' (1.2.77, 78) might have doubled as the devil's black robe listed in several stage inventories. 'Damnable faces' and 'devil-wear' may have been as much part of his antic repertoire as his clownish jig-making and pipe-playing (3.2.123, 341–42)." De Grazia, *"Hamlet" without Hamlet,* 194.

83. John Milton, *Paradise Lost,* ed. Alastair Fowler (New York: Longman, 1998), bk. 5, line 240. Compare Twycross and Carpenter, who write, "Morally and spiritually, this black is the opposite of divine radiance. Historically, they seem to have been charred when they fell from heaven: 'Fellen fro the firmament fendes ful blake.' Arrived in hell, the York Lucifer cries, 'My bryghtnes es blakkeste and blo now.'" *Masks and Masking,* 202.

84. To complete these costumes, many demons carried chains, clubs, or mauls (long-handled hammers), and surviving (or reclaimed) church iconography reflects this traditional gear.

85. See Beadle, *York Mystery Plays,* 1.

86. Mills, *Chester Mystery Cycle,* 415.

87. This translation is quoted from Mills, *Chester Mystery Cycle,* 426. The Latin stage direction reads: "[Descendet] Jesus quasi in nube, si fieri poterit, quia, secundum doctoris opiniones in aere prope terram judicabit Filius Dei." On the importance of vertical distinction in the hierarchical culture of the Middle Ages, see Davidson, "Falling and Rising on the Medieval Stage," in *Technology,* 81–100.

88. Beadle glosses "bield" as "dwell" in his *York Mystery Plays,* 279. For the various senses of the verb "to bide," see *OED.*

89. All quotes of Calvin's *Institutes* are taken from *Institutes of the Christian Religion,* ed. John T. McNeill, trans. Ford Lewis Battles (Philadelphia: Westminster Press, 1960), 1:676–83 (vol. 1, bk. 3, chap. 5, secs. 7–10). Article 22 of the Book of Common Prayer wholeheartedly agrees with Calvin's position on Purgatory, stating, "The Romish Doctrine concerning Purgatory, Pardons, Worshipping and Adoration, as well of Images as of Relics, and also Invocation of Saints, is a fond thing, vainly invented, and grounded upon no warranty of Scripture, but rather repugnant to the Word of God." Quoted from Low, "Hamlet and the Ghost of Purgatory," 450.

90. For various speculations by visionaries on the location of Purgatory, see Marshall, *Beliefs and the Dead,* 7–12.

91. According to Greenblatt, "In addition to the 150 surviving manuscripts of the Latin original, there are an equal number of copies in translation, diffused

throughout Europe from Madrid to Cracow, Edinburgh to Rome." Greenblatt, *Hamlet in Purgatory,* 75.

92. As Greenblatt explains, "The knight, acting as the reader's surrogate, insists upon a direct encounter, and the reader accordingly follows him into the black hole." Greenblatt, *Hamlet in Purgatory,* 82.

93. Mills, *Chester Mystery Cycle,* 414–15. In an e-mail to the author, Professor Mills explained that his comment is "a speculation deriving from the plural *sepulchris* in the original Latin stage direction," though he admits "the plural 'graves' may have its basis in texts such as John 5:28 [*omnes qui in monumentis sunt audient vocem eius*] rather than pointing to a staging method." Mills, e-mail message to author, 8 November 2010. In 1543 the Coventry cappers list a "sepvlcer" whose sides need repair ("paid for boordes abowt . . . ye sepvlcer syde"), and as they mended and painted their "hellmowthe" that same year, it seems that these items are not the same and therefore some distinction of understage spaces is assumed. REED: *Coventry,* 163.

94. Sheingorn and Bevington, "'Alle This Was Token Domysday to Drede': Visual Signs of Last Judgment in the Corpus Christi Cycles and in Late Gothic Art," in *Homo, Memento Finis: The Iconography of Just Judgment in Medieval Art and Drama,* ed. David Bevington, Early Drama, Art, and Music Monograph Series 6 (Kalamazoo, MI: Medieval Institute Publications1985), 126.

95. Beadle, *York Mystery Plays,* 267.

96. REED: *York,* 1:95.

97. N-Town fragment quoted from Sheingorn and Bevington, "Alle This Was Token Domysday to Drede," 129.

98. The latest record we have of the souls' wagon is 1467, when it was repaired: "warmanship [workmanship] whare ye saulys lyes." REED: *York,* 1:99–100. As Clifford Davidson notes, however, medievalists are unsure about the precise construction of the grave or graves on this cart: "Johnston and Rogerson speculate that the pageant was without wheels and was made in the shape of a coffin, but careful examination of examples in the visual arts from England during the period reasonably contemporary with the play will provide no absolute confidence with regard to the precise design." Davidson, *From Creation to Doom: The York Cycle of Mystery Plays* (New York: AMS Press, 1984), 185. Peter Meredith agrees with Alexandra Johnston and Margaret Rogerson that the souls' wagon was relatively smaller in comparison with the "great" wagon described in the 1433 indenture. Meredith, "The Development of the York Mercers' Pageant Waggon," *Medieval English Theatre* 1 (1979): 5–6.

99. According to Davidson, the separate pageant wagon in York was for "the souls both good and bad" and it "could be quite small and easily transported; its frame was of fir but was further filled out with lathe, and the whole was covered with five yards of 'now [new] canvays.'" Davidson, *From Creation to Doom,* 185.

100. See figure 23 in Davidson and Seiler, *Iconography of Hell.*

101. "Demons were clever," Greenblatt explains, "and it had long been understood that they were capable of insinuating themselves into human communities by pretending that they were souls in pain." Greenblatt, *Hamlet in Purgatory,* 209.

102. That is, "as if preparing for the Last Judgment." *The Norton Shakespeare: Based on the Oxford Edition,* ed. Stephen Greenblatt et al. (New York: Norton, 1997), 1720n9.

103. On "compulsive remembrance" in *Hamlet,* see Greenblatt, *Hamlet in Purgatory,* 205–58, esp. 214–29.

104. See Davidson's discussion of armored angels in drama and the visual arts such as the window of All Souls Church in York in *From Creation to Doom,* 30. A better illustration may be the Last Judgment panel painting by Hubert and/or Jan Van Eyck (c. 1420–25) at the Metropolitan Museum of Art, New York.

105. See York *Last Judgment,* lines 169ff.

106. "He addresses it directly," Greenblatt explains, "in words that would have been utterly familiar to a Catholic and deeply suspect to a Protestant: 'Rest, rest, perturbèd spirit.'" Greenblatt, *Hamlet in Purgatory,* 233.

107. Cooper, *Shakespeare and the Medieval World,* 159.

108. As de Grazia observes, eighteenth-century critics faulted the two clowns for holding up the play's tragic denouement, and the scene was often cut. De Grazia, *"Hamlet" without Hamlet,* 176.

109. On Hamlet's behavior as a stage devil and the long-standing reluctance of literary critics to make this connection with the medieval stage, see ibid., 188–94.

110. Ibid., 32.

111. For records of Adam's spade, see REED: *Coventry,* 167, 240, 334, 567.

112. *The Tragicall Historie of Hamlet Prince of Denmarke, by William Shakespeare. As it hath beene diuerse times acted by his Highnesse seruants in the cittie of London: as also in the two vniuersities of Cambridge and Oxford, and else-where* (London, 1603), sig. D4v.

113. It is no accident, de Grazia notes, that the transient dynasties of Caesar and Alexander "should be invoked in the shadow of Doomsday, as if all history in this world were in preparation for the kingdom promised in the next." De Grazia, *"Hamlet" without Hamlet,* 51. She subsequently adds, "Salvational history also spans the play: at the start the Incarnation is invoked to dispel the fear of the risen dead, and Doomsday looms over the remains of the dead at the end" (73).

114. With one glaring exception: The audience is never told whether Old Hamlet's "perturbèd spirit" (1.5.183) is finally put to rest after Claudius's death.

115. *The Tragicall Historie of Hamlet,* sig. I3v. See de Grazia, *"Hamlet" without Hamlet,* 188.

116. As Greenblatt notes, Purgatory, "while compatible with a Christian (and, specifically, a Catholic) call for remembrance, is utterly incompatible with a Senecan call for vengeance." Greenblatt, *Hamlet in Purgatory,* 237.

117. De Grazia, *"Hamlet" without Hamlet,* 7–8.

118. As Greenblatt has established, "There is something magnificently opportunistic, appropriative, absorptive, even cannibalistic about Shakespeare's art." Greenblatt, *Hamlet in Purgatory,* 254.

5. "Here's a Knocking Indeed!"

1. *OED Online,* s.v. "harrow," defin. b, http://www.oed.com. The Wakefield *Harrowing of Hell* refers to this episode as the "Extractio Animarum"—the Extraction or Deliverance of Souls—which, like the English word "harrow," conveys not just an attack on Hell but the plunder of its souls.

2. David Bevington, ed., *Medieval Drama* (Boston: Houghton Mifflin, 1975), 594.

3. On the manner in which the *Harrowing of Hell* reinforced a typological association between Adam and Christ for post-Reformation audiences, see V. A. Kolve, *A Play Called Corpus Christi* (Stanford: Stanford University Press, 1966), 60–61.

4. Paul Whitfield White, *Drama and Religion in English Provincial Society, 1485–1660* (Cambridge: Cambridge University Press, 2008), 96.

5. REED: *Cheshire,* 1:147.

6. Pope, Rowe, and Coleridge all quoted from John B Harcourt, "'I Pray You, Remember the Porter,'" *SQ* 12, no. 4 (Fall 1961): 393–402.

7. For example, both the 1997 *Norton Shakespeare* edited by Stephen Greenblatt and others and Stephen Orgel's edition of the play for Pelican (2000) note the contributions and revisions likely to have been made by Middleton in 3.5 and 4.1, yet neither editor disputes the Shakespearean authorship of 2.3. See *The Norton Shakespeare: Based on the Oxford Edition,* ed. Stephen Greenblatt et al. (New York: Norton, 1997), and *Macbeth,* ed. Stephen Orgel, The Pelican Shakespeare Series (New York: Penguin, 2000).

8. In addition to Harcourt's 1961 essay (cited below), Glynne Wickham's brief but important essay "Hell-Castle and Its Door-Keeper," *Shakespeare Survey* 19 (1966): 68–74, sees a connection between medieval drama and *Macbeth,* arguing that while there was "no attempt" by Shakespeare to write *Macbeth* as a "direct parallel," or political allegory, of the *Harrowing of Hell,* yet there is, he says, "ample evidence within the text of the play of a conscious attempt on Shakespeare's part to remind his audience of this ancient and familiar story" (70). See also Wickham's *Shakespeare's Dramatic Heritage: Collected Studies in Mediaeval, Tudor, and Shakespearean Drama* (New York: Barnes and Noble, 1969), 214–24. Richard Waswo's "Damnation, Protestant Style: Macbeth, Faustus, and Christian Tragedy," *Journal of Medieval and Renaissance Studies* 4 (1974): 63–99, is also exceptional for its study of the play as part of a tradition of English Christian drama.

9. Wickham, "Hell-Castle and Its Door-Keeper," 68.

10. O'Connell, *The Idolatrous Eye: Iconoclasm and Theater in Early-Modern England* (Oxford: Oxford University Press, 2000), as well as his "Vital Cultural Practices: Shakespeare and the Mysteries," *JMEMS* 29, no. 1 (1999): 149–68. Cooper, *Shakespeare and the Medieval World* (New York: Arden Shakespeare, 2010), esp. 64–71; also see her essay "Shakespeare and the Mystery Plays," in *Shakespeare and Elizabethan Popular Culture,* ed. Stuart Gillespie and Neil Rhodes (London: Arden Shakespeare, 2006), 18–41. Beatrice Groves, *Texts and Traditions: Religion in Shakespeare, 1592–1604* (Oxford: Clarendon Press, 2007), esp. chap. 2, "Shakespeare's Incarnational Aesthetic: The Mystery Plays and Catholicism," 26–59.

11. Like Holly Dugan, I "argue that visibility and materiality were not always historically linked. In doing so, I contend that many objects were valuable in the Renaissance precisely because *they were not meant to be seen;* they were meant to be touched, tasted, heard—or . . . smelled." Dugan, *The Ephemeral History of Perfume: Scent and Sense in Early Modern England* (Baltimore: Johns Hopkins University Press, 2011), 7.

12. Harcourt, "'I Pray You, Remember the Porter,'" 393–402.

13. Rebecca Lemon, "Scaffolds of Treason in Shakespeare's *Macbeth,*" in *Treason by Words: Literature, Law, and Rebellion in Shakespeare's England* (Ithaca: Cornell University Press, 2006), 79–106; Arthur Kinney, *Lies Like Truth: Shakespeare, "Macbeth," and the Cultural Moment* (Detroit: Wayne State University Press, 2001), 86–102; Steven Mullaney, *The Place of the Stage: License, Play, and Power in Renaissance England* (Chicago: University of Chicago Press, 1988). Yet Grace Tiffany has argued that *Macbeth*

upholds the myth of James's paternal kingship in *"Macbeth,* Paternity, and the Anglicization of James I," *Studies in the Humanities* 23, no. 2 (1996): 148–62.

14. Crashaw, *The sermon preached at the Crosse* (London, 1607), sig. Z1r.

15. Bruce R. Smith, *The Acoustic World of Early Modern England: Attending to the O-Factor* (Chicago: University of Chicago Press, 1999), 12–29.

16. Ibid., 107, 108–9.

17. For a discussion of Platonic and Aristotelean theories of memory available in the Renaissance, see Stephen Greenblatt, *Hamlet in Purgatory* (Princeton: Princeton University Press, 2001), 214–15.

18. Smith, *Acoustic World,* 114, 108–9.

19. Ibid., 112.

20. Ibid., 206, 209, 210.

21. However, Smith does not (that I am aware) discuss the knocking of the Porter scene.

22. Compare Dugan, who explains how scents like the damask rose could efficaciously recall previous significations and thereby transform and "control" distinct early modern spaces: "Infusing his physical body with fragrant scents previously associated with divinity, rose perfumes enabled [Henry VIII] to heighten the olfactory experience of kingship for those in his wake and to provide an olfactory reminder of his presence after he left." Dugan, *Ephemeral History of Perfume,* 45.

23. Shakespeare, *Mr. William Shakespeares Comedies, Histories, and Tragedies; A Facsimile of the First Folio, 1623,* ed. Doug Moston (New York: Routledge, 1998), fol. 137 (sig. mm3r).

24. See David Mills, ed., *The Chester Mystery Cycle: A New Edition with Modernised Spelling* (East Lansing, MI: Colleagues Press, 1992), 302.

25. William H. Hulme, *The Middle-English Harrowing of Hell and Gospel of Nicodemus.* Published for the EETS (London: Kegan Paul, Trench, Trubner and Co., 1907), 110.

26. E. K. Chambers, *The Mediaeval Stage* (Oxford: Oxford Clarendon Press, 1903), 2:4. Also see John Cox, *The Devil and the Sacred in English Drama* (Cambridge: Cambridge University Press, 2000), 16–17, as well as Wickham, *Shakespeare's Dramatic Heritage,* 217.

27. The Latin word *labarum* traditionally refers to Christ's *vexillum,* or standard; see Chambers, *Mediaeval Stage,* 2:73.

28. Quoted from the translation in Ann Faulkner, "The Harrowing of Hell at Barking Abbey and in Modern Production," in *The Iconography of Hell,* ed. Clifford Davidson and Thomas H. Seiler, Early Drama, Art, and Music Monograph Series 17 (Kalamazoo, MI: Medieval Institute Press, 1992), 147.

29. Kolve, *A Play Called Corpus Christi,* 195.

30. See Greg Walker, who cites Piers Plowman as an example of this heroic tradition: "York (The Saddlers), *The Harrowing of Hell,*" in *Medieval Drama: An Anthology,* ed. Greg Walker (Malden, MA: Blackwell, 2000), 143–49. On the tradition of representing Christ as a knight descended into Hell to do battle with the devil, see Gustaf Aulén's *Christus Victor* (New York: Society for Promoting Christian Knowledge, 1931), and J. A. MacCulloch's *The Harrowing of Hell: A Comparative Study of an Early Christian Doctrine* (Edinburgh: T. and T. Clark, 1930). More recent studies are found in Zbigniew Izydorczyk's collection of essays entitled *The Medieval Gospel of*

Nicodemus: Texts, Intertexts, and Contexts in Western Europe (Tempe, AZ: Medieval and Renaissance Texts and Studies, 1997).

31. Clifford Davidson, *Technology, Guilds, and Early English Drama,* Early Drama, Art, and Music Monograph Series 23 (Kalamazoo, MI: Medieval Institute Press, 1996), 84.

32. Mills, *Chester Mystery Cycle,* 302–3.

33. See R. W. Ingram, *Coventry,* Records of Early English Drama (Toronto: University of Toronto Press, 1981), 217, 221, 250, 257, 478 (hereafter REED: *Coventry*). Also see the numerous entries for gunpowder in the same volume, as well as Philip Butterworth, "Hellfire: Flame as Special Effect," in Davidson and Seiler, *Iconography of Hell,* 67–101. Jonathan Gil Harris argues that the scent of gunpowder may have encouraged Shakespeare's audiences to recall medieval stage devilry. Harris, "The Smell of Gunpowder: *Macbeth* and the Palimpsests of Olfaction," in *Untimely Matter in the Time of Shakespeare* (Philadelphia: University of Pennsylvania Press, 2009), 119–39.

34. According to Walker, "Battlements might also have been placed on the upper part of the wagon to represent the walled fortifications of Hell referred to at various points in the pageant." Walker, "York (The Saddlers), *The Harrowing,*" 143.

35. As R. M. Lumiansky and David Mills explain, there are variations in the surviving manuscripts of this text, with the Harley 2124 (1607) reading "materialis magnus" rather than "magnus materialis." Lumiansky and Mills, *The Chester Mystery Cycle,* EETS Supplementary Series 3 and 9 (Oxford: Oxford University Press, 1974; repr. 1986), 1:331, note to line 151.

36. Wickham, "Hell-Castle and Its Door-Keeper," 73; Mills, *Chester Mystery Cycle,* 308; Richard Rastall, "The Sounds of Hell," in Davidson and Seiler, *Iconography of Hell,* 112n27.

37. Wakefield *Harrowing of Hell,* lines 180, 183. Cited from Bevington, *Medieval Drama,* 600.

38. In his study of the prolonged stage career of devils before and after the Reformation, John D. Cox explains that "one reason devils endured on stage was that the material base of culture changed very little throughout the time they were popular: the slow pace of economic and technological change meant that costumes and the materials for assembling them remained the same." Cox, *Devil and the Sacred,* 5.

39. REED: *Coventry*, 308, 474.

40. As Andrew Gurr explains, "Thunder came from the 'roul'd bullet' on a sheet of metal, or a 'tempestuous drum.'" Gurr, *The Shakespearean Stage,* 3rd ed. (Cambridge: Cambridge University Press, 1992), 186.

41. Smith, *Acoustic World,* 211.

42. Shakespeare, *First Folio, 1623,* fol. 131 (sig. ll6r).

43. Gospel of Nicodemus 22:1, quoted from *The Apocryphal New Testament: Being the Apocryphal Gospels, Acts, Epistles, and Apocalypses,* trans. Montagu Rhodes James (Oxford: Clarendon Press, 1924).

44. The Bamberg service, Cox says, is a "more explicit rendering of the harrowing" in which someone "qui Diaboli personam simulans" recites the verse from Psalm 24, "Quis est iste Rex gloriae?" Cox, *Devil and the Sacred,* 17.

45. Weimann, *Shakespeare and the Popular Tradition in the Theater: Studies in the Social Dimension of Dramatic Form and Function.* Baltimore: Johns Hopkins University Press, 1978, 32–33. Cox offers an important caveat to Weimann's thesis regarding the "accessibility" of devils and vices to commoners. Satan and his cohorts, he observes,

are often courtly figures who speak from "various scaffold stages, not in the *platea.*" Cox, *Devil and the Sacred,* 223n4. Cox's insight is particularly apt to *Harrowing* plays, where Satan is often represented as seated upon (and eventually bound to) a high throne inside Hell Castle.

46. In medieval paintings of Last Judgments such as that in the Guild Chapel at Stratford, figures arising to hear their Doom are naked except for a badge of their rank, usually a hat of some sort: a crown, papal tiara, miter or monk's tonsure.

47. As David Mills explains, "In the 1607 manuscript, the play ends in triumph as the redeemed leave the stage singing the *Te Deum* while the Devil remains bound in a now empty hell. But in the other manuscripts there is a comic coda which changes the tone: as a Chester ale-wife enters to receive punishment for her 'sins' in contravening Chester's bylaws and defrauding her customers." Mills, *Chester Mystery Cycle,* 303.

48. Chester REED documents state that the alewife and her devil tormentors also appeared in the city's annual Midsummer parade: "The Innkeepers' records suggest that they are part of an activity called 'cuppes and canes,' in which the woman, atop a horse, carries a quantity of crockery which the devil breaks with his cane." REED: *Chester,* liii. According to Mills, this strange ritual, along with the alewife's appearance in the Innkeepers' *Harrowing* pageant, is probably related to a now-unknown folk custom. Mills, *Chester Mystery Cycle,* 303.

49. See *OED,* s.v. "morsell," defin. 1a. Also see the Chester *Antichrist* play, where devils enjoy "Many a fatt morsell" (677). A medieval church wall painting in Melbourne, Derbyshire, depicts two women, possibly witches, being gnawed by several devils that surround them. See the developing online catalog Medieval Wall Painting in the English Parish Church at http://www.paintedchurch.org/melbourn.htm

50. For example, the note on this line (2.3.8) in the *Norton Shakespeare* explains that the term "equivocator" is "possibly an allusion to the 1606 trial of the Jesuit Henry Garnet for involvement in the Gunpowder plot to blow up the Houses of Parliament; Father Garnet had written a treatise defending equivocation for Catholics being prosecuted for their beliefs." *Norton Shakespeare,* 2580n3. See also Greenblatt's introduction to the play, 2555–57.

51. Cox, *Devil and the Sacred,* 72.

52. Walker, "York (The Saddlers), *The Harrowing,*" 143.

53. Ibid., 147.

54. The term "divine duplicity" here is from Richard Beadle, *York Mystery Plays: A Selection in Modern Spelling* (Oxford: Oxford University Press, 1984), 98.

55. As Cox states, "Satan is defeated in the end only by the greater 'trick' of the Incarnation, Passion, and Resurrection." Cox, *Devil and the Sacred,* 72.

56. Wickham, *Early English Stages: 1300–1660* (New York: Columbia University Press, 1963), 4:87.

57. See Davidson, *Technology,* 84.

58. On devils and illusion, particularly theatrical illusion, see Cox, *Devil and the Sacred,* 152–53.

59. The Porter scene, in other words, does not quite fit Stephen Greenblatt's powerful thesis about how the Reformation made Catholic liturgy and dogma available to the commercial playhouses by transforming sacred signifiers into theatrical representations. See Greenblatt, *Shakespearean Negotiations* (Berkeley: University of California Press, 1988), 119.

60. Smith, *Acoustic World,* 242–43.

61. As Wickham states, "Thunder, cacophony, screams and groans were the audible emblems of Lucifer and Hell on the medieval stage." Wickham, *Shakespeare's Dramatic Heritage,* 224.

62. Cooper, *Shakespeare and the Medieval World,* 55; "Shakespeare and the Mystery Plays," 32. The Coventry devil-porter had been made famous by John Heywood's allusion to him in his play *The Foure PP* (c. 1543). See also Groves, *Texts and Traditions,* 36.

63. See Weimann, *Shakespeare and the Popular Tradition,* 114–15.

64. Wickham, "Hell-Castle and Its Door-Keeper," 72.

65. As Harris notes regarding the sulphurous squibs used in the play, "*Macbeth* is temporally double, evoking a past-in-the-present." Harris, *Untimely Matter,* 137–38.

66. *Othello,* 5.2.292–93. As Cox says, in *Macbeth* "literal stage devils" are eschewed. Cox, *Devil and the Sacred,* 176.

67. As Weimann states regarding the recollection of traditional Vice characters (particularly at 3.1.277 of *Two Gentlemen of Verona* ["Your old vice still"]), "The Vice was the *old* Vice, but *still* he could be used or referred to; and the words 'old' and 'still' indicate the dialectic of innovation and tradition by which Shakespeare's wordplay actually thrived." Weimann, *Shakespeare and the Popular Tradition,* 151.

68. I am neither claiming that knock-knock jokes were told in the seventeenth century nor that Shakespeare invents them in this scene. Rather, I draw a parallel between Shakespeare's play and this popular form of homonym in order to make the salient point that to get the joke of the Porter scene, a double hearing of the sound of knocking is required.

69. Lemon, "Scaffolds of Treason," 21, 86–87 passim.

70. Kernan, *Shakespeare, the King's Playwright: Theater in the Stuart Court, 1603–1613* (New Haven: Yale University Press, 1995), 76, 78.

71. Harcourt, "I Pray You, Remember the Porter," 393.

72. De Quincey, "On the Knocking at the Gate in *Macbeth*" in *The Norton Anthology of English Literature,* 6th ed., ed. M. H. Abrams (New York: Norton, 1993), 2:462.

73. Regarding various apotropaic rituals like the *Ordo Dedicationis Ecclesiae* performed to exorcise the devil, see Cox, *Devil and the Sacred,* 16–17.

74. Wickham, "Hell-Castle and its Door-Keeper," 70, 73.

75. Ibid., 74.

76. For, as Wickham then argues, "At this point in *Macbeth* Shakespeare has not yet informed us that Macduff is destined to avenge Duncan's murder, but in his use of the porter he gives us a clear hint of what to expect." Wickham, *Shakespeare's Dramatic Heritage,* 222.

77. James I, *Basilikon doron Devided into three bookes* (Edinburgh, 1599), sig. E3v-E4r.

78. "Why," asks Stephen Orgel, "in a play so clearly organized around ideas of good and evil, is it not Malcolm who defeats Macbeth? . . . What happens next, with a saintly king of Scotland, and an ambitious soldier as his right-hand man, and those threatening offspring, the heirs of Banquo, still waiting in the wings?" See Orgel, "introduction to *Macbeth* (Pelican), xliii.

79. "No one else in the play has a moral sensibility so intense or so visionary," writes Stephen Greenblatt, "no one else imagines so vividly the forces that lie beyond

the ordinary and familiar horizon of human experience." See Greenblatt's introduction to *Macbeth* in *Norton Shakespeare,* 2557.

80. As David Lowenthal writes, "Lady Macbeth, sleepwalking, thinks she is in hell.... And while she thinks of herself as already undergoing divine punishment in hell, [Macbeth] never ceases to anticipate a similar destiny for himself." Lowenthal, "*Macbeth:* Shakespeare's Mystery Play," *Interpretation* 16, no. 3 (Spring 1989): 313, 348.

81. What A. R. Braunmuller has noted regarding the malleability of the play's imagery is also true of its structure: "No simple code will decipher the play's chromatic figures. Black and darkness may often be evil, white and light good, red bloody, but the white of lily and linen is also cowardly, brightness Satanic, red the colour of courage and the 'painting' of a drunkard's nose, and dark night the time of restorative sleep." See Braunmuller, "introduction to *Macbeth* (Cambridge: Cambridge University Press, 1997), 53–54.

82. Cox, *Devil and the Sacred,* 23.

83. Barrett, *Against All England: Regional Identity and Cheshire Writing, 1195–1656* (Notre Dame, IN: University of Notre Dame Press, 2009), 80–82.

84. Cox, *Devil and the Sacred,* 22. Yet I agree with James Simpson that mystery drama's interrogation of power is more sophisticated, penetrating outwardly and inwardly so as not only to resist ecclesial and civic forms of tyranny but also to critique the regulation of labor by craft guilds. Indeed, for Simpson, the very society that produced the mysteries is open to their scrutiny. See Simpson, *Reform and Cultural Revolution, 1350–1547* (Oxford: Oxford University Press, 2002), 502–57.

85. James I, *Basilikon doron,* sig. E2r.

86. Stallybrass, "*Macbeth* and Witchcraft," in *Focus on Macbeth,* ed. John Russell Brown (New York: Routledge and Kegan Paul, 1982), 189–209.

87. Lemon, "Scaffolds of Treason," 86.

88. Gosson, *Playes Confuted in Five Actions* (London, 1582), sig. E5v–E6r.

89. Ibid., sig. E6v, E8r.

90. Cooper, "Shakespeare and the Mystery Plays," 22.

91. "Shakespeare deliberately locates the magic and mystery of his tale," Diehl states, "not in the remnants of the old religion but in the newly reinvigorated Pauline texts of the new." See Diehl, "'Does Not the Stone Rebuke Me?': The Pauline Rebuke and Paulina's Lawful Magic in *The Winter's Tale,*" in *Shakespeare and the Cultures of Performance,* ed. Paul Yachnin and Patricia Badir (Burlington, VT: Ashgate, 2008), 80. Diehl resists Michael O'Connell's account, which argues that Shakespeare "fully associates theatricality with [Roman Catholic] idolatry," and though this scandalous move is momentary, the playwright "embraces the charge" and "presses an audience into" idolatrous complicity "as it assents with Leontes to whatever reality the apparent statue may mysteriously possess." O'Connell, *The Idolatrous Eye,* 141. Yet Phebe Jensen has noted that the Counter-Reformation was equally Pauline; see Jensen, *Religion and Revelry in Shakespeare's Festive World* (Cambridge: Cambridge University Press, 2008), 226–67. For a similar argument, see Julia Reinhard Lupton, *Afterlives of the Saints: Hagiography, Typology, and Renaissance Literature* (Stanford: Stanford University Press, 1996, 226–27).

92. Shakespeare, Diehl writes, "teases his English audiences by arousing the anxiety that his marvelous theatrical spectacle might be 'popish' and therefore illicit and transgressive, only to relieve them of their anxieties by showing why his magic is, in

Paulina's words and according to Protestant teaching, 'lawful.'" Diehl, "'Does Not the Stone Rebuke Me?,'" 80.

93. REED: *Cheshire,* 1:333.

94. Stubbes, *Anatomie of Abuses* (London, 1583), sig. L5r–v.

Epilogue

1. Foucault, "What Is an Author?" in *Critical Theory since 1965,* ed. Hazard Adams and Leroy Serle (Tallahassee: Florida State University Press, 1986), 142.

2. The Latin stage direction following line 96 of the cooks' *Harrowing* (play 17) reads: "Tunc Sathan sedens in cathedra dicat daemonibus" ("Then Satan, seated on his throne, says to the demons").

3. See Barrett, *Against All England: Regional Identity and Cheshire Writing, 1195–1656* (Notre Dame, IN: University of Notre Dame Press, 2009), 81.

4. Dessen and Thomson, *A Dictionary of Stage Directions in English Drama, 1580–1642* (Cambridge: Cambridge University Press, 1999), 228.

5. See Jean Howard, *Theater of a City: The Places of London Comedy, 1598–1642* (Philadelphia: University of Pennsylvania Press, 2007), 19.

6. All citations of Jonson's *The Devil Is an Ass* are from *Ben Jonson: The Devil Is an Ass and Other Plays,* ed. Margaret Jane Kidnie (Oxford: Oxford University Press, 2000), 223–330, and will be cited by line number in the body of the text.

7. Williamson, *The Materiality of Religion in Early Modern English Drama* (Burlington, VT: Ashgate, 2009), 28.

8. Ibid., 68.

9. Noting that "a coffin-style prop appears not only in *Pericles* but in a series of plays produced by the King's Men in 1608, 1611, 1618, 1631, and 1637, indicating that the company probably owned one or more," Williamson argues that *The Winter's Tale* "ingeniously reworks existing conventions without using a tomb property, providing a new solution to the representational challenge of staging a character's resurrection." Ibid., 64.

10. The archangel Michael appears in both the Chester and York *Harrowing* plays, though it is unclear whether he is bearing the light. Yet, as Clifford Davidson notes, a continental version played at Mons, France, depicted Anima Christi "like a soul in a tent of fine gauze . . . with two angels censing before it." Davidson, *Technology, Guilds, and Early English Drama,* Early Drama, Art, and Music Monograph Series 23 (Kalamazoo, MI: Medieval Institute Publications, 1996), 84.

11. My translation. The Latin stage direction reads: "Et primo fiat lux in inferno materialis aliqua subtilitate machinate et postea dicat Adam." On the lighting effects in the *Harrowing* plays, see Philip Butterworth, "Hellfire: Flame as Special Effect," in *The Iconography of Hell,* ed. Clifford Davidson and Thomas H. Seiler, Early Drama, Art, and Music Monograph Series 17 (Kalamazoo, MI: Medieval Institute Publications, 1992), 67–101.

12. Davidson points to the "glorious gleme" at line 42 of the York play and line 30 of the Wakefield play, which was derived from the York text. Davidson, *Technology,* 84.

13. Middleton, *The Maiden's Tragedy,* 4.5.42 s.d., in *Four Jacobean Sex Tragedies,* ed. Martin Wiggins (Oxford: Oxford University Press, 1998), 216.

14. John Webster, *The Duchess of Malfi,* ed. John Russell Brown (Manchester, UK: Manchester University Press, 1997), 24.

15. For Williamson, Webster's play is more innovative "in that it eschews the standard material technology associated with the tomb, pointing around the thing to the power associated with it." Though Williamson is more interested in the affective power of conventional material technologies, she nevertheless seems to acknowledge the centrality of the empty tomb property: "Bracketed on either side by Bosola's sense of being haunted and by Antonio's vision of a face 'folded in sorrow,' the echo's incorporeality allows the empty tomb to become the focus of the scene." Williamson, *Materiality of Religion,* 59.

16. Ben Jonson, *The Alchemist,* 2nd ed., ed. Elizabeth Cook (New York: Methuen, 2010), 155.

17. On the "regulated vagrancy" of clothes as foundational practices for the professional playhouses, see Ann Rosalind Jones and Peter Stallybrass, *Renaissance Clothing and the Materials of Memory* (Cambridge: Cambridge University Press, 2000).

18. Jonathan Gil Harris and Natasha Korda, "Introduction: Towards a Materialist Account of Stage Properties," in *Staged Properties in Early Modern English Drama,* ed. Harris and Korda (Cambridge: Cambridge University Press, 2002), 7.

19. Andrew Gurr reproduces this title page illustration with a caption stating "a stage trap is clearly marked." Gurr, *The Shakespearean Stage: 1574–1642* (Cambridge: Cambridge University Press, 1992), 163. The trap does not appear to be visible in the Bodleian Library copy reproduced on EEBO, STC (2nd ed.) 21011.

20. Nathanael Richards, *The tragedy of Messallina the Roman emperesse As it hath beene acted with generall applause divers times, by the Company of his Majesties Revells* (London, 1640), sig. C3v, E3v, and E8v.

21. I am grateful to Cyrus Mulready for suggesting that the printer might have chosen this particular title page illustration for its mnemonic quality.

22. Richards, *Tragedy of Messallina,* sig. A5r.

23. Gurr, *Shakespearean Stage,* 163. See also John H. Astington, "The Origins of the Rosana and Messallina Illustrations," *Shakespeare Survey* 43 (1991): 149–69.

24. Christopher Marlowe, *Doctor Faustus,* ed. Sylvan Barnet (New York: Signet Classic, 2001), 82.

25. Richards, *Tragedy of Messallina,* sig. F6r–v.

26. Ibid., sig. A4v.

❧ Bibliography

Aers, David. "A Whisper in the Ear of Early Modernists; or, Reflections on Literary Critics Writing the 'History of the Subject.'" In *Culture and History 1350–1600: Essays on English Communities, Identities and Writing,* edited by David Aers, 177–202. Detroit: Wayne State University Press, 1992.

Alström, Torbjörn. "The Voice in the Mask." *Drama Review* 48, no. 2 (2004): 133–38.

Appadurai, Arjun. "Introduction: Commodities and the Politics of Value." In *The Social Life of Things: Commodities in Cultural Perspective,* edited by Arjun Appadurai, 3–63. Cambridge: Cambridge University Press, 1986.

Apuleius, Lucius. *The. xi. bookes of the Golden asse . . . Translated out of Latine into Englishe by VVilliam Adlington.* London, 1566. Early English Books Online. http://eebo.chadwyck.com.

Ashley, Kathleen. "Edmund Kerchever Chambers (1866–1954)." In *Medieval Scholarship: Biographical Studies on the Formation of a Discipline, Literature and Philology,* edited by Helen Damico and Joseph B. Zavadil, 2:313–24. New York: Garland, 1998.

Aulén, Gustaf. *Christus Victor.* New York: Society for Promoting Christian Knowledge, 1931.

Baldwin, Elizabeth, Lawrence M. Clopper, and David Mills, eds. *Cheshire including Chester.* 2 vols. Records of Early English Drama. Toronto: University of Toronto Press, 2007.

Bale, John. *The image of both Churches.* London, 1570. Early English Books Online. http://eebo.chadwyck.com.

Barish, Jonas. *The Antitheatrical Prejudice.* Berkeley: University of California Press, 1978.

Barrett, Robert. *Against All England: Regional Identity and Cheshire Writing, 1195–1656.* Notre Dame, IN: University of Notre Dame Press, 2009.

Barthlet, John. *The pedegrewe of heretiques.* London, 1566. Early English Books Online. http://eebo.chadwyck.com.

Beadle, Richard, ed. *The York Plays: A Critical Edition of the York Corpus Christi Play as Recorded in British Library Additional MS 35290.* Early English Text Society Supplementary Series 23. Oxford: Oxford University Press, 2009.

Beadle, Richard, and Pamela King, eds. *York Mystery Plays: A Selection in Modern Spelling.* Oxford: Clarendon Press, 1984.

Beckwith, Sarah. *Shakespeare and the Grammar of Forgiveness.* Ithaca: Cornell University Press, 2011.

——. *Signifying God: Social Relation and Symbolic Act in the York Corpus Christi Plays.* Chicago: University of Chicago Press, 2001.

———. "Stephen Greenblatt's Hamlet and the Forms of Oblivion." *Journal of Medieval and Early Modern Studies* 33, no. 2 (2003): 261–80.

Benjamin, Walter. *The Origins of German Tragic Drama.* Translated by John Osborne. London: Verso, 1977.

Bevington, David. *From "Mankind" to Marlowe: Growth of Structure in the Popular Drama of Tudor England.* Cambridge, MA: Harvard University Press, 1962.

———, ed. *Homo, Memento Finis: The Iconography of Just Judgment in Medieval Art and Drama.* Early Drama, Art, and Music Monograph Series 6. Kalamazoo, MI: Medieval Institute Publications, 1985.

———, ed. *Medieval Drama.* Boston: Houghton Mifflin, 1975.

The Bible and Holy Scriptures conteyned in the Olde and Newe Testament. London, 1560. Early English Books Online. http://eebo.chadwyck.com.

Bishop, Thomas. *Shakespeare and the Theater of Wonder.* Cambridge: Cambridge University Press, 1996.

Bloom, Harold. "Preface: The Anguish of Contamination." In *The Anxiety of Influence: A Theory of Poetry,* 2nd ed., xi–xlvii. Oxford: Oxford University Press, 1997.

Boaistuau, Pierre. *Certaine secrete wonders of nature.* London, 1569. Early English Books Online. http://eebo.chadwyck.com.

Brandes, Georg. "The Airy Dream." In *A Midsummer Night's Dream,* edited by Judith M. and Richard F. Kennedy, 339–42. New Brunswick, NJ: Athlone Press, 1999.

Briscoe, Marianne G., and John C. Coldewey, eds. *Contexts for Early English Drama.* Bloomington: Indiana University Press, 1989.

British Library MS Harley 2150. London.

Bullough, Geoffrey. *Narrative and Dramatic Sources of Shakespeare.* New York: Columbia University Press, 1957.

Burckhardt, Jacob. *The Civilization of the Renaissance in Italy.* Translated by S. G. C. Middlemore. New York: Modern Library, 2002.

Butler, Samuel. *Unconscious Memory.* London: Ballantyne Press, 1880.

Butterworth, Philip. "Hellfire: Flame as Special Effect." In *The Iconography of Hell,* edited by Clifford Davidson and Thomas H. Seiler, 67–101. Early Drama, Art, and Music Monograph Series 17. Kalamazoo, MI: Medieval Institute Publications, 1992.

Calvin, John. *Institutes of the Christian Religion.* Edited by John T. McNeill. Translated by Ford Lewis Battles. 2 vols. Library of Christian Classics 20 and 21. Philadelphia: Westminster Press, 1960.

———. "Short Treatise on the Holy Supper of Our Lord and Only Saviour Jesus Christ." In *Calvin: Theological Treatises,* edited and translated by J. K. S. Reid, 140–66. Library of Christian Classics 22. Philadelphia: Westminster Press, 1954.

Cary, Cecile. "'It Circumscribes Us Here': Hell on the Renaissance Stage." In *The Iconography of Hell,* edited by Clifford Davidson and Thomas H. Seiler, 187–207. Early Drama, Art and Music Monograph Series 17. Kalamazoo, MI: Medieval Institute Publications, 1992.

Chambers, Edmund Kerchever, *The Elizabethan Stage.* 4 vols. Oxford: Oxford University Press, 1923.

———. *The Mediaeval Stage.* 2 vols. Oxford: Oxford Clarendon Press, 1903.

———. *Sir Thomas Wyatt and Some Collected Studies.* London: Sidgwick & Jackson, 1933.

Charlton, Kenneth. "Holbein's *Ambassadors* and Sixteenth-Century Education." *Journal of the History of Ideas* 21 (1960): 99–109.

Cobb, Christopher. "Storm versus Story: Form and Affective Power in Shakespeare's Romances." In *Shakespeare and Historical Formalism,* edited by Stephen Cohen, 95–124. Burlington, VT: Ashgate, 2007.

Cohen, Stephen, ed. *Shakespeare and Historical Formalism.* Burlington, VT: Ashgate, 2007.

Clopper, Lawrence M., ed. *Chester.* Records of Early English Drama. Toronto: University of Toronto Press, 1979.

———. *Drama, Play, and Game: English Festive Culture in the Medieval and Early Modern Period.* Chicago: University of Chicago Press, 2001.

———. "The History and Development of the Chester Cycle." *Modern Philology* 75, no. 3 (1978): 219–46.

Coldewey, John C. "Some Economic Aspects of the Late Medieval Drama." In *Contexts for Early English Drama,* edited by Marianne G. Briscoe and John C. Coldewey, 77–101. Bloomington: Indiana University Press, 1989.

Coleman, David. *Drama and the Sacraments in Sixteenth-Century England.* New York: Palgrave, 2007.

Coletti, Theresa. "The Chester Cycle in Sixteenth-Century Religious Culture." *Journal of Medieval and Early Modern Studies* 37, no. 3 (2007): 531–47.

Coletti, Theresa, and Gail McMurray Gibson, "The Tudor Origins of Medieval Drama." In *A Companion to Tudor Literature,* edited by Kent Cartwright, 228–45. Malden, MA: Wiley-Blackwell, 2010.

Collier, J. Payne. *History of English Dramatic Poetry to the Time of Shakespeare: And Annals of the Stage to the Restoration.* London: George Bell & Sons, 1897.

Cooper, Helen. *The English Romance in Time: Transforming Motifs from Geoffrey of Monmouth to the Death of Shakespeare.* Oxford: Oxford University Press, 2004.

———. "Shakespeare and the Mystery Plays." In *Shakespeare and Elizabethan Popular Culture,* edited by Stuart Gillespie and Neil Rhodes, 18–41. London: Arden Shakespeare, 2006.

———. *Shakespeare and the Medieval World.* New York: Arden Shakespeare, 2010.

Cox, John. *The Devil and the Sacred in English Drama, 1350–1642.* Cambridge: Cambridge University Press, 2000.

Crashaw, William. *The sermon preached at the Crosse.* London, 1607. Early English Books Online. http://eebo.chadwyck.com.

Crawford, Julie. *Marvelous Protestantism: Monstrous Births in Post-Reformation England.* Baltimore: Johns Hopkins University Press, 2005.

Cummings, Brian, and James Simpson, eds. *Cultural Reformations: Medieval and Renaissance in Literary History.* Oxford Twenty-First Century Approaches to Literature. Oxford: Oxford University Press, 2010.

Davidson, Clifford. "'The Devil's Guts': Allegations of Superstition and Fraud in Religious Drama and Art during the Reformation." In *Iconoclasm vs. Art and Drama,* edited by Clifford Davidson and Ann Eljenholm Nichols, 92–144. Early Drama, Art, and Music Monograph Series 11. Kalamazoo, MI: Medieval Institute Publications, 1989.

——. *From Creation to Doom: The York Cycle of Mystery Plays*. New York: AMS Press, 1984.

——. *The Guild Chapel Wall Paintings at Stratford-upon-Avon*. New York: AMS Press, 1988.

——. *Technology, Guilds, and Early English Drama*. Early Drama, Art, and Music Monograph Series 23. Kalamazoo, MI: Medieval Institute Publications, 1996.

——. "'What Hempen Home-Spuns Have We Swagg'ring Here?' Amateur Actors in *A Midsummer Night's Dream* and the Coventry Civic Plays and Pageants." *Shakespeare Studies* 19 (1987): 87–99.

——. "York Guilds and the Corpus Christi Plays: Unwilling Participants?" *Early Theatre* 9, no. 2 (2006): 11–33.

Davidson, Clifford, and Thomas H. Seiler, eds. *The Iconography of Hell*. Early Drama, Art, and Music Monograph Series 17. Kalamazoo, MI: Medieval Institute Press, 1992.

Davis, Alex. "Living in the Past: Thebes, Periodization, and *The Two Noble Kinsmen*," *Journal of Medieval and Early Modern Studies* 40, no. 1 (2010): 173–95.

——. *Renaissance Historical Fiction: Sidney, Deloney, Nashe*. Cambridge: D. S. Brewer, 2011.

Dawson, Anthony, and Paul Yachnin, eds. *The Culture of Playgoing in Shakespeare's England: A Collaborative Debate*. Cambridge: Cambridge University Press, 2001.

de Grazia, Margreta. "Anachronism." In *Cultural Reformations: Medieval and Renaissance in Literary History*, edited by Brian Cummings and James Simpson, 13–32. Oxford: Oxford University Press, 2010.

——. *"Hamlet" without Hamlet*. Cambridge: Cambridge University Press, 2007.

——. "The Ideology of Superfluous Things: *King Lear* as Period Piece." In *Subject and Object in Renaissance Culture*, edited by Margreta de Grazia, Maureen Quilligan, and Peter Stallybrass, 17–42. Cambridge: Cambridge University Press, 1996.

——. "The Modern Divide: From Either Side." *Journal of Medieval and Early Modern Studies* 37, no. 3 (2007): 453–67.

——. "World Pictures, Modern Periods, and the Early Stage." In *A New History of Early English Drama*, edited by John D. Cox and David Scott Kastan, 7–24. New York: Columbia University Press, 1997.

de Grazia, Margreta, Maureen Quilligan, and Peter Stallybrass, eds. *Subject and Object in Renaissance Culture*. Cambridge: Cambridge University Press, 1996.

De Quincey, Thomas. "On the Knocking at the Gate in *Macbeth*." In *The Norton Anthology of English Literature*, 6th ed., edited by M. H. Abrams, 2:459–62. New York: Norton, 1993.

Dessen, Alan, and Leslie Thomson. *A Dictionary of Stage Directions in English Drama, 1580–1642*. Cambridge: Cambridge University Press, 1999.

Devitt, Amy J. *Writing Genres*. Carbondale, IL: Southern Illinois University Press, 2004.

Didi-Huberman, Georges. *Confronting Images: Questioning the Ends of a Certain History of Art*. Translated by John Goodman. University Park: Pennsylvania State University Press, 2005.

——. *L'Image survivante: Histoire de l'art et temps des fantômes selon Aby Warburg*, Paris: Minuit, 2002.

Diehl, Huston. "'Does Not the Stone Rebuke Me?' The Pauline Rebuke and Paulina's Lawful Magic in *The Winter's Tale.*" In *Shakespeare and the Cultures of Performance,* edited by Paul Yachnin and Patricia Badir, 69–82. Burlington, VT: Ashgate, 2008.

———. *Staging Reform, Reforming the Stage: Protestantism and Popular Theater in Early Modern England.* Ithaca: Cornell University Press, 1997.

Duffy, Eamon. *The Stripping of the Altars: Traditional Religion in England, 1400–1580.* New Haven, CT: Yale University Press, 1992.

Dugan, Holly. *The Ephemeral History of Perfume: Scent and Sense in Early Modern England.* Baltimore: Johns Hopkins University Press, 2011.

Dutton, Richard, Alison Findlay, and Richard Wilson, eds. *Region, Religion, and Patronage: Lancastrian Shakespeare.* Manchester, UK: Manchester University Press, 2003.

Early English Text Society: Lists of Publications. London: Oxford University Press, 1936.

Echard, Siân. *Printing the Middle Ages.* Philadelphia: University of Pennsylvania Press, 2008.

Emmerson, Richard K. "Contextualizing Performance: The Reception of the Chester *Antichrist.*" *Journal of Medieval and Early Modern Studies* 29, no. 1 (1999): 89–119.

———. "Dramatic History: On the Diachronic and Synchronic in the Study of Early English Drama." *Journal of Medieval and Early Modern Studies* 35, no. 1 (2005): 39–66.

Faulkner, Ann. "The Harrowing of Hell at Barking Abbey and in Modern Production." In *The Iconography of Hell,* edited by Clifford Davidson and Thomas H. Seiler, 141–57. Early Drama, Art, and Music Monograph Series 17. Kalamazoo, MI: Medieval Institute Press, 1992.

Foakes, R. A., ed. *Henslowe's Diary.* 2nd ed. Cambridge: Cambridge University Press, 2002.

Foister, Susan, Ashok Roy, and Martin Wyld. *Holbein's Ambassadors.* New Haven: Yale University Press, 1997.

Fortini Brown, Patricia. *Venice in Antiquity.* New Haven: Yale University Press, 1996.

Foucault, Michel. "What Is an Author?" In *Critical Theory since 1965,* edited by Hazard Adams and Leroy Serle, 138–48. Tallahassee: Florida State University Press, 1986.

Foxe, John. *Actes and monuments.* London, 1583.

Furnivall, James, and Paul Hamelius. *The Digby Plays.* London: Kegan Paul, Trench, & Co., 1896.

Gardiner, Harold. *Mysteries' End: An Investigation of the Last Days of the Medieval Religious Stage.* Hamden, CT: Archon Books, 1967.

Gerrish, B. A. *Grace and Gratitude: The Eucharistic Theology of John Calvin.* Minneapolis: Fortress Press, 1993.

Glendinning, Robert. "Pyramus and Thisbe in the Medieval Classroom." *Speculum* 61, no. 1 (1986): 51–78.

Gosson, Stephen. *Playes Confuted in Five Actions.* London, 1582. Early English Books Online. http://eebo.chadwyck.com.

———. *Schoole of Abuse.* London, 1579. Early English Books Online. http://eebo.chadwyck.com.

Grady, Hugh. "Shakespeare and Impure Aesthetics: The Case of *A Midsummer Night's Dream.*" *Shakespeare Quarterly* 59, no. 3 (2008): 274–302.

Greenblatt, Stephen. *Hamlet in Purgatory.* Princeton: Princeton University Press, 2001.

——. "The Mousetrap." In *Practicing New Historicism,* edited by Stephen Greenblatt and Catherine Gallagher, 137–62. Chicago: University of Chicago Press, 2000.

——. "Remnants of the Sacred in Early Modern England." In *Subject and Object in Renaissance Culture,* edited by Margreta de Grazia, Maureen Quilligan, and Peter Stallybrass, 337–48. Cambridge: Cambridge University Press, 1996.

——. *Renaissance Self-Fashioning: More to Shakespeare* (Chicago: University of Chicago Press, 1980.

——. *Shakespearean Negotiations.* Berkeley: University of California Press, 1988.

——. *Will in the World: How Shakespeare Became Shakespeare.* New York: Norton, 2004.

Greenblatt, Stephen, and Catherine Gallagher. *Practicing New Historicism.* Chicago: University of Chicago Press, 2000.

Greene, Henry Copley. "The Song of the Ass." *Speculum* 6, no. 4 (1931): 534–49.

Groves, Beatrice. *Texts and Traditions: Religion in Shakespeare, 1592–1604.* Oxford: Clarendon Press, 2007.

——. "'The Wittiest Partition': Bottom, Paul, and Comedic Resurrection." *Notes and Queries* 54, no. 3 (2007): 277–82.

Gurr, Andrew. *Playgoing in Shakespeare's London.* Cambridge: Cambridge University Press, 1996.

——. *The Shakespeare Company, 1594–1642.* Cambridge: Cambridge University Press, 2004.

——. *The Shakespearean Stage: 1574–1642.* 3rd ed. Cambridge: Cambridge University Press, 1992.

——. "The Shakespearean Stage." In *The Norton Shakespeare: Based on the Oxford Edition,* edited by Stephen Greenblatt, Walter Cohen, Jean E. Howard, and Katharine Eisaman Maus, 3281–301. New York: Norton, 1997.

Hammel, Gavin. "'Too Much Forwardnesse to Innouate': A Reformation Debate on Christ's Descent into Hell and Its Medieval Precedents." Paper presented at the Renaissance Medievalisms conference, University of Toronto, February 2006.

Hampton, Timothy. *Writing from History: The Rhetoric of Exemplarity in Renaissance Literature.* Ithaca: Cornell University Press, 1990.

Harcourt, John B. "'I Pray You, Remember the Porter.'" *Shakespeare Quarterly* 12, no. 4 (1961): 393–402.

Hardison, O. B. *Christian Rite and Christian Drama in the Middle Ages: Essays in the Origin and Early History of Modern Drama.* Baltimore: Johns Hopkins University Press, 1965.

Harris, Jonathan Gil. "The New New Historicism's *Wunderkammer* of Objects." *European Journal of English Studies* 4, no. 2 (2000): 111–23.

——. *Untimely Matter in the Time of Shakespeare.* Philadelphia: University of Pennsylvania Press, 2009.

Harris, Jonathan Gil, and Natasha Korda. "Introduction: Towards a Materialist Account of Stage Properties." In *Staged Properties in Early Modern English Drama,* edited by Jonathan Gil Harris and Natasha Korda, 1–34. Cambridge: Cambridge University Press, 2002.

Hegel, Georg W. F. *Introduction to* The Philosophy of History: *With Selections from* The Philosophy of Right. Translated by Leo Rauch. Indianapolis: Hackett, 1988.

——. *The Philosophy of History.* Translated by J. Sibree. Amherst, NY: Prometheus Books, 1991.

Helgerson, Richard. *Forms of Nationhood: The Elizabethan Writing of England.* Chicago: University of Chicago Press, 1992.

Heywood, John. *The playe called the Foure PP.* 1544. Early English Books Online. http://eebo.chadwyck.com.

Heywood, Thomas. *An Apology for Actors.* London, 1612. Early English Books Online. http://eebo.chadwyck.com.

Hodgdon, Barbara. "Shopping in the Archives: Material Memories." In *Shakespeare, Memory, and Performance,* edited by Peter Holland, 135–67. Cambridge: Cambridge University Press, 2006.

Holinshed, Raphael. *The Chronicles of England, Scotland and Ireland.* London, 1587. Schoenberg Center for Electronic Text and Image (SCETI), University of Pennsylvania Libraries. http://dewey.lib.upenn.edu/sceti.

Holland, Peter, ed. *Shakespeare, Memory, and Performance.* Cambridge: Cambridge University Press, 2006.

Howard, Jean. *Theater of a City: The Places of London Comedy, 1598–1642.* Philadelphia: University of Pennsylvania Press, 2007.

Hulme, William H. *The Middle-English Harrowing of Hell and Gospel of Nicodemus.* London: Kegan Paul, Trench, Trubner and Co., 1907.

Ingram, R. W., ed. *Coventry.* Records of Early English Drama. Toronto: University of Toronto Press, 1981.

Izydorczyk, Zbigniew. *The Medieval Gospel of Nicodemus: Texts, Intertexts, and Contexts in Western Europe.* Tempe, AZ: Medieval and Renaissance Texts and Studies, 1997.

James, Mervyn. "Ritual, Drama, and Social Body in the Late Medieval Town." *Past and Present* 98 (1983): 3–29.

James, Montague Rhodes, trans. *The Apocryphal New Testament: Being the Apocryphal Gospels, Acts, Epistles, and Apocalypses.* Oxford: Clarendon Press, 1924.

James I, King of England. *Basilikon doron Devided into three bookes.* Edinburgh, 1599. Early English Books Online. http://eebo.chadwyck.com.

Jensen, Phebe. "'Honest Mirth & Merriment': Christmas and Catholicism in Early Modern England." In *Redrawing the Map of Early Modern English Catholicism,* edited by Lowell Gallagher, 213–44. Toronto: University of Toronto Press, 2012.

——. *Religion and Revelry in Shakespeare's Festive World.* Cambridge: Cambridge University Press, 2008.

Johnston, Alexandra F. "The Feast of Corpus Christi in the West Country." *Early Theatre* 6, no. 1 (2003):15–34.

Johnston, Alexandra F., and Margaret Rogerson, eds. *York.* 2 vols. Records of Early English Drama. Toronto: University of Toronto Press, 1979.

Jones, Ann Rosalind, and Peter Stallybrass. *Renaissance Clothing and the Materials of Memory.* Cambridge: Cambridge University Press, 2000.

Jonson, Ben. *The Alchemist.* 2nd ed. Edited by Elizabeth Cook. New York: Methuen, 2010.

——. *The Devil Is an Ass.* In *Ben Jonson: The Devil is an Ass and Other Plays,* edited by Margaret Jane Kidnie, 223–330. Oxford: Oxford University Press, 2000.

Kernan, Alvin. *Shakespeare, the King's Playwright: Theater in the Stuart Court, 1603–1613.* New Haven, CT: Yale University Press, 1995.

King, Andrew. *The Faerie Queene and Middle English Romance: The Matter of Just Memory.* Oxford: Clarendon Press, 2000.

Kinney, Arthur. *Lies like Truth: Shakespeare, "Macbeth," and the Cultural Moment.* Detroit: Wayne State University Press, 2001,

Knapp, Jeffrey. *Shakespeare's Tribe: Church, Nation, and Theater in Renaissance England.* Chicago: University of Chicago Press, 2002.

Kolve, V. A. *A Play Called Corpus Christi.* Stanford: Stanford University Press, 1966.

Kopytoff, Igor. "The Cultural Biography of Things: Commoditization as Process." In *The Social Life of Things: Commodities in Cultural Perspective,* edited by Arjun Appadurai, 64–94. Cambridge: Cambridge University Press, 1986.

Kott, Jan. *The Bottom Translation: Marlowe and Shakespeare and the Carnival Tradition.* Translated by Daniela Miedzyrzecka and Lillian Vallee. Evanstan, IL: Northwestern University Press, 1987.

Kyd, Thomas. *The Spanish Tragedy.* Edited by David Bevington. Revels Student Editions. Manchester, UK: Manchester University Press, 1996.

Lake, Peter, with Michael Questier. *The Antichrist's Lewd Hat: Protestants, Papists and Players in Post-Reformation England.* New Haven, CT: Yale University Press, 2002.

Lane, Anthony N. S. *John Calvin: Student of the Church Fathers.* Edinburgh: T & T Clark, 1999.

Lambarde, William. *Dictionarium Angliæ topographicum & historicum.* London, 1730. Eighteenth Century Collections Online. http://gale.cenage.com.

Lange, Konrad. *Der Papstesel: Ein Beitrag zur Kultur- und Kunstgeschichte des Reformationszeitalters.* Göttingen: Vandenhoeck and Ruprecht, 1891.

Lemon, Rebecca. *Treason by Words: Literature, Law, and Rebellion in Shakespeare's England.* Ithaca: Cornell University Press, 2006.

Lesser, Zachary. "Typographic Nostalgia: Play-Reading, Popularity, and Black Letter." In *The Book of the Play: Playwrights, Stationers, and Readers in Early Modern England,* edited by Marta Straznicky, 99–126. Boston: University of Amherst Press, 2006.

Levering, Matthew. *Sacrifice and Community: Jewish Offering and Christian Eucharist.* Malden, MA: Blackwell, 2005.

Lodge, Thomas. *Defence of Poetry, Music, and Stage Plays.* In *Elizabethan Critical Essays,* edited by George Gregory Smith, 1:61–86. Oxford: Clarendon Press, 1904.

Low, Anthony. "Hamlet and the Ghost of Purgatory: Intimations of Killing the Father." *English Literary Renaissance* 29, no. 3 (Autumn 1999): 443–67.

Lowenthal, David. "*Macbeth:* Shakespeare's Mystery Play." *Interpretation* 16, no. 3 (1989): 311–57.

Luborsky, Ruth Samson. "The Illustrations to *The Shepheardes Calender.*" *Spenser Studies* 2 (1981): 3–53.

Lumiansky, Robert M., and David Mills. *The Chester Mystery Cycle: Essays and Documents.* Chapel Hill: University of North Carolina Press, 1983.

——, eds. *The Chester Mystery Cycle.* 2 vols. Early English Text Society Supplementary Series 3 and 9. Oxford: Oxford University Press, 1974; reprinted 1986.

Lupton, Julia Reinhard. *Afterlives of the Saints: Hagiography, Typology, and Renaissance Literature.* Stanford: Stanford University Press, 1996.

Luther, Martin. *A commentarie or exposition vppon the twoo Epistles generall of Sainct Peter, and that of Sainct Jude*. London, 1581. Early English Books Online. http://eebo. chadwyck.com.

——. "Against the Fanatics." In *Luther's Works*. American ed. Vol. 36, *Word and Sacrament II,* translated by Frederick C. Ahrens, edited by Helmut T. Lehmann and Abdel Ross Wentz, 329–61. Philadelphia: Fortress Press, 1959.

——. *D. Martin Luthers Werke: Kritische Gesamtausgabe*. Vols. 8, 11. Weimar: Hermann Böhlaus Nachfolger, 1883–1983.

——. "The Misuse of the Mass." In *Luther's Works*. American ed. Vol. 36, *Word and Sacrament II*, translated by Frederick C. Ahrens, edited by Helmut T. Lehman and Abdel Ross Wentz, 127–230. Philadelphia: Fortress Press, 1959.

——. *Selected Writings of Martin Luther*. Edited by Theodore G. Tappert. Minneapolis: Fortress Press, 1967.

Lynch, John T. *The Age of Elizabeth in the Age of Johnson*. Cambridge: Cambridge University Press, 2003.

MacCulloch, J.A. *The Harrowing of Hell: A Comparative Study of an Early Christian Doctrine*. Edinburgh: T. and T. Clark, 1930.

Malone, Edmund, ed. *Plays and Poems of William Shakspeare, in Ten Volumes; Collated Verbatim with the Most Authentick Copies, and Revised: With the Corrections and Illustrations of Various Commentators; to Which Are Added, an Essay on the Chronological Order of his Plays*. 1790. Reprint, New York: AMS Press, 1968.

Marlowe, Christopher. *Doctor Faustus*. Edited by Sylvan Barnet. New York: Signet Classic, 2001.

Marsalek, Karen Sawyer. "Marvels and Counterfeits: False Resurrections in the Chester *Antichrist* and *1 Henry IV*." In *Shakespeare and the Middle Ages,* edited by Curtis Perry and John Watkins, 217–40. Oxford: Oxford University Press, 2009.

Marshall, Peter. *Beliefs and the Dead in Reformation England*. Oxford: Oxford University Press, 2002.

Martin, Gregory. *The Nevv Testament of Iesus Christ, translated faithfully into English, out of the authentical Latin*. Rheims, 1582. Early English Books Online. http:// eebo.chadwyck.com.

McMillin, Scott, and Sally-Beth MacLean. *The Queen's Men and Their Plays*. Cambridge: Cambridge University Press, 1998.

McMullan, Gordon, and David Matthews, eds. *Reading the Medieval in Early Modern England*. Cambridge: Cambridge University Press, 2007.

Medieval Wall Painting in the English Parish Church: A Developing Catalogue. http://www.paintedchurch.org.

Melanchthon, Philipp, and Martin Luther. *Of two vvoonderful popish monsters*. London, 1579. Early English Books Online. http://eebo.chadwyck.com.

Meredith, Peter. "The Development of the York Mercers' Pageant Waggon." *Medieval English Theatre* 1 (1979): 5–18.

——. "The Iconography of Hell in the English Cycles: A Practical Perspective." In *The Iconography of Hell,* edited by Clifford Davidson and Thomas H. Seiler, 158–86. Early Drama, Art and Music Monograph Series 17. Kalamazoo, MI: Medieval Institute Publications, 1992.

The Middle English Dictionary. http://quod.lib.umich.edu/m/med.

Middleton, Thomas. *The Maiden's Tragedy.* In *Four Jacobean Sex Tragedies,* edited by Martin Wiggins, 161–232. Oxford: Oxford University Press, 1998.

Mills, David. *The Chester Mystery Cycle: A New Edition with Modernised Spelling.* East Lansing, MI: Colleagues Press, 1992.

———. *Recycling the Cycle: The City of Chester and Its Whitsun Plays.* Toronto: University of Toronto Press, 1999.

———. "Some Theological Issues in Chester's Plays." In *'Bring Furth the Pagants': Essays in Early English Drama Presented to Alexandra Johnston,* edited by David N. Klausner and Karen Sawyer Marsalek, 212–29. Toronto: University of Toronto Press, 2007.

Milton, John. *Paradise Lost.* Edited by Alastair Fowler. New York: Longman, 1998.

Mitchell, J. Allan. *Ethics and Exemplary Narrative in Chaucer and Gower.* Cambridge: D. S. Brewer, 2004.

Montrose, Louis. *The Purpose of Playing: Shakespeare and the Cultural Politics of the Elizabethan Theatre.* Chicago: University of Chicago Press, 1996.

Muir, Kenneth. *The Sources of Shakespeare's Plays.* London: Methuen, 1977.

Mullaney, Steven. *The Place of the Stage: License, Play, and Power in Renaissance England.* Chicago: University of Chicago Press, 1988.

Mulready, Cyrus. *Romance on the Early Modern Stage: English Expansion Before and After Shakespeare.* New York: Palgrave Macmillan, 2013.

Munday, Anthony. *A second and third blast of retrait from plaies and Theaters.* London, 1580. Early English Books Online. http://eebo.chadwyck.com.

Nagel, Alexander, and Christopher S. Wood. *Anachronic Renaissance.* New York: ZONE Books, 2010.

———. "Interventions: Toward a New Model of Renaissance Anachronism." *Art Bulletin* 87, no. 3 (2005): 403–15.

Nelson, Alan. "Some Configurations of Staging in Medieval English Drama." In *Medieval English Drama: Essays Critical and Contextual,* edited by Jerome Taylor and Alan H. Nelson, 116–47. Chicago: University of Chicago Press, 1972.

The Newe Testament in Englishe translated oute of the Greke, according to the translation of the greate Bible. London, 1569. Early English Books Online. http://eebo.chadwyck.com.

Nicoll, A. *Masks, Mimes, and Miracles: Studies in the Popular Theatre.* New York: Harcourt, Brace, 1931.

Nora, Pierre. "Between Memory and History: Les Lieux de Mémoire." *Representations* 26 (1989): 7–24.

———. *Les Lieux de Mémoire.* 3 vols. Paris: Gallimard, 1984–92.

North, John. *The Ambassadors' Secret: Holbein and the World of the Renaissance.* New York: Hambledon, 2002.

O'Connell, Michael. "Blood Begetting Blood: Shakespeare and the Mysteries." In *Medieval Shakespeare: Pasts and Presents,* edited by Ruth Morse, Helen Cooper, and Peter Holland, 177–89. Cambridge: Cambridge University Press, 2013.

———. *The Idolatrous Eye: Iconoclasm and Theater in Early-Modern England.* Oxford: Oxford University Press, 2000.

———. "*King Lear* and the Summons of Death." In *Shakespeare and the Middle Ages,* edited by Curtis Perry and John Watkins, 199–216. Oxford: Oxford University Press, 2009.

———. "Vital Cultural Practices: Shakespeare and the Mysteries." *Journal of Medieval and Early Modern Studies,* 29, no. 1 (1999): 149–68.

Orgel, Stephen. "Shakespeare Imagines a Theater." *Poetics Today* 5, no. 3 (1984): 549–61.

Orrell, John. *The Human Stage: English Theatre Design, 1567–1640.* Cambridge: Cambridge University Press, 1988.

Ostovich, Helen, Holger Schott Syme, and Andrew Griffin, eds. *Locating the Queen's Men: 1583–1603.* Burlington, VT: Ashgate, 2009.

Otter, Monika. *Inventiones: Fiction and Referentiality in Twelfth-Century English Historical Writing.* Chapel Hill: University of North Carolina Press, 1996.

The Oxford English Dictionary Online. http://www.oed.com.

Panofsky, Erwin. *Renaissance and Renascences in Western Art.* New York: Harper and Row, 1972.

Parker, John. *The Aesthetics of Antichrist.* Ithaca: Cornell University Press, 2007.

———. "What a Piece of Work Is Man: Shakespearean Drama as Marxian Fetish, the Fetish as Sacramental Sublime." *Journal of Medieval and Early Modern Studies* 34, no. 3 (2004): 643–72.

———. "Who's Afraid of Darwin? Revisiting Chambers and Hardison . . . and Nietzsche." *Journal of Medieval and Early Modern Studies* 40, no. 1 (2010): 7–35.

Parker, Matthew. *The text of the New Testament . . . with a confutation of all such arguments, glosses, and annotations, as conteine manifest impietie, of heresie, treason and slander, against the catholike Church of God . . . By William Fulke, Doctor in Diuinitie.* London, 1589. Early English Books Online. http://eebo.chadwyck.com.

Parker, Patricia. "Teaching and Wordplay: The 'Wall' of *A Midsummer Night's Dream.*" In *Teaching with Shakespeare: Critics in the Classroom,* edited by Bruce McIver and Ruth Stevenson, 205–14. Newark: University of Delaware Press, 1994.

Pechter, Edward. "Afterword: 'Performance,' 'Culture,' History." In *Shakespeare and the Performance of Culture,* edited by Paul Yachnin and Patricia Badir, 169–88. Burlington, VT: Ashgate, 2008.

Perry, Curtis, and John Watkins, eds. *Shakespeare and the Middle Ages.* Oxford: Oxford University Press, 2009.

Pilkinton, Mark, ed. *Bristol.* Records of Early English Drama. Toronto: University of Toronto Press, 1997.

Prynne, William. *Histrio-Mastix: The Players Scourge, or Actors Tragedie.* London, 1633. Early English Books Online. http://eebo.chadwyck.com.

Puttenham, George. *The Arte of English Poesie.* London, 1589. Early English Books Online. http://eebo.chadwyck.com.

Rainolds, John, *Th'overthrow of Stage-playes.* London, 1599. Early English Books Online. http://eebo.chadwyck.com.

Rastall, Richard. "Music in the Cycle." In *The Chester Mystery Cycle: Essays and Documents,* edited by R. M. Lumiansky and David Mills, 111–64. Chapel Hill: University of North Carolina Press, 1983.

———. "The Sounds of Hell." In *The Iconography of Hell,* edited by Clifford Davidson and Thomas H. Seiler, 102–31. Early Drama, Art, and Music Monograph Series 17. Kalamazoo, MI: Medieval Institute Publications, 1992.

Remnant, Mary. "Musical Instruments in Early English Drama." In *Material Culture and Medieval Drama,* edited by Clifford Davidson, 141–94. Early Drama, Art, and Music Monograph Series 25. Kalamazoo: Medieval Institute Publications, 1999.

Richards, Nathanael. *The tragedy of Messallina the Roman emperesse.* London, 1640. Early English Books Online. http://eebo.chadwyck.com.

Robinson, John W. *Studies in Fifteenth-Century Stagecraft.* Kalamazoo, MI: Medieval Institute Publications, 1991.

Rosenblum, Joseph. "Why an Ass? Cesare Ripa's *Iconologia* as a Source for Bottom's Translation." *Shakespeare Quarterly* 32, no. 3 (1981): 357–59.

Rossiter, A. P. *English Drama from Early Times to the Elizabethans.* New York: Barnes and Noble, 1950.

Rublack, Ulinka. *Reformation Europe.* Cambridge: Cambridge University Press, 2005.

Rust, Jennifer. *The Body in Mystery: The Political Theology of the "Corpus Mysticum" in Post-Reformation English Literature.* Evanston: Northwestern University Press, 2013.

———. "Political Theologies of the *Corpus Mysticum:* Schmitt, Kantorowicz and de Lubac." In *Political Theology and Early Modernity,* edited by Graham Hammill and Julia Reinhard Lupton, 102–23. Chicago: University of Chicago Press, 2012.

Salter, F. M. *Medieval Drama in Chester.* Toronto: University of Toronto Press, 1955.

Scanlon, Larry. *Narrative, Authority, and Power: The Medieval Exemplum and the Chaucerian Tradition.* Cambridge: Cambridge University Press, 1994.

Schleuter, June. "Rereading the Peacham Drawing." *Shakespeare Quarterly* 50, no. 2 (1999): 171–84.

Schroeder, H. J. *Canons and Decrees of the Council of Trent.* Rockford, IL: Tan Books, 1978.

Schwarz, Regina. *Sacramental Poetics at the Dawn of Secularism: When God Left the World.* Stanford: Stanford University Press, 2008.

Schwyzer, Philip. "Trophies, Traces, Relics, and Props: The Untimely Objects of *Richard III.*" *Shakespeare Quarterly* 63, no. 3 (2012): 297–327.

Scot, Reginald. *The Discoverie of Witchcraft.* New York: Dover, 1989.

Scribner, Robert W. *For the Sake of Simple Folk: Popular Propaganda for the German Reformation.* Oxford: Clarendon Press, 1994.

———. *Popular Culture and Popular Movements in Reformation Germany.* London: Hambledon Press, 1987.

Serres, Michel, with Bruno Latour, *Conversations on Science, Culture, and Time.* Translated by Roxanne Lapidus. Ann Arbor: University of Michigan Press, 1995.

Shakespeare, William. *Macbeth.* 2nd ed. Edited by R. A. Braunmuller. Cambridge: Cambridge University Press, 1997.

———. *Macbeth.* Edited by Stephen Orgel. The Pelican Shakespeare Series. New York: Penguin, 2000.

———. *A Midsummer Night's Dream.* Edited by Gail Kern Paster and Skiles Howard. New York: Bedford/St. Martin's, 1999.

———. *Mr. William Shakespeares Comedies, Histories, and Tragedies; A Facsimile of the First Folio, 1623.* Edited by Doug Moston. New York: Routledge, 1998.

———. *The Norton Facsimile of the First Folio of Shakespeare.* 2nd ed. Edited by Charlton Hinman. New York: Norton, 1996.

———. *The Norton Shakespeare: Based on the Oxford Edition.* Edited by Stephen Greenblatt, Walter Cohen, Jean E. Howard, and Katharine Eisaman Maus. New York: Norton, 1997.

———. *The Tragicall Historie of Hamlet Prince of Denmarke.* London, 1603. Early English Books Online. http://eebo.chadwyck.com.

Sheingorn, Pamela, and David Bevington. "'Alle This Was Token Domysday to Drede': Visual Signs of Last Judgment in the Corpus Christi Cycles and in Late Gothic Art." In *Homo, Memento Finis: The Iconography of Just Judgment in Medieval Art and Drama,* edited by David Bevington, 121–46. Early Drama, Art, and Music Monograph Series 6. Kalamazoo, MI: Medieval Institute Publications, 1985.

Shell, Alison. *Oral Culture and Catholicism in Early Modern England.* Cambridge: Cambridge University Press, 2007.

Sherman, William H. *Used Books: Marking Readers in Renaissance England.* Philadelphia: University of Pennsylvania Press, 2008.

Simpson, James. *Reform and Cultural Revolution, 1350–1547.* Oxford: Oxford University Press, 2002.

Singleton, Antony. "The Early English Text Society in the Nineteenth Century: An Organizational History." *Review of English Studies* 56 (2005): 90–118.

Smith, Bruce R. *The Acoustic World of Early Modern England: Attending to the O-Factor.* Chicago: University of Chicago Press, 1999.

Spector, Stephen, ed. *The N-Town Play: Cotton MS Vespasian D. 8.* 2 vols. Early English Text Society Supplementary Series 11–12. Oxford: Oxford University Press, 1991.

Spivack, Bernard. *Shakespeare and the Allegory of Evil: The History of a Metaphor in Relation to His Major Villains.* New York: Columbia University Press, 1958.

Spraggon, Julie. *Puritan Iconoclasm during the English Civil War.* Woodbridge, UK: Boydell Press, 2003.

Stallybrass, Peter. "*Macbeth* and Witchcraft." In *Focus on Macbeth,* edited by John Russell Brown, 189–209. New York: Routledge and Kegan Paul, 1982.

———. "Shakespeare's Desk: The Materiality of Authorship." Paper presented at the Shakespeare Association of America conference, Philadelphia, 15 April 2006.

Stallybrass, Peter, and Ann Rosalind Jones. *Renaissance Clothing and the Materials of Memory.* Cambridge: Cambridge University Press, 2000.

Steiner, Emily. "Radical Historiography: Langland, Trevisa, and the *Polychronicon.*" *Studies in the Age of Chaucer: The Yearbook of the New Chaucer Society* 27 (2005): 171–211.

Steinmetz, David. *Calvin in Context.* Oxford: Oxford University Press, 1995.

Stern, Tiffany. *Making Shakespeare: From Stage to Page.* New York: Routledge, 2004.

Stubbes, Phillip. *Anatomie of Abuses.* London, 1583. Early English Books Online. http://eebo.chadwyck.com.

Summit, Jennifer. *Memory's Library: Medieval Books in Early Modern England.* Chicago: University of Chicago Press, 2008.

Tappert, Theodore G., ed. *Selected Writings of Martin Luther.* Minneapolis: Fortress Press, 1967.

Tiffany, Grace. "*Macbeth,* Paternity, and the Anglicization of James I." *Studies in the Humanities* 23, no. 2 (December 1996): 148–62.

Travis, Peter W. *Dramatic Design in the Chester Cycle.* Chicago: University of Chicago Press, 1982.

Twycross, Meg. "The Chester Cycle Wardrobe." In *Staging the Chester Cycle,* edited by David Mills, 100–23. Leeds, UK: University of Leeds School of English, 1985.

——. "More Black and White Souls." *Medieval English Theatre* 13 (1991): 52–63.

——. "'With What Body Shall They Come?' Black and White Souls in the English Mystery Plays." In *Langland, the Mystics, and the Medieval English Religious Tradition: Essays in Honor of S. S. Hussey,* edited by H. Phillips, 271–86. Cambridge: D. S. Brewer, 1990.

Twycross, Meg, and Sarah Carpenter. *Masks and Masking in Medieval and Early Tudor England.* Burlington, VT: Ashgate, 2002.

——. "Masks in Medieval English Theatre." *Medieval English Theatre,* 3.1–2 (1981): 7–44, 69–113.

Voaden, Rosalynn. *The Discernment of Spirits in Late-Medieval Women's Visionary Writing (1300–1600).* Woodbridge, UK: York Medieval Press, 1999.

Waldron, Jennifer. "'The Eye of Man Hath Not Heard': Shakespeare, Synaesthesia, and Post-Reformation Phenomenology," *Criticism* 54 (2012): 403–17.

Walker, Greg, ed. *Medieval Drama: An Anthology.* Oxford: Blackwell, 2000.

Wallace, David. "Afterword." In *Reading the Medieval in Early Modern England,* edited by Gordon McMullan and David Matthews, 220–27. Cambridge: Cambridge University Press, 2007.

Ward, Adolphus William. *A History of the English Dramatic Literature to the Death of Queen Anne.* 2 vols. London: Macmillan, 1899.

Warton, Thomas. *The History of English Poetry.* 4 vols. London, 1774–81. Eighteenth Century Collections Online. http://gale.cenage.com.

Waswo, Richard. "Damnation, Protestant Style: Macbeth, Faustus, and Christian Tragedy." *Journal of Medieval and Renaissance Studies* 4 (1974): 63–99.

Watkins, John. "Bedevilling the Histories of Medieval and Early Modern Drama." *Modern Philology* 101 (2003): 68–78.

Webster, John. *The Duchess of Malfi.* Edited by John Russell Brown. Manchester, UK: Manchester University Press, 1997.

Weimann, Robert. *Author's Pen and Actor's Voice: Playing and Writing in Shakespeare's Theatre.* Cambridge: Cambridge University Press, 2000.

——. *Shakespeare and the Popular Tradition in the Theater: Studies in the Social Dimension of Dramatic Form and Function.* Edited by Robert Schwartz. Baltimore: Johns Hopkins University Press, 1978.

Welborn, Lawrence. *Paul, the Fool of Christ: A Study of 1 Corinthians 1–4 in the Comic-Philosophic Tradition.* New York: T and T Clark, Ltd., 2005.

Werth, Tiffany Jo. *The Fabulous Dark Cloister: Romance in England after the Reformation.* Baltimore: Johns Hopkins University Press, 2011.

White, Paul Whitfield. *Drama and Religion in English Provincial Society, 1485–1660.* Cambridge: Cambridge University Press, 2008.

——. "Reforming Mysteries' End: A New Look at Protestant Intervention in English Provincial Drama." *Journal of Medieval and Early Modern Studies* 29, no. 1 (1999): 121–47.

——. *Theatre and Reformation: Protestantism, Patronage, and Playing in Tudor England.* Cambridge: Cambridge University Press, 1993.

Wickham, Glynne. *Early English Stages, 1300 to 1660.* 3 vols. New York: Columbia University Press, 1963.

———. "Hell-Castle and Its Door-Keeper." *Shakespeare Survey* 19 (1966): 68–74.

———. *Shakespeare's Dramatic Heritage: Collected Studies in Mediaeval, Tudor, and Shakespearean Drama.* New York: Barnes and Noble, 1969.

Williams, Deanne. "Medievalism in English Renaissance Literature." In *A Companion to Tudor Literature,* edited by Kent Cartwright, 213–27. Malden, MA: Wiley-Blackwell, 2010.

Williamson, Elizabeth. *The Materiality of Religion in Early English Drama.* Studies in Performance and Early Modern Drama. Burlington, VT: Ashgate, 2009.

Wilson, Richard. "Introduction: A Torturing Hour—Shakespeare and the Martyrs." In *Theatre and Religion: Lancastrian Shakespeare,* edited by Richard Dutton, Alison Findlay, and Richard Wilson, 1–39. Manchester, UK: Manchester University Press, 2003.

Wolfe, Jessica. *Humanism, Machinery, and Renaissance Literature.* Cambridge: Cambridge University Press, 2004.

Womack, Peter. "Imagining Communities: Theatres and the English Nation in the Sixteenth Century." In *Culture and History, 1350–1600: Essays on English Communities, Identities and Writing,* edited by David Aers, 91–145. Detroit: Wayne State University Press, 1992.

Woolf, Rosemary. *English Mystery Plays.* Berkeley, CA: University of California Press, 1972.

Yates, Julian. "Accidental Shakespeare." *Shakespeare Studies* 34 (2006): 90–122.

———. *Error, Misuse, Failure: Object Lessons from the English Renaissance.* Minneapolis: University of Minnesota Press, 2003.

Zachman, Randall C. *The Assurance of Faith: Conscience in the Theology of Martin Luther and John Calvin.* Minneapolis: Fortress Press, 1993.

Zwingli, Ulrich. "On the Lord's Supper." In *Zwingli and Bullinger,* Library of Christian Classics 24, edited and translated by G. W. Bromiley, 185–238. Philadelphia: Westminster Press, 1953.

Index